John Thein

Answer to difficulties of the Bible

John Thein

Answer to difficulties of the Bible

ISBN/EAN: 9783742863393

Manufactured in Europe, USA, Canada, Australia, Japa

Cover: Foto ©Lupo / pixelio.de

Manufactured and distributed by brebook publishing software (www.brebook.com)

John Thein

Answer to difficulties of the Bible

ANSWER
TO
DIFFICULTIES
OF
THE BIBLE

BY
REV. JOHN THEIN.
Priest of the Cleveland Diocese; Author of "Christian Anthropology."

"I say to you, that if these shall hold their peace, the stones will cry out."
—*Luke XIX. 40.*

"For the stone shall cry out of the wall; and the timber that is between the joints of the building shall answer.—*Habacuc II. 11.*

B. HERDER
BOOKSELLER AND PUBLISHER
NO. 17 SOUTH BROADWAY, ST. LOUIS, MO.
1897

PREFACE

EACH century has its peculiar intellectual life, and divine Providence always holds in reserve the proper nourishment. This nourishment especially consists in three things: In the faith, arms and study; these three form the Christian, the soldier and the savant. The one who prepares himself by the study to combat for his faith; the one who seeks the truth, not only to know it, to possess it, but also to propagate and defend it, can lay claim to these three titles. This was true at all times. Every Catholic, even moderately acquainted with the course of modern science, must be painfully aware that its professed relations to faith are simply hostile. Weapons are sought in every region of enquiry and speculation, with which to beat down revealed truth, or to assail its defenders. In our epoch error adorns itself with the most pompous and captivating names, with the cloak of science and thus enters our schools and workshops, in order to deny God and His revelation, the Church and her doctrine. Historical facts are misrepresented and used to calumniate God's Church and her most sacred institutions. Geology, Palæontology, Ethnology, Biblical Criticism, and above all, the new Science of Comparative Religion yield arguments that must be met, and difficulties that must be answered if we would save educated Catholics, perhaps from loss of faith, but certainly from painful perplexity of mind. Questions of faith and science are now in the forefront of our modern intellectual life. They confront us at every turn. To enable the Catholic to cope with them, the present work will furnish to him some weapons in a simple and condensed form, its scope is instructive, critical and apologetical.

We do not claim any originality for the present work; its articles are culled from various authors. The works especially used in the composition of this book are: "Dictionnaire Apologetique," by J. B. Jaugey; "Les Livres Saints et la Critique Rationalist," 5 vols. by Rev. F. Vigouroux; "La Bible et les Deconvertes Modernes," 5 vols. *idem;* and Mgr. Meignand, " Le monde et l'homme primitif."

Since we wrote the work under the pressure of the various pastoral duties, no doubt some inaccuracies and omissions will be discovered, in regard to these we trust to find indulgence with the reader.

THE AUTHOR.

TABLE OF CONTENTS

	PAGES
CHAPTER I.—RATIONALISM, ...	13–16

CHAPTER II.—THE AUTHENTICITY OF THE PENTATEUCH.—Moses is its Author—Proofs drawn:—1. From the Bible—2. From the Samaritan Pentateuch—3. From the Egyptian Monuments—4. From the Language of the Pentateuch—5. Arguments of Prescription or Possession—6. Answer to Objections, ... 17–33

CHAPTER III.—HISTORICAL OBJECTIONS AGAINST THE AUTHENTICITY OF THE PENTATEUCH.—1. Unity of Sanctuary—2. The Sacrifices at the Hebrews—3. Feasts of the Hebrews—4. The Priests and Levites at the Hebrews—5. The Endowment of the Clergy, ... 33–59

CHAPTER IV.—THE DIFFERENT NAMES OF GOD, . . . 59–63

CHAPTER V.—THE FATHERS AND THE MOSAIC COSMOGONY.—1. Importance of the First Chapter of Genesis—2. The Work of the Fathers—3. The Fathers could not explain the Biblical Cosmogony without touching on Science—4. In explaining human things the Fathers were deprived of Divine Revelation—5. In Matters of Science the Fathers spoke as Private Doctors—6. The Accessory becomes the Principal—7. Neither the Patristic Tradition nor the Church has fixed the Scientific Sense of the First Chapter of Genesis—8. Different Opinions on the First Chapter of Genesis—9. The Results from this absence of Accord among the Fathers—10. How far have we Deviated from Patristic Teaching—11. We Adhere to the Rules laid down by the Fathers—12. Meaning of the Word Day and teaching of the Fathers—13. The explanations of the Fathers are completely in Accord with modern Discoveries—14. The Catholic Exegesis has never changed in Principle, ... 64–81

CHAPTER VI.—THE HEXÆMERON OR THE SIX GENETIC DAYS.—Four Principal Systems: The Literal System; System of Intervals; Ideal System; and the Concordistic System—I. Criticism of the Literal System—2. Genesis abounds in figurative Expressions—3. The Meaning of the Hebrew Word Yom—4. Testimony of the sedimentary Grounds—5. Microscopic remains in the Chalk and Limestone Formations—6. The Coal Measures—7. Conclusion—II. The System of Restitution or Intervals—1. Criticism of the System of Restitution—2. This Theory is against Reason—3. This Theory is opposed to the Bible—III. The Ideal System—1. Criticism of the Ideal System—2. Chaldean Cosmogony—3. Accord between Geology and Sacred Scripture—4. Objections refuted—5. Evidence of a Primitive Revelation—IV. The Concordistic System—1. Criticism of the Concordistic System—2. The Cosmogonic Tradition of diverse Nations—3. The Concordistic System establishes the most complete Accord, ... 82-124

CHAPTER VII.—THE HEXÆMERON OR THE SIX GENETIC DAYS—(Continued) I.—1. "In the Beginning God created Heaven and Earth"—2. Criticism of the First verse of Genesis—3. Organization of the Elements of Matter—4. And the Spirit of God moved over the Waters—II.—1. First Day's Work—2. Objection—3. The Meaning of the Words Evening and Morning—4. Objection—5. Second Day's Work—6. Third Day's Work—7. Fourth Day's Work—8. Fifth Day's Work—9. Objection—10. Sixth Day's Work—11. Seventh Day—Conclusion, . . 125-161

CHAPTER VIII.—MAN FROM THE SCIENTIFIC POINT OF VIEW.—I. The animal Origin of Man—1. Physical Difference between Man and the Brute—Upright Position—2. Facial and Cerebral Formation—3. Volume of the Brain—4. Embryology—5. Rudimentary Organs—6. Intellectual Qualities—Speech—7. Conscience—8. Religion—II. Has the Primitive Man been a Savage—III. Antiquity of Man—1. No Traces of Tertiary Man—2. Kitchen Refuse, ... 161-188

CHAPTER IX.—CHRONOLOGY AND THE PRINCIPAL MONUMENTS.—I. Biblical Chronology—II. Chronology and the Principal Literary Monuments of Antiquity:—1. Of India—2. Of China—3. Of Egypt—4. Of Chaldea and Assyria—5. Conclusion, ... 189-208

TABLE OF CONTENTS

CHAPTER X.— UNITY OF MANKIND.— 1. Biblical Account — 2. Science compelled to acknowledge a common Humanity — 3. Common Characteristics — 4. The various Races — 5. Other Differences — 6. Higher and Lower Races — 7. All Men are Social — 8. All the human Races are endowed with the Gift of Speech — 9. The various Languages — 10. Conclusion, ... 209–216

CHAPTER XI.—THE EARTHLY PARADISE AND ITS SITE, 216–219

CHAPTER XII.—THE CREATION OF EVE, ... 220–222

CHAPTER XIII.—THE FALL AND ORIGINAL SIN, . . . 222–226

CHAPTER XIV.—THE PATRIARCHAL RELIGION OR PRIMITIVE MONOTHEISM, ... 226–231

CHAPTER XV.—THE BOOK OF EXODUS.— 1. The Persecution of the Hebrews in Egypt — 2. The Existence of the Tabernacle, ... 232–242

CHAPTER XVI.—THE TEN PLAGUES OF EGYPT.— Their miraculous Character — Examination of each of the Plagues and its Supernatural Character — 1. The Water of the Nile turned into Blood — 2. Invasion of Frogs — 3. The Musquitos — 4. The Flies — 5 and 6. The Pest over both Animals and Men — 7. The great Hail — 8. Invasion of Locusts — 9. The Extreme Darkness — 10. Extermination of the First-born of the Egyptians, ... 242–249

CHAPTER XVII.—THE CROSSING OF THE RED SEA.— 1. The Hebrews did not pass along the Mediterranean Sea — 2. They did not profit by a Low Sea, but, according to the Biblical Text, the event was Miraculous, ... 249–252

CHAPTER XVIII.—MYTHIC SYSTEM, ... 252–256

CHAPTER XIX.—CAIN, CAINITES AND SETHITES, . . . 256–259

CHAPTER XX.—LONGEVITY OF THE FIRST MEN, . . . 259–262

CHAPTER XXI.—THE ANTEDILUVIAN GIANTS, ... 262–264

CHAPTER XXII.—THE SONS OF GOD AND THE DAUGHTERS OF MAN, ... 264–267

CHAPTER XXIII.—THE NOACHIAN DELUGE.— 1. Biblical Account — 2. Cuneiform Inscriptions — 3. Other Traditions — 4. The Question as to the Universality of the Deluge: As to the Earth — 5. As to the Animals — 6. As to Mankind, ... 267–275

viii   DIFFICULTIES OF THE BIBLE.

                                                                    PAGES

CHAPTER XXIV.—ETHNOGRAPHIC TABLE OR DISPERSION
OF THE NATIONS.—Tableau of the distribution of the
Primitive Peoples upon earth — It existed before Moses
— Objections raised by the Rationalists and Solution, . 275–284

CHAPTER XXV.—THE PATRIARCH ABRAHAM.— Objections
raised against the History of Abraham : — 1. Origin — 2.
Abraham's Journey to Egypt — 3. Abraham's Victory over
Chodorlahomor, ... 285–292

CHAPTER XXVI.—SODOM, THE ORIGIN OF THE DEAD SEA
AND LOTH'S WIFE, ... 293–296

CHAPTER XXVII.—THE PATRIARCH JACOB AND THE MAN-
DRAKES OF RUBEN.— 1. Jacob buys Esau's birthright —
2. The Blessing of Isaac — 3. Causes of Jacob's Voyage —
4. The Sheep of Jacob and the Manner he obtained them
— 5. The Mandrakes of Ruben, ... 296–306

CHAPTER XXVIII.— THE PATRIARCH JOSEPH.— 1. The
History of Joseph confirmed by scientific Discoveries — 2.
Answer to Objections — 3. The Collar given to Joseph
by the Pharaoh — 4. Divination by the Cup — 5. The
Possession of all the Egyptian soil by the Pharaoh — 6.
Answer to Objections made by the Rationalists against the
Authenticity and Veracity of the History of Joseph, . . 306–315

CHAPTER XXIX.—THE BOOK OF JOSUE AND GALILEO.— 1.
Antiquity of the Book of Josue — 2. Historic and Scientific
Difficulties — 3. The Circumcision at Galgala — 4. The
Conquest at Palestine — 5. The Miracle of Josue com-
manding the sun to stand still and the Condemnation of
Galileo, ... 315–335

CHAPTER XXX.—JEPHTE AND THE IMMOLATION OF HIS
DAUGHTER, ... 335–337

CHAPTER XXXI.—GEDEON AND THE MADIANITES, . . 338–341

CHAPTER XXXII.—THE BOOKS OF KINGS.— 1. Difficulties
drawn from the Books of Samuel or 1st and 2d Books of
Kings — 2. Difficulties drawn from the Chronology of the
3d and 4th Books of Kings — 3. King Josias and the High
Priest Helcias, ... 341–358

CHAPTER XXXIII.—THE PARALIPOMENONS.— 1. The Captivity of King Manasses — 2. The Annals of Assurbanipal
— 3. The restoring of Manasses to the Throne, . . . 359–364

CHAPTER XXXIV.—THE BOOK OF TOBIAS.— 1. Difficulties
— 2. Objections — 3. Anachronism — 4. The Demon
Asmodeus, ... 364–371

TABLE OF CONTENTS

CHAPTER XXXV.—THE BOOK OF JUDITH.— 1. Pretended historic and geographical Errors — 2. The site of Bethulia — 3. Historical Difficulties — 4. Assurbanipal, the Nabuchodonosor of Judith — 5. Anachronisms — 6. Discourse of Achior — 7. The Heroine Judith, ... 371–383

CHAPTER XXXVI.—THE BOOK OF ESTHER.— 1. Esther, the wife of King Xerxes — 2. The delay of Aman's vengeance — 3. The immense number of the Dead — 4. The Facts justified by History — 5. Living proofs of the reality of the History of Esther — 6. Additions in the Greek and Latin Bibles, ... 383–391

CHAPTER XXXVII.—THE BOOKS OF THE MACHABEES.— Book I.: — 1. Alexander the First that ruled over Greece — 2. The Division of Alexander's Kingdom among his Generals — 3. Judgment on the Romans — 4. Ties of Relationship between the Jews and Spartiates — Book II.: — 1. Letters of the Jews of Jerusalem to those of Egypt — 2. The Sacred Fire — 3. The Ark hidden — 4. The Death of Antiochus — 5. Name of the Temple pillaged by Antiochus — 6. The Letter of the Jerusalem Jews — 7. The Martyrdom of the Seven Machabean Brothers — 8. The Letters of Antiochus V., Eupator and of Lysias — 9. The Anniversary of the Birth of Antiochus Epiphanes, . . 392–428

CHAPTER XXXVIII. — THE PSALMS. — Objections: — 1. Against the Origin — 2. Against the Doctrine of these Sacred Chants, ... 428–431

CHAPTER XXXIX.—THE BOOK OF PROVERBS, ... 432–434

CHAPTER XL.—THE BOOK OF ECCLESIASTES. — Objections: — 1. Epicurianism — 2. Scepticism — 3. Materialism — 4. Pessimism, ... 435–439

CHAPTER XLI.—THE CANTICLE OF CANTICLES, . . . 439–441

CHAPTER XLII.—THE BOOK OF JOB. — Various Objections: — 1. The Probability of all the Details — 2. Pretended Contradictions — 3. The Friends of Job — 4. The Reality of the Epilogue — 5. Names of the Daughters of Job — 6. Authenticity of the divers parts of the Book of Job, ... 442–449

CHAPTER XLIII.—THE PROPHET DAVID. —1. The Holiness of the Life of David — 2. David merits the praises of Scripture — 3. Abisag, the Concubine of David — 4. David and the Prophecy of Nathan, ... 450–457

CHAPTER XLIV.—THE PROPHET ISAIAS.— 1. The Authenticity of Isaias — 2. First Objection: The Epoch of the Prophecy — 3. The Place of its Composition — 4. The Style of the Prophecy, ... 458–464

CHAPTER XLV.—THE PROPHETS JEREMIAS AND BARUCH.— 1. The Prophecy against Babylon — 2. Letter of Jeremias to the Jews in Captivity — 3. Baruch, ... 465–472

CHAPTER XLVI.—THE PROPHECIES OF EZECHIEL AND THE VISION OF THE CHERUBIM.— 1. The Authenticity of the Prophecies of Ezechiel — 2. Objections — 3. The Eating of a Book — 4. The Cherubim of Ezechiel, ... 472–477

CHAPTER XLVII.—THE PROPHET DANIEL.— 1. Authenticity of the Book of Daniel — 2. First Objection — 3. Musical Instruments — 4. Other Objections — 5. The Statue of Nabuchodonosor — 6. The Lions' Den — 7. Balthazar, King of Babylon — 8. The Canticle of the Three Children in the Fiery Furnace — 9. The History of Susanna — 10. Bel and the Dragon, ... 477–489

CHAPTER XLVIII.—THE PROPHET JONAS.— 1. Attacks against This Book — 2. These Objections are very Weak — 3. Jonas in the Whale's Belly, ... 489–493

CHAPTER XLIX.—THE PROPHET ZACHARIAS, ... 493–495

CHAPTER L.—AUTHENTICITY OF THE GOSPELS IN GENERAL, 495–499

CHAPTER LI.—AUTHENTICITY OF THE GOSPEL ACCORDING TO ST. MATTHEW.— 1. Formal Testimonies of Antiquity — 2. Indirect Testimonies — 3. Intrinsic Arguments, . 500–505

CHAPTER LII.—AUTHENTICITY OF THE GOSPEL ACCORDING TO ST. MARK.— 1. Formal Testimonies of Antiquity — 2. Indirect Testimonies — 3. Intrinsic Arguments, . 505–508

CHAPTER LIII.—AUTHENTICITY OF THE GOSPEL ACCORDING TO ST. LUKE.— 1. Formal Testimonies of Antiquity — 2. Indirect Testimonies — 3. Extrinsic Arguments, . 508–511

CHAPTER LIV.—OBJECTIONS AGAINST THE AUTHENTICITY OF THE THREE SYNOPTIC GOSPELS, ... 511–516

CHAPTER LV.—AUTHENTICITY OF THE GOSPEL ACCORDING TO ST. JOHN.— 1. Intrinsic Arguments — Formal Testimonies of Antiquity — 2. Indirect Testimonies — 3. Intrinsic Arguments — 4. Objections of the Rationalists Against the Authenticity of the Gospel of St. John . . 517–528

TABLE OF CONTENTS

CHAPTER LVI.—INTEGRITY OF THE GOSPELS.— Proofs for the Substantial Integrity — Passages Contested by the Critics, ... 529–537

CHAPTER LVII.—VERACITY OF THE GOSPELS.— Competency of the Historians of the Facts they relate — Sincerity of their Relations — It was Impossible for them to deceive their Readers — Seal of Sincerity imprinted upon their Work — Objections: — 1. The Double Genealogy of Our Lord — 2. The Census of Quirinus — 3. The site of Emmaus — 4. The Name Joanna — 5. The flat Roofs — 6. Christ's Public Life; The Portrayal of Jesus given by the Synoptics — 7. The Beginning of the public Ministry of Jesus — 8. Place of residence of the Holy Family — 9. The Name Levi — 10. The Demoniacs of Gadara — 11. Another Pretended Contradiction — 12. The History of the Vocation of the Apostles — 13. Finally — 14. The Magi and the Flight into Egypt — 15. Conclusion, . . 537–567

CHAPTER LVIII.—DEMONIACS AND DEMONIACAL POSSESSION.— The Word Demon — Demoniacal Possessions, . 568–579

CHAPTER LIX.—THE SO-CALLED BRETHREN OF OUR LORD.— The Arguments of Helvidius and Answer — By what title the term Brother of Jesus is given to certain Evangelical Personages, ... 579–585

CHAPTER LX.—THE ACTS OF THE APOSTLES.— Authenticity of the Acts — 2. Their Integrity — Their Veracity — Answers to pretended Errors, ... 585–595

CHAPTER LXI.—ST. PAUL'S EPISTLE TO THE GALATIANS— 1. The Cephas of the Epistle to the Galatians, ... 595–603

CHAPTER LXII.—ST. PAUL'S EPISTLES TO THE THESSALONIANS, ... 604–607

CHAPTER LXIII.—PASTORAL EPISTLES OF ST. PAUL, . 608–614

CHAPTER LXIV.—THE EPISTLES OF ST. JOHN, . . . 614–616

CHAPTER LXV.—THE EPISTLE OF ST. JAMES, . . . 616–619

CHAPTER LXVI.—ST. PAUL'S EPISTLE TO THE HEBREWS, 620–625

CHAPTER LXVII.—THE APOCALYPSE, ... 626–628

CHAPTER I.

RATIONALISM.

THE Sacred Scriptures have become in our time the point aimed at by infidelity. Against them the rationalistic criticism directs all the weight of its efforts. Since the foundation of the Church, our Sacred Books have been mingled with all its wrestlings, but in a manner very different formerly from to-day. Formerly they were unanimously acknowledged as the word of God; after the extinction of paganism both heretics and orthodox accepted their authority and divine origin; they often disputed about the meaning one had to attach to the oracles which they contain, but never about the submission and obedience that are due to them; the soldiers of every camp pretended to enroll themselves under their banner and combat for their triumph. To-day, all is changed. Many heads bow down no longer with respect before the divine pages; error does not accept the Bible as judge and umpire in the combats which it delivers to Christianity. Revolting reason or Rationalism, as they call it, has thrown off the yoke of faith. It believes no longer in revelation, it denies the inspiration of the Sacred Scriptures, the existence and possibility of miracles, and sometimes even the existence of God. For Rationalism, the supernatural is only an illusion; the efficaciousness of prayer, a revery; grace, an idle fancy; heaven and hell, phantoms; nothing exists except what falls under our senses, or, at least, does not surpass the bearing of our intelligence. Thus it lays violent hands on all the great Christian truths, and because all these truths are founded upon Scripture which teaches them to us, they attack the Scripture with a blind fury, without truce and without mercy, knowing very well that if they will succeed in overthrowing this column, the entire building of Jesus Christ would tumble with it, as the temple of the Philistines ruined by the force of Samson.

Such is the origin of the war undertaken by the rationalistic criticism against both the Old and New Testament. Between the two antagonists, there is a deadly duel. If infidelity is right, the Bible is not what the Church believes; it is a purely human book, as the Iliad or Odyssey of the Greeks, as the Vedas or the Mahabharata of the Hindoos, not an inspired book of supernatural and divine origin. If, on the contrary, the Church is not deceived in adoring in the Scriptures the authentic word of the Holy Ghost, rationalism is an error, its principles are false, its conclusions inadmissible.

Hence the efforts of infidel criticism against our revealed Books; hence also the necessity to oppose a dam to it. The numberless accusations launched against the Bible justify only too well the opportuneness of the present work. Since we are attacked, we have to defend ourselves. Since God has intrusted us to guard His Word, we have to keep this divine deposit intact. It is our duty, as well as our right and consolation.

Certainly, we know, the most efficacious means to dispel the clouds which one gathers around our Sacred Books, is not to carry therein the flame of discussion.

To those who calumniate the light of the sun, we only need to say: Look. To those who outrage the Gospel, we only need to say: Read. The Gospel, indeed, needs only to be read with simplicity of heart in order to enlighten and touch the souls. Even those who have been gnawed by the worm of doubt cannot resist to the divine charm of the words of Jesus Christ, when they are upright enough to impose silence upon their prejudices, and to listen only to this heavenly voice. Then they will experience what Silvio Pellico experienced, after he had abandoned his errors: "The Bible—thanks be to heaven, I now knew to read,"—he relates to us in his Prisons, "the Bible was no longer for me as in the time when I judged it with the critical uprightness of Voltaire, turning into ridicule expressions which are ridiculous or false only in the eyes of ignorance or of bad faith, incapable to penetrate its sense. I saw clearly that, under many titles, it is the true code of holiness and therefore of truth; how little philosophical is that delicacy which becomes shocked at certain imperfections of style, and which resembles the pride of those who despise all that has no elegant forms."

Those who will read the Gospel with the same sentiments as Silvio Pellico will admire therein, like he, the true code of holiness and truth, and the doctrine of its detracters will then appear futile to them; they will be no longer dazzled by the dust one sees appear in the midst of the bright rays of the sun.

The direct study of the Sacred Books, for those who are capable to do so, in conforming themselves to the rules wisely established by the Church, is the most efficacious means to triumph over the objections. But the honor of the Scriptures requires that we defend it against those who combat it, however unjust their attacks may be. It must be avenged for the outrages of its enemies. One must show to misled souls, who, without having ever opened it, insult it on the faith of authors of renown, how their guides are deceivers. One must also put into the hands of the champions of the Church the weapons with the help of which they can avenge the insults which they have attempted to inflict upon it. Therefore, this book is especially addressed to the instructed Christians, to both priests and laymen, desirous to render an account to themselves of their beliefs, and also desirous to justify them against false accusations. But it is equally addressed to all men of good faith, friends or enemies, because truth is made for all upright souls. "Blessed," says the Lord, "are the clean of heart, for they shall see God." God will manifest Himself in His Scriptures to all those that shall seek Him with purity of heart and simplicity of intention. The scales will fall from their eyes as from those of the converted Paul, and there, where previously they beheld only shadows and spots, they will perceive only radiant truths, worthy of their belief and adoration.

CHAPTER II.

THE AUTHENTICITY OF THE PENTATEUCH.

THE word Pentateuch signifies a work embracing five books. It is the collective name which we give to the first five books of the Bible, that is, Genesis, Exodus, Leviticus, Numbers and Deuteronomy.

Moses is at once a historic personage and a historian. He is a historic personage, because he directed the exodus of the Hebrews, gave to them a legislation, and led them until to the gates of Palestine; he is a historian, because he has related the history of his people since the beginning of the world, and because he has insisted quite particularly upon his own history: he is *the author of the Pentateuch.* Now, the rationalistic criticism makes efforts in our days, with a real madness, to make Moses disappear as a historian, and even as a historic personage; it feels that, if it succeeds in this task, it would destroy the character of the religion of Israel, and consequently it would deal a great blow to Christianity, for on account of the intimate connection that exists between Christianity and the religion which was destined to prepare its coming, every attack, either against the supernatural character of this religion, or even against the traditional history of the people chosen by God, falls back on the religion of Jesus Christ. Therefore, it is more important to-day than ever, to establish solidly these two beliefs of tradition: Moses is the legislator of the Hebrews; Moses is the historian of the people of God, and the author of the Pentateuch. There is between these two assertions an intimate bond, although not necessary: an intimate bond, for when Moses is the historian, one cannot deny that he is the legislator; a not necessary bond, for if Moses were not the historian, it would not necessarily follow from this that he was not the legislator. Therefore, there are two distinct questions, that of Moses as legislator, and that of Moses as historian.

I. Moses as Legislator.

Both the Jewish and Christian tradition has always presented to us Moses as the legislator of the Hebrew people, and as the author of the book which contains this law, that is, of the Pentateuch. The rationalists understanding very well the whole importance of this truth from the point of view of Christianity, have at first tried to rob Moses of the composition of the Pentateuch, as we shall see further on. Then, emboldened by their audacity, they went further and have refused to Moses, not only the historical authorship, but even the promulgation of the law. According to the rationalistic school, Moses would not be even the author of the most of the laws which carry his name. Perhaps he is the author of the Decalogue and of some rare laws promulgated in the same epoch as that fundamental rule of religion and morals. Not even this is certain according to the modern doctors, but which, according to them, is outside of dispute, is that Moses is neither the author of the ritual laws of Leviticus nor of Deuteronomy. What they affirm is, that the legislation of the Pentateuch, attributed to Moses, is in great part posterior to him.

How do the rationalists explain the formation of this law? Their hypotheses in regard to this subject are exposed and refuted in various chapters of this work; what is sufficient to keep in mind here, is the affirmation that Moses is not the legislator of the Hebrews: an affirmation completely erroneous and given the lie to, not only by faith, but also by science, as we are going to see.

1. In the first place, the authenticity of the Pentateuch, in considering it in its lgislative portion as well as in its dogmatic portion, we shall prove in the second part of this chapter. When, therefore, Moses has drawn up these laws, it is naturally impossible to pretend that they are posterior to him.

2. But, in making abstraction of the authenticity of the Pentateuch, in supposing even, if you wish, that this authenticity is not proved, the role of Moses as legislator of the Hebrews is thereby not less established upon incontestable proofs. And indeed, the rationalists do not make the attempt, we believe, to deny the fact, that in the epoch of the captivity the Hebrew people was universally persuaded that Moses was its legislator. Rigorously taken, this would be sufficient for us, for there is not question here, as in the question of the authenticity of the Pentateuch, of a literary fact so to say: there is question of a social fact, of an extreme simplicity as well as of a capital importance. Now, the existence of a general belief of a people upon a point of this kind, at a given moment, can be explained only—at least by convincing proofs of the contrary—by the antiquity of this belief and by the veracity of the fact in question. As a brilliant apologist has correctly remarked, "If tradition were not admitted as a proof of a similar fact, entire history would fall to pieces."

3. But when one cannot deny that Moses has been the legislator of the Hebrews, one pretends that his role has not been so extensive as the Pentateuch makes us suppose, that the ritual laws in particular are not derived from him, and date only from the time of Esdras. To this we answer: 1. How could one make us believe that the contemporaries of Esdras, instructed as all the peoples upon their history, permitted themselves to be imposed upon, and to believe that laws, which were unknown until the captivity, came from Moses; and especially when these laws were, as the rationalists claim, in contradiction with the history of the Israelites; when they imposed upon them one single sanctuary, sacrificial rites, and even a sacredotal caste unknown until then? A certain rationalist treats the Hebrews as horned brains; indeed, one must regard the Hebrews as stupid beings, when one supposes that they, on the invitation of Esdras, and by admitting as Mosaic a new legislation, have consented to see in their whole history the contrary of what they had seen thus far. 2. Besides, we have the right to invoke here the argument of *Possession*. We possess the ritual laws, about the unity of the sanctuary, about the Levitical priesthood, etc., as emanating from Moses; now possession is equal to a title, and to rob us of this, our adversaries will be obliged to prove, not only that the things might have passed as they say, but that they could not pass otherwise. Now, do they prove this? Far from this, for their hypotheses have not even the merit of probability, as we remarked before, and as one can easily convince himself by reading the next chapter in regard to the Sanctuary, Priesthood, etc.

Thus, it can be seen, that even by clinging to the

scientific point of view, one is not authorized to deny tradition which beholds in Moses the author of the Hebrew legislation. As to the dogmatic point of view, we have to make a remark in ending. As we have said elsewhere, when the authenticity of the Pentateuch was a point regarded by the theologians as semi-dogmatic, certain Christians believed that they could make some concessions in regard to this subject. We do not pretend here to judge this tendency but we will remark that the question of Moses-legislator presents itself with a character more strictly dogmatic than that of Moses-historian. How could a Catholic refuse to Moses the laws of the Pentateuch, when the official title under which all the laws, the civil as well as the moral or ceremonial laws, is this: "God said to Moses: Thou shalt speak thus to the children of Israel?" The Christian who believes in the inspiration of the Bible cannot suppose that the Sacred Books attribute to Moses laws which are not derived from him; to suppose this would be attacking the very origin of these laws, not only their Mosaic origin, but also their divine origin; this would be supposing that the inspired authors from whom these laws are derived had made an abuse of the belief of the Hebrews, at the authority of Moses, to impose upon them, in the name of God, painful and very heavy laws. From that time one would find himself in the following dilemma: either these laws are divine, and then it is a peculiar mark of respect towards the divine law to introduce fraud at its promulgations; or these laws are human, and then one supposes that the Bible, in giving them as divine, has committed an error upon a dogmatic point. Hence, we must conclude that the thesis in question belongs to faith.

II. Moses as Historian.

In the first place, what is the degree of dogmatic certitude of the assertion: The Pentateuch is from Moses? Theology which allows generally a great liberty to the discussions in regard to the human authenticity of the Sacred Books, and ordinarily contents itself to require that one respects their canonicity and their inspiration, shows itself more rigorous in regard to the books of Moses, and the most of the theologians consider tradition which refers to this prophet the entire composition of the works that are attributed to him, as having a semi-dogmatic character, and do not believe it permitted to remove from this. The Church, however, has not pronounced herself officially upon this question, and the exact limit which orthodoxy allows upon this point does not seem, as long as the Church has not spoken, that it can be traced with a complete certitude. Certain Catholics, exaggerating perhaps the liberty which the Church permits, in this point, to her children, show, since some years, a pronounced tendency to break with the traditional thesis which sees in Moses the author of the Pentateuch considered, either in its ensemble, or in each of its parts. Always believing in Moses-legislator, a point which we consider as dogmatic, as we have seen, they tend, it seems, to suppress or to diminish, at least in part, the role of Moses-historian, in spite of the intimacy of this point with the first. We will not follow them upon this ground, and, without inquiring whether this point belongs to Catholic belief, what we maintain here, is the traditional thesis: the Pentateuch, taken in its ensemble, is the work of Moses. This thesis, we shall prove successively by the Bible itself, by the Samaritan Pentateuch, by the language of the Pentateuch, by the Egyptian monuments, and finally by the argument of possession, and then we shall examine the objections opposed by the rationalists to the authenticity of the Pentateuch.

1. The whole Bible testifies in favor of the mosaic origin of the Pentateuch:—1. The Pentateuch itself must contain, as all the books, certain allusions by means of which it is possible to designate its author. Now these allusions are really found therein, and the one which they designate is Moses. For the *legislative portion*, there cannot be any doubt. About this point the very text of the Pentateuch is formal. It affirms that the laws have been revealed by God to Moses himself, and promulgated by this prophet to the people of Israel. The legislative formula constantly repeated, the official title under which are inscribed all the laws, the civil as well as the moral or ceremonial laws, is this: "God said to Moses: Thou shalt speak thus to the children of Israel." On the other hand, it is said (Ex. xxiv. 4; Deut. xxxi. 9) that the law was not only promulgated aloud, but also written by Moses. As to the *historic portion*, several passages equally suppose its historic origin. In Exodus (xvii. 14), for instance, God commands Moses to write, not in a book, but in the Book, according to the Hebrew text, the account of the battle against Amalecites, which supposes the existence of a book concerning the history of Israel. The same reflection is introduced by Num. xxxiii. 1-2, etc. 2. All the other books of the Old Testament confirm the Mosaic origin of the Pentateuch, for all make allusion to it, all presuppose it, either in the events which are

related therein, or in the laws which are contained therein. *Josue* could not be understood without the Pentateuch, and besides he names several times the book of the law (I. 7, 8, etc.). The *Judges* suppose it, either at their first appearance, by recalling to mind the order contained in the Pentateuch to exterminate the Chanaanites, or in the discourse of the angel (II. 1-3), which reproduces passages from Exodus (xxiv, 12), from Deuteronomy (vii, 2), etc. In I and II of Kings, we see God honored in the tabernacle according to the Mosaic law, and a passage of Deuteronomy (xiii, 3) reproduces word for word I Kings, ii, 13. Beginning with III Kings all the *historical books* make mention of the Pentateuch, and history itself supposes it forcibly. And indeed what do we see therein? a people carried by its taste to idolatry, and falling therein frequently: why therefore does it always leave this, after having fallen therein? because its law is monotheistic, because it has the Decalogue and the Mosaic legislation. Suppress these, and you understand nothing in the history of this people; admit for a moment the absence of the Mosaic law at the outset of the history of the Hebrew people, and you will ask yourselves how it comes that a people carried invincibly, so to say, towards idolatry could end in making for itself a law in complete contradiction with its tastes and inclinations. The history of the Hebrews supposes the Mosaic law as a stone ascending towards heaven, in spite of the force that attracts it downward; it supposes a foreign force which has impressed upon it this movement. When finally we run over the Psalms, the Books of Wisdom and the Prophets, we again arrive at the same conclusion: they all suppose the Pentateuch; they are its echo; they quote it sometimes word for word, thus proving not only that the facts related by the Pentateuch were known to the Hebrews, but also that this book itself was known and employed by them. 3. As to the new Testament, what stronger words can one desire than the words of our Saviour addressed to the Jews: "If you did believe Moses, you would perhaps believe me also, for he wrote of me; but if you do not believe his writings, how will you believe my words?" (John v, 46.) Elsewhere we see the Messiah interpreting to the two disciples of Emmaus, all the prophetic writings in regard to Him, beginning with Moses (Luke xxiv, 27), etc. The New Testament is therefore fully in accord with the Old to tell that Moses has written, and that his book has always been religiously guarded by the Hebrew people.

2. The high antiquity, if not the mosaism of the Pentateuch, is confirmed by the existence of the Samaritan Pentateuch. This is a Pentateuch written in Hebrew, but with the ancient letters, in the Phoenician form. It is substantially the same as that which is printed in our Bibles; it distinguishes itself from this by the absence of the archaisms. We know that Samaria was repeopled by means of foreigners conquered by the Assyrians, after the transportation of the Israelites to Ninive: these pagans afflicted by God on account of their iniquity, obtained from the king of Assyria that one of the priests transported could return and settle among them in order to teach them the worship of his God. It is quite natural to suppose that it was this priest who brought the Pentateuch along. To believe many critics, who reject after the captivity the appearance of this Pentateuch, it cannot be seen why the

Samaritans should have then accepted a book written in a foreign language, and one can see neither why the Pentateuch should not have been accompanied by the books of the Prophets.

3. The new science of Egyptology has furnished to us another proof for the authenticity of the Pentateuch. All that is related of Egypt, at the occasion of the sojourn of the Hebrews in this country and of their exodus, is in perfect accord with the state of Egypt such as it appeared under the Rameses; now this state was very different from what it should be later on, for example, in the epoch of Solomon or in that of the prophets. The Egypt of the Pentateuch is very different from that of the prophets: in the first, one sole state, in the second, an empire parcelled out into small principalities; in the first, complete silence about the kingdom of Ethiopia, in the second, this kingdom appears; in all the details we recover the same exactitude, proving that the Pentateuch is much anterior to the prophets. As to the Egyptian customs, we recover them faithfully depicted until to the smallest details: for striking examples, see chapters, Abraham, Joseph, Plagues of Egypt, etc. To be so exact the author of the history must necessarily have lived himself in Egypt with the people whose exodus he relates.

4. Even the language of the Pentateuch is a confirmation of its high antiquity; we meet therein, indeed, with linguistic archaisms which we find no longer in the other books of the Bible. The principal ones are: 1. The frequent employ of the masculine for the feminine, for example, in *hohou, hî,* for he, she, and in *na'ar,* young man, for *na'arah,* for young girl. 2. The employ of *yod* in order to connect two substantives. 3. A peculiar con-

struction for the infinitive. 4. Certain poetic phrases, as to cover the eye with earth. 5. The absence of foreign words except Egyptian, which shows that the Hebrews, during the composition of the Pentateuch, were not in relation with the Assyrians and other nations, as they should be under the kings.

5. The proofs we come to give are not all of equal value: that drawn, for example, from the Samaritan Pentateuch, is not so convincing as that founded upon the constant testimony of the Bible; but these proofs taken in their ensemble, do they give us a real certitude about the authenticity of the Pentateuch? All the rationalists and, we have to admit, some Catholics, more audacious in criticism than prudent, deny this. For us, it seems that these proofs have or have not that character of evidence, according as one joins them or not to another argument, the argument of *Prescription*, or, if you wish, of Possession. Thus, supposing that the Pentateuch was unknown until now, or, lost as so many other books, were found to-day, and that one would have to assign to it a date and an author, one would be led, by the reasons exposed above, to conclude with a quasi-certitude that these books emanate from Moses; but we would have no perfect certitude about this, on account of the arguments which another would bring forward, and which would not leave any doubts to arise. But in reality the question does not pose itself thus, and it is this what one forgets too often. In fact, we possess from immemorial times the Pentateuch, and we possess it as being from Moses. Now, possession is equal to the title. We have received the Pentateuch from the Jews; they themselves, as far as they may go back in their history, have no knowledge of any

protestation made against the Mosaic origin of this book, which would be inexplicable if the Pentateuch would not come from Moses; we have therefore every possible reason to say: the Pentateuch is from Moses. And behold after a possession of more than twenty centuries, critics come and tell us: But prove that the Pentateuch is from Moses! We are therefore in the same position as so many proprietors to whom one would come and say, after several centuries have seen their ancestors possessing the same good: But prove that this same good belongs to you! We have the right to answer to the Rationalists: It is for you to prove that the Pentateuch is not from Moses. Messrs. critics, shoot first!

In placing ourselves upon this ground we are invincible; for to overthrow our thesis, it is not sufficient to show that such or such a fragment of the Pentateuch, or even the entire Pentateuch might not be from Moses; to this we would answer: admitted, but in fact it is from Moses. It would be sufficient neither, whether it was possible, that such or such a fact related by the Pentateuch offers improbabilities; we would answer: The true may sometimes not be very probable, and this fact is true, authentic, we know it; because we possess the Pentateuch. Even it would not be sufficient to erect skilfully a system which, adorned with the whole apparatus of science and with the artifices of language, might appear from the human point of view more probable than the system of the Mosaic origin of the Pentateuch; then even we would answer: This is not sufficient! If it were you that had discovered the Pentateuch and brought it to us, and if there were simply questions of doing critical work and inquire who might be its author, your theory might make an impression upon us; supposing even, if you wish, that it could conquer adherents among us. But, once more, the question does not pose itself thus: We have always possessed the Pentateuch as being from Moses, and to destroy this traditional belief, more than ingenious hypotheses are required, more than probabilities; we must have certain and invincible proofs, and you do not furnish these to us.

But when, as we have said, a traditional possession can be destroyed only by convincing proofs, there remains for us to show, to complete the argument of possession, that the reasons brought forward by the rationalists in favor of their system are not at all convincing. One knows that all the imagined theories by the critics in regard to the subject of the Pentateuch can be about reduced to the following system: The Pentateuch must be considered as an assemblage of fragments of different epochs rehandled and more or less well joined together in an epoch which one can put back until to the return of the captivity. Now, the reasons produced in favor of this thesis can be summed into three, which we shall successively refute:

1. OBJECTION.

The principal argument of the Rationalists is drawn from the diversity of names of God in the Pentateuch: beginning with the 6th chapter of Exodus. God is called indifferently Elohim or Jehovah, but in the whole of Genesis there are fragments where Elohim is found exclusively, and others where God is called only Jehovah. The Rationalists conclude from this that Genesis is due at least to two authors, and that tradition which attributes it to Moses is apocryphal. In order that the conclusion of the critics might be founded, they would have to show that the name of Jehovah was unknown in the time of Moses; then one would have some foundation for denying to him the Jehovistic passages; but in fact, according to Exodus (iii, 13-15), it is precisely to Moses that He revealed Himself as Jehovah. As for the explanation of this distinction of the Jehovistic and Elohistic passages, we can do it, either in supposing that Moses had in hands and inserted into the Pentateuch more ancient documents wherein God is called Elohim, or in noticing that God is generally called Elohim when one represents Him as the God of the universe, and Jehovah when one speaks of Him as the God adored by the Hebrews. In every case it is absolutely impossible, in placing aside the Elohistic passages, which are very numerous, to arrive to make thereof something that has resemblance to a well connected history. Finally, we will ask whether we must regard as Elohistic or as Jehovistic the quite numerous passages where both names are united together.

2. OBJECTION.

Again the critics believe of being able to deny the authenticity of the Pentateuch, in supporting themselves upon certain contradictions which they pretend to discover therein; according to them, these contradictions can be explained only by the plurality of authors, who would have related the same fact in different manners. According to what we have said before, in order that this argument might have some value against us, the Rationalists would have to establish a contradiction in a manner, not only probable, but absolutely certain.

Now these pretended contradictions are so easy to reconcile, that they have not even the merit of probability. Thus, they oppose to us examples of this kind: Jacob goes to Mesopotamia, here to seek a wife (Gen. xxvii, 46, etc.), and there to fly from the wrath of Esau (xxvii, 41-45); the wealth of Jacob is attributed here to the blessing of God (xxxi, 4-48), and there to the industry of the patriarch (xxx, 25-43); Joseph is sold by his brethren, here to Ismaelites (xxxvii, 25), and there to Madianites (28); the Hebrew slave must recover his liberty here after six years of service (Ex. xxi, 1-6), and there at the moment of the Jubilee year (Lev. xxv, 39-41). No long reflection is needed to see that there are things here which add and do not contradict themselves: the flight of Jacob has two different motives; his wealth was caused by his industry, but the latter was blessed by God; the Madianites of Joseph were Ismaelites at the same title as the Yankees are Americans; finally, when the Hebrew slave should not serve more than six years, he had moreover the advantage to recover his liberty before this time, when meanwhile a Jubilee year took place. All the other contradictions imagined by the Rationalists are about as easy to solve, and it seems useless to insist any further on them.

3. OBJECTION.

Finally, certain analogous facts, which are repeated several times in the epoch of the patriarchs, are, for this reason several times related by the Bible, and the Rationalists have believed to see in these repetitions the proof for the existence of several documents put together. Here again the answer is easy: why should there not be some analogous accounts, when several analogous facts produced themselves? Can the critics prove, for instance, that Sara was not carried off twice: in Egypt and at Gerara (Gen. xii, xx); that Abimelech did not contract an alliance, with Abraham first, then with Isaac (xxi, xxvi); that God could not send twice quails to the Hebrews in the desert, nor to cause to spring forth water twice from a rock (Ex. xvi, xvii; Num. xi, xx)? Evidently the critics can prove nothing in this regard, and between their hypothetical affirmations and the repeated accounts of the Pentateuch, there can be no hesitation.

Thus the objections of the Rationalists against the authenticity of the Pentateuch serve absolutely for nothing. We are deceived: they have a great usefulness, they conform more strongly its authenticity. Indeed, a thesis must be very solid for having been able to resist to so many, and, let us tell it, to such skilful attacks. Now, the Catholic thesis resists and subsists in spite of all. On the contrary, what do we see from the side of our adversaries? The systems change constantly, and the Rationalists themselves would laugh if one would make the attempt to resurrect some of the theories of their predecessors. In reality, they are agreed only upon one point, namely to deny the authenticity of the Pentateuch, and their accord upon this point is too complete not to be suspicious, especially in the presence of their disaccord, quite as complete, when there is question to elaborate a positive theory and to make anew the history of the composition of the Pentateuch. We do not need to enter here into detail of these theories; we keep ourselves only in the defensive; but nevertheless we have to remark in ending, what a beautiful confirmation of the authenticity of the Pentateuch, is this disaccord of the Rationalists when there is question for them to explain its origin outside of Moses! Disaccord so perfect, that the same passage, studied intrinsically by five different Rationalists, will be attributed by them to five different epochs and separated by an interval of several centuries! When the intrinsic criticism gives such scientific results, it would be from its part more just, and more modest at the same time, not to despise the intrinsic testimonies: these, at least, have never varied, and have only one sole voice to proclaim that the Pentateuch is from Moses.

CHAPTER III.

HISTORICAL OBJECTIONS AGAINST THE AUTHENTICITY OF THE PENTATEUCH.

1. UNITY OF SANCTUARY.

DIFFERENT to the Catholic religion, where God multiplies His presence in thousands of churches, the Jewish religion admitted only one Ark of Covenant, one sole Temple, and before this Temple, one sole Tabernacle. Thereby God wished to impress more profoundly into the minds of the Hebrews the monotheistic idea. He had promised to dwell in a particular manner in the Tabernacle (Ex. xxv, 8) and, consequently, the unity of the sanctuary quite naturally reminded them on the unity of God.

The Rationalists deny this teaching of the Bible: to believe them, the Hebrews have no knowledge at all of the unity of the sanctuary; on the contrary, they had in a permanent manner a great number of local sanctuaries, and this since their first beginnings until their transportation into Assyria and Chaldea.

"Deuteronomy," says Mr. Wellhausen, "permits to render to God a solemn worship only in one sole place. This is an important prescription. Now, there is nothing of the kind. Nowhere do we meet with the allusion to a law of this kind. The prophets often rise against idolatry, but never against the plurality of places consecrated to worship. The "Book of the Covenant" approves of the multiplication of altars (Ex. xx, 24-25). Deuteronomy is the first that preaches the centralization of worship, favored by the fall of Samaria. The Sacerdotal Code goes still further and removes the institution of one sole place in the time of exodus by the double fiction of the central Tabernacle and the Ark it placed therein.

To answer to this objection, let us examine the texts themselves whose Mosaic origin they contest. It is drawn from Exodus (xx, 24-25). This law does not prescribe the unity of altar; on the contrary, it says that one may raise one, either of earth or of non-polished stone, all over where God will honor its name, that is, in very different places. The Rationalists themselves being agreed to this, we do not need to insist thereon; this passage is the destruction of their thesis. In the desert they offered sacrifice to God wherever they camped. Later on they did this in various places, because the law of Exodus permitted it: at Siloe (Judges xviii, 31); Cariathiarim (1 Kings vii, 1); Masphat (vii, 6-9); Ramatha (vii, 17); Galgala (x, 8); Bethlehem (xvi, 2); Gabaon (3 Kings iii, 4) etc., to speak only of the time previous to the building of the Temple. In order to raise an altar in any place, it was sufficient "that the memory of God's name was made there" (Ex. xx, 24).

The prescription reported above was promulgated upon Mount Sinai, the third month after the departure from Egypt, immediately after the Decalogue, whose complement it is. Some time afterwards, after the erection of the Tabernacle and the organization of worship, Moses, in the name of God, carried the law as found in Leviticus (xvii, 3-9). The law contained in this passage forbids to slaughter any of the animals which might be offered as a sacrifice, without offering them to Jehovah, even then were one to immolate them only to eat their flesh. According to Wellhausen, this law is posterior to the captivity. To maintain a similar opinion, to pretend that it was in the time of Esdras when it was forbidden to immolate victims, in the camp or outside the camp, and to offer them elsewhere except at the door of the Tabernacle, when there was neither camp nor Tabernacle, is a perfect nonsense. Wellhausen himself acknowledges that the interpretation which he gives to the text is, "according to its contents, impossible to execute and to put into practice," but nevertheless, he concludes that this passage forbids "to slaughter an animal, even for profane use, outside of Jerusalem, contrarily to the concession which Deuteronomy had made" and of which we shall speak very soon. When one is forced to explain the texts thus; when one pretends that a law promulgated by a reasonable man, and regarded as divine by an entire people, prohibited to this same people, then dispersed not only in the whole of Palestine, but also in Assyria, Chaldea, Persia and Egypt, to eat, under pain of death, the flesh of any animal that was not killed at Jerusalem; when one attributes to a writer such an absurdity to maintain a hypothesis which is in contradiction with the tradition of all centuries, does he not furnish himself the proof that he maintains a false and erroneous hypothesis? If a Catholic author would emit similar explanations to defend the Mosaic origin of the Pentateuch, what would one say of him and of such kind of arguments?

As much as the explanation of Wellhausen is contrary to common sense, so much is that furnished by tradition, in being conformant to real chronology, simple, natural and logical. As one might have, under pretext to kill an animal for eating, offered it to false deities, "to devils," says the text, within or without the camp, the legislator, in order to prevent all danger of idolatry, prohibits to slaughter any of the victims which might be offered into sacrifice, without offering them to the true God, at the door of the Tabernacle, even when one has no other reason to kill them than that to use the flesh thereof as nourishment. The remedy was very efficacious and cut short to idolatry; it could be easily executed in the desert, because every Israelite was near the Tabernacle and the usage of flesh meat was very rare among the Israelites in the desert, as it is still at all the nomad and pastoral peoples of the Orient.

But when it is easy to observe this law in the peninsula of Sinai, this was the case no longer, when the twelve tribes were dispersed in the east and west of the Jordan; also about forty years later, in the time when Israel went to take finally possession of the Promised Land, Moses abrogates the law of Leviticus which now could be observed no longer (Deut. xi, 31-32).

The spirit of the new law is the same as that in Leviticus; it has for chief end to prevent idolatry. Just as God had forbidden to offer in the desert of Sinai sacrifices to the devils, to the deities of the desert, He now forbids to offer them upon high places to the idols which the Chanaanites adored. In the peninsula of Sinai, in order to hinder all the abuses, He prescribed to offer no sacrifice, except before the Tabernacle; as henceforth this will be impracticable, He ordains to destroy everything that reminds of the Chanaanite worship. The Israelites, under the influence of the belief then dominating among the nations, that each country, as each people, had its particular gods, must have been strongly tempted to adore the false gods of the land of Chanaan, in associating them with the worship of the true God. Moses foresees this danger and to hinder his people to underlay to the temptation he prescribes to destroy everything that reminds of idolatry.

After having passed this ordinance, Moses, by the abrogation of the law of Leviticus, expressly authorizes the Israelites to eat in all places, without being bound to any particular rite, the flesh of animals offered into sacrifice, even that of game and of clean animals which cannot be offered to the Lord. The right to eat all over the flesh of clean animals is so natural that the permission given here can be explained only because it abolishes an anterior defense, carried in special circumstances. As much as everything is consequent and easily intelligible, in the traditional and chronological order, so much is everything forced and incomprehensible in the interpretation of the Rationalists. One can grant to somebody the authorization to do what everybody does only in the case where one did formerly forbid it to him for exceptional reasons. Deuteronomy abrogates therefore, at the leaving of the desert, a law which could be observed only in the desert. In future one will be bound no longer to present before the Tabernacle the ox, the sheep, or the goat one desires to eat.

Finally, let us remark that the new law does not prescribe to offer all the sacrifices before the Tabernacle. Neither Exodus nor Deuteronomy tells this. There is no longer question here, as in Leviticus, of the Tabernacle. All the Lord ordains is to offer the holocausts in the place He will choose. The place which He selected subsequently was Jerusalem, where the Temple arose, and which became the dwelling of His holiness. Then they should render to Him, upon the mountain consecrated to His worship, the homages and adorations of all the people. Until that time, before the divine selection, we cannot see why it should have been illicit to offer to God's sacrifices "in all the places where they made memory of His name," according to the expressions of Exodus. Moreover, even after the building of the Temple, we discover nowhere any formal and absolute defense to offer sacrifices, when there are reasons to do so, outside of Jerusalem. The law of Exodus is not expressly abrogated in Deuteronomy. In the last book, Moses has not attached to his prescription the completely exclusive sense, which the Rationalists give to it. When one reads carefully the terms which we have quoted, a measure prescribing the centralization of worship can be seen therein, indeed, but we find nothing therein which expresses the defense to offer sacrifices outside the place selected, when extraordinary circumstances may require this. The object of the law is to favor the unity of worship, in authorizing the official and ordinary service of religion only in one place, but it is good to remark that the legislator employs no absolute and quite restrictive term; he does not pronounce the pain of death against the prevaricators, as he had done in Leviticus; he does not say: you shall offer all your holocausts, *without exception, only and inclusively* in the place which God has selected, but simply: "you shall offer your holocausts in the place which God shall choose." When one keeps account of the Oriental habits and of the genius of the Hebrew language, which so easily employs universal expressions and formulas that are hyperbolical in our eyes, this reserved manner to announce the law is very significant. Hence there is nothing astonishing that the Israelites did not understand the ordinance in an absolute sense and they did not believe that if, in ordinary cases, it was in the Temple itself they had to offer all the sacrifices, in extraordinary cases and when they had reasons to act differently, one did not violate a law which was not imposed in a strict manner and without exception. The Pentateuch and the example of Moses justify this interpretation. Not only had the liberator of the Hebrews raised himself an altar after the victory over Amalek (Ex. xvii, 5), but he had prescribed, in Deuteronomy, to build one upon Mount Hebal, after the conquest of the Promised Land, which Josue faithfully executed.[1] Therefore the Rationalists alter the meaning of the prescription of Deuteronomy and are more rigorous than the Jews themselves in

---

[1] Deut. xxvii, 5, etc.; Jos. viii, 30, etc. Josue also raises an altar at Sichem, Jos. xxiv, 26. As to the altar built in the east of the Jordan by the transjordanic tribes, the latter are reproached, not to violate the law, but for desiring to cause a schism.

interpreting the text as they do, in a partisan and interested spirit.

Indeed, the Jews believed that God could authorize His prophets to abrogate certain prescriptions of the law. The history of the temple built by the Jews of Egypt at Leontopolis furnishes us a remarkable example of this. The law of Deuteronomy prohibited incontestably to raise a temple outside the territory of the twelve tribes, and when that of Jerusalem had been constructed, they considered as illicit to build another one elsewhere. In consequence of this regulation, the Jews did never wish to acknowledge the temple of Mount Garizim as legitimate, and very probably because all the Israelites believed that there could be in Palestine but one house of God which, before the arrival of the Samaritans in the north of Palestine, the kings of the ten tribes, even the most powerful, even those who were most ambitious to erect buildings and raise temples to Baal, raised never any to the true God. Nevertheless when the Jews of Egypt, under the reign of Ptolemy Physcon, built a temple at Leontopolis, although those of Jerusalem beheld this undertaking with a very evil eye, they did not condemn it as they had done for the temple on Mount Garizim, and the Talmud teaches us that when the priests who had served in the Egyptian temple were not admitted to fulfill their functions in that of Jerusalem, they were not however excluded from the assistance in the exercises of worship. The Egyptian Jews were never treated as schismatics. What was the cause of this difference of conduct? The following: To justify themselves, the Jews of Egypt had supported themselves upon a text of Isaias, announcing that "Jehovah would have an altar in the midst of Egypt."[1] Did this prophecy really legitimate their conduct? We do not need to examine this here. It is sufficient for us to state that the Jews did not doubt that the Lord could inspire His prophets with things in contradiction with the law, and that when they could interpret the law in this manner in this circumstance, they could interpret it in others in an analogous manner. Consequently supposing even that Moses had really forbidden in Deuteronomy to offer any sacrifice outside the place chosen by God, the prophets, the men of God, by an order or by an inspiration from His part, would have had the right to offer sacrifices in any place of Palestine, and the conduct of Gedeon, Samuel and Elias, would be only a derogation to an ordinance which obliged neither its author nor those who represented him.

Therefore we do not need to enter into a detailed discussion of the facts alleged by Messrs. Wellhausen, Reuss and Kuenen to establish that the law of the unity of the sanctuary did not exist before the last years of the kingdom of Juda. In fact it did not exist and it never did exist in the absolute sense which they attribute to it. The prescription of Deuteronomy indeed dates from the time of Moses, but they did not understand it, and with right, as they understand it, and this simple observation is sufficient to make crumble their whole thesis. They pretend to prove that Deuteronomy was not yet written in the time of Samuel and of the prophet Elias, because, they say, these personages offered sacrifices in different places, contrarily to the ordinances of Deuteronomy, which they never would have done, if this book would have already

---

[1] Is. xix, 19; Josephus, Ant. Jud. xiii, iii, i.

been known in their time. Certainly, if they had believed that God prohibited it indeed or that He did not dispense them from this general law, by virtue of the mission which He had intrusted to them; but when they did not believe themselves bound to observe what the Rationalists suppose or when they believed themselves dispensed therefrom, what can one infer from their conduct against the existence of Deuteronomy? Absolutely nothing.

Thus, in summary, Exodus permits to offer sacrifices in various places, and in the desert even they offer sacrifices to God all over where they camp. Leviticus ordained to offer all the sacrifices before the Tabernacle, and forbidded to slaughter, even for a simple, profane usage, any of the animals which might be offered to God, without offering them in effect, in order to hinder thereby more easily every act of idolatry. On the eve of taking possession of the Promised Land, Moses abrogated this double law of Leviticus; he commanded in Deuteronomy to offer the sacrifices in one sole place, to preserve more easily the purity of the dogma and to hinder the people from adoring the false gods; but he formulated his ordinance into such terms that they did not imply an absolute prohibition to offer victims elsewhere. One can apply them only to ordinary cases and interpret them in the sense that it was not illicit to erect also in other places, at least transitorily, altars to the true God. The explanation of the three legal texts concerning the place of worship, made also in the traditional and chronological order, offers therefore no difficulty, whilst on the contrary that of the Rationalists, who refuse to admit their Mosaic origin, obliges them to exaggerate

HISTORICAL OBJECTIONS. 43

the bearing of the law of Deuteronomy and to attach to that of Leviticus an inadmissible and quite unreasonable meaning.

2. THE SACRIFICES AT THE HEBREWS.

The Bible tells us that the sacrifices, although anterior at the Hebrews to the appearance of Moses, were regulated by him, and that he fixed with precision the nature, the epoch, the rite of the various sacrifices to be offered to Jehovah. But the Rationalists do not wish to behold in Moses the legislator of the Hebrews; for them the ritual, the *Sacerdotal Code*, dates only since the return from the captivity and must be ascribed to Esdras.

What the Rationalists call Sacerdotal Code must have indeed for object, before all, to regulate the rites and ceremonies because it is drawn up solely for this purpose, but to conclude from this that the Code is posterior to the captivity, it is very far. When historical books do not reproduce this ritual, it is because they had to record only the events. And when one tries especially to show that the sacrifice has been offered to the true God, not to idols, it is because the people had a marked inclination towards idolatry, whilst the sacrificer was not moved by any passion to violate the sacrificial laws and, consequently, had to dread no transgressions from this side. "They had besides seldom an occasion, as can be easily imagined, to describe the sacrificial rite." It is Mr. Wellhausen himself who avows this. He is also obliged to acknowledge that the language of the prophets proves that in their time, that is, according to his opinion, before the creation of the Levitical rites, they attached the greatest importance to worship and to the sacrifices, because the prophets often rise against the excessive formalism which induces both priests and people to attach themselves more to the exterior of worship than to the reform of the dispositions of the heart.

But it is not only the legal ritual which they ignored before the Captivity, according to Wellhausen, but the division itself of the sacrifices. The Sacerdotal Code distinguishes four kinds of them: the holocaust, *olah;* the sacrifice for sin, *hatta't;* the sacrifice for crime, *asam;* and the peaceable sacrifice, *selem.* The professor of Marburg agrees that the holocaust and the peaceable sacrifice have always been in use, because the Bible mentions them frequently, but he assures us that before Ezechiel one does not find "any trace" of the sacrifice for sin, "neither in the Jehovist nor in the Deuteronomist, nor in any historical and prophetic book." This assertion is not correct. The sacrifice for sin is expressly mentioned in one of the most ancient Psalms: "Sacrifice and oblation, O Lord, thou didst not desire. . . . Burnt offering and sinful offering thou didst not require." (Ps. xxxix, 7.)

We find a very clear allusion to this kind of sacrifices in the history of Heli, when the Lord said to the young Samuel: "I have sworn to the house of Heli, that the iniquity of his house shall not be expiated with victims nor offerings forever." (1 Kings iii, 14.) The prophet Osee speaking of the priests, names expressly the *hatta't:* "They shall eat the *hatta't* of my people" (Osee iv. 8), that is, the victims offered for the Israelites as sacrifices for sin, for the word *hatta't*, as we have seen, is the Hebrew word of the sacrifice for sin, and the priests, after having burned the fatty parts of the immolated lamb or ram, ate the flesh which belonged to them by right.

The *hatta't* is, therefore, mentioned in the Sacred Scriptures, outside the Pentateuch, long before Ezechiel. It is the same with the sacrifice for crime, the *asam*. The latter resembled so much the preceding that the commentators are not in agreement until to-day to point out the differences which distinguished the one from the other; but, be it as it may, there is question thereof, in the same time as of the sacrifice for sin, in a passage of the Book of Kings, where we read, in regard to the revenues of the Temple, in the time of king Joas: "The money of the *asam* and the money of the *hatta'ot*, they did not bring into the Temple of the Lord, because it belonged to the priests"(4 Kings xii, 16). This manner of speaking supposes that these two kinds of sacrifices are perfectly known. In a still more ancient epoch, in the time of the Judges, the Philistines who had captured the Ark, and who had been struck on this account with different evils, returned it to the God of Israel with asam to obtain pardon for their fault. The *hatta't* and *asam* have therefore been known at all times at the Hebrews, but on account of their nature itself, they have been named only occasionally, because they did not enter into the great acts of public worship, as the holocaust and the peaceful sacrifice, which were an essential part of the rejoicings and of the feast, and were associated with all the great events of the history of the people of God.

When among the writers of the Old Testament, outside the Pentateuch, Ezechiel alone has spoken in detail in regard to the worship and ceremonies, the reason is quite natural; it is because he, like Moses, is the only writer that treats upon this subject. Where will one find, for instance, details about the military tactics, except in the writings where one studies them? Where can one equally meet with the Levitical ritual, if not in the prophet who announces its restoration? The second part of the prophecy of Ezechiel is destined to picture the glorious future reserved to Juda after the Captivity. Israel should reobtain its lost country; the new kingdom of God will rise again and religion will flourish again more brilliant and more beautiful than ever. From the depth of his exile the seer greets already the splendors of this bright aurora. Under the conduct of an angel, he visits beforehand the restored Temple, and perceives with his own eyes the Promised Land restored to the race of Jacob; as in the days of his youth, he is upon Mount Moriah, and this priest of the ancient Temple delays willingly in the description of the new, which he sees already erect; he exposes with delight the rites followed in the sacrifices and in the various ceremonies of the worship of Jehovah; his heart overflows with joy in picturing those tableaus which revive in him the so dear past and make him forget the pains of the present. The abundance of the details which we read in his prophecy, compared to the small number of allusions which we find in the other books, explains itself therefore without difficulty by the very nature of the subject which he treats, namely, that of the ritual portion of the Pentateuch. The historical writings have not furnished to us the same indications, because a ritual act is not an historical act; the other historical writings do not teach us anything neither, because the prophets arose only against the reigning vices and did not need to reproach the priests for neglecting the observation of the sacred rites, to which the people attached rather a too great an importance. Ezechiel was no longer in the same situation as the other prophets; he wrote in a moment when, the Temple being destroyed, the sacrifices, with their traditional rites, had ceased to be offered at Jerusalem. To console himself and to console his brethren in mourning for Sion, he shows the worship rising again in the future and in his prophetic pictures he recalls to mind the events of the past and of the country, always so dear to the unfortunate and exiled.

Not only the numerous recollections of the Levitical rites contained in Ezechiel explain themselves by the very character of his prophecy, they are moreover, independently from all the other proofs we have given, a strong presumption in favor of the pre-existence of these rites. In fact it is only through a manifest inconsequence that the rationalistic critics pretend to make Ezechiel the inventor of the Israelitic ritual. They generally acknowledge that the second part of his book is only an embellished tableau of what he had seen in Jerusalem in his youth. The Temple which he describes is not a purely ideal temple; it is the temple of Solomon; the number of buildings, the sacred implements, the whole of his description, is only a faithful picture, except some details added for ornament, of what has remained deeply engraved in his memory. How, therefore, could he have invented the ritual with all its particulars, since in all the rest he has mainly reproduced only what existed already before? Undoubtedly, this is not impossible, but is contrary to all analogies, and since tradition has always placed the composition of the Pentateuch a long time before Ezechiel, and since we find in all the other Hebrew accounts manifest allusions to the ceremonial laws before this prophet, we are not permitted to maintain that these laws date only from his epoch. Besides can one imagine that there existed no ritual in the time of Solomon? No; because it was necessary for worship; there were some rites in all the temples. The Phenician inscription of Marseille furnishes the proof of this for the temples of Phenicia. Hence, Ezechiel must have made known to us this ritual anterior to the Captivity, as he has made known to us in his descriptions the ancient temple itself.

3. FEASTS OF THE HEBREWS.

The Hebrews had five great annual feasts: The Pasch, Pentacost, the feast of the Tabernacles, that of Expiation and that of the Trumpets. These five feasts are indicated and their celebration was regulated by Moses. But to believe the Rationalists these feasts are of recent institution, not Mosaic. "Primitively," says Mr. Wellhausen, "they were all profane feasts and had no other end in view but to celebrate the commencement and the end of harvest (Easter and Pentecost) or the vintages (feast of the Tabernacles). The Sacerdotal Code not only changed their character, but increased also their numbers by introducing the feast of the Trumpets and the solemnity of the Expiation or the great day of fast inaugurated during the Captivity. The Sabbatic year, and especially the Jubilee year are also of recent date. We meet with them only in the collection of the laws of Leviticus, xvii-xxvi, accepted and rehandled by the Sacerdotal Code."

All these affirmations of negative criticism are not supported by any proof. Here, as in all other cases, it is forced to avow that it has no other argument to allege but that of silence of the texts; it cannot bring forward the least historical argument and testimony in favor of its system. All what it finds to tell is that, if the feast of the Jubilee year, dated from the Mosaic time, we ought to discover traces thereof in the writings anterior to the Captivity of Babylon, outside the Hexateuch, that is, of the Pentateuch and Josue.

Even were this really the case, the demonstration would be insufficient, but what criticism advances is false. First it is deceived by what it tells of the Jubilee year, prescribed by Leviticus (xxv, 8) and called in this book "the year of propitiation, the year of remission"(xxv, 9-10). Isaias makes allusion like Ezechiel to the legal Jubilee (Isaias lxi, 1; Ezechiel xlvi, 17). Nehemias expressly attributes to Moses the institution of the Sabbatic year (x, 29-31). As to the feasts we have already established their Mosaic origin. The historians did not note, as can be easily understood, the observation of the legal solemnities, when they had no reason to do so; however they speak of them when circumstances furnished occasion for this. Thus we see that the great feast of the Pasch is celebrated by the Israelites, according to the ordinances of Moses, right away after having entered the land of Chanaan (Jos. v, 10) and in different epochs of their history. The author of Kings relates that under Josias, they celebrated it with greater solemnity than they had done since the time of the Judges (4 Kings xxiii, 21-22). Therefore, the historian did not doubt that they had celebrated it since the time of the Judges, although with less pomp and magnificence. Osee (xii, 9-10) makes allusion to the feast of the Tabernacles; the Book of Nehemias (viii, 14) assures us that it was Moses who instituted this solemnity during which the peoples dwelt under tents. Isaias speaks of the cycle of the feasts (xxix, 1; xxxii, 9; etc.).

As to the feasts which Wellhausen pretends to have been added by the Sacerdotal Code to the three ancient feasts, that of the Trumpets and of the Day of Expiation, his affirmation is not correct. Chapter xxxiii of Leviticus does not enumerate the feasts, but simply the time fixed to celebrate what they called the "Holy Convocation." Neither the Book of the Covenant in Exodus, nor Deuteronomy makes mention of the time, because they enumerate only the feasts which obliged the Israelites to render themselves into the place where the sanctuary of Jehovah was. Hence, it comes that the Sabbath is not even mentioned at the occasion of the laws about these feasts. The solemnity of the feast of the Trumpets and of the Day of Expiation, not requiring the presence of the faithful before the Tabernacle, are omitted for this reason. They are neither mentioned in the other books of the Old Testament; but this argument from silence proves nothing against their existence, because the sacred writers had no occasion to speak thereof, so that if the silence were conclusive, it would follow that the feast of Expiation would not have existed before Herod, in 37 B. C., because there is no mention made of it before this epoch.

4. THE PRIESTS AND LEVITES AT THE HEBREWS.

Not content to deny the Mosaic origin of the feasts at the Hebrews, Wellhausen also denies the Mosaic origin of the priesthood, in order to draw from this a new argument against the authenticity of the Pentateuch. He pretends that the distinction between priests and Levites is of recent invention: "Ezechiel is the first Hebrew author," he says, "who makes a distinction between priests and Levites. . . ."

In spite of the affirmation of the Professor of Marburg, it is not less true that all what concerns the priesthood is of Mosaic institution, and nothing is more historical and more certain than that which we read in regard to this subject in the Pentateuch.

Nothing is easier to explain than the establishment of the priesthood in Israel. There was at the Egyptians since the most remote antiquity, a hierarchical constituted priesthood, which was very numerous and influential. What is there astonishing that Moses, whose special end in view it was to establish solidly the religion in Israel, did institute a priesthood, "reminding by many traits of the Egyptian priesthood?" What is there astonishing that in order to fulfill its functions he chose his own family and his own tribe? What is there astonishing that he gave to it a ritual during his leisure hours of the nomadic life in the desert, when the daily offering of sacrifices caused often unforeseen cases to arise which required to be regulated? Also the ancient existence of this ritual is established by the writings themselves whose origin anterior to the Captivity the most extreme critics are forced to admit.

Besides nothing is less "legendary" than the details

which the Book of Numbers (xvi) furnishes about the opposition which Moses met with when he conferred the sacerdotal rights upon the family of his brother Aaron. Members of the tribe of Ruben, eldest son of Jacob, to whom belonged by right the sacerdotal functions, according to the patriarchal customs, refused to accept the new institution, and even descendants of Levi jealous of the privileges conferred upon Aaron, made common cause with the Rubenites and revolted with them. If the priesthood of Aaron were not historical, as Wellhausen claims, it would have been attributed to Moses. Moses would have been both the high priest and chief of his people; his sons and not Josue would have succeeded him in the commandery; they would have had like the latter, a select portion in the division of the Promised Land, and the author of the Paralipomenons (Par. vi.) would have not described so carefully the genealogy of Aaron and of his descendants, after having mentioned only that of Moses. Similar facts are not at all "mystic inventions," but bear the seal of the reality. Besides the whole history of Israel confirms what the Pentateuch teaches. It is sufficient to read the episode of Michas, in the Book of Judges, to recognize that the tribe of Levi was in Israel the sacerdotal tribe. What is more significant, among other things, than the word of Michas when the Levite has consented to fulfill in his house the functions of the priesthood: "Now I know that God will do me good since I have a priest of the race of the Levites?"[1] Mr. Wellhausen assures us that this Levite

---

[1] Judges XVII, 13. We read the name priests thirty-four times in the two Books of Samuel, sixty times in the Third and Fourth of Kings, etc.

"drew his value from its great rarity," but he does not dare to contest the antiquity of the passage which contains this account, and thus we have a sufficient proof of the existence of the Levites, in the epoch which immediately followed Moses and Josue. When this passage does not prove by itself the distinction of the priesthood and of the Levitic ministry, it proves at least the distinction between the clergy and the people. On the other hand, the difference of attribution between the descendants of Aaron and the other Levites is clearly pointed out in the institutions of David (1 Par. xxiii-xxvi).

At the commencement of the schism, under the reign of Roboam, nephew of David, one of the crimes with which Jeroboam, the first king of the ten tribes, is reproached, is for having established priests that were not of the race of Levi (3 Kings xii, 13), Jeremias (xxxiii, 21) expressly distinguishes between the *leviyim* and the *kohanim*, "the Levites and the priests." And before Jeremias, long before the copy of the law had been recovered in the Temple, the Books of Kings, in relating the feast of the dedication of the Temple of Solomon, mention separately the priests and the Levites. When the sacred writers do not always explicitly distinguish between the priests and Levites, the reason is to be brief. The priests were really Levites or of the tribe of Levi. This manner of speaking is so natural that the biblical authors who have lived after Ezechiel often express themselves as their predecessors, in a general fashion and without making any distinction, from which one could conclude, if one would reason like Wellhausen, either that the priests and the Levites were not yet distinct from one another, or that the Paralipomenons, Esdras, and Nehemias are more ancient than the Pentateuch. Undoubtedly, when we compare the priesthood and its attributions such as they go forth from the last prophets, with that which we read in the Pentateuch, we remark a development and a progress, due to time and circumstances, but we also behold that the most ancient form is the Mosaic form.

The prescriptions in regard to the priesthood are the same in Moses and in Ezechiel, for instance, as to the exterior behavior, the abstaining of intoxicating liquors during the exercise of their functions (Lev. v, 9; Ezech. xliv, 21), marriage (Lev. xxi, 13-14; Ezech. xliv, 22,) the removing of corpses (Lev. xxi, 11; Ezech. xliv, 25). When we see sometimes kings offer sacrifices, as Saul and Ozias (1 Kings xiii, 9-14; 2 Par. xxvi, 16-21), the chastisements which they incurred are a confirmation of the Law instead of proving that it did not exist. One pretends, it is true, that Ezechiel permits to the king to offer the sacrifice of Expiation (xlv, 17), but this is a false interpretation. When the sovereign has the right to present victims in the name of the people, he does not offer them as God's minister: the prophet tells explicitly: "The priests shall offer his holocaust and his peace-offerings" (Ezechiel xlvi, 2).

As to the high priests, not only can we establish their existence, but we can draw up the almost complete list of them since Aaron, the brother of Moses and the first pontiff of Israel, until the time of Our Saviour. Josephus has given us a summary of the history of the sovereign pontificate in his "Hebrew Antiquities." He might have had in hands documents which we possess no longer, but it was sufficient for him to open the Sacred Books to draw therefrom the most of the accounts which he has given to us. Aaron had for successor his son Eleazar, who himself leaves the priesthood to his son Phinees (Jos. xxiv, 33; 1 Par. ix, 20; Judges xx, 28). Heli, descendant of Aaron, exercises the office of the high priesthood about the end of the period of the Judges (1 Kings ii, 27-33; Judges xvii). In Saul's time and in that of David and Solomon, Abimelech, Abiathar, Sadok, Azarias (1 Kings xxii, 9; 11-20; 2 Par. viii, 17; 1 Par. vi, 10), fulfilled the functions of high priest. We see in the first Book of Kings that not only does the high priest exist, but also that he occupies a high position in the kingdom of Juda. Who does not know of the capital role which Joiada played in the history of Joas whom he restores on the throne, usurped by Athalia? The sacred author calls him explicitly the high priest (4 Kings xii, 11). Helcias, Seraias also carry this title (xxii, 4; xxiii, 4; xxv, 18). Moreover, the first Book of Paralipomenons (vi.) gives us the list of the high priests of the successors to Aaron. When therefore, as the rationalistic criticism claims, the sovereign priesthood was unknown before the Captivity, when the Levites formed no distinct class from the priests, all historical books of the Hebrew Old Testament would be the most monstrous fraud that was ever practiced; the Levites themselves who accepted this subordination to the priests, when the most ancient among them could still perfectly remember that before the ruin of the temple there existed no distinction between priests and Levites, would have been the most simple of men, and all the people of Juda, who received as deriving from Moses and as something which was practiced for centuries, would have been the most stupid peoples had they accepted an institution which previously never existed. How could it be possible that old men, who had seen the ancient Temple, and deplored the poverty of the new, would not have remarked that nothing was done any longer as in the ancient Temple.

Mr. Curtiss, in a book wherein he treats *ex professo* the question of the Mosaic priesthood, has established according to the authorized testimony which Franz Delitzsch renders to him, that the whole history of Israel presupposes a hierarchical distinction between the priests and Levites; that this distinction goes back to Moses, and that it has existed since the establishment of the people in Palestine until the ruin of Jerusalem; that the books written after the Captivity do not favor in any manner the opinion according to which the organization of the Aaronic priesthood would date from the time of Esdras, and, finally, that Deuteronomy contradicts in nothing the other books of the Pentateuch concerning not only the existence, but also the rights peculiar to the priests and Levites.[1]

5. THE ENDOWMENT OF THE CLERGY.

Mr. Wellhausen does not limit himself indeed to deny the Mosaic origin of the priesthood in the family of Aaron, he maintains moreover that the Dues due to the clergy, according to the Law, are equally a recent institution. In antiquity, according to him, the sacrifices were essentially sacred repasts to which they invited the priests, where there were any. The

---
[1] S. J. Curtiss, "The Levitical Priests," Edinburg, 1877.

one who possessed a sanctuary, instituted priests, by means of a salary, but he had no legal right to any portion of the victim. Deuteronomy commences to attribute this to them; the Sacerdotal Code notably increased them. As to the forty-eight cities given to the Levites (1 Kings ii, 12-17), it is a fiction of which the first germ is found perhaps in the visions of the future Israel by Ezechiel.

Mr. Wellhausen would like therefore here, as in the points we have already examined, to make of the second part of the prophecies of Ezechiel one of the sources of the legislation of the Pentateuch. Ezechiel should have suggested the idea of a part of the Sacerdotal Dues. But the truth is that the second part of Ezechiel clearly supposes the Books of Moses. The history of the children of Heli confirms in an irrefutable manner the existence of the Sacerdotal Dues a long time before the Captivity (1 Kings ii, 12-17). The Books of Kings mention, in the time of Joas, the money that was given to priests as prize of the sacrices for sin and crime (4 Kings xii, 16). The author of the Paralipomenons relates that, under the reign of Ezechias, they gave to the priests the tithes and first fruits (2 Par. xxxi, 4-6). The offering of the first fruits is such a natural thing that it exists still as a practice of devotion in many countries. The nations whom the Hebrews knew were in the habit to offer to their deities gifts of the soil; they did this in Chaldea and in Egypt. In an Accadian inscription found at Birs-Nimrud, near Babylon, an ancient Semitic king of Erech, who lived long before Abraham, offers in the temple of his god measures of grain, twelve mines (about six bushels) of wool, oil, etc. The Egyptian monuments are filled with enumerations of the gifts of grain, wine, vegetables, offered in the temples of all the cities of the Nile valley. Moses, in fixing what the children of Israel should offer to the ministers of worship, regulated only ancient customs and which he had seen practiced in the kingdom of the Pharaohs.

As to the existence of Levitical cities, which is denied by the Rationalists, it is established by facts. The impossibilities which Wellhausen pretends to point out, are not real. The sacred history shows, long before the Captivity, that there were sacerdotal cities. At Bethsames where we see Levites receive the Ark in the time of the Judges (Jos. xxi, 16; 1 Par. vi, 59; I Kings vi, 15), at Anatoth whither Solomon banishes Abiathar and where Jeremias was born, who was of the sacerdotal family (Jos. xxi, 8; 1 Par. vi, 59; Jer. i, 1, etc.).

Hence there is nothing founded in the allegations of the Rationalists against the antiquity of the law of Moses. It was the liberator of the Hebrews who regulated the divine worship; it was he (Moses) who instituted the ritual of the sacrifices and of the Levites and fixed the right of the sacred ministers. Esdras by whom the infidels pretend that the Pentateuch was written, explicitly attributes the same to Moses: "They built an altar to the God of Israel, that they might offer holocausts upon it, as it is written in the law of Moses, the man of God (I Esdras iii, 1-4). Nehemias speaks in the same manner (i. 7; viii, 14; xiii, 1).

Hence all the arguments which the infidels allege against the Mosaic origin of the Pentateuch are without value, and the ancient tradition is not shaken by modern criticism. The sacred history, far from proving that the Law is the work of time, a natural development of the Hebrew civilization, establishes, on the contrary, that the Mosaic legislation is a divine work. It is not the people of God that made the Law; but the Law made the people of God. The history of the race of Abraham and Jacob is really miraculous. The answer of the chaplain of Frederick II of Prussia remains always true. When this infidel prince asked him for a short and decisive proof of the divinity of the Scriptures, the chaplain answered by the sole word: "*Israel.*"

CHAPTER IV.

THE DIFFERENT NAMES OF GOD.

TO GOD, though in Himself most simple, we give different names to express even imperfectly our knowledge of Him. As we cannot comprehend His essence in itself, we can know Him only through His perfections as they are manifested in creatures. The first revealed name of God which we meet with in Scripture is Elohim. "In the beginning," writes Moses, "God (Elohim) created heaven and earth." In nearly every verse of the first chapter of Genesis the same name occurs. It is in the plural number, and according to Genesis is a developed form of El, which radically means power. Other scholars would derive it from the Hebrew word "Alah," to swear. What is peculiar about the name is that, though in plural number, it is constantly, when used for the true God, joined with verbs and adjectives in the singular. And on the other hand, when applied to denote false gods, it is invariably united to verbs and adjectives in the plural. This marked distinction in the use of the name has thoroughly convinced some Rationalists of the original monotheism of the Hebrew race.

Another peculiar feature of the name Elohim is, that it has a singular Eloah, which, though used by Moses, is found in Job and Habacuc, as Pererius points out (Comm. in Genesim, t. i, p. 11). Again when Elohim is united to a verb in the plural (which occurs, in any form, critics say, at most twelve times against some two thousand instances for the contrary usage) its sense is determined by the word Jehovah which accompanies it. This constant use of the name Elohim, theologians following the opinion of the Master of Sentences uphold, was not without design. By it Moses wished, they say, to indicate the Trinity of Persons in the Godhead, and by the singular verb to teach the unity of Divine nature.

The name Elohim, however, as being generic, was sometimes given to created beings. "In Scripture," writes Pererius, "it is given not only to God, but also to angels, to judges, and princes. Since properly it signified those who, on account of their great authority and power, especially in the vindication of justice, are objects of fear to others" (Op. cit.). When men fell away from the true faith they called their gods and their idols Elohim.

The exclusive use of the name in first chapter of Genesis seems to suggest that by divine inspiration it was chosen by Moses to denote the exercise of the power and the beneficence of the one true God.

But the name which the Israelites looked upon as the proper name of God was Jehovah. It is derived according to Hebraists, from the Hebrew *haia* "is," and means "He who is." The Jews style it "the name of substance," "the name of being," "the venerated and terrible name," "the name reserved or incommunicable," "the mysterious name," "the ineffable name," "the name tetragrammatical" (literally, the name, product of four letters—Hebraism). Jehovah, therefore, as Masius, quoted by Cornelius a Lapide says, is the same as He " who exists from eternity, who is His own essence, and from whom depends the essence of all things." So sacred was this name to the Jews that it was only the high priest who pronounced it, and that amid the most solemn rites. In common discourse or in reading the people substituted the name Adonai for Jehovah. Literally Adonai means Lord, and this meaning the Septuagint version adopts, translating Jehovah by the word *kurios*, while the Vulgate renders it by the word "*Dominus*." Being first revealed to Moses, the name Jehovah was not known to the Patriarchs. To them God revealed Himself as the Almighty (El Shaddai), for thus He spoke to Moses: "I am the Lord that appeared to Abraham to Isaac and to Jacob by the name God of Almighty (El Shaddai), and my name Adonai (Jehovah) I did not show them." (Ex. vi. 2-3).

Modern infidels have undertaken to prove that Jehovah stands for the sun, which in Grecian and Phenician mythologies is called, according to the different seasons, by different names. They report that the

Grecian oracle of Apollo at Claros said: "Jao is the greatest of the gods; he is styled Hades in winter, Zeus in spring, the sun in summer, and the tender Jao in autumn." This story, however, about the Grecian oracle has been rejected by all learned critics, among them, Gesenius and Jablonsky. The fabrication they attribute to one of the early judaizing Gnostics. But in itself the story is puerile and sophistical. We prove from the authentic teaching and religion of the Hebrews, as far back as the time of Moses and Abraham, that they worshiped Jehovah as the one and only true God; but, notwithstanding this evidence, opponents insist that for our proof we must go to Phenician and Grecian mythologies, even though these have no connection whatever in time or in place with the subject of our thesis; or, what the Greeks and Phenicians thought of their gods in the beginning of the Christian era, is to be the basis of proof for what the Hebrews thought about Jehovah in the time of Abraham. There is no need of enlarging further on the absurd in such reasoning.

But so far were the Hebrews from worshipping the sun that they were forbidden to do so under the penalty of being stoned, as we read in Deuteronomy. And on the other hand they were taught to sing, "Praise ye the Lord (Jehovah) from heavens . . . praise ye Him, O sun and moon; praise ye Him, all ye stars and light" (Ps. cxlviii, 1-3).

Another name generically used in Scripture for God is the word *El.* Primarily it means power. Thus in Genesis Laban says to Jacob: "It is in my power (El) to return the evil," and Moses speaking to the people, says: "May thy sons and daughters be given to another people . . . and may there be no strength (El) in the Land" (Deut. xxviii, 32). But generally El, when applied to God, takes an adjective denoting the one or other of the divine attributes. Hence, as we have seen, He revealed Himself to Abraham as El Shaddai, that is, God all-powerful and munificent (Shaddai), while He revealed Himself to Melchisadech as "the most High" (Elyon). Of Abraham it is written, "I lift up my hand to the Lord God, the most High (El Elyon), the possessor of heaven and earth" (Gen. xiv, 22).

Besides the names just enumerated and given by St. Jerome, he also adds El Sabaoth, that is, according to Aquila, "the God of armies." Strictly speaking Sabaoth is not a name but a surname, hence says Cornelius a Lapide, "it is always united to some other name of God." Then there is the *Ja*, which is an abbreviated form of *Jehovah* and is one of the component words of Halleluia, made up by *hallelu*, praise ye, and *ya*, the Lord.

CHAPTER V.

THE FATHERS AND THE MOSAIC COSMOGONY.

ALTHOUGH the authority of the Fathers extends only to matters of faith and morals, Christian teachers have always maintained that outside the sphere of the divinely revealed religious doctrines, there exists yet a vast realm of profane or purely natural sciences—a boundless field in which the human mind may freely exercise itself. This privilege the Fathers have exercised on many important occasions, especially on points growing out of the first chapter of Genesis.

Notwithstanding the Fathers were deprived of divine inspiration in explaining the cosmogony of the Bible, yet they knew that the inspired writers were personally not exempt from the erroneous views of their contemporaries on matters purely profane, and though they knew it was not the object of divine revelation to enrich purely profane knowledge with direct instructions on purely scientific subjects, yet they fully believed and taught, that the *Spirit of Truth* could not sanction with His authority any such error on even purely profane matters, in the writings which He inspired.

The very nature and importance of the first chapter of Genesis, in the work of the Fathers, necessitated their touching on science when explaining the cosmogony of the Bible. But, neither the patristic traditions nor the Church have fixed the scientific sense of the first chapter of Genesis. In matters of science, the Fathers spoke as private Doctors. "The authority of the Fathers, as also the authority of the Church, extends only to matters of *faith* and *morals*, and truths essentially connected with them. Consequently, purely scientific views of the Fathers have no greater value than the scientific principles on which they rest. . . For sufficient reasons, we may reject them, however unanimously they may be held by the Fathers."[1]

How far do we deviate from the teaching of the Fathers? Do we adhere to the rules laid down by them on the meaning of the word "Day"? These questions can be briefly answered by saying that, the explanations of the Fathers are completely in accord with the discoveries of modern science—the Catholic exegesis has never changed in principle.

I. IMPORTANCE OF THE FIRST CHAPTER OF GENESIS.

The first chapter of Genesis is a pen picture of the visible crowning glory of Almighty God and His wonderful works, as manifested in the creation of heaven and earth, the sun, moon and stars, the plants, animals and man. It is a worthy frontispiece to the inspired writings, and shows the grandeur, sublimity, order, harmony, and completeness of God's works: an awe-inspiring, withal ravishing manifestation of His power and glory, and solicitude for man. It is at the same time the basis of theology—the fundamental dogmas

---

[1] Dr. J. B. Heinrich, "Dogmatische Theologie," vol. I, p. 810.

of religion—unity of God—creation out of nothing, or rather out of what did not exist before. Providence, unity of the human species, dependence of man on his Creator; also a complete annihilation of the errors of the ancients—a condemnation of polytheism, naturalism, and materialism.

The importance of the Biblical cosmogony has drawn forth many theological and philosophical speculations concerning its origin, each epoch considering it from its own point of view. In our days it has become more interesting from the fact, that science assumes sponsorship and dictatorship of all natural phenomena. At the beginning of Christianity, attention was directed to it, chiefly from the theological side; this the Christian Doctors awakened by their masterly logic and eloquence. The earliest of the venerable teachers enraptured by admiration of the first chapter of Genesis, clearly pointed out the wonderful beauty, power and majesty displayed in the creation of the visible universe, in their controversies with pagans and heretics, showing the superiority of the Biblical cosmogony over the mythological and philosophical cosmogonies of the Greeks, Romans and Gnostics.

St. Theophilus of Antioch, who after his conversion from polytheism to Christianity, had become bishop of that city, speaks with fervor and enthusiasm of the account of creation, in the most ancient work on the hexæmeron, handed down to us from the Fathers. He comments on the first chapter of Genesis, to some length, in his defence of Christianity against the pagan Autolycus, and devotes the greater part of the second book of his "Apology" to enumeration of the beauties of the Mosaic cosmogony; so clear, so precise, and so convincing are his arguments, that pagan errors dissipate themselves before the exposition of the truth.

2. THE WORK OF THE FATHERS.

The ancient systems of cosmogony had, in turn, raised the problem of the origin of things, and diverse philosophies followed in explanation; they being only ingenious or rough attempts at solution. But the Book of God—the Bible—had given its own, and the Fathers desired to point out its superiority over all other systems of cosmogony. The pagans lulled thus far by the poetic imaginations of Hesoid and Ovid, and the Greeks misled by the philosophies of Plato, of Zenon, of Epicurus and of Lucretius, they had to present the dogma of a God, free, almighty, eternal, and unique Creator of heaven and earth; and to the Manicheans, prepossessed with the idea that the natural creation was bad and absolutely unworthy of the Deity, they had to justify the marvelous beauty and adaption of this superhuman work, and make them behold therein its relations with the supernatural world and the life of the soul.

This is the work which the Fathers accomplished; necessarily an arduous and unremitting task, considering the subtle theories of the ancient philosophers and poets, and the crude views of the unlearned and ignorant classes, which had to be overcome. Bossuet summed up the teaching of those champions of truth, in a wonderful manner, in a page of his book—"Discourse on the Universal History"—which is substantially a translation of their own words:

"The conduct of God in the creation makes us see that all proceeds immediately from His hand. The nations and philosophers who have believed that the earth, mixed with water, and assisted, if you wish, by the heat of the sun, had produced by itself, by its own fecundity, the plants and the animals, did deceive themselves very much. The Scripture gives us to understand that the elements are sterile, if the word of God does not render them fruitful. Neither the earth, nor the water, nor the air, would ever have produced the plants or animals which we behold, if God, who had made and prepared the matter, had not formed them by His all-powerful will, and if He had not given to each thing the seeds proper to multiply themselves in all the centuries. Those who behold the plants take their birth and growth from the heat of the sun, might believe that it is their creator; but the Scripture tells us that the earth clothed with herbs and all kinds of plants before the sun had been created, in order that we might perceive that all depends upon God. This great Workman was pleased to create the light, even before reducing it to the form which He has given to it in the sun, and in the stars, because He wished to teach us that these grand and magnificent lights, of which they wished to make deities, had not by themselves neither the precious and shining matter of which they have been composed, nor the wonderful form to which we behold them reduced. Finally, the account of creation, such as it is made by Moses, reveals to us that great secret of real philosophy, that in God alone resides the fecundity and the absolute power. . . . If, after the established order in nature, one thing depends upon the other, for instance, the rise and the growth of the plants, of the sun's heat, it is because this same God who has made all the parts of the universe, wished to unite them among one another, and make shining His Wisdom by this wonderful connection."[1]

3. THE FATHERS COULD NOT EXPLAIN THE BIBLICAL COSMOGONY WITHOUT TOUCHING ON SCIENCE.

Evidently, it was impossible for the Christian Doctors to explain the Biblical cosmogony, without touching on science, for Genesis itself, necessarily touches on it. To combat the pagan philosophers, they had to enter upon their physical theories, and to root out the worship of the astres, they had to touch on astronomy; and to teach the faithful how to lead a good life, they had to draw useful lessons from the works of creation. The preacher had to become more or less a naturalist, and present to the people God's solicitude for man as manifested in the fruitfulness of the earth in plants, animals, and fish in the waters, and clothe these illustrations with fitting anecdotes and moral sentiments. Man has always shown much interest and curiosity about the things of nature, especially the animal kingdom, and this was shown among other things, at the dawn of Christianity, by the singular but significant books entitled: "Bestiarü." Marvel not then at the motives which prompted the Christian teachers to enter the domain of natural science, though their teaching before all was dogmatic and moral.

4. IN EXPLAINING HUMAN THINGS THE FATHERS WERE DEPRIVED OF DIVINE REVELATION.

By entering the domain of profane science, the Fathers no longer had the aid of revelation, and had

---
[1] Bossuet, "Discours sur l'Histoire Universelle" 2, part, chap. 1.

to depend on the light of their own intelligence. There is a revealed religion, but not a revealed science. This is so true, that the scientific ideas which we meet in the works of the Fathers are mainly borrowed, not from the Bible, but from the Greek philosophers and other profane sources. As already noted, God did not wish to teach us in Holy Scripture, physics, chemistry, biology, astronomy, or in fact, any abstruse science. His only purpose was to give us the means to save our souls and inherit the kingdom of heaven. On this point, St. Thomas observes very correctly, that when the Bible speaks of nature, it is mentioned incidentally, and it conforms itself to the popular language: "One must consider that Moses spoke to an ignorant people and that, condescending to its weakness, he proposed to it only the things which fell clearly under the senses."

The first chapter of Genesis forms an exception to this, in one sense, for, although it is susceptible to different interpretations, its subjects seem to imply in themselves great outlines and a real scientific foundation. But that which it teaches, though important in itself, is little, comparatively speaking, to the vast domain of science. Indeed, the whole sums itself up in the following points, confirmed by geological and paleontological discoveries, that in the creative work there is an ascending gradation. God created matter first, and afterwards He drew forth the world from chaos; He produced the lower forms of life first, then higher beings, rising from the less perfect to the more perfect, in a regular ascending scale; the mineral kingdom, the vegetable kingdom, the animal kingdom, and lastly, the human kingdom above all. Outside of this record, Moses teaches us nothing precise about the nature of things.

5. IN MATTERS OF SCIENCE THE FATHERS SPOKE AS PRIVATE DOCTORS.

When the Fathers had occasion to discuss scientific points, they did not assume to have found any special light in the Sacred Books, aside of the dogma of creation, consequently they spoke of these things, not as depositaries and witnesses of Catholic tradition, but as private Doctors; therefore, their assertions have no binding effect, as they are the expressions of individuals making no claim to scientific knowledge, and for which the Church does not hold herself responsible, though in matters of faith and morals, their unanimous testimony carries authority with it. Providence raised these great men to propagate Christianity, and preserve and defend its doctrines in their purity and integrity, and not to teach physics or chemistry, or delve in geology. We do not find a Copernicus, nor a Cuvier among them; their science partook of the times in which they lived, consequently it was defective.

6. THE ACCESSORY BECOMES THE PRINCIPAL.

The cosmógony of the Fathers, nevertheless, deserves more than a passing notice, not so much from its scientific value, but on account of the use some wish to make of it in our times to ridicule the Bible and Catholicism.

Now, that what was in the early centuries of the Church the accessory in the first chapter of Genesis, has become the principal in the present century. The wonderful progress of astronomy, physics and geology, has stimulated general attention to the first chapter of Genesis. Is it in accord with modern discoveries? The faithful will answer Yes; the infidel will say No. In support of their allegations they will refer to the exegesis of the Fathers. When the Christian savants affirm that the cosmogony of the Hebrews, well understood, embraces a series of successive epochs, during which were formed the diverse layers of the earth with the fossils which characterize them, the enemies of religion cry out at the newness of this interpretation, and accuse us of holding opinions contrary to ecclesiastical tradition.

7. NEITHER THE PATRISTIC TRADITION NOR THE CHURCH HAS FIXED THE SCIENTIFIC SENSE OF THE FIRST CHAPTER OF GENESIS.

Hence it is important to give a general view of what is the real cosmogony of the Fathers, and what duties it imposes on the exegetist of our times. Contrary to the general belief of the enemies of religion, we shall prove that the patristic tradition no more than the authority of the Church, has never fixed the scientific meaning of the first chapter of Genesis. The Fathers, as well as the theologians who succeeded them, were not unanimous on this point, some understanding it in one sense and some in another. Consequently, there does not exist, strictly speaking, a traditional interpretation of the Mosaic cosmogony, binding on the Catholic. The exegetist of our times has the right to choose the one which appears to him the most conformable to the accounts of real science. And so far as the ancient Church writers are not in accord with the manner of explaining the Mosaic cosmogony in our days, it is because they found themselves in face of undemonstrated hypotheses, and had no authorized commentaries, as in modern times, to furnish the necessary points on geology and paleontology. Theology, in our century, can march only in the track, and conform itself to the true principles, by interpreting the word of God by the aid of the light which science furnishes to it, just as it has the duty to profit by the archæological, historical and geographical discoveries, to explain obscure or even badly understood passages of Scripture, so also, it is obliged to make use of scientific discoveries, when they are certain, in order to fix the meaning of passages which they can clear up, so far as being unfaithful to the traditions of the Church, it follows only the example of the past.

8. DIFFERENT OPINIONS ON THE FIRST CHAPTER OF GENESIS.

Certainly, it cannot be our object to enter into details about the ideas of the Fathers regarding the Biblical cosmogony, as each school held particular views, and we can only summarize the many points at issue.

That what strikes us in the first place, is, the diversity of opinion on the scientific interpretation of this chapter, while there is perfect accord on the dogmatic sense of the same, so much do they differ on the manner, mode and details of creation, that they instituted two opposing schools on the leading point, namely: *the time the creation lasted.* Not only the Jewish writer Philo, but also many of the Levantine and Latin Fathers, particularly Clement of Alexandria, Origen, and Procopius, considered those *six days* not as ordinary days of twenty-four hours, but as periods of time of unknown duration, while others held the opinion that creation took place instantaneously. The great St. Augustine says: "What kind of Days they are, is either most difficult or impossible for us to guess; how much more so to decide." The diversity of opinion on all particular questions was even much greater. We may mention here, that the fame of the Alexandrian school for profane knowledge was world wide. Indeed, it may be said, that all the early Christian teachers, not only studied the Bible and traditions of the Church, intelligently and profoundly, but also the writings of profane, even pagan, authors. St. Jerome, in his letter to the orator Magnus, gives the names of many Christian teachers, from the days of St. Paul to his own time, of whom he says, "that one knows not what to admire more, their profane science or their knowledge of the Sacred Scriptures."

9. WHAT ARE THE RESULTS FROM THIS ABSENCE OF ACCORD AMONG THE FATHERS.

Even if these venerable writers were in accord on the scientific explanation of the origin of the world, we would not be obliged to accept their interpretation, because science is not a deposit preserved by tradition, like the revealed truth. We must believe, in matters of faith, *quod semper quod ubique.* We must accept in the scientific domain, the sure progress brought about in the series of centuries through the accumulation of observations and experiments. We are no more bound to the scientific ideas of the Fathers than are the savants of to-day to those of the savants of former times. We can reject them without losing respect for their authors, with the same liberty contemporary astronomers reject the system of Ptolemy.

But when the exegetist has preserved his independence, even though the Fathers were in accord, with much greater reason has he preserved the right to form a personal opinion in the midst of conflicting views. Even the theologian has the right to choose the opinion which pleases him most in dogmatic matter, when the ancient tradition is divided and unsettled, so long as the Church has not given her opinion or judgment on any side of the question in dispute. Now, the infallible authority has never expressed itself on the scientific interpretation of the Biblical cosmogony, nor on the question of the simultaneous creation. Hence we may say, it is a self-proved fact, that the Catholic can explain the Mosaic cosmogony by giving to it the meaning which appears to him the most conformable to the accounts of true science, under the sole condition to observe the rules of Hermaneutic and of the interpretation of the Sacred Books.

After stating the independence and rights of the exegetist in scientific matters, let us now examine the points we have deviated from patristic teaching:

10. HOW FAR HAVE WE DEVIATED FROM PATRISTIC TEACHING?

That which forms the basis of the present question is not in the details themselves, because the Fathers are not in accord, but in the principles which they followed, and which are common to all. These principles embody the following: We must make use of reason, of science in its sure accounts to interpret the Mosaic cosmogony. The motive, for instance which urged the Alexandrian school to take up the question of simultaneous creation, was to reconcile the Bible with the then existing philosophical systems which appeared consistent with reason. Most of the ecclesiastical writers have personally supported their individual views on some points, just as the science of their times directed and assured them. St. Augustine for example, proclaimed forcibly the necessity of putting the exegesis in accord with what is true in science: "Acquired by reason and experiment."

II. WE ADHERE TO THE RULES LAID DOWN BY THE FATHERS.

The principle of our teachers in faith is also ours. When we are not in accord with them in details, it is not because the principle has changed, but because science has advanced—outgrown its environments. We do what they would have done had they lived in our times. They accepted what the savants had taught them, just as we accept what the savants are teaching to-day. Hence, there is only a change in the interpretation, because there is a change in science, and this change cannot be imputed to theology but to science itself, which by its nature is progressive and searching, changing, remodeling or modifying former hypotheses; adding something new, or refuting what had been generally accepted demonstrated facts yesterday, by experiments to-day. Of course, it does not enter one's mind to reproach science for its rapid strides and every day discoveries, but why should scientists withhold their approval and forbid us to make use of these progressive changes, because we do not abandon our traditions, that which we hold fundamental and essential and because we continue to apply the principles which have guided the interpreters of Holy Scripture, at all times. For, the more knowledge of nature is diffused the more clear is the Sacred Text to us, but its authority does not change; it is always the same.

We can also observe, that not only do we preserve the rules laid down by our Fathers, but that we keep an important part of their explanations, though as already stated, we are not obliged to accept their scientific ideas, inasmuch as they were not savants by profession, the great majority being distinguished for intelligence and exalted virtue, but the penetration of their keen intellects enabled them to discover in the Sacred Books truths ignored by the common people, which are confirmed by the discoveries of our age.

12. MEANING OF THE WORD DAY AND TEACHING OF THE FATHERS.

Among the many truths handed down to us from the Fathers, let us point to the one that is necessarily connected with our subject, namely, the meaning we must attach to the word *day*, as given in Genesis. Contemporary exegetists who accept the results of geology, maintain that the word cannot be taken in its literal meaning, that is for a duration of twenty-four hours, but in a figurative sense, simply signifying time. Now, contemporary exegetists are not the authors of this opinion, for we find this already advanced by the Fathers.

True, none of the Fathers teach expressly that the six days of creation were periods of time, though St. Justin and St. Gregory, of Nazianz, admit a long interval between the creation of matter and that of light. Clement of Alexandria, Origen, and Procopius, considered those six days not as ordinary days of twenty-four hours, while the words of the Venerable Bede can be readily taken to mean periods of time of indefinite length.

St. Augustine and the Venerable Bede say that the seventh day had no evening, but neither of them had foreseen what is called epochal days of creation. All the efforts that have been made to interpret some of the texts of the great Bishop of Hippo to the latter sense, is fruitless. How could he affirm that the six days of creation must be taken in the sense of long periods of time when he taught instantaneous creation? However, we find in the writings of some of the Fathers a particular emphasis on the word *day* as employed in passages of the Bible, to mean an indefinite period of time, but they could not advance this view in their days and conform to the universal interpretation of the first chapter of Genesis. Fifteen hundred years have passed without a change in the literal interpretation, and no doubt, many of the Fathers, conformably to their principles, would have adopted the system of epochal days, had they lived in a later age.

As to the points of detail it matters little, but it is certain that the famous school of Alexandria, in the Orient, and a large number of the Fathers of the Occident, with St. Augustine at their head, have maintained that the word "day," as occurring so often in Holy Scripture, must not be understood in its literal sense, but rather in its figurative sense, though they have not explained it in the same manner as we do. Hence, we do not innovate by interpreting the word in a metaphorical sense.

Moreover, some of the reasons alleged by the Fathers for establishing their opinions on the word *day*, may be summed up in the words of Origen; that the Bible itself gives us to understand that the Genesical days are not ordinary days—solar days, because it teaches itself that during the first three days the sun did not exist. We have the right to couple his words with those of St. Augustine, that the word "day" in Scriptural language does not designate a space of twenty-four hours, because at the beginning of the second chapter of Genesis, it designates the whole period of creation: "These are the generations of the heaven and the earth when they were created, in the *day* that the Lord God made the heaven and the earth, and every plant of the field before it springing up in the earth" (Gen. ii, 4).

13. THE EXPLANATIONS OF THE FATHERS ARE COMPLETELY IN ACCORD WITH MODERN DISCOVERIES.

The Fathers not only furnish us reasons which are favorable to the discoveries of modern science, but really their explanations are in accord with them. Most of the savants of our day admit that the universe existed first in an informal state; that it was only successively that matter first transformed itself, and produced the diverse creatures which compose the world to-day.

This is the opinion of St. Ephrem, St. Basil, St. Gregory of Nazianze, St. Gregory of Nyssa, St. Ambrose, Severinus Gabalis, and many others. Although St. Augustine admits simultaneous creation, he explains it in certain passages of his writings in terms which one might consider befitting a modern treatise on the origin of things. In first Book on Genesis against the Manicheans, he says: "'At the beginning God created the heaven and the earth.' Under the name of heaven and earth is designated every creature made and produced by God. The creature is thus called by the name of visible things, on account of the weakness of the unlearned ones, who are so little apt to understand the visible things. Matter has, therefore, been created first in a confusive and informal state, in order that the individual beings and which have a form might be drawn from this; this is, I believe, what the Greeks call chaos. . . . This informal matter, which God has drawn from nothing, has therefore been called first heaven and earth, and it is written, 'In the beginning God created heaven and earth,' not because it was this already (heaven and earth), but because it was destined to become this. When we consider the seed of a tree, we say it contains the roots, the stem, the branches—the fruits and the leaves, not because they are there, but because they should proceed from it. It is in this sense that it is said, 'In the beginning God created the heaven and the earth,' that is, the seed of the heaven and of the earth, when the matter of heaven and earth was yet confounded (in one whole); because it was certain that the heaven and the earth should go forth from this; this matter is called already (by anticipation) the heaven and the earth. . . . We find in the Holy Scriptures numberless examples of similar locutions."

Thus it is seen that a great number of the Fathers, both of the Orient and the Occident, are in accord on the texts of Scripture relating the origin of the world, with our modern savants. Some of the Fathers, like some of the savants, did not believe that the sun was, properly speaking, created on the first day, though the details which they give on this subject are wanting in exactness, on account of the prevailing ignorance of their times about the real nature of the light, nevertheless, it is conceded, that they approached theories commonly admitted by the moderns.

14. THE CATHOLIC EXEGESIS HAS NEVER CHANGED IN PRINCIPLE.

We could add other points of detail to this subject, if we thought it necessary to extend our space, but believe we have given all that is sufficient for the purpose we had in view. It seems to us that we have shown that the Catholic exegesis has never changed in principle, and that it is the same to-day it has been in the past. It beholds in Holy Scripture the word of God itself, but put down after the meaning and manner of men, and consequently so expressed in human language. At all times Christians have made use of the sciences to interpret the Bible; every scientific discovery throws new light upon some point of the Sacred Text. The Fathers made use of established truths when the science of their times permitted them. We continue their work by making use of the science of our times, and like them and with them, we believe, that, "*No real discord can exist between reason and faith.*"

CHAPTER VI.

THE HEXÆMERON OR THE SIX GENETIC DAYS.

MAN having been created last of the visible world, he could not have witnessed the acts of creation. The tradition of the ancients, whether civilized, semi-civilized or savage, agree in the main points with the inspired text. Since man was unaided by science, through the long years of his existence, it was natural he should accept the Mosaic account of the creation as he finds it in Genesis.

The time has come when man must take a more comprehensive view of creation. The progress of the natural sciences makes it essential that one should inquire into the interpretation of the Mosaic account and see wherein it falls short of the demands of science. In the present chapter we review the objections made against the literal system, and with such tangible evidence in the strata and in the fossils imbedded therein, we can no longer accept this system as being in harmony with science.

The study of geology shows us that our globe is composed of superposed strata or layers, distinguished from one another by the elements and different fossils which are proper to each. To explain the existence of these layers and fossils, the learned have instituted four principal systems: The Literal system, system of Intervals, Ideal system and the Concordistic system.

THE LITERAL SYSTEM consists in understanding the Sacred Text in the proper and literal sense. It maintains that God created the earth as it is, with its plants and petrified animals. Hence, this system takes all the words of Genesis literally and substantially as they are written, without change of meaning. Consequently, it adheres to the interpretation that the universe was created in six ordinary days of twenty-four hours each, of an evening and morning—a night and day. This system is still maintained by some rare theologians or exegetists, and by the majority of the unlearned, who consider the fossils "freaks of nature."

I. CRITICISM OF THE LITERAL SYSTEM.

Geologists of the present day are unanimous in rejecting this system. Whoever has seen with his own eyes, or has given the least study to geology and paleontology, will not hesitate to discard this system as untenable in the face of such unquestionable testimony. If Holy Writ did not abound in figurative expressions; if it did not convey meanings hard to be understood; if it did not use words, expressions and forms of speech peculiar to the age, country and people to whom they were addressed, and if it were free from the criticism of science, on matters pertaining to nature, then there would be good reason to adhere to its literal meaning. But the Bible imposes no theory of creation; it does declare this universe not to be uncaused and orphaned; it asserts Creation, Providence and Fatherhood; but how matter was created, and how, after its creation, the divine agency was correlated to it in producing new forms of life and beauty, Genesis does not declare. God has given to man *faith* and *reason* as a means of reading the Book of Revelation and the Book of Nature. He can exercise the former in reading the Book of Nature, without losing the latter in the Book of Revelation. He must take into consideration the mistakes of translators and copyists; and that on matters purely scientific or profane, they are mentioned only incidentally. Therefore, the Church has never by solemn decisions of general councils, or by definitions *ex cathedra*, interfered in settling purely scientific questions.

Although we should ordinarily preserve the proper sense of the words of Holy Writ in its integrity, it is certain that we must understand some words in a figurative or metaphorical sense, when, if taken in their literal acceptation would, strictly speaking, convey an erroneous meaning. Now, this is the case with the literal system, because geology and paleontology prove that the world in its actual state was not produced within an ordinary week of six days, and that many centuries must have elapsed before animal life, and before man appeared upon the earth.

2. GENESIS ABOUNDS IN FIGURATIVE EXPRESSIONS.

The first chapter of Genesis abounds in figurative expressions, and must be explained as such by all the exegetists without exception. Even the adherents of the literal system are obliged to admit a great number of figurative locutions following the record of the days of Creation: "So the heavens and the earth were finished, and all the furniture (or ornament— 'ornatus,' as the Vulgate has it) of them. . . . These are the generations of the heavens and the earth, when they were created in the day that the Lord God made the heavens and the earth."

3. THE MEANING OF THE HEBREW WORD YOM.

There is no one conversant with Holy Scripture but will agree it is by metaphor that God is, at times, represented expressing words; seeing what He did is good, calling the light *day*, and the darkness night. Science shows us that the Hebrew word *Yom*—day—is also employed in a figurative sense. Certainly, Moses does not designate before the fourth day the ordinary succession of day and night, because the sun did not yet shine in the horizon; hence, it is taken in a figurative sense, and so is the latter part of the account. With our more accurate use of language it might appear strange that the inspired writer would make use of the word day for an indefinite period, and yet, the word *day* is frequently used in our languages in an analogous manner. Modern languages are rich in such expressions: duration, epoch, age, time, etc., but the Hebrew has only the word Yom, to express both a *day*, and *an indefinite period of time*.

By following the dictates of reason, we must conclude it was unnecessary that God should employ twenty-four hours to create the light, twenty-four hours to create the stars, the planets or the animals; an instantaneous act of His will was sufficient for Him to bring forth all these things, as God could not employ an entire day's work to give existence to every one of the species of creatures, which appeared during the Genesical days; therefore, there is good reason to believe that the word day is figurative, and denotes here an epoch of time.

The Arabs call a period of time *Jaumun*, which word is evidently related to the Hebrew *Yom*. That what proves the word *Yom* to mean here an epoch (as we shall show more fully when we come to explain the Hexæmeron) is, that the earth contains in its bosom remains of plants and animals beyond computation, and that the geological layers are immense graveyards where the dead are heaped up:—

> The earth has gathered to her breast again
> And yet again, the millions that were born
> Of her unnumbered and unremembered tribes.

It is not possible to preserve to the word *Yom* the meaning of twenty-four hours duration, except in supposing that God did create in the fossil state those numberless remains of plants and animals found in the strata. Such a hypothesis cannot be accepted by one that has studied geology. We cannot suppose that all these fossils had been deposited in the terrestrial layers since the creation of man: 1. Because we should then have to give to man a much greater antiquity: 2. Because in the ancient layers there is nowhere a trace of man, which proves that the animals which have left their remains had lived before the creation of man.

4. TESTIMONY OF THE SEDIMENTARY GROUNDS.

The sedimentary grounds or deposits have a thickness of many miles. By adding the thickness of each layer together, where they are the most complete, if not the most developed, will aggregate from 105,000 to 120,000 feet. The thickness of the united Palæozoic formations alone has been estimated at 40,000 feet. Of course, this estimate is wanting in actual measurement, but we can give reliable data for a few well known formations. One division of the Permerian system, the Rothliegende, is divided at Mansfeld and Thuringia, Germany, into three layers, which are respectively 500, 800, 200 and 80-300 feet thick. The Vosges sandstone, one stratum of the three divisions, in the Triassic system, is 1200 feet thick; another is 150 feet, and in some localities of the Vosges, others are over 400 feet thick.

5. MICROSCOPIC REMAINS IN THE CHALK AND LIMESTONE FORMATIONS.

We think enough has been said to show that the theory of the formation of these strata since the advent of man, may be set aside as untenable. But if we are to suppose that the formation took place in preadamite ages, the theory that only six days had elapsed before the creation of man, must also fall to the ground. We would have to admit in this case, that the millions and millions of plants and animals imbedded in the terrestrial layers, were created in fossilized form; and that species and whole kinds, like the tribolites,[1] which characterize the primary and disappear in the secondary grounds, have had a like creation, or like the ammonites,[2] which characterize the secondary and no longer appear in the Tertiary. The multitudinous plants of

---

[1] An ordinary group of articulated animals which existed in the Paleozic period, and have been extinct since the close of the Carboniferous. It is conceded by all that their nearest representatives are the horse crabs.

[2] So-called from their resemblance to a ram's horn. One of the fossil shells of an extensive genus of extinct cephalopodous mollusks (cuttle fishes) of the family *ammonitidæ*, coiled in a plain spiral and chambered within, like the shell of the existing nautilus, to which the ammonites were allied.

the coal measure, and the countless shells which form the Cretaceous grounds, the nummulites[1] of the Tertiary, or the debris of crinoides,[2] which form the limestone, etc., are solely *lusus naturæ* — mere freaks of nature — cannot for a moment be entertained.

In order to be more explicit in details, we will add, that the Cretaceous grounds or composition of chalk, form the soil of a considerable part of Asia, Northern America, Europe, and especially France—in the neighborhood of Picardie, Champagne and Paris (Mendon Bongival). It sometimes attains a thickness of many hundred feet, and is almost entirely composed of the debris of countless millions of microscopic organisms — foraminifers, belonging to the *globigerina* kind Ehrenburg counted ten millions of *carapaces* in a single pound of chalk, and Alfred Maury, has made the curious calculation that the soldier who cleans his helmet with a cubic inch of tripoli, handles no less than forty-one millions of animalculæ, and at each rubbing he crushes about twelve millions of fossil animals.

To-day, as in primitive times, the chalk formations constitute a large part of the bottom of the Atlantic Ocean, and also of those countries which were covered with sea water, through the deposit of globigerine

---

[1] The nummulities comprise a great variety of fossil foraminifers, having externally much of the appearance of a piece of money (hence the name), without an apparent opening, and internally a spiral cavity, divided by partitions into numerous chambers, communicating with each other by means of small openings.

[2] A class of Metazoic animals containing globular or cup-shaped echinoderms, having normally joined arms, furnished with pinnules and stalked and fixed during some, or all of their lives; so-called from the resemblance of their rayed bodies borne upon a jointed stem, to a lily or tulip.

mud, consisting almost exclusively of carapaces, foraminifers and diatomites. The Tertiary formation in many parts, consists of an enormous mass of compact limestone, which extends from Spain to Morocco, to India and China; and contributes largely to the formation of the Pyrenees, Alps, Lebanon, Caucasus, Altai and Himalaya Mountains.

The fossils which are imbedded in these terrestrial layers are of all sizes, ages and shapes. Some are in their infancy, some in their growth and full development, and some in their old age. We meet fragments of shells, bones and skeletons of animals, and even the remains of their food, with the coprolites, imbedded with them. The coprolites or fossil excrements, are spread in several sedimentary layers, and may be used to enrich the soil, as they contain valuable properties for vegetable growth, they being chiefly derived from reptiles.

6. THE COAL MEASURES.

The development of vegetable life in the Carboniferous epoch, gives us an idea of the long ages before the creation of man. How can we explain without the aid of numerous centuries the origin of coal beds? They are composed of heaps of humble plants, and transformed into their present state by the aid of time and heat. The luxuriant growth of plants in those days of great heat and moisture, may be sufficient for the formation of coal beds, but we can believe with the majority of geologists, that they were formed by the vegetation which the waters had piled up at the mouth of lakes, rivers and low grounds. However, it is certain that this vegetation must have grown somewhere.

In further proof of the necessity of long ages for the transformation of vegetation into coal, of great thickness, we will state here, that the ordinary thickness varies from a few inches to many feet. In a few cases it exceeds 40 feet, for instance, at Drombrowa, in Russian Poland, there is a seam 48 feet thick, which extends without interruption for a distance of 7000 feet. Thick beds of coal are often divided by intermediate strata into several seams, of greater or lesser thickness, and generally the seams are fewer and less thick than these intermediate layers of sandstone and slate. At Newcastle-on-Tyne, there are 40 coal beds; some of these do not show much thickness in the alternate layers of sandstone and slate. In Wales, we find from 50 to 100 beds over one another, and the same can be seen in a few places in this country. The entire thickness of the coal beds in the south side of Hundsrück, Prussia, is 338 feet. Some of the English and American coal beds, may be traced continuously on the surface to the extent of 15-20 geographical miles in length, and 5-10 in breadth, while the subterranean extent is much greater, and may reach 50 geographical miles. As a rule, the American coal beds have a larger extent than those of Europe.

In view of the foregoing facts, and in further proof of the long ages of time which intervened between the creation of the world and the creation of man, we shall for example, adduce the wonderful vegetation of the Carboniferous age, from which the coal beds of the world were formed. The great heat of the earth, with the sun, the humidity which naturally followed, and the excess of carbonic acid contained in the air, not yet thoroughly purified, must all be abandoned for a system unsupported by modern science.

7. CONCLUSION.

What could have been God's motive to imprint in the coal measure, like a seal, false roots, leaves, blossoms and fruits of plants, which never grew? What could have been His motive to imbed shell fragments and countless generations of microscopial animals, if they never had existed? What could have been His object to seal the deep strata with bones, skeletons, and even with animals, surprised at the moment of eating, and with the remains of the food yet undigested, if they had not partaken food?[1] The testimony of the strata as well as the alluvial deposits, in fact, the whole circle of natural science, is opposed to the literal system of the cosmogony.

Following this, we meet in the fossil grounds, traces of rain drops with the imprints of bird claws and animal feet. How can we believe that the birds and animals which left these marks in the soft strata, had never trodden the plastic formations? We think enough has been adduced to show, that the literal system of creation is untenable, and in direct opposition to the discoveries of modern geology and paleontology, which demand long ages of time for these formations and fossils, before the creation of man.

II. The System of Restitution or Intervals.

The second system founded on the interpretation of Genesis is known as the system of Restitution or

---

[1] They have found in the stomach of one of the fossil ichthyosaurus, the scales of the fish which it had eaten.

the system of Intervals. It has few supporters among modern exegetists or savants, for the reason, that it is opposed to modern science and Sacred Scripture. It consists in supposing that an indefinite period had elapsed between the act of creation, properly speaking, and the Hexæmeron or six days work, described by Moses. During the interval in question and the six days, God restituted or reëstablished the creation. By the first creative act, the earth was rendered fit for the dwelling place of organized beings, a long time before the six days mentioned in Genesis. It was, however, during this *interval*, that plant and animal life had come into existence, as we find them to-day in the fossil state among the terrestrial layers. It was at some period of this interval, when the earth with all its living creatures and productions were destroyed by a great cataclysm; and one can draw inference from the allusion: "The earth was void and empty," that is, in a chaotic state, that such a catastrophe really took place. Now, the chaotic state indicated in Genesis, can hardly apply to the divine work, such as went forth from the hands of the Creator. It presupposes a revolution having been brought on which destroyed all the order of anterior things, and must be considered as the starting point of a new creation, which interests us more directly, because it should terminate by the creation of Adam, our first father.

This system was first brought forward by Dr. Thomas Chalmers, a Scotch clergyman; defended by Buckland, and afterwards adopted, modified and developed by Kurtz and Wagner of Germany. What can we say of this system; is it geologically and exegetically admissible? We shall examine its claims and see if it has any foundation that can be supported by science and Holy Scripture.

1. CRITICISM OF THE SYSTEM OF RESTITUTION.

Although the first system has little to support it from science or Sacred Scripture, in truth it is opposed to science, but this and the other systems advanced by geologists and exegetists, appear as if they could be maintained according to the theories put forward by the supporters of each system. Now, the system of *Restitution* or *Intervals* has the especial merit to preserve to the word *day* its ordinary signification of duration of twenty-four hours. This of itself has led several exegetists to accept this system, though we cannot, with our present knowledge, see that it is founded on reason, because the Sacred Text does not indicate such a catastrophe, supposed by this explanation between the creation of the first matter and that of the actual world. It has no scientific basis, and the result of paleontological inquiries shows that the actual world was not created in six days, but had developed itself slowly through long periods of time.

The defenders of this theory support themselves on the hypothesis, that the creation of matter is not expressly mentioned in Genesis, as a part of the work of the six days; that certain Fathers and Doctors of the Church have believed in the existence of an interval between the origin of things and the *fiat lux* (Be light made), which, after this, opens the first day. They add, that their hypothesis has the advantage of rendering all conflict impossible between the Bible and science. But when all these arguments are thoroughly sifted, they will not be able to bring them in harmony with science.

True, several Fathers have admitted that the first Genesical day had begun by the apparition of light, thus placing the creation of matter outside the six days. Some even went so far as to acknowledge, though in general they keep silent on this point, that matter once created, remained for a long time in a confused mass as described in Genesis. But it is far from this to admit that, during this period anterior to the first day, all the plants and animals developed themselves, whose remains we find in the fossil state.

2. THIS THEORY IS AGAINST REASON.

It is difficult for us to form an idea of a revolution which was sufficiently powerful to annihilate both plant and animal life from the face of the earth, and cause the light to disappear completely, so that one could have said of our globe, "it was formless and void, or invisible and confused; *invisibilis et incomposita*, after the language of the Septuagint. And then, is it not repugnant to conceive that a God infinitely wise, who pursues His work by progressive development during countless ages, would annihilate the same afterwards before the appearance of the being created after His own image, and who was destined to become its crown and king?

Let us suppose for argument sake, that some kind of a cataclysm had annihilated at this point, all organized life from the surface of the earth, and reduced the latter to a formless and confused mass, according to the words of Genesis, the same laws would undoubtedly govern the development of the new creation. But God is an unchangeable Being; the image of His divine attributes is manifest in all the work of creation, sealing by His providential plan order, unity, stability and harmony throughout the laws of nature. One may theorize in a general way about the working of these laws, and draw conclusions from the results of science or the interpretations of Genesis to satisfy his searching and inquisitive mind, but no one has the right to boldly affirm without a special revelation, that God destroyed His own works to make room for a new creation, because such a hypothesis has no support from science, reason or Scripture. But the authors of this theory acknowledge with us that plant life of the ancient world appeared gradually and developed slowly during long periods of time, prior to the coming of man. Why should not it be the same with the new creation? Why the long periods of development in the first interval, and only six days of twenty-four hours each in the latter creation? Most assuredly, it is not easy to find a satisfactory answer to this question

3. THIS THEORY IS OPPOSED TO THE BIBLE.

There is another question not much less embarrassing. If the history of the globe is divided into two great periods, and one totally foreign to the Bible, can one tell at what epoch of this history the first one ended to give place to the second? Was it at the end of what they agree to call the geological ages, that is, the end of the Tertiary epoch? Now, to believe recent discoveries man must have lived in this epoch, and it is bold to deny that he was not contemporary with the mammoth and other extinct species considered characteristic of the Quaternary epoch. Hence man would be preadamite and prehistoric, and would have formed a part of the ancient world as well as of the ages of the animals now living to-day whose ancient remains are found associated with the mammoth in the deluvian deposits. The adherents of the theory of Restitution cannot reconcile these two prominent questions, and must flinch before this exposition.

Again, will they maintain that the reorganization of the world took place at the end of the Tertiary epoch? Man did not exist at this early age, though a few have endeavored to make man very much older than he is. But another difficulty presents itself in this case; most of the Tertiary species have passed into the Quaternary epoch, and several of them exist to-day. Hence it is out of question to admit there was an universal cataclysm which caused the total annihilation of previously existing beings, and there is nothing to authorize us to consider this date the starting point of a new era and complete reorganization of the globe.

It would be vain and short sighted in us to ascend yet higher in the series of the geological ages to find a starting point. Nowhere will one find this line of demarcation, which they believe exists between the anterior and actual world. Neither the flora nor fauna which characterizes each epoch disappear immediately with its respective epoch. Hence it is not apparent from the beginning that a universal cataclysm violent enough to entirely annihilate life upon earth, and cause the absolute need of reorganization of a new order of things, complete in every manner, had ever taken place.

THE HEXÆMERON OR THE SIX GENETIC DAYS. 97

This system is faulty in many respects, and the idea of such a cataclysm is obviously without foundation. To accept it one would be forced to reject the whole pregenesical theory, for this event could not have taken place except in very remote geological ages, especially since the secondary formation, for we have ample testimony to prove that such a catastrophe did not take place since the latter epoch. Now, in order to understand the development of life in times posterior to the reorganization of the globe, one would be forced to accept long periods of time, six days of twenty-four hours each are insufficient to represent one sole period of the history of the entire globe.

We could bring forward many other proofs to show the falsity of the system of *Restitution* or *Intervals*, if we thought it necessary. Buckland and his supporters contend that the Bible favors it. How can that be? The work of all creation is described as the work of six days. Moses proclaims that in six days the Lord made heaven and earth and the sea, and all the things that are in them. He also adds, "These are the generations of the heaven and the earth, when they were created, in the day the Lord made the heaven and the earth." (Gen. ii, 4). It would be difficult to find a more formal or conclusive text than the one just quoted.

The adherents of this system affirm that the world was organized at two different times. The first organization took place immediately after the creation of matter and during the early geological ages, and the second took place just before the advent of man. They also assert that the latter organization took place before creation, and is supported by Moses. Now, it is evident by Holy Writ, that Moses answers this assertion in a formal and emphatic manner. He tells them that the generations he describes as the work of six days, are those which took place when the heaven and the earth were created. It is impossible to be more explicit and to the point.

With regard to the word *create*, so often mentioned here, it is from the Hebrew word *bara*, which means "*create*" in its fullest sense, and nothing else. Further on, we shall explain this word more fully, and show it has a special significance which cannot be changed or modified in any manner from its original meaning. This word is always employed by Moses with design, in opposition to the word *hasah* "to make," "to shape." It is the same word which the sacred writer employs in the beginning of his book when describing that heaven and earth have been drawn from nothing; it is the same word which he uses afterwards to qualify the appearance of animal life and of man upon the earth. In the latter case, however, man's creation was a special act of God, and not due to the sole forces of nature.

It can be seen that the hypothesis of Buckland and his followers is not only against science and reason, but also Holy Scripture. It finds little favor to-day among savants. One of whom uses the following language: "The theory of Restitution supposes cataclysms, which in diverse epochs, and especially before the creation described in Genesis, would have annihilated all life upon earth and established a sharp line of demarcation between the beings previously created and those which have come posteriorly to inhabit the earth. Now, the most attentive study of the grounds and of the fossils which they contain, shows that these revolutions which one believed that could be admitted, have not existed; that among the flora and fauna of one geological period and the flora and fauna of the period following, there has not been any solution of continuity. The species of one epoch encroach on the epoch following and reciprocally. Among the mollusks which live actually in our seas, and even among the mammifers contemporary with man, there are several which have lived many centuries, and perhaps even thousands of years, before his advent upon earth. Therefore, we cannot suppose that these animals have been created only a few days before the creation of man."[1]

The foregoing quotation is alone sufficient to overthrow the system of *Intervals*. Hugh Miller supports the opinion and uses the same language of Lavaud de Lestrade,[2] and adds the following:

. . . "We are led also to know that any scheme of reconciliation which separates between the recent and the extinct existences by a chaotic gulf of death and darkness, is a scheme which no longer meets the necessities of the case. Though perfectly adequate forty years ago, it has been greatly outgrown by the progress of geological discovery, and is, as I have said, adequate no longer; and it becomes a not unimportant matter to determine the special scheme that would bring into completest harmony the course of creation as now ascertained by the geologist, and that brief but sublime narrative of its progress which forms a meet introduction in Holy Writ to the history of the human family."[3]

---
[1] Lavaud de Lestrade, "Accord de la Science," pp. 30–31.
[2] "Testimony of the Rocks," p. 121.
[3] "Testimony of the Rocks," p. 122.

III. The Ideal System.

The third system founded on the interpretation of the six days of creation, is known as the Ideal system, or Ideal explanation, and also called the allegorical or mystic explanation. This system is substantially composed of the following questions: It admits with St. Augustine, that God created all things simultaneously by a single act of His will, and that the distinction of the works of creation in the Mosaic account, has no other end than to place the cosmogony more easily within the comprehension of our intelligence, by presenting the same to us in a series of six tableaux, rather than by one direct presentation. Therefore God did not make use of six days to produce the universe and all things therein. He drew the same from nothing through an act of His will. Only its exposition is described figuratively by six successive days, in order to classify the principal works and impress us with the magnitude of His creative acts.

In modern times, those who have adopted the Ideal explanation of St. Augustine, have modified it in the following way: Moses did not describe the creation objectively but subjectively. He does not relate what passed in fact interiorly or constituently in the production of the universe, but what took place within himself, as it were, when God revealed to him His works in a series of visions. The distinction of days is nothing more than the distinction of the visions. In order to make known to Moses His creative powers, God permits him to behold in six visions the works which had taken place in the six successive days, or the creative acts presented in six tableaux, which the sacred writer describes to us in the first chapter of Genesis.

According to the author of this theory, Mgr. Clifford, bishop of Clifton, Moses did not wish to give us a history of the creation. His sole end in describing the works of God was to dedicate to the memory the days of the week consecrated by the Egyptians to so many special deities. For this purpose he had to adopt some order, but the one already mentioned does not answer anything real; it is not based upon facts, therefore we are not enjoined to accept it.

1. CRITICISM OF THE IDEAL SYSTEM.

Now, regarding this system, there is much about it that seems to please its supporters, because it cuts short all the difficulties of reconciliation which have arisen between the Mosaic account and the results of science. Moses does not describe in what manner the universe organized and developed itself. He only traces an imaginary picture, consequently, there is no longer contradictions nor reproachments possible between his poetic description and the rigid demonstrations of geologists.

The basis of the system, which Mgr. Clifford and his followers have adopted, as already shown, is in the existence of the week consecrated by the Egyptians to their special gods. There is no real foundation for this thesis, inasmuch as the origin of the pagan and Egyptian week cannot be maintained the present day. T. H. Martin,[1] a member of the French Institute, tells us: "It had been already successfully combated in the midst of the seventeenth century, in the Memoirs

---

[1] Annales de Philosophie Chrétienne, Jan. 1882.

of the Ancient Academy of Inscriptions and Belles Lettres,[1] by the learned Abbe Sallier, who at that time had given it a blow from which it could not raise itself since; and in the nineteenth century, the finishing blow was given to this erroneous thesis by a distinguished member of the new Academy of Inscriptions, Alfred Maury, together with an illustrious and very Christian astronomer, Jean Baptist Biot. . . . Among the nations of antiquity, one cannot prove that there has been ever a single one that did not employ the week as a chronological period, abstracting from all religious intention, without having received it from the Hebrews, or better, from the Jews, who were the propagators thereof."

The bishop of Clifton made a great mistake when he referred to Herodotus and Dion Cassius to help him on this point, for the former tells us of the Egyptian months, but not a word about a period of seven days composing the week, and this silence is quite significant. Dion Cassius expressly states that the period of seven days in use in Rome and elsewhere, "is originally from Judea."

Besides the authors just quoted, we learn from Champollion, what was the exact division of time among the ancient Egyptians. In the whole, it was the Republican Calendar of the French Revolution; division of the year into twelve months, divided into three decades of ten days, and followed by five complementary days. The week of seven days does not appear therein.

Hence, Moses could not borrow the idea from the

---

[1] Vol. IV.

Egyptians, nor is it probable that he borrowed it from other sources, not even from the Chaldeans. Therefore, we cannot attribute to him the intention of putting the polytheistic week in place of the monotheistic, and substituting to the pagan deities, who presided over the days, the works of creation arbitrarily divided.

For argument sake, let us suppose such was the object of Moses, the proposed system receives no benefit from this, because there is first a difficulty which immediately presents itself to the mind. The sacred writer does not content himself in describing the different works of God, but tells us in plain language that one took place on the *first* day, the other on the *second* day, and so on to the *seventh* day, when God finished the work of creation (Gen. ii, 2). It seems to us there is here every evidence of succession of days. We find this statement corroborated in Exodus (xx, 11): " In six days the Lord made heaven and earth, and all things that are in them and rested on the seventh day."

All this is of no importance to the author of the new theory. He tells us that both texts are borrowed from a historical work. The first is extracted from a sacred hymn, such is, in his eyes, the nature of the first chapter of Genesis. The second is a liturgical formula, the terms of which must not be taken in their ordinary sense, hence there is no reason to attach any importance to them.

This is a very easy and off-handed way of solving such a grave question; for, texts so clear as those which precede do not lose their meaning, even were they found in a ritual or liturgical book. The thought of the sacred writer seems to be evident, and we do not believe that until now there has been two manners of seeing in this regard.

Moreover, it is not proved that the first chapter of Genesis has the character of a hymn, or sacred chant. In the first place, it is in prose, an observation which has already sealed its importance. Then, it is unquestionable, that the book to which it belongs is absolutely historical. To refute this quality of the first chapter, Mgr. Clifford appeals to the difference of style, especially in the employment of the word *Elohim* to designate God, instead of Jehovah which appears later. This distinction of rationalistic origin tends, it is true, to establish that Moses would have inserted in his work ancient documents to which he preserved their primitive form, but it does not follow from this that these documents are void of all historical character.

2. CHALDEAN COSMOGONY.

In support of his thesis, the learned prelate appeals to the recent discoveries of Assyriology. Now, it happens that these discoveries completely upset his hypothesis. We already owe to Berosus a Chaldean cosmogony, which presents the appearance of things in an order analogous to that indicated in Genesis, but with an idea of a yet more marked chronological succession. A cuneiform inscription, unfortunately incomplete, has been discovered and preserved for public use, which substantiates this idea.[1] It is a detailed account of the primitive state and progressive development of the universe. "A great number of days and a long time elapsed," it says in the middle of the account. It

---

[1] See George Smith's Chaldean account of Genesis, pp. 62-63.

gives us clearly to understand that there was a succession in the formation of the globe. It does more, it expressly tells us that the days of Genesis were not days of twenty-four hours but periods of unlimited duration.

The Chaldean inscription has another advantage. To the description of the work of six days, it joins the account of the fall of man. From this it results, that these two accounts, which some would like to see separated, and one not confirming the other, are intimately connected, and serve to prove the texts in Genesis relating to the works of creation and the fall of man. Therefore, when the one is historical the other must likewise be the same.

We must not assimilate or confound the two cosmogonies, that is, the Biblical and Chaldean, for the reason, that the latter is disfigured by myths, which takes away much of its value at first sight, of what it has preserved of its primitive features. Nevertheless, it must be taken into serious consideration by the exegetist, for everything proves that it is, if not in its actual form, at least, in its essential account anterior to Moses, perhaps even to Abraham. That it has preserved to us in its alteration, an ancient tradition, which the sacred author, on the contrary, has transmitted to us in all its primitive purity. Mgr. Clifford is astonished because God has revealed to Moses geological facts, which are within the domain of natural sciences. This revelation would explain itself sufficiently by the importance of the fact in question; but nothing obliges us to believe it was made only to Moses. It is quite probable that it is much anterior to him and that God communicated this revelation to Adam himself.

Thus we can trace the source from which they drew the records of these Chaldean documents which seem anterior to the Hebrew legislator.

Whatever way we may regard the case, it appears that the first chapter of Genesis traces for us the real history of our globe before the coming of man. Were this page, as one pretends, a hymn placed by Moses at the head of his book, we ought yet expect a truth therein. Its adoption by the inspired writer would give to it the same character of veracity as to other Biblical accounts, and we must always hold as certain that the things have succeeded in the order so exactly indicated by the same.

We may admit that the number of six days into which Moses has divided the works of creation, is, in a certain sense, an arbitrary number. Perhaps, it was only adopted because the number *seven* was already a sacred one among the Hebrews (Gen. iv, 15-24; vii, 2-34). Moses could with the same facility divide this work between *ten* periods, for there is nothing to prove that a precise line of demarcation separates the diverse days. But we cannot refuse to admit, because Moses declares this in a formal manner, that the order which he presents to us is really the chronological order, the one in which appeared in their turn, at the will of the Creator, both the inanimate and animate beings which as a whole constitute the universe. If it were different, we would have to say that the sacred writer has expressed himself in a manner to lead into inevitable error all the future generations. This is inadmissible, and we cannot think for a moment that the Holy Ghost who inspired him permitted him to commit a false statement which would produce such grave consequences.

3. ACCORD BETWEEN GEOLOGY AND SACRED SCRIPTURE.

It is strange that the truth of the Biblical cosmogony would be contested at a time the geologists, who are free from party prejudice and not blind to reason, willingly render it homage. Nowhere, perhaps, is this accord more striking between the accounts of science and those of the Sacred Books, than on geological ground. Here we find such an astonishing coincidence that it cannot be the effect of chance. Geology has never tried hard to remain orthodox, and never proposed to come to the assistance of the defenders of Biblical truth, nevertheless, it has divided the history of the globe into three great periods anterior to the advent of man; characterized the one by its wonderful vegetation, the other by the prominence of aquatic animals, and the third by the number of land animals. This is precisely the order we find in Genesis, and which represents the third, fifth and sixth days of creation. We do not need to speak of the other days, for they are consecrated to recall to our minds the creation of light, the firmament, and finally, the celestial bodies. It is not the business of geology to make inquiries about this order of things, but it is certain, that in all researches where its control has been possible, it has turned to the glory of our Sacred Books whose indications it has confirmed.

Mgr. Clifford asks: "Who would risk to affirm that the study of Genesis has ever led to the discovery of one single geological fact?" We can readily answer his question and say, that the succession into three distinct periods and of three great series of beings which compose the organic kingdom, that is, the vegetable, aquatic and terrestrial, is a geological fact of the first order, and this was known to Genesis before the study of the terrestrial layers had been made a scientific truth. The relatively recent appearance of man upon earth, is a fact of the same order, which the Sacred Books made known to us before it was proclaimed by geology.

And what difficulties arise before the views of the bishop of Clifton, when he beholds the acceptation of the generally received theory of the period-days?

"The Biblical account" he says, "seems in disaccord not only with the discoveries of modern science, but also with the wisdom of Egypt, in which Moses had been educated. The Egyptians knew very well that the vegetation depends, for its development, upon the action of the sun. . . . When the date of the creation of this astre must be taken in a historical sense, and as implying that the earth existed, that it turned upon its axis, that it was covered with vegetation before the sun, the centre of the system of which the earth forms a part, came to its existence, it is useless to make the attempt to reconcile such a proposition with the unquestionable facts of science."[1]

Now we behold Moses caught in the fact of error, if, with the great majority of interpreters, we set him up as a historian!

4. OBJECTIONS REFUTED.

We believe that the error is on the side of the new exegetist, who gives here proof of a singularly incomplete science. Moses, we must remember, does not

---

Annales Phil. Christ.—Nov. 1881.

tell us that the sun was created on the fourth day, but only that it appeared on that day. Hence, we may believe it had previously existed as the centre of the planetary system, perhaps even as a luminous body. All we are obliged to admit, and this is not against the geological accounts, is, that in this epoch, supposing reasonable inhabitants of the globe had really existed at the time, did perceive for the first time the disk of the sun, the immense cloud, which before surrounded the earth, having finally torn itself to give passage to the solar rays. It would be easy to prove by analogy, in showing what passes in certain equatorial regions, that these conditions were precisely those which combined to the development of the immense vegetation of the anterior period — the Carboniferous period. What is needed for the tropical forests, in order to grow luxuriantly, is great heat, to be sure, but a diffusive heat and light more than the direct action of the solar rays.

When we can believe that the sun existed, but masked by thick clouds before the fourth day of creation, then nothing hinders us to admit that then it only became luminous. The theory of Laplace, which is now generally received, proposes to our belief, that each of the bodies of our planetary system did in its turn play the role of the sun, favors this hypothesis, for the central astre, precisely because it is immensely greater than the others, and must have entered into this phase of its existence a long time after. By this hypothesis, one would not be embarrassed to find the primitive source of light, which sprang forward since the beginning at the word of the Creator, and which, enlightened the earth during long periods of time, in the way of its formation. Without seeking any further, we may believe the moon was that incandescent body which first gave light to our globe, and thus contributed to entertain life upon its surface.

Mgr. Clifford vaguely opposes other difficulties to the system of periods. He assumes, for instance, that the progress of geology has condemned them; that this science in substituting the theory of the *actual causes* for that of cataclysms, does not permit any longer the division into periods having, as Genesis tells, a *morning* and an *evening*, a beginning and an end.

The theory of causes, readily accepted by some, is far from having brought forward its proofs. It always had among the best geologists decisive adversaries, and, if there is something in it, nothing at least authorizes us to completely eliminate the violent cataclysms of our globe's history. Were it true, it would not at all shake the theory of the day-periods. Nothing obliges us to believe that each of the Genesical days has been limited by a violent phenomenon; the passage, even insensibly, from one work to the other, is sufficient to mark the end of one period and the beginning of another. When the sacred writer appears to insist on the precision of this separation; when, repeatedly, he employs, to mark it better, the expressions evening and morning, it is undoubtedly that the expressions evening and morning convey to us the idea, that he wishes us to behold in the seven periods of the creation the figure of the seven days of the week.

Mgr. Clifford speaks of new difficulties which the progress of geology would create to the theory we defend. Perhaps he has in view what Genesis says about the creation of plants before that of animals.

Now, geology shows us certain fishes already living in the Silurian, which is anterior to the Carboniferous epoch, the latter showed the greatest development which vegetation ever reached, because it is to this we owe our immense coal deposits. Moreover it shows us below the Cambrian ground, consequently quite to the origin of life, an animal of a very inferior order — the Eozoon Canadense, which the Evolutionist has just put into bold relief for the needs of his theory when hard pressed; but every scientist knows that the existence of this pretended zoöphite is very questionable. In every case, it is of no importance to our question; for Moses, who evidently does not assume to be a naturalist, mentions only the superior animals — those which could attract the attention of man.

Finally, if even some of these animals were found imbedded in the transition grounds belonging to the primary epoch; if even the secondary layers would reveal to us the debris of some representatives of the terrestrial mammifers and reptiles, which appear in masses only later on, it would be true to say that the primary period has been characterized by the extraordinary development of the vegetable kingdom, the secondary period by its aquatic animals of variable forms, and the tertiary period by the abundance of terrestrial animals, exclusive of man who, according to science and the Bible, was the last in the order of created beings which appeared.

5. EVIDENCE OF A PRIMITIVE REVELATION.

There is, here we repeat, such a remarkable concordance that it is, according to our views, both the effect and proof of a primitive revelation. It was impossible to take the things in their whole and without entering into details which circumstances did not permit, to describe in a more exact manner the work of creation. And we ask those who see errors, irregularities, or even "absurdities" therein, how they would proceed to give us in so few words a cosmogony which would be more in accord with science, and which would offer us more titles to our acceptation.

In summary, the reasons which Mgr. Clifford brings forward against the almost unanimous opinion, that sees in the first chapter of Genesis the *historical* account of the creation of the world, will not stand a serious examination. It is, therefore, wise to preserve the weapons used up to the present to defend the Sacred Books. Those they offer us in exchange appear too weak and futile; others may say, perhaps with good reason, that they are dangerous.

IV. The Concordistic System.

The fourth system of the interpretation of the first chapter of Genesis, is known as the theory of *day-periods*, because it considers each of the six days to represent an epoch or period of unlimited time, and not an ordinary day of twenty-four hours. It is also called Concordistic, because it affirms to be in concord between Genesis and the sciences, and therefore in opposition to other theories in which they deny this accord between the Mosaic account and the researches of geology. The adherents of the day-periods understand by the Genesical days long periods, during which the world organized itself progressively and conformably to the physical laws; by gradual development and perfection it was rendered a fitting abode for all organized life, and when sufficiently prepared, God produced by His immediate action, the plants and animals. These reproduced and developed themselves, bringing forth and dying with the march of time, in obedience to the laws of their nature. Man was the last to appear; he was the crowning work of the Creator, being created in a special manner by the hand of Him who fashioned everything according to His will, and who breathed into him a soul immortal. The theory of day-periods was adopted by Cuvier in 1821.

1. CRITICISM OF THE CONCORDISTIC SYSTEM.

We adopt the theory of day-periods, which continues to regard the first chapter of Genesis as historical, but understanding it in the following manner, and by being careful to not exaggerate the Concordistic relations between the Biblical cosmogony and geology.

There has been a development, an ascending scale of progression in the divine work from the beginning. The Creator, at first, produced the elements of matter, as we are told in the first verse; these have, through their diverse combinations, formed the inorganic and mineral matter; after which appeared successively the plants, the lower and higher order of animals, and finally man.

Genesis does not assume to be a scientific treatise by any means. It only gives the principal features of the cosmogony, and does not enter into details. Consequently, all the attempts which have been made to make particular points of geology agree with the sacred accounts, are merely conjectural. The natural sciences have established the fact of the production of inorganic and organic beings, in the same ascending gradation as mentioned in Genesis. This of itself is sufficient to affirm an accord between them. The following clear, succinct and logical examination of this accord, by the distinguished savant, M. Barrande, who covers the whole ground, and leaves no doubt in the unbiased mind that there exists an irreconcilable conflict between the accounts of Genesis and the researches of geology:—

"With regard to the creation of the organized beings, the whole account of Genesis reduces itself to establish three great facts, about which it is in perfect harmony with the scientific accounts acquired thus far by the geological science. These facts can be formulated as follows: 1. The vegetable life has preceded the animal life in both the seas and upon the earth. 2. The animal life has been at first represented by the animals living in the sea and by the birds. 3. Consequently, the animal life has been developed posteriorly upon earth, and man has appeared only after all the created beings.

I. . . . We know that the marine vegetables, known under the name Fucoids, have preceded the apparition of the ancient fauna. . . . It is the schists placed above the fucoid grit, and consequently posterior to this, that we meet the first traces of animals constituting the primordial fauna, chiefly represented by the crustacea of the family of the tribolites. With regard to the terrestrial plants, there exists no trace in the rocks of the Silurian system, except perhaps in England, in the so-called tilestone layers, which border upon its upper limit. . . . After the facts we come to indicate, the most ancient earthly plants ascend to the epoch where the Silurian ground ends in depositing itself. Now the only vertebrate animals known in the epoch consisted in some species of fishes, yet very rare. They have discovered no trace of any earthly animals ascending to this period. The most ancient of all the animals which have breathed the air and the traces of which have been known until this day, has been found in the upper part of the old red sandstone or Devonian ground of Scotland, that is, above the horizon which is assigned to the Devonian plants of which we come to speak. It is a small reptile whose length did not attain ten centimeters. It is known under the name *Telerpeton elginense.* The facts considered until at this moment agree therefore to show that the vegetation has preceded the apparition of the animals, as well upon earth as in the sea. As to this point, Genesis is therefore in perfect accord with the discoveries of science.

"We must also consider that the gradation established by Moses in the creation of the vegetable kingdom agrees well with the facts observed by science, which acknowledges that the plants offering the most elevated organization have appeared much later than the inferior types of the vegetable kingdom. Moses, after having enumerated the three principal degrees in the vegetable organization, did not occupy himself to fix exactly the epoch in which each of them has made its apparition, either through the effect of a slow transformation of types primitively created, and in virtue of a law of development which was imposed upon them, or by a direct and repeated action of the Creator. In other words, Moses only seems to have wished to establish the relative order of the epochs in which God was pleased to create the prototypes of the classes of beings which had already succeeded one another, and which succeed themselves yet in the series of times. He made abstraction of the history of the development of these beings, the chief successive forms he enumerates however.

"II. The animal life has been at first represented by the animals which live in the sea and by the birds. As to the sea animals, the fact of their existence before that of the earthly animals goes forth incontestably from all geological observations made until this day. . . . The primordial fauna on the globe explored, composes itself almost solely of articulate animals of the class of the crustaceæ, constituting the family of the tribolites. The mollusks are hardly represented therein except by some lower types of the class of the brachiopodæ.[1] The second fauna enriches itself chiefly by the apparition of a great number of types of mollusks, representing nearly all classes of this branch. The third fauna shows the yet more considerable development of the mollusks, and distinguishes itself from the two preceding faunas by the apparition of some rare fishes, which are the first representatives of the branch of the vertebrates on the globe. In the Devonian faunas, the fishes take in their turn a great and a rapid development, in harmony with that of the mollusks. . . . After these considerations . . . it is evident that the animal life in the seas has been anterior to the animal life upon earth.

"As to the birds, one conceives naturally that cer-

---

[1] The brachiopodæ, a class of the mollusk-like animals, distinguished by the development of two labial appendages diverging from either side of the mouth.

tain kinds must have existed in the most ancient epochs, because they live of fishes, of mollusks and other sea animals. However, the most ancient traces which we know to-day do not ascend beyond the Triassic epoch.

"After having exactly fixed the point of origin as to the marine animals and the birds, Moses enumerates in a remarkable manner the principal types of the animals which have peopled the seas, starting with those which are crawling, that is mollusks, until the fishes and the large cetaceæ. The order followed in this enumeration corresponds perfectly with that which we observe in the series of geological formations. But after these general indications, although sufficient in a book which is no scientific treatise, Moses does not occupy himself to determine the precise epoch when each of the animal classes has made its particular appearance in the seas. . . .

"III. Since it is proved that the animal life has been at first represented by the animals living in the sea and by the birds, it follows necessarily that the animals which inhabit the surface of the earth ascend to a less ancient origin. But we must well remark that after having fixed the relative epoch of their appearance, Moses has not sought to instruct us about the diverse epochs when types of the animal life upon earth have made their particular apparition. It appears certain however, that they have not been created all at once, but successively, like the sea animals of which we come to speak. Each of the ancient types has disappeared after a more or less long existence, to make room for new types.

"Thus, in summary, the sacred historian appears

to have proposed to himself principally for end to fix the relative epoch of the apparition of the plants, of the marine animals and of the terrestrial animals, without entering into historic detail with regard to the subsequent development neither of the vegetable reign nor of the animal reign. This development took place in the series of time, either through a new and repeated action of the Creator himself, or through the effect of the laws originally established by Him in nature and which He has not judged proper to reveal to us.

"In studying from this point of view the history of the creation of the vegetable kingdom and of the animal kingdom given by Moses, one recognizes that it is in perfect harmony with that geology has drawn from the observation of the facts, that is, from the strateographic study of the sedimentary rocks and of the organic remains, either vegetable, or animal, which they contain."[1]

Astronomy also shows the necessity of long periods to the Genesical days. The telescope makes us behold stars so distant that, if we are to believe astronomers, they need over 10,000 years to transmit their light to us, which travels over 225,000 miles per second. They even speak of 1,000,000 years for certain nebulæ lost in the depths of space. If the world had existed only 6,000 or 8,000 years, as it was formerly believed, all these astres would still be invisible to us.

We may ask why the Genesical days should be days of twenty-four hours? A day is usually measured according to the rising and setting of the sun. The sun, as we know, appeared only on the fourth day. One can see the difficulty which comes in the way of this

---

[1] Geological note of M. Barrande.

hypothesis, though declared by its adherents the most natural and the one most acceptable.

Will they tell us that the first three days are measured by the duration of the rotation of the earth upon its own axis? Surely, they would be days without nights, and the words evening and morning, to which they attach a proper and literal meaning, must be taken in the figurative sense, as well as in the theory of the day-periods.

Let us add that these days would have more than twenty-four hours. The duration of the rotation of a celestial body upon its own axis, diminishes indeed with its volume. Now, according to the theory almost universally accepted, a theory which everything confirms, even the text of Genesis (*terra erat invisibilis et incomposita*), our globe was primitively in the gaseous state.

There was an epoch when its surface extended itself to the actual lunar orbit and even beyond it, for the moon, in the system of Laplace, is only a fragment of the terrestrial nebula detached from its periphery and condensed afterwards. In this epoch the earth required the time to turn round upon its own axis that our satellite employs now to accomplish its revolution round our globe, a little more than twenty-seven days. The Genesical days, even agreeably to the hypothesis we combat, were therefore very different to the actual days. This is the negation itself of the hypothesis that the creation took place within the space of six days, of twenty-four hours each.

Another grave question is presented in Scripture. The sacred writer tells us that God rested on the seventh day. According to the common opinion of theologians, this seventh comprises the whole time which followed the apparition of man and always continues. Hence, it is not a period of twenty-four hours, and everything goes to show that the other days are of the same nature.

2. THE COSMOGONIC TRADITION OF DIVERSE NATIONS.

The cosmogonic traditions of the diverse nations of antiquity confirm this interpretation. The Chaldeans, Phenicians, Persians, Etruscans, etc., have believed in the division of the creation into six periods of long duration. May these traditions be derived from a Hebrew source, or may they be connected, like the Biblical cosmogony, with one and the same primitive revelation. However, they are no less significant.

"In all the pagan cosmogonies" says Pozzie, "the world has been at its origin a chaos; it was inclosed in an egg which broke and whose half has formed the heavenly vault, the other the earth. Whence this idea which we find among all the nations? This is not a simple idea, which rises spontaneously in the human brain, because among the philosophers, the one suppose the universe to be eternal, whilst others make it rise from the fortuitous meeting of atoms hooked in the space. Besides, the chaos has no analogy in the actual nature. We behold no being going forth from a confused and informal mass. And then, how can we reconcile the chaos, the ideal of the disorder and of death, with the egg, which is the most beautiful symbol of life and harmony? Hence, because we find this idea among all the nations, it must have come to them from a common source, it must form part of those primordial beliefs which constituted the religion of primitive humanity and which the nations, during the dispersion, carried along with them. It is thus that we can explain the numerous resemblances of these cosmogonies. It is thus that we can explain equally those not less striking which they present with Genesis, with that difference, however, that the cosmogony of the Hebrews is much more correct and better united, and that which gives us the key to all the others. By the latter the two contradictory notions of the egg and of the chaos complete themselves. The earth was void and empty and darkness was upon the face of the deep: Behold the chaos. And the spirit of God moved (brooded) over the waters (like a bird); behold the idea of the egg of the world, idea which we find from one end of the world to the other until at the natives of the Sandwich Islands. ' In the time when all was sea,' they say, ' an immense bird was hovering over the waters and laid an egg from which went forth the Island of Haouaï.' But, these reserves made, everything goes to show that the Hebrews, like the other nations, had drawn the account of the creation, which is at the head of Genesis, in the primitive tradition of humanity, from which all the pagan cosmogonies went forth."[1]

3. THE CONCORDISTIC SYSTEM ESTABLISHES THE MOST COMPLETE ACCORD.

From all the facts we have adduced here and in the preceding section, the results fully show that the Concordistic system alone establishes the most complete accord between Genesis and science. Let us observe, however, that it goes forth from what has been said on all points intimately connected with the six days

---

[1] Pozzie, "La terre et le recit Biblique de la Creation," 1874, pp. 244, 245.

of creation, that the Mosaic days are metaphorical, not only as to their meaning, but also as to their number. The figure six in Genesis must not be taken in a rigorous and absolute sense; it does not signify that one counts only six epochs in the series of the productions of the Creator; we must understand in the sense that there have been several successive periods of development. This number was chosen only in order that the divine week might correspond with the human week, in which six days are given to labor, and the seventh, the Sabbath, is consecrated to rest. Moreover, we may remark that the Mosaic cosmogony points out only the chief features in the work of creation. The details which are of less importance in the eyes of mankind in general are neglected.

Hence we may say there are three kinds of omissions: 1. The little striking objects (mollusks, marine plants) are omitted or included in the general affirmation of marine life; 2. The meagre beginning as to the number or importance of the objects of a work, which had its full development in one of the following days. Thus, on account of this secondary importance regarding the large aquatic reptiles, the fishes, properly speaking are passed over in the third and fourth days when they were abounding, and named only in the general recapitulation, which refers to the fifth day-epoch of the great creation of marine life; 3. Also the continuation or repetition of a work already mentioned under one day, is passed over in silence; for instance, the continuation of the emersion of the continents, the substitution of one species to another in the same general category of living beings; thus, although the creation of the actual species did not take place before the sixth day, one could however place the creation of plants in the third, and that of the marine animals in the fifth.

As to the creation of the plants on the third day, which fact gives rise to a particular objection, the sun having been created only on the fourth, we shall answer this objection when we come to examine more fully the Hexæmeron.

The Mosaic account therefore contains no detail which is irreconcilable with the sure accounts of science, and, in summary, the Concordistic theory or day-period, seems the most acceptable. It is, however, like the other theories on which we have commented, only a system; a fact which we must keep in mind. It was especially the desire of Moses to impress on us the belief of a God Creator, and show Him gradually preparing the earth to serve as a dwelling place for man, and His great solicitude for his well being.

How long did this preparation last? This is a secondary question whose solution has no theological importance. When one admits that the Genesical days are periods of undetermined length, it is evident that we cannot fix after the Bible the origin of the universe, because we ignore how many years—how many centuries—these periods have lasted. But were one to maintain that the six days were only ordinary days of twenty-four hours, we would still not know in what epoch the universe was created. In fact, the Sacred Text teaches us that only the elements of which heaven and earth are composed, have been produced by the divine power. "In the beginning of time;" it does not explain to us what interval separates us from this initial point; it does tell us how many years or centuries the chaotic state prolonged itself, the state in which all was confounded before the work of the first day. The duration of this primitive period is, therefore, totally unknown to us. Science may calculate and speculate at will its probable length of time, but it can never be scientifically established beyond doubt. The American geologist, Professor Dana, has calculated on the respective thickness of the sedimentary stages, that the Primitive era must have lasted about 36,000,000 of years, the Secondary era 9,000,000, and the Tertiary era 3,000,000,[1] in all 48,000000 of years. Our Sacred Books do neither approve nor contradict these calculations, for on this subject they are absolutely silent. "I have discovered neither in Scripture, nor in reason, nor in the monuments of other historians, any chronological character which might help us in the inquiry of the time of the creation," wrote Des Vignoles in 1738, and he renounced all attempts at ever discovering its date. Indeed, it belongs to the savants, and not to the exegetists nor the historians to make this inquiry. And we can say to the paleontologists and the geologists, attribute to the universe as many centuries as you judge proper, you will have to give an account of your calculations or of your hypothesis only to science—theology is disinterested in this question.

---

[1] Dana, Manual of Geology, New York, 1876, p. 591.

CHAPTER VII.

THE HEXÆMERON OR THE SIX GENETIC DAYS.
[Continued.]

I.

MUCH importance is attached to the first two verses of the Bible, as they are the groundwork and superstructure of the world's history from the beginning, and stand to-day as they have in the past, impregnable to all attacks, misrepresentations and false theories. "In the beginning God created heaven and earth, and the earth was void and empty, and darkness was upon the face of the deep, and the Spirit of God moved over the waters."

1. "IN THE BEGINNING GOD CREATED HEAVEN AND EARTH."

There exists in no language any sentence which contains in so few words so many important dogmas. The Mosaic cosmogony is the condemnation of all the errors of the ancient world. The sacred writer does not speak in an abstract or philosophical manner, but in concrete terms. As a historian, he announces the fact, without delivering himself to any commentary, and the first verse alone of his book is sufficient to make all the errors of ancient and modern times detestable and insignificant. "In the beginning God created heaven and earth." Consequently there exists only one God, contrary to the general belief of all nations at that time with the exception of the Hebrews; the former adored several gods and had a "divinity in every bush." This sentence also summarily disposes of the subject of matter. Matter is not eternal, because it did not exist before God created it. God has drawn matter from nothing by an act of His all-powerful will. He is the absolute master of the world as the world, and all things contained therein were created by Him. With all this evidence before him, man has been prone to error from the earliest times. Peoples and philosophers have believed that matter was not distinct from God himself; they were called Pantheists; others again believed that matter had always existed—they were known as Hylozoites — the same as our modern Materialists. Moses overthrows all these erroneous systems with one sentence: "In the beginning God created heaven and earth."

2. CRITICISM OF THE FIRST VERSE OF GENESIS.

The first verse of Genesis has been understood in three different ways: 1. As a summary of the whole chapter and the work of the six days; 2. As indicating a complete creation, quite distinct from the following, from which it should have been separated by a geological revolution marked in the second verse; 3. As signifying the creation of the first matter or elements of matter. This last sentence is the only one admissible, because the second verse is inexplicable in the first two cases, as we have shown in another place. Moses could not say at first that the earth was void and empty, if there had been no creation of the first matter, before the organization of this matter. There is seemingly a sequel between the first and second verse, but only under the condition of admitting that God primitively created all the elements—heaven and earth, which in Hebrew designate the universality of the beings. Most of the Fathers too, have understood it in this sense.

Let us inquire further: What does Genesis mean by the word *bârâ*, which our Vulgate translates here as elsewhere, *creare*—"to create." The true meaning of the verb *bârâ*, employed by the original text here, is to produce *ex nihilo*—"of nothing." The equivalent of the word *ex nihilo* is not found in the Hebrew Pentateuch, because the language of Moses has no corresponding expression, but the sense which the Bible attaches to the verb *bârâ* is beyond question. However, some contemporary infidels deny this as the following will show:

"Modern exegesis rejects the interpretation of the creation *ex nihilo*, which they often give to the Hebrew verb *bârâ*. This verb signifies essentially to cut, to pare, to shape, in the sense to cut the trees of a forest, etc. Far from excluding the idea of a preëxisting matter, it implies the same. Also passages like Gen. i, 27, and ii, 7, for instance, prove that the notion of a creation *ex nihilo* has no foundation in the Hebrew text."[1]

Nothing is more at variance with the spirit and meaning of the texts just quoted than these assertions. In the first two chapters of Genesis, we find four different verbs to express the creative action of God: 1. *bârâ* — to create; 2. *âsâh* — to make; 3. *yoâsâr* — to form;

---

[1] Saury, "Theories Naturalistes du Monde," pp. 48, 49.

4. *bânâh* — to build. *Bârâ* is used for the creation of the universe as in Gen. i, 1; the great fishes of the sea, in verse 21, and of man, in verse 27; elsewhere, God makes His creation from the substance already created, as in verse 17, 16, 25; or He forms the beasts of the field from the earth, ii, 9; or, finally, He builds the woman, ii, 22.[1]

Not only here but in almost all the passages of Scripture, where we meet the word *bârâ*, it expresses the creation *ex nihilo*. This word is reserved to God, particularly associated with His creative work, and He is always the subject thereof, to mark the creation of heaven and earth. Moreover, God produces the creature by His sole will. The mode of creation in Genesis, is the word, that is, an act of the will:

> He spoke and they were made;
> He commanded, and they were formed.
> — *Ps. CXLVIII*, 5.

The words following " heaven and earth," expressed two ideas, and mean the universe, the same which the Greek books of the Old and New Testament call the Kosmos. According to St. Augustine, we would have to understand here only that primordial mass out of which was formed "heaven and earth." This primitive mass would be meant by the words "earth and water." This explanation has not only the clear expression of the text against the ideas of many other interpreters, that "heaven and earth" mean here two different things, but is more conformable to the meaning of other passages. No doubt, this difference of explanation comes from verse 2; the " earth " about which there is

---

[1] Cf. Is. xliii 7. In this sole verse, Isaias employs the first three words.

question, in opposition to "heaven and earth," as in verse 1, cannot possibly signify the primitive heaven and primitive earth at the same time. It is just what the name tells without any exegesis—the earth itself; under the expression "heaven," we have to understand the material heaven, not the heaven which is the abode of angels, as was formerly accepted. Against the latter interpretation other passages are decisive, because, several texts speak of the destruction of heaven and earth at the end of time. "In the beginning, O Lord, thou foundest the earth, and the heavens are the work of Thy hands. They (heaven and earth) shall perish, but Thou remainest."[1] We cannot find a passage in Scripture wherein heaven and earth is mentioned that means both the spiritual and material creation, and it is less allowable here, because in the following verses, heaven does not mean the spiritual (9-10) and the earth the material world (2-10). If the angels are meant to be included in the first verse as the creatures of God, it is reasonable to infer it is only in so far as they belong to the world, but it does not mean that they are especially denoted by the word "heaven."

3. ORGANIZATION OF THE ELEMENTS OF MATTER.

After having affirmed in the first verse the creation of the elements of matter, Moses makes known to us the organization of the same. God puts in order the elements which had remained in a state of confusion until then, *thohu vabohu* (void and empty) as the sacred writer tells us. *Thohu vabohu* does not express chaotic shapelessness, as we learn from the following

---

[1] Ps. CI. 26-27; Cf. Math. xxiv. 35; Peter iii, 7, 10. 12, 13; Acts xxi; Is. lxv. 17; lxvi. 22.

texts: "He did not create (the earth) in vain (or desolate)" says Isaias xlv, 18, "but formed it to be inhabited." and Jeremiah says: "I beheld the earth, and lo it was void and nothing; and the heavens, and there was no light in them. I looked upon the mountains; and behold they trembled; and all the hills were troubled. I beheld, and lo there was no man; and all the birds of the air were gone. I looked and behold Carmel was a wilderness, and all its cities were destroyed at the presence of the Lord, and at the presence of the wrath of his indignation. For thus saith the Lord, all the land shall be desolate."[1] Thus, what were the heavens without the light, what were the mountains and hills without firm foundations, what was the universe without man and birds, what was the land of Carmel without its cities and fruitfulness: That was the earth in the state of *thohu vabohu*. Indeed, it is yet earth, but deprived of its proper ornament, it is "void and empty." All this stands as the effect of a divine desolating judgment. "All the land shall be desolate." From this, it is to be understood that also *thohu vabohu* cannot be rendered to indicate "formless, shapeless, bottomless," for the "*invisibilis et incomposita* (invisible and confused)" of the Septuagint, must be translated according to the Hebrew text, with "invisible and unadorned." which is about the same as "void and empty." One cannot appeal here to the text of Wisdom xi, 18: "Thy Almighty hand which made the world of matter without form," because the primordial formlessness need not to be understood as an absolute one, but only as a relative one, consisting in the want

---

[1] Jer. iv. 23-27.

of form and beauty essential to the world for its development and full completion. When we designate a person ill shaped, we do not mean by this that he or she is shapeless or devoid of form. The *thehom*, which St. Jerome translated with abysus—"abyss," following the Septuagint — does not point to a chaos. It is nothing else but the *tihamtu* of the Assyrians, the same the Chaldean account of Genesis makes use of in this place, and which designate the "sea," meaning the same as the "waters." In this, it agrees with Laplace's theory, which assumes that the earth was at first a vast globe of vapor, then a liquid spheriod.

4. AND THE SPIRIT OF GOD MOVED OVER THE WATERS.

During the interval which separated the creation of the first matter from the apparition of the light, the Spirit of God (considered by some Fathers, the Third Person of the Blessed Trinity, and by others, the wind which agitated the waters, as rendered by the Hebrew *rouakh*, signifying both spirit and wind), worked at the elaboration of the universe. It is this that Moses expresses by saying: "And the Spirit of God moved over the waters," or as the Hebrew text more correctly translates it, and as translated by some of the Fathers: "The Spirit of God brooded over the waters." Chaos is therefore under the influence of the Divine Spirit; it is intended that life shall come forth from it as from the egg on which the bird is brooding. The chaotic mass as it is, is unworthy of God, as it has not been produced to remain inert, but that it may supply the raw material for more perfect forms; and by the words: "The Spirit of God moved (or brooded) over the waters," Moses declares that the chaos contains the germs of these more perfect forms, or that the divine purpose and the divine power are ruling over this inorganic matter, in order to form it into varied, beautiful and perfect organic types.

The interpretation of this passage as given by both ancient and modern rationalistic and believing writers, is this: "And a wind of God hovered or passed over the waters." "This translation is exegetically inadmissible," says Reusch. No doubt the first meaning of *Rouakh* is "breath," and so of course a "wind," and the expressions "mountains of God," "cedars of God," may be quoted as parallels to that of "wind of God," would mean a mighty storm. But these expressions are strictly poetical, and *Rouakh Elohim* never has this meaning in the Old Testament, although it very often has that of "Spirit of God." And besides this, the word *rachaph*, whether it is translated hovered or brooded, does not apply to a storm.

After clearing up and explaining the objections and false interpretations of the first two verses of Genesis, we shall proceed to examine in the next section, the account of the six day's work, in order to show how it accords with the results of the natural sciences.

II.

Having examined the first two verses of the Bible, the various systems of their interpretation touching the Mosaic cosmogony, we shall now enter more into detail concerning certain results of natural science, in so far as they are in accord with Genesis. For this purpose we shall examine each day's work in the order given, and trust we shall be able to prove, so far as the actual state of knowledge will permit, that it essentially corresponds with the scientific history of our globe.

1. FIRST DAY'S WORK.

Gen. i, 3-5. (3) "*And God said: Be light made, and the light was made;* (4) *And saw that the light was good; And He divided the light from the darkness;* (5) *And He called the light Day and the darkness Night, and there was an evening and morning one day.*"

The first day we can call the *cosmic period*. This period embraces the cosmogony in general or the creation of the elements of matter. It comprises the long space of time indicated in the first five verses of Genesis, and corresponds both to the time which preceded the first Mosaic day as well as to the first day itself; science knows nothing of this period except by induction.

Certain savants have made all kinds of objections against the creation of light on the first day, in the name of science. "How can we understand that the light did exist before the sun," they say. To this Phaff replies: "When we seek in the works of the physicists the answer to this objection, What is light? then either do we not find it therein or we meet therein the following avowal: We do not know what light is; we can only study its properties, and these make us consider it as very probable that it is a kind of an infinitely subtle fluid, spread in the space like ether, and put into movement by bodies what we call luminous. They are the undulatory movements of this ether which produce in us the sensation of light. How does all this take place? We do not know. The true nature, the essence of the light, is totally unknown to us.

"When we consider in what circumstances the terrestrial bodies develop the light, we discover that it is generally in the following manner: 1. A great elevation of temperature renders luminous the bodies which are not this; the incandescent metals; the incombustible objects between the poles of an electric battery emit a lively light, without that we can notice any other change in their properties. 2. The intense and rapid chemical combination of two bodies in the combustion, for instance, is equally accompanied of a disengagement of light. 3. The disengagement of electricity produces also a blending light, like the flashes of lightning prove. Such are the best known and more ordinary phenomena which associate themselves to the manifestation of light upon earth, but in no case can we tell what the essence of light is. All we know are the facts which pass thus, without being in the state to explain why.

"As to the different celestial bodies which appear to us luminous by themselves, in studying them by the means of the spectroscope, we see that we must consider them as incandescent gases or as bodies in fusion. When we observe now that the nebula and the comets disengage themselves from the light, we must conclude from this that the gaseous masses, even in the state of the greatest rarefaction, can already be luminous. In what epoch in the formation of the universe the emission of light began, the natural sciences cannot tell, but they can affirm that the light could have manifested itself long before the separation of matter and the formation of the particular bodies. Consequently, there cannot be question of a contradiction between the accounts of Genesis and those of natural sciences, relatively to the origin of light."[1] In other words, the first part of the Mosaic account is unassailable from a scientific point of view.

The third verse says, that it became light only in consequence of an act of the divine will, that is, one quality of chaos — darkness, was removed. Darkness, however, was not quite removed, but it is no longer absolute; having lost its sole supremacy, it is kept within certain limits, and its relation to light is fixed. God divided the light from the darkness. This relation is that of a regular change; and this alteration between light and darkness is called day and night, so that when Moses says God called the light day, and the darkness night, he means that the alteration between light and darkness, called day and night, rests upon a divine ordinance. This alteration began at once; God creates light, and so it is day. After a time, the length of which is not mentioned, darkness sets in again, and it is night; this in turn gives place to light, the second appearance of which is the beginning of the second day. "And the evening and the morning were the first day."

However, we have shown in another place that the word *yôm* — "day," must be taken in a figurative sense. Certainly, it does not designate before the fourth day, the ordinary succession of day and night, because the sun did not yet shine in the horizon, therefore, it is reasonable to accept it in a metaphorical sense, and the same will apply to the first part of the account. Although the word day has a literal meaning in our language, and does not necessarily express an indefinite period, never-

---

[1] Phaff, "Schophungsgeschichte," pp. 745-746.

theless we employ it often in an analogous manner. Modern languages, though giving the word day its ordinary sense, are still very rich in expressions denoting long time, such as duration, epoch, age and period, but in Hebrew it is different, there is only the word *yôm* — " day " to indicate an indefinite duration, the same as we understand by the word epoch or period. Hence, the Hebrew word *yôm* may signify, and does signify in a geat number of Scriptural passages, an indefinite period.

The foregoing reasons fairly establish the possibility of the sense of epoch given to *yôm*. There are other considerations to prove that Moses does not employ it in this chapter to signify a solar day of twenty-four hours, but to mean an indefinite time. He tells us that the sun, which serves now to regulate the day, did not appear before the fourth *yôm;* consequently, the first three *yômûn* were not solar days, and analogy authorizes us to understand the following three days in the same sense as the three preceding ones.

The cosmogonic traditions of other nations consider the days of creation long periods. According to Hindoo tradition, Brahma remained 360 days in the cosmic egg, of which he formed the heaven and the earth. Each of these days were 12,000,000 years.[1] In the Persian tradition, the creation was divided into six stages, which form six equal epochs, in an order similar to that of Genesis. Each of these epochs was 1,000 years. We find in the old Etruscan tradition, the Supreme God had employed 12,000 years at the production of His works; 1,000 at the organization of heaven and earth; 5,000

---

[1] Cf. W. Jones, "Institutes of Hindoo Law," 1794, pp. 9-10.

years at the engendering of animated and inanimated beings, and 1,000 years at the formation and duration of man.[1] The Phenician cosmogony appears to have admitted a like interval of time between the different works of creation. This appears after a passage of Philo of Byblos, abbreviator of Sanchoniaton; the chaos and the surrounding air were at first extended to the infinite, and had found limits only after a long series of centuries. The Chaldean cosmogony referred to in a previous chapter, probably admits also that the days of creation were long periods.

2. OBJECTION.

To establish that the days of creation are ordinary days of twenty-four hours each, they explain the origin of the week, and that the rest of God on the seventh day is the reason for the institution of the Sabbath. Ex. xx. 10-11.

Although the creation of the world explains the origin of the week, we must not conclude from this, that the word *yôm* must be taken in the literal, and not in the figurative sense. On this point, Father Palmieri, very sensibly remarks: "There is good reason why those seven spaces of time or epochs were called days, rather than by any other name, namely: the series of those epochs will exist as a type of the week, which is a kind of a measure of our time; the seventh future day was the type of that day, when one must rest and praise God." Therefore, the work of creation was divided into six days, followed by rest on the seventh day, in order to impress more profoundly on the mind

---
[1] Suidas, Lexicon.

of the primitive people, the obligation of sanctifying the Sabbath. Hence, the natural employment of the words day, evening and morning, as being the most proper to represent the division of the great Sabbatic week.

3. THE MEANING OF THE WORDS EVENING AND MORNING.

Having examined the meaning of the word *yôm* or "day," we shall now inquire into that of *éreb* and *bogêr* — evening and morning. Moses has metaphorically used the word day to designate each of the revolutions of the world and the creative acts, and continued the metaphor by calling the total space of time which elapsed between one revolution and another, evening and morning. He placed the evening before the morning according to the usages of the Hebrews, who reckoned journeys, etc., from evening, with us from midnight, a custom of which we have yet traces in the Offices of the Church. As to proof that the Hebrews sometimes employed the words evening and morning figuratively we have only to read Daniel viii, 26-14: "The vision of the evening and the morning. . . . Unto evening and morning, two thousand three hundred days. . . ."

A fact worthy of remark, and which seems to indicate that the words evening and morning are only figurative terms, is the creation, properly speaking, that is, the production from the bosom of nothing of the elements of matter, which had not been preceded by a cosmic revolution, is related without any other designation of time but "In the beginning." It is only after the first organization of the elements, that there is question of evening and morning.

4. OBJECTION.

The chief objection, and a very weak one too, against the foregoing explanations is, that it is new and in opposition to tradition. But it is easy to answer that there is no unanimous and constant tradition as to the manner we have to understand the cosmogony of Genesis. Since Moses did not speak scientific language with precision and rigor, his account is susceptible of many interpretations, a fact borne out in every epoch, as it was diversely explained by the Fathers and theologians. Doubtless, none among the ancients understood the word day exactly in the sense of epoch or indefinite time, because in their days they lacked the geological knowledge which could have enlightened them on this point, and helped to discover its true meaning. But a great number among them, particularly the whole exegetic school of Alexandria, with St. Augustine, beheld only figurative expressions in the words day, evening and morning. In this respect we come to the same conclusion, and attach to these words only the signification required by demonstrated scientific discoveries, as surely as the Fathers would have done had they lived in our times, because in their days they have had recourse to science to explain the Mosaic creation.

5. SECOND DAY'S WORK.

Gen. i, 6-8. (6) "*And God said: Let there be a firmament made amidst the waters; and let it divide the waters from the waters;* (7) *And God made the firmament, and divided the waters that were under the firmament from those that were above the firmament, and it was so;* (8) *And God called the firmament heaven, and the evening and morning were the second day.*"

The terrestrial nebula which remained gaseous during the length of the first day, continued to condense itself during the second day, and soon passed into the liquid state. Then a crust formed itself on the surface of this mass, and the waters, that maintained till then a vaporous state through natural heat, became partly condensed and gave rise to the seas. This is the separation of the waters of which mention is made in the sixth verse. The atmosphere meanwhile remained charged with thick clouds, which up to the fourth day hindered the light of the sun and other bodies from being seen.

The separation of the upper waters from the lower waters, or in other words, the atmospheric vapor from the terrestrial waters, has been considered as the formation of the firmament, but this term, quite scientific, is not found in the original text; hence, it is wrong to reproach the sacred writer for making use of inaccurate terms, and putting forth false ideas concerning matter of cosmography. Nothing obliges us to believe that Moses had a knowledge of the terms such as we possess to-day, but at the same time we must acknowledge that the expressions which he had used are not at all contradictory to actual science. What he relates as the work of the second day, is the formation of the atmosphere, and this did not really exist while it contained in a vaporous state the totality of the earthly waters.

Some commentators wished to behold in the waters, of which there is question, at the entering of the second day, the gaseous matter of the primitive nebula, and the separation of the upper waters from the lower, the breaking of this nebula into solar and terrestrial nebula. But this comment is too distorted and far fetched from the literal meaning of the words as intended by Moses. The sacred writer always spoke the ordinary terms of the language so as to be clearly understood by the people; scientific expressions at that epoch were unknown to all, as they are of modern origin, and " coined " from time to time to meet the exigencies of modern progress in science. However, in making the second day accord with a more advanced phase of our globe's history, we have still the advantage of preserving to the word waters its literal meaning. This signification is much more probable, as the precipitation of a part of the atmospheric waters must have naturally preceded very closely the third day, characterized by the development of vegetation. Plants could not live without water to moisten their roots, nor without a certain light to maintain the chlorophyl or green of their leaves.

Besides this, if the foregoing interpretation were established, there would be a serious break in the Bible. The time, though undoubtedly very long, which elapsed between the first formation of the earthly crust and the appearance of life upon its surface, would not be represented in Genesis, whilst according to our explanation it corresponds with the second day.

The period of the formation of the universe is called by geologists the Primary or Azoic Age, because it offers no trace of life. It was during this period that the amorphous, crystalline and metaphorical rocks, gneiss and the primitive granites, first rudiments of the continents, showed themselves, yet quite bare in several places in Europe and America. The thickness of the grounds of this epoch, which can be recognized by the absence of all traces of animal and vegetable life, is, according to Zittel, about 45,000 feet. This period is also called *Geogenic*, to distinguish it from the first day, which is called the *cosmic* period.

6. THIRD DAY'S WORK.

Gen. I, 9-13. From hypotheses we pass to the domain of facts, and find accord with Holy Scriptures no less striking. (9) "God also said: Let the waters that are under the heaven be gathered together into one place; and let the dry land appear, and it was so done. (10) And God called the dry land Earth; and the gathering together of the waters, he called seas, and God saw that it was good. (11) And he said: Let the earth bring forth the green herb, and such as may seed, and the fruit tree yielding fruit after its kind, which may have seed in itself upon the earth, and it was so done. (12) And the earth brought forth the green herb, and such as yielded seed according to its kind and the tree that beareth fruit, having seed each one according to its kind, and God saw that it was good. (13) And the evening and the morning were the third day."

The third and fourth days correspond to what geologists call the Paleozoic or Transition Age, thus named, because we find in it the most ancient traces of life, debris of submarine flora and fauna, cryptogamiæ, algæ, crustacea, mollusks, tribolites, echinites and corals.

At the beginning of this age, the solid crust was recovered by precipitated waters. The first islands emerged in consequence of contraction of the terrestrial envelope. The atmosphere, coarsely purified, permitted only a diffuse light to reach the earth, but this light, though feeble, was sufficient for the first development of the terrestrial vegetation. No other age has left such traces of luxuriant vegetation. It was then that the carboniferous and coal flora arose, not in multiplicity of kinds or brightness of colors, for it was rank and coarse, but its grandeur consisted in colossal dimensions. The coral flora contained about 800 species, while the actual flora is composed of 80,000 to 100,000 species of plants. The former was far more luxuriant than the vegetation of our tropics, and most of the extinct species surpass their like of to-day.[1] Shave grasses, which may be seen in our marshes, attained the marvelous thickness of a man's body, and reached from sixty to seventy feet in height. Mosses and ferns too attained such size over that of corresponding species now known, that comparison would be out of question. But no flower with brilliant colors, no fruit tree with blossoms, relieved the gigantic growth of vegetation, for the coal flora bore no other ornament than its green color.

"Another striking character of this flora," says Zittel,[2] "was the rapidity of its growth. Our ferns were annual plants, and the stem of the calamites (species of reeds which have with them so much affinity) must have attained, probably in a few months, a thickness from one to thirty feet in diameter. Such a vegetation is possible only in a damp and tropical climate. Those competent to judge estimate that the temperature was at that time seventy-five centigrade degrees[3] (on the Spitzburg, where one finds the coal)."

---

[1] With regard to the creation of vegetation, we must observe that Moses refers the creation of all the species to the same geological day; but he seems, as we shall show further on, to have expressed himself only in the way of anticipation, in order that he would not be obliged to re-enumerate or return to the same subject, because science shows that the most elevated types of the vegetable kingdom appeared only later on.

[2] Zittel, "Aus der Urzeit," p. 253.

[3] The centigrade thermometer introduced by Celsius, and universally used by physicists, divides the interval between the freezing and boiling points of water into 100°, the zero of the centigrade thermometer being placed at the freezing point; 5° centigrade are

To-day we can hardly form any idea of the development of this vegetation without variety, and without inhabitants. What gives the greatest charm to our forests is the song of birds, hum of insects, and the movement and voice of mammifers, but all these were wanting. Its vegetation in some respects resembled that of New Zealand, where yet dominates the primitive flora; the tree-like ferns and the majestic araucaræ (species of large evergreen trees with verticillate spreading branches, covered with stiff, narrow, pointed leaves, and bearing large cones, each scale having a single large seed). "No bird balanced itself yet in the branches of the trees," says Hochstetter, "no mammifers animated the depth of the forests. All was desert and silent. Hardly a few isolated scarabæi and scorpions were erring in the moss."[1]

During the coal period there was not yet, as Moses tells us, any mammifers nor any birds. There were already, but in limited number, some low amphibia, fishes, and a few low animals in the marshes and shallow waters, where they were covered by thick vegetation.

The flora of the carboniferous grounds displayed itself during long centuries.[2] We can imagine during

---

equal to 9° Fahrenheit, and the point marked 10° on the centigrade scale corresponds to the point marked 50° on the Fahrenheit scale.

[1] F. von Hochstetter, "Geological Tables of the Primitive World," p. 16.

[2] It is in place to remark that a certain number of geologists have attributed to the coal period a very exaggerated length of time. Grand Eury has done justice to these exaggerated statements by showing that the carboniferous layers were made with vegetable and floated bark, and not with vegetables that grew on the place. Hence the necessary time for the formation of these layers is infinitely less than one supposed, when it is remembered that there has not yet been any displacement in the plants transformed into coal, and that they had grown successively on the spots themselves. Annales des Mines, Paris, 1882.

this long period a series of warm and damp days. Let us present to ourselves a greenhouse intensely heated, its glass covering and sides blackened in a manner so as to partly intercept the solar rays, and its chief light that of an electric flame burning inside. What would be the result of vegetation under such conditions? Colossal plants without lively colors — giants with greenish heads; and such was the coal vegetation.

The character of the coal vegetation furnishes an answer to one of the objections brought against the Mosaic account, and really confirms the latter. How could the plants develop themselves without the action of the solar rays? they ask. To this Pfaff replies with fairness and conciseness: "It is not that the plants stand in need of the sun, but only of the light and heat. Now both light and heat existed unquestionably before the sun; this is a certain fact in natural history."

Moreover, recent experiments have directly and completely solved the difficulty. It has been proved that electric light possesses all the necessary qualities for the development of the green parts of the plant. Mr. Faminzin, in all his experiments with the algæ, always made use of a very strong light from a coal oil lamp, to obtain the development of these vegetables.

The coal flora being characterized by the absence of bright colors, what must we conclude from this, but that the sun did not yet act upon our globe. It is an established fact, that the plants which have formed the coal beds, belong to species which need shade and humidity, and the same can be said of the class of living creatures which appeared about that time.

Following these, some batrachians began to appear; also the *archegosaurus, dendrerpeton, lepterpeton,* pro-

triton, petrolei, similar to our actual salamander. We also find traces of the *labyrinthodon*, a breathing vertebrate, and seventy-four species of fishes. "But the amphibia at that time," says Zittel, "were small, and their form could hardly be noticed; they were, however, the most elevated beings of the paleolithic creation." Moreover, they are rare, specially when we consider the great spreading of life which followed. Hence, Moses could not enumerate the number of lower species, and, therefore, passed them over in silence. He mentions only the class of beings which characterized each epoch.

7. FOURTH DAY'S WORK.

Gen. i, 14-19. (14) "*And God said: Let there be light made in the firmament of heaven, to divide the day and the night, and let them be for signs, and for seasons, and for days and years;* (15) *To shine in the firmament of heaven and to give light upon the earth, and was so done.* (16) *And God made two great lights, a greater light to rule the day, and a lesser light to rule the night, and the stars.* (17) *And he set them in the firmament of heaven to shine upon the earth;* (18) *And to rule the day and the night, and to divide the light and the darkness, and God saw it was good.* (19) *And the evening and the morning were the fourth day.*"

The work of the fourth day escapes the control of geology, because there is question not of the earth but of the celestial bodies. There is, however, every reason to belive that it coincides with the end of what is called the Primary or Transition Age, that is, with the formation of the Permian ground. Indeed, as we shall show further on, the lower or carboniferous stage represents the third day, and the Secondary Epoch, doubtless represents the fifth day; hence, we have to place in this interval the apparition of the stars.

We say apparition and not creation, because Holy Scripture does not say that the astres were created on the fourth day. They were in their own proper spheres, revolving silently and unobserved for a long time, but their light was hidden by thick clouds, and only became visible after the clouds had been rent asunder for the first time.

Undoubtedly, we could believe, without placing ourselves against the cosmogonic theory as generally accepted, that the sun commenced at this epoch to emit both heat and light, but then we might ask ourselves, from whence the source of heat which caused the rapid growth of vegetation of the preceding epoch? It could not have emanated from the moon, for that orb is much smaller than the earth, and must have been covered with a crust ere this; neither is it probable that the earth furnished its own internal heat, though its crust, yet so thin, and the poor conductibility of the rocks, which constituted the same, had, during that time, hindered the internal fires from exercising such a sensible action upon its surface. The simple fact that the sun, moon, and the stars date from the same day, proves there is question only of their apparition, for it would be contrary to science to say that all these astres were created or had become luminous at the same epoch.

The hypothesis of a thick cloud until the fourth day, that is, until the beginning of the Secondary Epoch, completely concealing the astres from view, is entirely conformable to science. In the first place, it is natural to suppose that the atmosphere was not thoroughly purified at the beginning; the elevated temperature that reigned upon the surface of the globe, and attested by the living beings and plants of this primitive epoch, must have maintained in a vaporous state, many bodies, either liquid or solid to-day. The carbon actually stored up for the future needs of utility and industry in our coal mines, was undoubtedly, at that time, scattered in the atmosphere in the form of carbonic acid, which composition was largely absorbed by the luxuriant plants of the coal period, and helped greatly to clear the sky.

Moreover, as already mentioned, if there is one fact demonstrated in vegetable biology, it is, that the inferior plants, analogous to those which produced the coal, attained nowhere such luxuriant development than in this warm, damp and murky atmosphere. The animals of this epoch attest the absence of the direct action of the sun. The reticulated eyes of the tribolites prove at once the existence and poverty of the light. M. Heer has established that most of the insects, like the blattidæ and termites of the coal epoch, were "nocturnals."

Hence, everything concurs to establish that the thick clouds hindered the direct action of the solar rays to make themselves felt on the surface of the earth, until the coal vegetation helped to purify the atmosphere of carbonic acid. Like the Bible, science teaches us that the appearance of the sun and the astres had to follow, and not precede, the extraordinary development of vegetation, which inaugurated the geological times. Here again, one cannot imagine a more striking accord, and this accord can hardly be the effect of chance. It was impossible for Moses to make such a true record without revelation, a fact formerly considered improbable, but which so clearly goes forth from the scientific accounts recently established, that it can no longer be doubted by the rational savant.

8. FIFTH DAY'S WORK.

Gen. i. 20-23. (20) *"God also said: Let the waters bring forth the creeping creatures having life, and the fowl that may fly over the earth under the firmament of heaven.* (21) *And God created the great whales, and every living and moving creature which the waters brought forth according to their kinds, and every winged fowl according to its kind, and God saw that it was good;* (22) *And he blessed them, saying: Increase and multiply and fill the waters of the sea; and let the birds be multiplied upon the earth.* (23) *And the evening and morning were the fifth day.*

The fifth day coincides with the Secondary or Mesozoic Epoch of geologists. By describing it under the preceding features, it really seems that Moses had a view of all animated nature, and of all the landscapes of this epoch.

That which characterized the fifth day, were, he tells us, the marine monsters, the aquatic reptiles and the winged creatures. Now, when we cast a glance at one of the tableaux in which geologists have tried to reconstitute some scenes of the secondary times, we are amazed at the sight of these marine monsters, those enormous aquatic reptiles which give to the fauna of this epoch a special physiognomy. Among the aquatic or amphibious animals we point to the Ichthyosaurus and Plesiosaurus, two gigantic saurians. The former was a fish-like reptile, thirty feet long, having somewhat the shape of a cetacean mammal, with an enormous head, whose jaws were garnished with one hundred and eighty teeth, devouring turtles, mollusks, and even those of similar kinds. Its neck was short, a tapering body, with four paddle-like flippers, and probably a fin-like expansion of the caudal region. The latter was a lizard whose length was more than thirty-six feet, had a serpent-like head with a jaw six feet long, its swan-like neck was from fifteen to eighteen feet long, and had from twenty to forty cervical vertebræ, whilst the giraffe has only seven. Both the fore and hind limbs constituted flippers or paddles, like those of the cetacean mammals, having numerous phalanges inclosed in a common integument like a fin. Others, like the Teleosaurus, something similar to our actual crocodiles, but which surpassed them in dimensions; the Mosasaurus, called also, animal of Mæstricht, an immense lizard, which also had aquatic habits; finally the Megalosaurus and the Iguanodon, othr lizards of dreadful aspect, which attained colossal proportions. The Megalosaurus, whose gigantic body measured about sixty feet in length. " Whose teeth," says Mr. Figuier, " seemed to be at once a knife, sword and saw." The epoch to which Moses refers the creation of the reptiles, is so characterized by this class of living creatures, that some geologists have called it, " the era of reptiles."

As to the flying creatures, we can hardly imagine anything more remarkable than the Pterodactylus, and its relative the Ramphorhynchus. Both were a kind of flying dragon or lizard, provided with a lengthened muzzle in the form of a bill, with teeth similar to those of the crocodile, sharp claws like those of the tiger, and wings like those of the bat. The imprints of real gigantic birds are not wanting in the secondary grounds. They complete the series of succession of dominant types as recorded by Moses, and authorize us to identify the Secondary Epoch with the fifth day's creation.

The first appearance of birds corresponds to the epoch of the great saurians, conformably to what Moses tells us. The Mesozoic Age comprises three stages of grounds: the Triassic, Jurassic and Cretaceous. The Jurassic and Cretaceous grounds presents imprints of large, long-legged birds of the genus ostrich. But until now, which confirms the account of Genesis, they have not met in these grounds any mammifers, except a very small number of insectivorous rodents, and later on in the chalk deposits, a kind of oppossum didelphis. Mammifers appeared only in a posterior epoch; it was towards this end of the Tertiary Age that their reign had actually begun; they are the work of the sixth day.

9. OBJECTION.

Some translators do not understand the work of the fifth day as indicated by the foregoing explanation. The Vulgate, for instance, translates the passage: " Let the waters bring forth the creeping creatures, and the fowl that may fly over the earth." They have concluded from these terms, that there is here a question of fishes and birds, properly speaking. Now, the original text has not quite this sense. If Moses had wished to speak of fishes, he could have done so in the clearest manner, for the Hebrew has a word which conveys a precise meaning. In making use of the word *cherets*, which in a general sense signifies reptile, and especially when the word is accompanied with the qualifying clause, " having respiration of life," it seems that the sacred writer wished to include the fishes, which do not creep, and which, deprived of lungs do not breathe, properly speaking. It is also saying too much with regard to the birds. The proper meaning conveys the idea, "to be flying," which also applies with equal force to these strange creatures with wings, like the pterodactylus, which animated the terrestrial landscape of the Secondary Epoch.

When one wishes to make the Bible say that the waters brought forth the aquatic animals, it is from all points of view an error, for the Hebrew word *cherets* which they translate in this manner, has not this meaning, for it signifies "creeping," and can also be translated in the present case "to abound."

Some commentators, preoccupied wrongfully with geological discoveries, have believed that here there was not a question of aquatic animals but of reptiles, properly speaking. Undoubtedly the Hebrew word *cherets* has two meanings, but the context shows clearly that there is question of animals that live in the water. Indeed, we read immediately after:

"And God created the great whales (*cetos magnos-belluas marinas*, according to Gesenius), and every living and moving creature which the waters brought forth." Further on (i, 26-28) "God said: Let us make man, . . . and let him have dominion over the fishes of the sea and the fowls of the air, and all living creatures that move upon the earth. And God created man; male and female he created them, and he said to them, . . . rule over the fishes of the sea and the fowls of the air, and all living creatures that move upon the earth."

In these passages, the animals are evidently mentioned in the order in which they were created. Now the fishes and the other aquatic animals precede the birds, which, according to the general opinion, belong to the fifth day. Hence, these animals were also created on the fifth day; the creation of the exclusively terrestrial reptiles was put off till the sixth day.

Geology confirms in the most expressive manner this order of apparition. Indeed it is wrong to consider the Secondary Epoch as being par excellence the epoch of reptiles. The truth of the question is, that it was the era of aquatic animals, no matter to which class they belong. We believe they did not meet in the whole secondary grounds a snake, the only animal universally and at all times looked upon as a reptile. The chelonians (turtles), the saurians (lizards), and the batrachians (frogs), abound it is true, in these grounds, but we know that these three orders are quite arbitrarily classed as reptiles, and have very little resemblance to ophidians or serpents, the typical animals of the class. The serpents, that is, those animals which are completely deprived of members, are at the bottom, the very ones agreed upon, and about which the learned and unlearned have always agreed to call reptiles. Moses spoke the language of the people, and was not bound to adopt the more or less systematic classification of modern savants. We may add more, for it is our belief that all the chelonians, saurians and batrachians discovered in the secondary grounds, are more or less aquatic species.

There cannot be any difficulty as to the subject of batrachians, for they are almost all amphibious, and all breathe through the gills during the first stage of their development. Hence, they are not terrestrial animals, strictly speaking. Besides, they are quite rare in the secondary grounds. We can add that the majority of naturalists make a special class of them, which thus places them outside of that of reptiles.

As to the chelonians or turtles, we can say that they confirm the exactitude of the Biblical account in the most remarkable manner. The marine, fluviatile and paludal turtles abound in the secondary grounds, but they have not discovered one that is surely and exclusively terrestrial.

The saurians found in the same grounds are equally aquatic. One finds no difficulty in this respect regarding two species, the megalosaurus and iguanodon, a kind of gigantic lizard, which characterize the Wealden formation.[1] These two kinds are between lizards and crocodiles, and difficult to find out their chief regimen. If they were not exclusively acquatic, it is believed that they always frequented the water. Hence they belonged to the fifth day's creation, and their presence in the secondary layers must not surprise us any longer.

However, let us suppose they would succeed in discovering some reptile exclusively terrestrial outside the Tertiary grounds wherein they are abundant, what then? Nothing would result from this against the

10. SIXTH DAY'S WORK.

Gen. i, 24-27. (24) " And God said: Let the earth bring forth the living creature in its kind, cattle and creeping things, and beasts of the earth, according to their kind, and it was so done. (25) And God made the beasts of the earth according to their kinds, and cattle and everything that creepeth on the earth after its kind, and God saw that it was good. (26) And he said: Let us make men to our image and likeness, and let him have dominion over the fishes of the sea and the fowls of the air, and the beasts, and the whole earth and every creeping thing that moveth upon the earth. (27) And God created man to his own image, to the image of God he created him, male and female, he created him. . . . "

---

[1] In geology the name of a formation extensively developed in the Weald of England, and interesting from its position and organic remains.

exactitude of the Mosaic account. The Secondary would be always that of the aquatic animals, and the following epoch that of terrestrial animals.

Moses tells us that on the sixth day God created the mammifers, at first the animals, and man afterwards. This last creation corresponds to the Cænozoic or Tertiary Age, and also to the Quaternary Age.

Geologists divide the Tertiary grounds into three stages — Eocene or Lower Tertiary (plastic clays, rough limestone, gypsum), Miocene or Middle Tertiary (pebbly and flinty stone, travertin,[1] molasse,[2] faluns),[3] and Pliocene or Upper Tertiary (crags,[4] Roman and sub-Alpine hills). The Tertiary ground is especially characterized by nummulites; the Quaternary is charac-

---

[1] The calcareous deposit from springs which occurs in many localities in Italy and extensively quarried for the use of building; it is a soft, porous, straw-colored rock, easily wrought when freshly quarried, which afterwards hardens and seems durable under the climate of Italy. The interior walls of the Colosseum and St. Peter's are built of this material.

[2] A name given in Switzerland to an important geological formation belonging in part to the Miocene, and in part to a position lying between the Eocene and Miocene. The formation is in places over 6,000 feet thick, and chiefly of lacustrine origin. The fossil vegetation of the molasse is of great interest, being sub-tropical in character, containing palms of an American type, and also the coniferous genus sequoia, now limited to California. It is the upper member of the molasse which contains these plant remains, and this part of the series is made up of red sandstones, marls and conglomerate (*nagelfluh*). The lower division of the molasse is a sandstone containing marine and brakish water shells.

[3] Strata of Miocene or Tertiary Age occurring in Touraine, France.

[4] Certain strata of Pliocene Age found in the southeastern countries of England. They consist of sandy and shelly deposits similar in character to those now forming in the North Sea, and contains the white, red or Suffolk and Norwich, the latter containing many bones of the elephant, mastodon, hippopotamus, rhinoceros and other large mammals.

terized by crags and erratic blocks, the gray and red diluvian; the Bonecaves and osseous breccias.[1]

They occur in widely extended but isolated patches, rarely more than fifty feet thick, and have long been used for fertilizing. The rock consists of coarse breccia of shells and shell fragments mixed with sand, and in places passing into limestone. It also contains numerous bones of mammals, of species indicating a warmer climate than that of the region at the present time.

The beginning of the Tertiary Age manifests itself by the apparition of mammifers, great and small quadrupeds. In the upper part of the Eocene, in the gypsum of Paris, we meet the remains of vast herds, composed of diverse species of the paleotherium, herbivorous animals, a kind of tapir, varying from the dimensions of a hare to the thickness of that of a horse; from the paleotherium, a kind of hippopotamus, with a horse-like form, short legs, and its dimensions varied from those of a boar to those of an ass; the xiphodon, chamois, with long and slim legs, and a gracefully lengthened neck; bats, marsupials, reptiles, and a multitude of fishes have left their fossil debris in the gypsum and marls of the Upper Eocenè.

In the molasse layers and faluns, which are the two chief divisions of the Miocene ground, and which form a great part of the actual soil, are found traces of the first gigantic mammifers, extinct to-day. The dinotherium or "terrible animal," the largest of all the

---

[1] Bone caves and osseous breccias are fissures in the old rocks, which are open from above, and have been filled up with fragments of bones, teeth of large and small mammals, besides shells, the remains of plants and wood, pieces of limestone and other rubbish, all of which has been cemented into a solid mass by calcareous cement or clay.

terrestrial animals known, was a species of phoca or elephant, armed with two hooks of extremely hard ivory, which served to dig up the soil for roots and bulbs, which formed its chief nourishment. It measured about nineteen feet in length. The megatherium, a kind of living mountain, and the mylodon, with a snout like a hog, and immense claws for tearing up the earth. The huge mastodon, larger than the actual elephant, with four defenders, of unequal length, bent forward so as to reach food readily, roamed the marshy lands, or rather lowlands. The dinornis, the dodo and the epiornis, gigantic birds of Australia and Madagascar, measured over nine feet in height.

Later in the period which forms the transition of the Tertiary to the Quaternary Epoch, the mammifers approached more to the species of our days. In 1806, a specimen of the mammoth was found at the mouth of one of the rivers of Siberia, perfectly preserved in a block of ice in which it had perished. Its flesh and hair were intact, its intestines contained the leaves of the larch-tree of Siberia from which it received nourishment, and dogs ate of its flesh. It was somewhat like an elephant, but with wooly hair, long bent and sharp teeth, reaching out of its mouth, ears protected by long tufts of hair, and a large black mane. Some naturalists believe the mammoth still lives in certain unexplored boreal regions. The bos primigenius, with a massive head, then filled the prairies; the cervus megaceros, a stag with large horns which measured over nine feet in length, and which can be seen in the leading museums of Europe; the ursus spelæus (cave bear). etc., animated the plains and forests in early days.

Finally, man appears when the great mammoth had

disappeared, and buried in slime or entombed in ice. The majority of geologists locate human fossils only in the Quaternary ground. It is only there where we find certain traces of his presence. Conformably to Genesis, man appeared the last on the stage of creation. This is the last confirmation which geology brings forward in favor of the Biblical account.

As to the subject of the sixth day's work, we may add to what has been said before in regard to some interpreters, who have attributed to the fifth day, the creation of reptiles, correctly speaking. The proof that there was question only of the aquatic animals is shown by the word *remesh*, employed on the sixth day, unquestionably designates terrestrial reptiles.

Some commentators have applied this word to all the small terrestrial animals, even mammals, such as the hare and marten. Perhaps they are right, but it is impossible to furnish proof of this. The sacred writer, in the concise and rapid enumeration of the sixth day's work, may have overlooked or neglected to mention these small animals, just as he neglected speaking of the fishes.

It is useless to insist on the precision of the distinction regarding the two acts which gave rise successively to animals and to man. It is proof that our species is not naturally derived from anterior species, as certain transformists endeavor to make us believe. It is expressly said that man was created (*bárá*), a significant word which thus far has been only employed in two important circumstances, one of which we find in the first verse with regard to the creation of matter, and in the other, the twenty-first verse, to announce the advent of the first animal. Hence when the Bible does not directly contradict the theory of Evolution, limited to plants and animals, it does not permit to apply the same to man.

11. SEVENTH DAY.

It is said in the beginning of the second chapter of Genesis, that God rested on the seventh day, that is, He ceased to create immediately after the apparition of man. Here too, science confirms the inspired text in the most expressive manner. In proving that man had lived since the Quaternary Epoch or Post Pliocene it has equally proved that all the animals which surround us, have existed since this epoch. Several species have disappeared since the creation of man, but no new species have appeared.

CONCLUSION.

The Mosaic cosmogony and the natural sciences are in accord, particularly in their main features. Thus, science — true science — must ever be in accord with the Mosaic cosmogony, because God the Creator could not permit a real contradiction or conflict between His revelation and the creation itself. If one observes striking difference between the Mosaic account and the discoveries of science, it is certain that Holy Writ is wrongly interpreted, or that science has not demonstrated beyond possibility of doubt, the question at issue. Hence, we may safely say, there is no contradiction, no necessary conflict between the two. We have shown this in the present work, and the reader cannot help but admire this striking harmony.

" When we compare the scientific accounts with the Biblical history of the creation," says Phaff, " we see that this latter harmonizes with these accounts as much as one has the right to expect. Indeed, we discover in both science and the Bible, the same kingdoms, equally distinct in themselves, by not keeping account of the historical changes they might have undergone; the chronological following of their apparition is exactly given by Moses. The primitive chaos, the earth covered at first by the waters, emerging afterwards; the formation of the inorganic kingdom, followed by the vegetable reign, then of the animal kingdom which has for its first representatives the animals living in the water, and, after them, the terrestrial animals; finally man appearing the last of all; such is really the succession of the beings, such are really the diverse periods of the history of creation, periods designated under the name of days."

What must we conclude from this? "We can observe," says Dana, our eminent American geologist, "that if the (Mosaic) document is true — and it is true, because the order of the events in the cosmogony of Scripture corresponds essentially with that which is given (by geology)— it follows that it is of divine origin. For no human intelligence has been witness of the events, and no human intelligence in the primitive age of the world, at least if it had not been endowed with a supernatural penetration, could have invented such an arrangement; it would never have placed the creation of the sun, source of the earth's light, so long after the creation of the light, on the fourth day, and what is equally singular, between the creation of the plants and the animals, although this astre may be as important for the first as for the second. Neither could anybody have reached to the depths of the philosophy which manifests itself in this plan. . . . The Biblical account is profoundly philosophical in the tableaux by which it presents the creation to us. It is at once true and divine. It is a declaration on the first page of the sacred volume, that both the creation and the Bible have the same author. Here there cannot be any real conflict between the two books of the great Author. Both are revelations which He made to man."[1]

CHAPTER VIII.

MAN FROM THE SCIENTIFIC POINT OF VIEW.

ONE denies to-day, in the name of a false science, all that Holy Scripture teaches about the first man. It is our object to answer briefly to all the difficulties they allege against the Sacred Books in treating the three following questions:

1. Was the first man an intermediary being between the animal and actual man? 2. Was he a savage? 3. In what epoch did he make his appearance?

I. The Animal Origin of Man.

For the adherents of Monism, who admit the evolutionary theory with all its consequences, and reject all idea of creation, there has not been, properly speaking, a first man. Evolution which has ended by giving to one or several animals, placed amidst favorable conditions, the traits which distinguish us, has been so insensible, that it is impossible not only to fix the date of the

---

[1] J. D. Dana, "Manual of Geology," 2 ed. pp. 767-770.

appearance of our species, but even to tell of an individual that he was its first representative. The chief adept of contemporary Darwinism, Hæckel, a professor in the University of Yena, Germany, formally tells us: "This passage has been so slow that one cannot speak at all of a first man."

Hæckel teaches, however, that the species which preceded ours, and to which we owe existence, belonged to the family of apes, the first of the order of quadrumanes. The man-ape, whom they have called more learnedly the pithecanthropus or the anthropopithecüs (of Mortillet), would have lived about the end of the Tertiary Epoch, perhaps even earlier, according to M. de Mortillet, who attributes to him the so-called worked flints of the Miocene layers of Thenay, France. It was an anthropoid, a brother of the actual anthropoids, but more similar to man by his anatomical or physiological characters; for nobody pretends to-day to make us derive from apes which belong to the contemporary fauna, so considerable is the distance that separates us from them.

The opinion of Darwin, author of the evolutionary system most in vogue, does not differ in this respect from that of his disciple Hæckel. He also makes us descend from an anthropomorphous ape. According to Darwin it was a hairy mammifer, endowed with a tail and pointed ears, which undoubtedly lived on trees and dwelt in the ancient continent.

Not all the adversaries of the creation of man make us descend from the ape. According to a great number of them this honor would be still too great to attribute to us this origin; we have to look for our ancestors among the lowest marsupials or didelphydæ. At least they claim that the laws which preside at the general development of the beings are opposed to our origin from some quadrumane. This opinion is shared by the Professors Huxley, of England, Fillippi, of Italy, and Vogt, of Geneva, although the latter seems sometimes to attribute to us for ancestors the actual ape, for he said that he " rather preferred to be a perfectioned ape than a degenerated Adam."

Hence we have to do rather with the animal origin of man than with his simian origin. However, this point matters little; for, whatever may be the different views that separate them with regard to the human genealogy, our adversaries have recourse to the same arguments when there is question to prove their general thesis — the descent of man from some inferior type. The arguments alleged that we descend from some animal species are of three kinds: 1. The general conformation of the body of man; 2. The development of the human embryo; 3. The presence in man of the rudimentary organs; 4. Intellectual qualities.

1. PHYSICAL DIFFERENCE BETWEEN MAN AND BRUTE. — UPRIGHT POSITION.

Vegetative and sensitive life is common to man and animals. For this reason man's organization is very similar to that of the animal. The organs and method of nutrition, respiration, and propagation are the same in man and the higher mammals. Neither is there any essential difference in the action of the senses. Thus, the sense of touch, the yellow speck of the retina, the iris in the apple of the eye, and the ear lobule, are shared by man with the anthropoid ape. Nevertheless, the physical difference between man and the highest animal (the anthropoid ape) is greater than the physical difference between any two closely allied animals. Man's entire build and habitus are essentially different from those of the animal. If man was not created in his present fully-developed condition, then he is a product of historical evolution in every organ and system of his complex body, and in the uniform spiritual development that has accompanied the corporal development. In several animals this or that organ or sense is more perfect than in man; but no animal can compare with man's organization as a whole. One chief difference is man's attitude and gait. "Man alone," says Aristotle, "among living beings walks with head upright. To make his upper parts light and easy to carry, nature removed the weight from the above and placed it below. Hence, his thighs and haunches and the calves of his legs are covered with flesh, and he is without a tail. The nutrition goes in the direction of these parts, in order to clothe them with flesh." Aristotle is undoubtedly right in making man's upright bearing the keystone of his entire organization. The lower extremities were lengthened, and their supports strengthened, while the upper extremities were dispensed from locomotion, and fitted up into an organ of all work. The hand, that organ of organs, as Aristotle calls it, with its thumb turned inwards, has a suppleness and daintiness of sense unrivaled by any organ of the animal kingdom. Apes have, it is true, four hands; but as all four are locomotory, they have none of that nimbleness and flexibility which are peculiar to the human hand. Anthropoid apes occasionally lay hold of stones and clubs in self defense; but this is the highest use to which they put their hands. There is also a considerable difference in the relative lengths. The arm of the ape is disproportionately longer than the human arm. Neither has any man a prehensile foot, although savages are sometimes credited with it. But the story is just as fabulous as the fiction which represents men with tails. Anthropology and ethnography have no information of man's capacity to turn his toes inwards like an ape. Man can, it is true, in exceptional circumstances, write or paint with his feet; still the foot never becomes prehensile. The relations of the several parts (e. g. toes) are very different in men and apes. The proportion of the shin bone to the foot is as 82.5 to 52.9 in man, and as 80 to 72.8 in the chimpanzee.

2. FACIAL AND CEREBRAL FORMATION.

Connected with man's upright bearing is his facial and cerebral formation. The position of the nose and jaw determines the form of the face. The more the jaw protrudes, the greater the animal tendency to sensible pleasure which, on the contrary, is in inverse ratio to the frontal and nasal projections. The high forehead too, stamps the human face as something more than material. Since the days of Camper the relation between forehead and jaw has been regulated by the facial angle, the lines of which pass over the highest part of the forehead and the middle of the orifice of the ear and meet in the upper front teeth. In normal skulls the facial angle varies from 75 deg. to 85 deg. In the Caucasian race 90 deg. is not infrequent, while in races low down in the scale, and in idiots, the average falls as low as 70 deg. These lower numbers, however, are uncertain. In any case the lowest outside limit must be set down at 64 deg. The facial angle averages 35 deg. in a full-grown chimpanzee and 30 deg. in the orang-outang. When these apes are in their youth their facial angle comes much nearer to that of man. Then it reaches 60 deg. and 64 deg., but youth cannot be taken as the standard, because the jaw is only fully developed as age advances.

3. VOLUME OF THE BRAIN.

"In proportion to his size," says Aristotle, "man has more brain than all living beings, and men have more than women." Aristotle's words still hold good. In size and richness of convolution man's brain is superior to that of all animals, apes included. The size of the brain may be determined by measuring either the upper surface or the inner space of the skull—the latter being the easier and surer method. Then an estimate is made of the weight of the contents. To obtain a sure result many measurements have to be made. According to Morton, the maximum size of the skull varies between 112.5 and 77 cubic inches; whereas the minimum size oscillates between 91 and 58. The mean is 96 to 75.3, and the average ranges from 93.5 and 80.3. If we allow the limit of 63 cubic inches assigned by Morton, man's skull has still the very considerable balance in its favor of 34.5, as compared with the largest gorilla skull. Some of the great mammals have absolutely a far larger brain than man, but in proportion to the weight of his body man scores a decided advantage. Man's brain compared with his total weight is as 2 to 47; the dolphin's is as 1 to 66; and the elephant's 1 to 500. The importance of this fact should not be overrated, since in birds the proportion is even smaller than in man, being as 1 to 14 in the greenfinch; still it is not wholly devoid of significance as regards man and apes. A full-sized gorilla or orang-outang is nearly doubly as heavy as a Bushman or as many a woman, but his brain is at least one-third lighter than the smallest human brain. Even the lowest human skulls, those of the Papuans, are far ahead of the skulls of the highest apes, even morphologically. History also bears witness to the distinctive character of the human skeleton in general, and of the human skull in particular. Modern peoples are branded with the characteristic peculiarities of their forefathers. Not a single skeleton that has been discovered differs from our own in formation. Nowhere are we on the trail of an abnormal formation or impeded development. Doubtless strange specimens existed then as now, and were as exceptional in olden times as they are now. The skull capacity is the same in all.

4. EMBRYOLOGY.

The argument drawn from the embryogenic development moves us little. It is true that man starts by an egg, like all animals. To believe Hæckel, the human embryo, in its development, would be by turn a zoöphyte, fish batrachian, reptile and mammal; but these pretended successive states are more than contestable, and, even if they were real, they would have no bearing on the origin of man.

First they are contestable. It is not sufficient, indeed, that Hæckel affirms them in order that we may be convinced thereof. We know that good faith is not the dominant quality of the German naturalist. To-day it is admitted by everybody that, in order to render more striking the resemblance of the embryos of man and the animal, he greatly altered the cuts which pretend to represent them in one of his books. The striking resemblances there depicted are, therefore, in reality the result of a fraud. In his turn, Doctor Jousset establishes " an enormous difference " between the human embryo depicted in his book and that which is represented in the " Encyclopedique Dictionnaire des Sciences Medicales."

According to the judgment of the most competent naturalists the similarities appealed to are purely illusive. That there are certain analogies between the successive stages through which the human embryo passes and the different groups of the animal series, we do not contest, and this is quite natural, because in both cases there is a progress from the simple to the complex; but from the analogy to a complete resemblance it is pretty far. " In no moment of his existence," teaches a famous anatomist, Gratiolet, " does man resemble any other species. . . . In all the epochs of the fœtal life, man is man in power, and definite characters distinguish him." " The forms of the embryo have a wonderful relation with the future forms," says the same anatomist; " they complicate themselves, it is true, but according to a specific mode; in all the epochs, the future man foretells himself. . . . A fundamental difference notably distinguishes the primitive forms of the encephalon of man in the embryogenic state from those presented by the lower animals arrived at their definitive term; it consists in the peculiar incurvations at the nervous axle of the encephalic hood of the embryo. . . . In no epoch, is the brain of the human fœtus similar to that of an ape; on the contrary, the more it becomes developed the more the difference appears." ("Cf. Anatomie compareé du Systeme Nerveux," p. 251, 248, 253.)

Although these are facts, and not merely personal impressions, one might object that Gratiolet permitted himself to be influenced by his prejudices favorable to the fixity of the species, and to the superiority of the human nature. One will not make the same reproach to Carl Vogt, one of the champions of Evolutionism and of free thought. Now, Carl Vogt protests still more energetically than Gratiolet against the pretended similarities of the human embryo and the lower animals. "It has been supposed," he says, "that the embryos pass in abridgment the same phases which the stem passed during its development through the geological epochs. It was my belief for a long time that this law was well founded, but it is absolutely false in its basis. A careful study of embryology shows us, indeed, that there exists a certain harmony among them, but that they differ in their development." Also, Agassiz says: "It has been maintained in the broadest terms that superior animals pass, during their development, through all the phases which characterize inferior classes. Thus formulated, this proposition is entirely contrary to truth. . . . In their primitive condition the eggs of all animals are alike, but as soon as the embryo begins to show characteristic traits, these reveal such peculiarities that the type of the animal can be distinguished." "On the Species," pp. 278-279.

The ovules of mammals in their primitive state resemble one another, so that they cannot be physically distinguished, and nevertheless, an ovule in the course of its development may become a horse, a dog, or a whale. Therefore, there must be in the ovule a special principle, a something which distinguishes its physical composition, although in the present state of our knowledge, and with the resources at present within our reach, this escapes the eye of the naturalist; it being impossible to ascertain these physical differences on account of the imperfection of our senses.

5. RUDIMENTARY ORGANS.

The rudimentary organs will retain us less long. One can maintain of these organs what we have said of the pretended embryogenic phases: they have neither the importance nor the signification one attributes to them. Their presence in man can be explained by the simple consideration that all the organized beings are subject to the same physiological laws.

The argument they bring forward has the defect of proving too much. The rudimentary organs are so numerous and so different in man, they approach in this respect so many animals in which they are completely developed, that, if they would suppose an identity of origin, we would have to conclude that man has anteriorly passed through all the classes of the various vertebrates. Now who will believe, for instance, that he counts birds among his ancestors because man in his embryogenic state possesses their nictating membrane? One would arrive at still more strange consequences, if one would persist in beholding in these rudiments a remainder of developed organs and utilized in an anterior state. The atrophied breasts which the males possess in the class of the mammifers are first-class rudimentary organs, and the most striking of all. Must we conclude from this that the males were formerly females? These rudimentary organs are common among the animals, and until at present it entered nobody's mind to behold in them the traces of an anterior state. Thus the whale possesses teeth which never arrive in piercing the gums. It is the same with the incisives with which the calf is endowed in its fœtal state. Must we conclude from this that the whale and the ox have passed through anterior states when they had the teeth of which they are wanting to-day? The Evolutionists themselves would hardly dare to affirm this.

When Darwin considers the rudimentary organs as useless, he tells something which is not by any means proved. Indeed, we are far from knowing perfectly the functions of all the parts of organized beings. It is, therefore, very possible that all the rudimentary organs, like the wings of the apteryx, serve an end which is unknown to us. The uniformity of plan adopted by the Creator in His works may very well explain the presence of organs without apparent use in some animals, whatever the Transformists may say. God has impressed in them in some manner the seal of their parentage. "Instead of being an argument in favor of evolution," remarks Agassiz, "does not the existence of a rudimentary eye discovered by Doctor J. Wyman in a fish (*amblyopsis spelaeus*) of the mammoth cave of Kentucky, prove rather that this animal, like all others, had been created with all its peculiar characteristics by the fiat of the Almighty, and that this rudimentary eye has been left to it as a reminiscence of the general plan of structure on which is constructed the grand type to which it belongs."

Other drawbacks to the human organism tell as little in favor of evolution or rather of "natural selection," as the advantages. The most striking is the absence of a *tail.* For this deficiency no sufficient reason can be assigned, as man is quite singular in this respect. The incipient tail in the fœtus shows at most a disposition, without giving any clue to its deterioration. Want of use is insufficient to account for it. The coiling tail could be dispensed with, if the animal had gradually exchanged its climbing propensities for walking, but many monkeys still climb and use their tails. Evolutionists, to be consistent, must hold that the coiling tail was transformed into a walking organ. Many land animals, in spite of living on land, walk on all fours, and yet have a tail which renders good service in other ways besides climbing. This change in their mode of life would have either destroyed or improved the tail, as may be seen from the ape's clumsy walk on level ground, and the waddle of the gorilla supporting himself on his bended hands.

Take again the want of a hairy coat. It is admitted that selection could not have dictated its abandonment, since the man without hair has less chance of withstanding the climate, and enduring wind and weather. If it be universally true that the organism which is simple and developed all round is better adapted for the struggle for life than the organism which is complex and has only one-sided development, then the want of a fur coat cannot be explained on the principles of selection. On such principles it would indeed be most surprising if a hairy coating were not formed, since the disposition is already there (the embryo being covered with down) and individuals have a luxuriant growth of hair in various parts. Then, too, what a bulwark it is against the subtle encroachments of climate? Sexual selection does not lift us out of the bog. If hairness were universal, how could a stray male with less hair be an attraction to a female, or *vice versa?* But, letting that pass, we would further ask, how this fashion was enabled to gain the ascendant, and to extirpate all hairy individuals in the teeth of the fact that hairness is useful in the struggle for life? We are crediting our great animal ancestors with advanced æsthetic tastes that are hardly to be found among modern savages. Nor can the beard which occurs in animals also, be explained in this way. For it would be too exacting to expect æsthetic females to renounce the beard as well as the hairy coating. Each race, as Darwin says, has a predilection for those characteristic peculiarities which have been gradual in their growth. And Wallace rightly thinks that a hairy race would have admired great hairness as much as modern bearded races admire a fine bushy beard. Thus a liking for partial hairlessness would have been as rare and as abnormal as a preference for partial baldness, or for the few straggling hairs of which women can boast. No effect could follow from an individual having a taste for such an abnormal peculiarity. But it is in the highest degree improbable that such a fashion should have become a general favorite with our semi-human forefathers and resulted in total hairlessness. Such a phenomenon is without parallel in the history of the animal kingdom. The "porcupine" man, the descendants of an Englishman of Euston Hall, Suffolk, who was covered with warts half an inch long and as thick as a string, dried out in the third generation. Extinction is the lot of all monstrosities. To build a calculation on them is to build science on the extreme edge of hazard. The abnormal succumbs to the normal.

Man is not, on the whole, so well accoutered for the battle of life as the animal. He is more sensitive to wind and weather, and a prey to many maladies. His diet is limited. When he first comes into the world, he is more helpless than any other organic being. He needs the support of his parents longer. Is this the outcome of the struggle for existence? Surely this cannot be the goal of its ambition! " Man can provide himself with food and raiment from animals and plants," says St. Thomas, " since he presupposes both." Hence, nature leaves him naked, because he can clothe himself. Nature supplies him with no food but milk, because he can procure other food for himself. Supposing the difference between man and animal to be as represented above, this is the simple explanation of man's present condition. For man has, indeed, the power to set nature at defiance and bid her do her worst. He can procure for himself the best of food and clothing; he can till the ground and make fire his servant; he can make his armor proof against all nature's shafts, and can forge for himself weapons that enable him to hold the field against all comers. But the need in itself is not enough. Man must have also the capacity to use them. It is arguing in a circle to say that the needs of living organisms are gratified for the same reason that they exist. There is a recognized limit to the need of animals. Many faculties which seem to supply a need, are really born of instinct and desire. The spider weaves its web from pleasure, not from hunger, and the bird sings from sexual excitement. Hence, we are led to suppose the existence of a spiritual element in man.

The physical differences between men and animals should not, however, be exaggerated. Nor should they be underrated in such a statement as the following: " In form, in build, and throughout his organic tendencies man is an ape." For not only is the similarity not proven, but the spiritual activity for which the organism is destined involves physical differences. It cannot have been, in the first instance, the product of education. Education can work wonders, but it cannot change the natures and peculiarities of the human species. Physiology and morphology have not yet succeeded in laying hands on the parents that gave birth to the first human being. The scouts of science have explored the whole earth, but they can find only men and animals. Their search for a being half man and half animal has been fruitless; they were never even on the track. Even the Bushmen are men, and not semi-apes. So far, as Wallace, Huxley and Virchow allow, the excavations of science have brought no fossil-ape-skull or skull of a man-ape that can have belonged to a human being. Even the oldest skulls that have been found are human. "Dolicocephalic or brachycephalic," says Quatrefages, "large or small, orthognathous or prognathus, quaternary man is always man in the full acceptance of the word. Whenever the remains have been sufficient to enable us to form an opinion, we have found the hand and the foot which characterized our species; the vertebral column has displayed the double curvature. . . . The more we study the subject, the more are we convinced that every bone of the skeleton, from the most massive to the smallest, carries with it in its form and proportions, a certificate of origin which it is impossible to mistake." The crude theory of Vogt, according to which man is descended from one of the extant kinds of anthropoid apes, must be set down as obsolete. For the human body has but few similarities with the highest representatives of this class, that is, with the Asiatic orang-outang, the gibbon, the African chimpanzee and gorilla.

The hairy pithecanthropos primigenius is accepted by Hæckel and Darwin as the common progenitor of man and gorilla. "Both male and female wore beards. Their ears were probably pointed and moveable. A tail hung from the body. Veins and nerves took a different course. A first parents, too, had prehensile feet, climbed trees, and inhabited a warm well-wooded country." At a still earlier period they must have been water-animals, for the lung is a modified swimming bladder. The traces of our primitive forefathers lie not on the earth but under the earth. Africa is the spot selected by Darwin and Huxley; Hæckel prefers southern Asia, but suggests the Indian Ocean as an alternative; Lemuria is its name. So this hypothesis, alas! has tumbled overboard into the sea. Hence, Darwinians are forced to admit that the animal forms, to which they ascribe the origin of the human race, have long since perished. Not even a bone has yet been found.

6. INTELLECTUAL QUALITIES — SPEECH.

Articulate speech and man's erect attitude are said to be the chief proof that the human organism has undergone an essential change morphologically. These two physiological functions ought to have produced great morphological changes, and to have given a spurt to the development of the powers of the soul. From speechless or pithecoid man to rational man a complete transition has been effected, owing, it is said, to the acquisition of language as the articulate expression of words and concepts. But the begging of the question is so shining and so evident that it will glimmer through a blind man's eye. Surely the upright position and language must themselves be accounted for before they are made a stepping-stone to evolution. The upright position is universal among men, and universally absent in apes. If the perfection of brain and larynx is dependent on the evolution of speech, then a properly developed larynx and brain must be the companions of speech that already exists. But how did these arise? The "gradual acquisition of the upright position" is not proved, nor has it anything whatever to do with the organs of speech. However, even if this unwarranted assumption be let pass unchallenged, it has still to be explained how vocal organs, intended originally for the production of rude inarticulate sounds, have been made capable of speech. If this change was preceded by a partial formation or transformation of parts of the brain, the puzzle has veered round to its first position. Not the faintest ray of light breaks through the mysterious darkness. Man is man only by speech; to have speech he must be already man. How comes it that only this branch of the original tree has "luckily" been able to adapt itself to this development? One would suppose now, that it would be much easier for the other branch to grow to the same height since in man who walks erect and speaks, it has before its eyes a fine model and excellent instruction. But all the efforts of selection and education have been unavailing to train man's first cousin to walk upright or to talk. He is and remains a climber, in nowise a *homo alalus* but a *simia alala*.

In speech lies the broadest and most powerful distinction between man and the brute. No brute has speech; no properly developed man is without it. Man speaks, but no animal has ever uttered a word. Speech is our Rubicon, and no animal will dare to cross it. Speech is the great distinguishing feature of man. Animals are speechless because they are thoughtless.

7. CONSCIENCE.

Besides language, and other manifestations of intellect, there are identical moral characters which are wanting in no human race. Conscience is there, with its rewards and its remorses, its hopes and its fears, the same that have inspired the white-robed army of heroes and martyrs; the heroes in thought and action, the martyrs to honor or to truth.

Here, too, we have been rudely awakened to the fact that the moral problem contained in the beautiful sentiments of conscience has been solved by that intrusive species of modern science, as with the touch of a master. An eminent observer points to his dog, in the act of refraining from eating his master's dinner, when it might. See, says the master, there is the moral sentiment, in its first stage of evolution — conscience in embryo! Such is the explanation vouchsafed as for the moral order and its origin; and it is an explanation, we must confess, which suggests pregnant reflections.

They become more fertile still upon the further statement being contributed to the question, that the dog looks up to its master as its god? A compliment, indeed! though not so disinterested as you might think, if the master meanwhile is looking back at the brute as his progenitor.

8. RELIGION.

We have no proofs of man's aboriginal belief in a God, the Darwinists tell us. "Fear of the supernatural," says Vogt, "of the unknown, the germ of religious ideas, is found developed in a high degree in our intelligent animals, the dog and the horse; men only developed these farther, and formed them into a system of faith. Lawgivers and priests invented the belief in a God." Had the belief in a Supreme Being, and the desire to know more about Him, not dwelt in man, neither lawgivers nor priests could have spoken at all about God; and if they had done so, nobody would have understood them. No nation or tribe has yet been found that had not some idea of religion and of the Supreme Being. Even the poor Andaman Islanders, who were once considered the missing link between man and the ape, have ideas about a God which are superior to those held by the Romans.

Let us pass to our second question:

II. Has the Primitive Man Been a Savage.

From the foregoing it can be seen that it is not probable that man, intellectually and morally, is a physical evolution from the brute. Ethnography has blown to atoms Rousseau's ideal child of nature. But the Darwinian substitute, namely, speechless primitive man, the brutal savage, we have to subject to a further inquiry. Little as the savage is an ideal of innocence, from his birth he is and remains a man. Every man has something of the animal in his nature; the savage has a greater quantity and a grosser kind, but he is still a human animal. Characteristic peculiarities crop up at every turn. Australians and Tasmanians, Botocudos and Pescheros in South America, Bushmen in South Africa, are all men, whichever is to have the device " Lower Race " emblazoned on its banner. So little was known of the earth in the days of Lucretius that there is some excuse for his hazarding the hypothesis that aboriginal man was a semi-animal, using neither fire nor clothing. Now, however, the earnest student cannot plead the backward state of knowledge. Darwin's blunder in relation to the people of Terra del Fuego, which first brought home to him the idea of man's animal origin, was corrected long ago. No people is destitute of certain abilities and capacities, which are the sign of a free intelligence. To this even prehistoric science bears witness. The carved bones of wild animals found in the south of France and in the cave of Thainger reveal a fairly developed æsthetic sense, and a delicacy of artistic skill for which we seek in vain among modern savages. The same thing may be observed in America. The old mound-builders were more civilized than modern Indians, who were more civilized at the Spanish Conquest than they are now. The Indians are a degenerated race. The arms and implements used by them in the Stone Age were doubtless rude and primitive; but to this day no animal has attempted to manufacture or use such weapons, rude as they were. The ideas that form the basis of social and moral life are familiar to all peoples. A certain social organization and tribal divisions obtained even among the most primitive races. The drawings above alluded to (which are modeled from nature) are suggestive and significant. So far only one small detached figure, representing a sort of *Venus impudica*, has been discovered. In museums may be seen crowds of such objects that have come down to us from the Greeks and Romans, whose advanced civilization is beyond question. Savages have the idea of Mine and Thine and of good and evil, although they both steal and work evil. A little while ago an effort was made to forge an intermediate link between man and animals out of the Mincopians of the Andaman Islands who, represented as cannibals, are wholly devoid of moral and religious ideas. It has, however, since transpired that they have a horror before human flesh, believe in a life to come, devoutly worship their ancestors, and are superior to many civilized nations in morality. The same may be said of the inhabitants of the Nicobar, who were visited by the Novara Expedition. Many wild and uncivilized peoples are no doubt sitting in darkness, but the darkness should not be artfully intensified. Their ignorance and moral depravity are pitiful and harrow up the soul, but the traces and germs of civilization must not be passed over and ignored. The responsibility of savagery, then, need not rest with man's animal origin; for savagery must be regarded in great measure as a degradation and a decadence. This will be apparent when it is shown that the different races of mankind have a common origin. History states that many nations, Egyptians, Syrians, Persians, and other Asiatic tribes have actually relapsed into barbarism from a high state of civilization. The ruins of Egypt, Mexico, and South America, and the monuments recently discovered at Yukatan, are a clear proof that the career of some nations has taken a downward course. In the seventh century the barbarians of Central Asia were highly civilized. The Redskins have retained a fairly pure notion of religion, but among other races in the same part of the globe civilization has given way to idolatry and human sacrifice. Faith and science both declare that man's condition in the beginning was purer and nobler than at present. Thus races degenerate, although progress is the general law. A backward and forward movement may be seen going on side by side. The organic connection is often wanting, but it is of no moment in the universal history. But the mere power of man is inadequate to explain this progressive tendency even in the remotest periods. Thus the difference between palæolithic and neolithic is considerable. Domestic animals have taken the place of cave animals; the nomad has become a settler, and the huntsman has turned husbandman. Shapeless arms and implements have been cast aside for polished axes that would do credit to a modern artificer. Dolmens (stone erections) and menhirs (monoliths) were erected as temples or sepulchral monuments; nets were plaited, garments woven, and houses more securely built. What is the cause of this vast difference? Such advanced culture was not within the unaided reach of the cave men, and of those whose remains have been found in the quaternary strata. In many places immigrations were frequent. Whence came the new settlers? Whence their civilization? Palæontology can give no answer to these questions. The Science of Language comes nearer the mark, but it also halts before arriving at the beginning.

III. Antiquity of Man.

Since Holy Scripture nowhere tells the age of the earth, we are not directly called upon to deal with the random calculations of palæontologists. As long as it was customary to interpret the days of creation as ordinary days, the earth and the human race were naturally supposed to be coeval; now, however, that it is fashionable to lengthen the days into periods, or take them as merely formal determinants, the partnership is dissolved. And yet palæontology has still some voice in the calculations. The swollen figures given by geologists and palæontologists are still pregnant with mischief. Moreover, it should not be forgotten that palæontological explorations brought to light the first traces of man by unearthing human fossil remains, and by giving an insight into prehistoric man's mode of life.

Human fossil remains were first discovered at Canstadt in 1701, part of a human skull being found in the clay, imbedded in mammoth remains. In 1774 the cave of Gailenreuth yielded a human jawbone and shoulder blade. In 1835, three human skeletons were discovered in the cave of Enghis on the Meuse, and many others were found in a cave of England on the opposite bank of the Meuse, with the bones of the mammoth, rhinoceros, great bear, and other such ancient animals as their companions. A skull was found at Neanderthal near Elberfeld in 1856, and the right half of a human lower jaw, with its row of teeth, in the sandpit of Moulin-Quignon, near Abbeville, in 1863. Many other discoveries followed, especially in France. In 1866 the district of Soloutre in the Maconnais Department, so bristled with discoveries that it was nicknamed the "charnel house." The position in which the skeletons discovered lay, indicated that they had been buried. All these discoveries are supposed to form a cumulative argument that man inhabited Europe at a time when the cave-bear and the great feline species represented the great carnivorous animals, and the mammoth, the rhinoceros and the pachyderms. But — accepting as a starting point the one admissible distinction of the Stone Age — these animals belong to the palæolithic period. Of course, it cannot be concluded with absolute certainty that primitive man lived on the earth with these animals, but the bone implements seem to suggest that men killed these animals for food. All the remains, it is quite clear, cannot be referred to this distant date. The age of the Canstadt skulls is still a bone of contention. Then, again, the bones, in many instance, have not the characteristics of great age. A more recent date is rendered highly probable, owing to volcanic agency, e. g., at Le Puy in the Department of Loire, and Calaveros in California, for these volcanoes were active in the fifth century of our era. Still, all this notwithstanding, we have to face the probability that man and beasts were contemporaries.

And now another difficulty looms in sight: to determine the period at which the animals of the Lower Quaternary Epoch (diluvial) lived. It is all very well to invoke the aid of a higher temperature, to appeal to the beginning of the Ice Age, and so forth; but these climatic conditions set up only a relative standard of measurement. Eminent geologists have declared with unmistakable emphasis, that man did not appear on the scene till after the Ice Age. The Ice Age and the Quaternary Epoch coincide in their beginnings, and man must certainly be referred to the second glacial epoch. It has still to be ascertained whether there have been one or more Ice Ages. Now, historical proof is forthcoming that the temperature has been on the increase in many countries since the days of Herodotus, and that the glaciers generally have receded. Hence, there is no necessity to suppose that glacial man has been in existence for an immense number of years. When the fact is grasped, that within the last hundred years several species of animals have perished in Australia, and that the buffalo and the auerochs are even now on the point of dying out, it will be more clearly understood how, in an earlier age, when no quarter was given, sets of fauna were, owing to climatic action, completely swept away.

1. NO TRACES OF TERTIARY MAN.

So far the Tertiary Epoch has been sterile in fossil bones. Of no single bone that has been found can it be predicated with certainty that it is of the same age as the Tertiary deposits from which it was taken. Other footprints of Tertiary man have proved equally illusory. The Abbe Bourgois set the ball rolling by labeling the many flints he had found in Thenay (France) as the workmanship of Tertiary man. At first he succeeded in enlisting several men of science on his side; but the matter, on investigation, became so thickly enveloped in the mists of doubt that it vanished at last in utter improbability. The repeated works of art, with indented surfaces, are much like shapeless works of nature. Again, other flints, lances, arrowheads, spears and such like found in St. Prest, probably belong to a later formation. To determine the age of objects found in mud or sand deposits is most difficult, as these may easily have been buried subsequently at a greater depth. In like manner man's handiwork in conjunction with natural causes may have shifted the deposit. Moreover no standard is at hand for gauging the time of the deposits in the several periods. Recent researches, even in the much belauded Somme Valley, have shown that the layers of sand were formed in historic times. Furthermore it was alleged that drawings, which none but the hand of man can execute, adorned the bones of some Tertiary animals. Bones, too, have been produced which had been fractured, so it was said, by the hand of man. Colored impressions were also said to be distinctly perceptible on the bones of a petrified Hipparion recently discovered in Greece. How transparently fragile these reasonings are, he who runs may read. On inquiry it turns out that the holes and indentures were made by contemporary animals. Many of the alleged marks and drawings are accidental chinks wrought by mechanical causes.

2. KITCHEN REFUSE.

These remarks bear also on other remains of human life and industry found in the lower strata. Heaps of refuse, mussels, crabshells, bones, pots, and stone implements have been found in every country and on every coast. The edible mussels, oysters, and snails cannot be a natural deposit, but are a heap of the refuse of man's meals, whence they were called kitchen refuse or kjokkenmoddings. This opinion is borne out also by the remains of ashes, coals and wood (beech, oak, pine) with which they are mingled, and by the fire places that have been discovered. But it is unsafe to assume that these were contemporary deposits, and unsafer still to compute their age. The deposits in the deltas proceed at a slow rate, but historical times can point to a great change. The configuration of lands and continents is other than it was. Elevations and depressions, upheavals and subsidences have likewise had their share in effecting the change. Alluvial deposits, peat formations and stalagmites often attain a considerable thickness, but, as is well known, such formations are most irregular. The surroundings of the Quaternary Epoch were totally different from ours; the causes at work to transform the earth's surface throbbed with such fierce abnormal intensity, that their duration cannot be measured by their results. Compared with the thickness of the deposits, their duration must have been short. On this point geologists are agreed. So far the assumption of vast numbers of years lacks confirmatory evidence.

With regard to the so-called "lake dwellings" discovered in various parts of Europe, especially in Swizerland, they cannot be regarded as evidence of the great antiquity of the builders. For it has transpired that pile-builders dwelt near most lakes, even in historic times.

In dealing with history and philology (see next

chapter) no less than with geology, we must take care not to lose our heads over big figures. All apologists of note now agree in allowing that the antiquity of the human race is somewhat greater than it had been commonly supposed. The lowest estimate varies between eight and ten thousand years, but even the highest is not double the Septuagint computation.

And now we may safely leave the reader to draw his own conclusions in regard to both the essential difference between man and the brute and his antiquity. As to the latter, we just come to see that man is not as old as some geologists and palæontologists pretend. In regard to the former we have shown that man alone is self-conscious; he alone, unlike the whole of irrational nature, knows himself to be a personal being; he alone is conscious of moral obligations and responsibilities which he often fulfills in opposition to his own nature and to the world around him. By being born with head erect he is destined to gaze upwards from the earth to heaven, to God his Creator.

CHAPTER IX.

CHRONOLOGY AND THE PRINCIPAL MONUMENTS.

I. Biblical Chronology.

THE Biblical chronology presents extreme difficulties. As far back as St. Jerome it was regarded as insoluble, although in his time and long after the objections which have been formulated against this chronology were not imagined. A learned religious of Citeaux, Father Perron, wrote in 1687: "The antiquity of the epochs is much greater than is believed to-day. It is a great deviation from the truth to disregard the opinion of the Fathers and the ancient authors in regard to this subject. . . . All the Christians of the first centuries have counted about six thousand years until the arrival of the Messias. The history of the Chaldeans, Egyptians, and Chinese confirm this chronology and cannot be made to agree with the Hebrew of to-day."

The learned Father Touremine, S. J. said in this regard, in 1719: "The Jewish calculation appeared to me always too short and little in accordance with certain monuments of history. It takes from the chronologists several centuries necessary for the agreement of profane history with sacred history."

The most of the chronologists down to this century, have confounded the epoch of the creation of the world with that of the creation of man, because they believed that the one was separated from the other only by an interval of six days of twenty-four hours. Certain more perspicacious minds had, however, avoided this confusion. "St. Gregory, of Nazianz, following St. Justin the martyr, supposes," says Cardinal Wiseman, "an indefinite period between the creation and the first regular arrangement of things."

All savants who have occupied themselves with the chronology of primitive times have taken for the basis of their inquiries the genealogical lists of the antediluvian and postdiluvian patriarchs contained in Genesis, and which extend, the one, from Adam to Noe, and the other, from Noe to Abraham (Gen. v. and xi). These are the only documents upon which it is possible to erect a calculation, because they are the only ones that have been preserved to us. Whence, therefore, the disagreement of the chronologists? Because the figures on which their calculations are founded are not the same in the original text, which has descended to us, on the one hand, through the Jews, and, on the other, through the Samaritans, as well as in the most ancient version of Genesis, that of the Septuagint.

Now witness the totals of the antediluvian lists. The Hebrew and the Vulgate give 1656 years; the Greek, 2242; the Samaritan, 1307. The postdiluvian lists, to the time of Abraham, give these totals: The Hebrew and the Vulgate, 307 years; the Greek, 1147; the Samaritan, 1017. Which gives, by adding the two lists since the creation of Adam to the time of Abraham: The Hebrew and the Vulgate, 2023 years; the Greek, 3389; the Samaritan, 2329. Such are the usual figures; but in the case of the Septuagint, there exist numerous variations, resulting from the calculations of individual writers. It is thus that, in the first list, the total computed by Julius Africanus is 2262, and that, in the post-diluvian list, Clement of Alexandria finds 1250 years to the time of Abraham. These two totals taken together would give, consequently, 3512 years from Adam to the time of Abraham.

The savants not being able to agree among themselves, the sacred text being uncertain on this point, the Church did she not, at least, express herself in regard to this matter, and has she solved the difficulty? No! It is not within the province of the Church to regulate questions of chronology; she always left this subject to the historians with entire liberty to opine what conjectures and facts they might; she has not even manifested a marked preference in favor of any system. If the shortest chronology has predominated since the sixteenth century, it is not without notable exceptions, and the favor which it has enjoyed was due to the authority attributed to the Protestant Scaliger in this character of inquiry. This savant having expressed himself for the Hebrew text, to which the reformers attached in many things an exaggerated value, his opinion was generally accepted.

The celebrated annalist of the Church, Cardinal Baronius, while acknowledging the obscurity of the question, expressed himself in favor of the calculation of the Greek Bible, as more conformable to ecclesiastic tradition. All the doctors of the Greek Church, and all the ancient writers of the Latin Church have, indeed, accepted the figures which the Septuagint give. The Roman Martyrology has always preserved them, and it assigns as date of the birth of our Lord "the year 5199 after the creation of the world." Some ancient

Fathers, including Julius Africanus, had recognized the impossibility of reconciling the chronology of the Hebrew text with the history of the Chaldeans and Egyptians.

In more modern times, the Jesuit missionaries in China declared themselves also in favor of the Septuagint, by means of which they could reconcile the testimony of the annals of the country they evangelized with Holy Scripture, and their opinion was approved by their general. To eliminate all doubt, Father Adam Schall drew up, nevertheless, a memoir wherein he rendered account of the foundation of the Chinese chronology, and sent the same to Rome, where it was examined. It is not said whether or not the Holy Father was consulted, but a letter written from Rome, December 20, 1657, in answer to the consultation, does not hesitate to affirm " that one can without scruple follow the Chinese chronology," placing the reign of the Emperor Yao in the year 2357 B. C., because it is not in contradiction with the Septuagint, the chronology of which " is supported on the authority of the Fathers of the Church."

What must we conclude from all these facts? First, that " the Church does not warrant the exactitude of either of these two chronologies (of the Septuagint and of the Hebrew text), and that her authority does not oblige us at all to follow rigorously the text transmitted by tradition, nor the sense which has been attributed to it down to the present." " *Quam floxifaciat illam numerorum varietatem testantur duo Ecclesiæ lumina, S. Hieronymus et S. Augustinus,*" says Noel Alexandre (" Hist. Eccles. Vet. Test." vol. i, p. 76). Moreover, it is impossible to fix the date of the creation of man with certitude; the more competent savants unanimously concede this. "The number of the years which elapsed since the creation to the Nativity of Christ is uncertain," says Pagi, the learned annotator of Baronius. . . . "It will never be definitely ascertained what the age of the world was in the epoch of the Incarnation."

The reason of this avowed incertitude is, that in supposing the genealogical lists of Genesis to be complete, it is impossible to know the real figures written by Moses. It is even certain, because the list of the figures of the three most ancient and most respectable versions differ notably from one another, that two of these versions, as to the figures they give, are erroneous; consequently, it is not at all proved that any of the three versions gives actually the figures written by Moses.

"The genealogies of the Bible, having for object to give us the filitation of early man, and not the succession of time, and, consequently, might have omitted intermediaries," observes M. Wallon ("La Sainte Bible resume," 1867, vol. i, p. 435), "no calculation descends for certain beyond Abraham." What authorizes the supposition of these omissions in Genesis, are the analogous omissions remarked in other books of the Scripture where it is possible for us to establish them. The latter have been acknowledged at all times, because they are evident. "It is possible," says Father Lequien, "that Moses considered it advisable to mention only ten principal patriarchs who preceded the Deluge, and ten others who followed it before Abraham, by omitting the others for reasons which are unknown to us, as St. Matthew has done in the genealogy of our Lord, the author of Ruth, and that of the first book of the Paralipomenons, in that of David and of the high priests. . . ."

But the most remarkable example of breaks in the genealogical trees is that which Father Lequien first called attention to, that is, that which occurs in the Gospel of St. Matthew. The sacred author has excluded, with evident object, from the list of the ancestors of our Lord three well-known royal personages: Ochosias, Josias, and Amasias. But the suppression of generations means years, even centuries, which cannot be calculated in remote epochs.

Consequently, the epoch of the appearance of man upon earth is altogether uncertain, not only because we are in ignorance of the exact figures which the author of the Pentateuch had written, but, moreover, because we are also totally unable to ascertain the number of omissions in the genealogical series. When the alteration of figures can modify the estimate of the antiquity of man only in a limited manner, such is not the case where generations have been omitted, because it depends entirely upon how many these omissions were, and the periods of time which they represent, and thus how far back we may have to place the creation of man.

Man is not as old as certain savants maintain; it has been determined, however, that he is of more ancient origin than has been generally believed. It is impossible to uphold at present that the first man appeared upon earth only 4004 years, B. C., and to preserve that date which chronology derives from the Hebrew text. It is well established by geology and palæontology that our species ascended from a very remote epoch. Certain of these authorities have exaggerated this antiquity on the basis of hypothetical calculations. The existence of the Tertiary man is not proved at all, and he counts many more adversaries than adherents. Science is not conditioned to furnish us with precise figures in regard to the periods into which it has divided creation, much less is it enabled to assign the date of the appearance of man.

"What eminent geologists have written in regard to fossil man and his coexistence with preadamitic animals, etc., has to-day become without object," says Mr. Jakob, summing up the opinion of the savants on this subject. It is not regarded seriously in the present day at what date the glacial epoch took place, and how long it continued. The geologist knows no dates, but only a succession in the things; to the question of time, he must answer: "We do not know." It is thus that M. de Lapparent, whose name is an authority, concludes one of his most beautiful dissertations: "It is sufficient for us to have established how far all those calculations are lacking in a substantial foundation which distribute so generously hundreds and millions of centuries between the different phases of the Quaternary Epoch."

It remains, nevertheless, not less true that, while rejecting these exaggerations, it must be admitted that man is much more ancient than was believed before the progress of geological research. The human races existed from a very remote antiquity; we find the prinpal ones already pictured, such as they are to-day, on the most ancient monuments of Egypt. Humanity was, therefore, already very ancient in this epoch, because, issued from one single pair, it had time to become so greatly diversified. Philology furnishes an analogous conclusion; for in a very remote epoch we meet with a number of languages completely different from one another and as there could have been but one mother tongue, it required many centuries to have produced these different forms of speech.

However, to appreciate the duration which these changes and revolutions have claimed in the languages and in the physical conformation of man, the chronometers are entirely wanting, and thus we can arrive only at vague and indefinite results.

The historical monuments which have descended to us, and of which a great number have been discovered only in this century, will permit us to be a little more precise. We have already seen that it was the knowledge of the annals of China which obliged the Jesuit missionaries in this country, as well as several savants living in Europe in the seventeenth and eighteenth centuries, to abandon the short chronology then in vogue, of the Hebrew text, and to return to that of the Septuagint, which had been followed before the adoption of the Hebrew. When the Sanscrit studies began to be cultivated in Europe, the Indianists claimed in their turn for India a high antiquity. But since the rise of the Egyptiology and Assyriology, the savants who devoted themselves to the deciphering of the hieroglyphics and the cuneiform characters have been still more exacting. Therefore, we will have to examine successively the chronology of India, China, Egypt and Chaldea.

II. Chronology and the Principal Literary Monuments of Antiquity.

1. In regard to India, its chronological pretensions are not justified. Those who occupy themselves with

Sanscrit studies acknowledge this themselves; they avow that their predecessors have exaggerated the antiquity of its history and literature. Those best versed in the literature of primitive India are the first to agree that it was completely void of historic weight. "The Hindoos," says Kruse, "do not possess any work of history. They have wrapped up the ancient events in a poetic cloak of myths, without determination of time."

It is generally supposed that the separation of the Aryans and the Indo-European migrations, starting from Bactriana to disperse themselves to the four winds of heaven, took place anteriorly to the year 2500 B. C. This is only a hypothesis, but it is quite probable. The antiquity which the Hindoos attribute to themselves is, therefore, fabulous. Talboys Wheeler commences their history only about 2500 years before the Christian era, and he has nothing to say about this epoch except of legends which he derives from the Mahâbharata.

M. Dunker asserts that one cannot with exactness go further back than the year 800 before the Christian era.

The most ancient epigraphic monument of certain date, in which mention is made of the ancient Hindoos, is the thrilingual inscription of Darius, King of Persia, at Persepolis. The son of Hystaspes enumerates the land of the Hindush, the India, among the countries which are subject to his dominion.

In the country itself no historic records, dated anterior to the third century before the Christian era, have been discovered. The inscriptions of Acoka (250 B. C.), the most ancient of the native inscriptions, give some historic details of certain date. "The civilization and literature of India must be referred to a remote period in profane antiquity, there is really no doubt on the subject . . . but nobody assigns to them that fabulous antiquity which was hastily attributed to them, because of a fame. . . . There is no Sanscrit work anterior to the body of the sacred writings, called Vedas. After a most scrupulous examination of the books, Indianists of eminent authority have not dared to set back the composition of the most ancient parts beyond the fourteenth century B. C. The learned editor of the Rigveda, Max Müller, has traced with a master's hand the picture of the ancient Sanscrit literature, and he has placed its complete development into a period of about one thousand years, of the twelfth to the second century before our era." (Cf. Bartholemey Saint Hilaire, 1860-61, F. Neve, 1883.)

According to Max Müller, the ancient Hindoos did not originate the idea of a chronology; this idea came to them from elsewhere, like the alphabet and the use of money, and it was the influence of an association with the Greeks that led the Hindoos to date their historic documents.

Therefore, the Sanscrit literature cannot furnish any imporant evidence of the antiquity of man, and we can conclude with Bartelemy Saint-Hilaire: " Ceylon alone, in the world of India, has regular annals and what might almost be called history. . . . Everywhere else history is absent altogether; or, when it tries to show itself, it is so disfigured that it is absolutely unrecognizable. . . . Since India did not wish to discard its dreams, one cannot historically invoke it from its tomb."

2. Quite different in this respect from India, China

presents itself to us with a long series of regular annals. The Jesuit missionaries who first studied the Chinese chronology, were struck by the connection and unity which they remarked therein; the majority of the missionaries accepted the chronology without hesitation, and their testimony influenced several Sinalogues of Europe, who displayed a great avidity for this question in the seventeenth and eighteenth centuries. The Fathers Cibot and Premare conceived, nevertheless, doubt regarding the authenticity of the primitive dates contained in the Chinese histories, and they were followed by Guignes, Klaproth, Renaudot and some others. Even to the present day a diversity of opinion in regard to this subject exists.

Father Martini commenced his history of China, published in 1658, with the reign of Fo-Hi, who inaugurated, according to the native savants, the period in 2952 B. C., which is designated as that of a " very high antiquity." Father Gaubil who placed still farther back the reign of the Emperor Fo-Hi, " to the body of the dragon, and to the head of the bull," was careful, however, not to fix any event before the Emperor Yao, whom he believes ascended the throne in 2357 B. C., according to the calculation of the eclipse mentioned in the annals of China. Only, he observes, China was at that time well populated, the people knew how to write in verse, fix the points of the solstices and of the equinoxes, manufacture articles of leather and of iron, weave the silk, etc. . . . " And, necessarily, it must be admitted that there were people in China before the time of Yao."

In spite of the reflections of the learned Jesuit, several modern Sinalogues have little faith in the

Chinese chronology; what renders very suspicious the Chinese dates and calculations is, that they rest upon no solid basis, and that all means of control are wanting. The inhabitants of the Celestial Empire had not formerly an era, properly speaking, like that of Nabonassar or of the Seleucides; the era of Hoanghti, commencing the year 2367 B. C., was adopted officially by the Chinese government at a time when it was impossible to verify its exactitude; also it is not universally accepted by the natives themselves. "Who knows what occurred in remote antiquity," asks the Chinese Yangts, "because no authentic document has descended to us? . . . In the primitive times historic documents were not preserved." Our modern authors cannot be more exacting than the Chinese authors.

In 213 B.C., the Emperor Chi-Hoang-ti, founder of the dynasty of Tsin, commanded, under pain of death that all the historic books of the empire should be burned. The Chinese literators have never questioned this annihilation of the documents of their ancient historic literature, and, if they are correct in this, all that is related in regard to times anterior to the dynasty of the Tsin, merits little confidence. However, modern critics cannot believe that a certain number of copies of the Chou-King and of other historic works did not escape the flames in an empire so vast as that of China.

But a number of those even who admit as very probable that the destruction of the historic literature was not total, have another complaint to make against the Chinese chronology, namely: that the ancient monuments which would verify it are wanting. One of the most ancient historians of China, Sigismond of Fries, divides his work into two parts: the mythic period and the historic period, the latter commencing in the year 775 B. C. Not, he says, that all events related after this date are historical, and that all those which precede it are fabulous, but "because this is the first fixed point for a comparative chronological study, whilst all the anterior dates can be considered only as estimation." What we do not meet with in China, neither do we find outside of this country; we have no other foreign testimony in favor of the great antiquity of the Chinese. For the commercial relations which we are assured existed, during three thousand years, between the Celestial Empire and Egypt, Chabas has proved that the monuments of ancient Egypt do not contain any mention of the Celestial Empire, although we recover therein all the other nations known at that time.

3. The accounts we possess of the *Egyptian* chronology come to us from three different sources: from the narratives of the Greek travelers who had visited Egypt; from a history written in Greek by a native writer of great reputation, Manetho, shortly after the conquest of Alexander, and, finally, from the original monuments, inscriptions, and papyri, recovered in the valley of the Nile since the beginning of this century.

The Greek writers attribute to Egypt a very high antiquity. The priests of Heliopolis related to Solon that their monarchy ascended to 9,000 years. A century later, the priests of the same temple of Heliopolis, told Herodotus that the annals of their kings ascended to 11,340 years, that is, 2,240 years more. According to Varro (116-126 years B. C.), on the contrary, the Egyptian monarchy had hardly existed, in his time, more than 2,000 years. Diodor of Sicily, who visited Egypt under the reign of Augustus, dates back the epoch of Menes to a period little anterior than 5,000 years before his time. But little satisfaction can be derived from these vague and contradictory accounts. The figures of the Greek travelers do not merit much confidence, and do not enjoy any great authority. They communicated with the Egyptians only through interpreters and besides, it is evident, that the value of their testimony must be controled and appreciated with the help of native documents.

Among the latter we possess only one which is anterior to the Egyptiological discoveries of our century, namely, the history of Manetho.

Manetho, an Egyptian priest, born at Sebeunyt (now Semnoud) in the Delta, about the year 300 B. C., wrote in Greek a history of his country for his new masters, under the reign of Ptolemy Philadelpus. Unfortunately, the writing of Manetho was lost, but the chronological part has been preserved. He attributed to Egypt an antiquity of 3,000 years before the epoch of Alexander. The reign of the gods occupies 13,900 years, that of the heros 1,250, the reign of the other kings 1,817 years, of thirty Memphites 1,790, of ten Thinites 350 years, that of Menes and of the heros 5,813, and, finally, the reign of thirty dynasties 5,000 years.

The most critics correctly consider as historical the thirty dynasties beginning with Menes and ending with Nectanebo II. The greatest embarrassment for the historian, is that the lists of Manetho enumerate the dynasties as if they had been successive, while it is, nevertheless, certain that there have been certain dynasties which were contemporaneous. Moreover,

Manetheo never associates two kings on the throne. We know, however, through the monuments, that during certain periods, there were kings that jointly reigned in Egypt. The best known example is that of Ramses II of the nineteenth dynasty, who, when only twelve years of age, was associated on the throne by his father Seti, and reigned conjointly with him about 20 years, after this he continued to reign about 36 years. Manetho assigns to these two kings a reign of 101 years; the monuments attribute 77 years. Finally, the historian of Egypt exaggerates frequently the duration of the reign of his kings. In thirty-seven cases where we can control his figures by those of the papyrus of Turin, they exceed the latter twenty-two times, and are deficient only six times. The total of these thirty-seven reigns is, according to Manetho, 984 years, and, according to the papyrus of Turin, 615 years; there is, therefore, an excess of more than one-third (Cf. G. Rawlinson, "The Antiquity of Man"). The authority of Manetho, even in the thirty dynasties, needs therefore, to be regulated by the monuments.

The authentic and original monuments of the Egyptian chronology are the royal lists, the most important is that which is contained in the papyrus of Turin. Unfortunately, the papyrus, entire at the time of its recovery, was broken when they transported it to Turin, and is not now complete. The Egyptians had no era; they had not, consequently, a chronological system. The accounts which are preserved to us state how long each king reigned, but do not connectedly determine when one king begins to reign at the time when the reign of another terminated. The only effort of chronology existing to-day is in a stela of Tanis, where there is mention of the year 400, but this is an isolated fact, besides even now but poorly understood. (Cf. Mariette, *La Stele de l'an* 400. in the " Revue Archeologique," 1865, vol. xi, p. 169-190.)

When the shortest chronologies are doubtful and suspicious, the longest are certainly false; even their authors themselves have been cautious to assert their truthfulness. " In the actual state of things," says Brugsch, " no living man is capable of removing the difficulties which prevent the restoration of the original list of kings contained in the fragments of the Turin papyrus. . . . It appears certain, besides, that the long duration of kings which the papyrus formerly contained, had been arranged by the author according to his own ideas and individual views." The preceding paragraph explains why there exists such a great discord among the different modern historians who have occupied themselves with the history of Egypt. It is, therefore, with Egypt, to a certain degree, as with China: the historic monuments and the dates they furnish are insufficient to establish an exact chronology, and of themselves, they do not prove that the chronology of the Septuagint is not of sufficient antiquity.

4. Chaldea and Assyria offer more precise figures than Egypt. They are furnished to us not through the ancient authors, but through the native monuments discovered in the last years. We possess no other ancient native accounts of these countries except those which are contained in the Chaldean history of Berosus, priest of Bel, at Babylon, in the time of Antiochus II, King of Syria (261-246 B.C.); but what fragments which have arrived to us from him teach in regard to chro-

nology is, in great part, fabulous, and has not met with credence, even among the Greeks and Romans. According to Berosus, there had elapsed 36,000 years since the Deluge until the Persian conquest.

The Babylonians alleged also, in favor of their antiquity, their astronomical observations which they made descend beyond 45,000 years. But this allegation thenus to study the Chaldean astronomy, after the Greeks. When Aristotle charged his disciple Callisthenus to study the Chaldean astronomy, after the taking of Babylon by Alexander, this savant stated that his observations embraced only a period of 1,903 years. The ancient authors teach us nothing more than Berosus about the Chaldean antiquity, and, until the second half of the nineteenth century, no further knowledge was obtained; but the Assyriological discoveries of the last century have totally changed the order of things.

The cuneiform documents have furnished us, indeed, new accounts of the Babylonian chronology, and it is especially through the Assyrians that they have been furnished. The Assyrians are the first people of antiquity among whom we discover some chronology. The historic inscriptions which they have left us, and which the contemporary explorers have excavated from the ruins of their ancient capitals, contain the most precise details, and are carefully dated. This people did not count like the Egyptians and the Chinese, by the years of reign of their sovereigns, but by the name of eponym officers, called Limmi, who gave their name to the year, like the Archonts at Athens, and the Consuls at Rome. They drew up canons or eponymous lists, and some of these documents have been recovered and published. Unfortunately, we possess only a very small portion of them. The fragments recovered give us an exact chronology of the history of the Assyrian Empire, from 913 to 659 B. C., but we have the assurance that the institution of the Limmi descended at least to the fourteenth century before our era, for the inscription of Binnirar I is dated by the eponymy of Salmankarradu. Thanks to this system of chronology, the Assyrians were enabled to give precise dates for past events, an exactitude, which, in a similar respect, is not met with among any other people. Sennacherib (705-681), the enemy of Ezechias, mentions in one of his inscriptions that a seal having belonged to Tuklath-Ninip, had been carried to Babylon 600 years previously and that 418 years had elapsed when he himself invaded Babylon (692), since the defeat of Teglath-Phalasar I (about 1130) by the Babylonians. Teglath-Phalasar I says, in his turn, that he restored at Khalah-Chergat (the antique city of Assur) a temple built by Samsibin, son of Ismidagon, 701 years before.

The son of Sennacherib, Assurbanipal (668-626), relates on his part, that an idol which he recovered in 639 in the country of Elam, had been forcibly carried away from Erech, that it was then 1,635 years, consequently 274 years before our era. This is the most remote date which the Assyrian documents have as yet furnished. We may, however, entertain some doubt regarding the veracity of the last figures. The carrying away of the idol of the goddess Nana, being an event in the history of Chaldea, we have not in favor of its date the same guarantees as for the facts which regard Assyria.

M. Pinches, in 1882, made known to the Biblical Archæological Society of London, a cylinder of Nabonidus, King of Babylon, found at Abou-Abba, and preserved now in the British Museum. We read thereon that Ligbagas or Urbagas, King of Ur, lived 700 years before the epoch of Hammuragas, the time of which is, however, unknown. But we read thereon, moreover, that Naramsin, son of Sargon I, had founded the temple of the god Samas (the sun) at Sippara, 3,200 years before the reign of Nabonidus, that is, about the year 3750 before our era. This positive date would set back the Deluge, known to the Babylonians as well as to the Hebrews, to more than 4000 years B.C.; for, before Naramsin and before Sargon, there had been already, according to the testimony of the monuments, a certain number of kings posterior to the great cataclysm.

However, we must remark, that although the date given by Nabonidus has been vigorously maintained by certain Assyriologists, it should only be accepted reservedly. Indeed, nothing vouches for the exactitude of this calculation of so remote an antiquity as made by the King Nabonidus, or those who furnished him this date in regard to an epoch greatly removed from them, and we must also remark that, until a recent date, no trace of a chronological canon, similar to that of the Assyrians, was met with among the Babylonians. How, therefore, could Nabonidus calculate to a certainty, the time which separated him from Naramsin? May not the priests of Sippara have exaggerated the antiquity of their temple, and may not the figures of the inscription be fabulous, or extended beyond the warrant of truth, like so many others we read of in Berosus?

An exact chronology of Chaldea and Babylonia

commences only with the era of Narbonassar in 747 B. C., but all means of verification are wanting for the anterior epochs, except in the Assyrian monuments, which do not go back far enough.

5. In conclusion, the history of India, and even that of China, in their authentic portions, can be inclosed without very great difficulty in the centuries admitted by the Greek and Latin Fathers. As to Egypt, the high antiquity of Menes is far from being proved, and numerous reasons tend to lower its date; finally, the ancient civilization of Egypt and Chaldea offers no basis for an exact calculation, and we may, at least, give this advice to the archæologues and savants: Establish on good proofs the antiquity of man and of the ancient peoples and the Bible will not contradict you. It presents no obstacle to the path of these researches, provided one remains within the limit of a wise criticism. Suffice it to say that all knowledge obtainable on this subject can but verify the revealed truth of Him, "Who hath numbered the sand of the sea, and the drops of rain, and the days of the world."

CHAPTER X.

UNITY OF MANKIND.

1. THE whole human race, according to Holy Scripture, is descended from one physically united pair, Adam and Eve. Preadamites are impossible. Apart from Adam there has been no race. An exegetical difficulty arises out of Genesis iv, 14-16; but it affords as little ground as Romans v, 14, for Isaac Pereyre's contention, that Genesis represents Adam as the progenitor of none but the Jewish race. The Old and New Testaments repeatedly proclaim that the human race is one, in the strict sense of the word (Acts xvii, 26; Heb. ii, 11). The doctrines of original sin and redemption are based on this community of descent. By one man sin and death, and by one man grace and life have come into the world. This intimate connection between unity of race and the dogma of redemption prompted Augustine, Lactantius and others to deny the existence of the antipodes.

2. Science, too, has been compelled to acknowledge this common humanity. The discovery of America unexpectedly brought to light a new race. The learned were as much perplexed as Pliny of old, when he set eyes on the black Ethiopians. Their convictions were shaken. Naturalists and missionaries assigned the Redskins to another Adam, or denied that they were

created by God. Pope Paul III had to issue a Brief asserting that the Indians had equal rights with other men. Later on, selfish slave-traders, egged on by the learned, tried to widen to the uttermost the rift between whites and blacks, by declaring dominion and slavery to be their respective birthrights. This, however, notwithstanding proofs of the common origin of all races are now coming in thick and fast. The Darwinians, in direct antagonism to their own principles, obstinately maintained the stability of the various races. But, despite all obstructions, modern naturalists have marched forward towards the goal of unity. Polygenists are fast sinking into disrepute, and the unity of the species is coming to be recognized. Philologists have likewise grown in prudence and discretion. The physical and spiritual differences existing between men still present many difficulties; there is, however, no danger to faith as long as a common origin is allowed to be possible.

3. However much people differ in size and color and hairiness, in the skeleton, the formation of the skull and so forth, still *common characteristics* are at hand that unite the several groups into races. The very name of *race* indicates the meaning of the principle of division. For it was chosen on the supposition that all races form one species. The fact that all races cross and are fertile, affords one among several verifications of this supposition. Cross breeds are often more fertile than alliances in the same race. As long as this common characteristic holds good, the unity of the human species is a necessary consequence. Clearly, therefore, the differences of race are not essential nor absolutely unchangeable. The characteristics of each race are

found in isolated and exceptional instances in other races. Differences of race are as old as history, yet no classification has been generally accepted. The bulk of the population of Central Africa are generally designated as Negroes, and it is usual to characterize the negro type by black, woolly hair, prominent cheek bones, pouting lips, and black skin. Later researches, however, have shown that this type exists in only a few of the wild stocks on the slave coast. At length these characteristics get so toned down, that this race forms a transition to the inhabitants of Melanesia and the other islands. The same is true of the Mongolians. It would seem, therefore, that race differences were not formed till the tribes had migrated and settled, and that they now remain constant unless interfered with from without. Once the type has set firm through hundreds and thousands of years, individuals easily lose all capacity for variation. Even change of abode and of climate is unable to revive it.

Nevertheless, the experience gained in America during three hundred years has shown that the color and facial expression of negroes are undergoing a slow change. And the change would have been still more marked, had not slaves been constantly imported from Africa. It is very striking in those who have mixed with other races.

4. *Race* is the gradual outcome of the mutual action and reaction of people and country on each other. In nothing is this brought out so clearly as in color. Color is not merely external. Its foundation lies deep down in organism. It supposes a greater change than is usually ascribed to the power of the sun. Color is caused by the carbon pigment found in the Malpighian

cells. These cells are also found in the colored places of the white man's skin. The sun cannot suddenly effect this transformation, but may further it in the course of time. A change in the color of the skin may have easily been caused by the sun acting in conjunction with moisture, temperature, manner of living, and other climatic factors. The *physiological* explanation is that respiration, being retarded by heat, fails to change all the carbon into carbonic acid. The light playing on the surface materially aids the process. Parts not exposed, like the sole of the foot and the palm of the hand, are less dark even in the negro. Arabian women, who go about well wrapped up, are as white as Europeans. Even in the same country and climate this influence acts in different degrees, although the skins are generally darkest in hot countries. Anyhow, side by side with secondary and accidental causes, light and climate will always be regarded as the chief factors in producing the change.

5. Other differences, in the skeleton and formation of the skull for example, are less important. Occupation and manner of living, and malformations, intentional or otherwise, may have had their share in producing a clear but variable type in a short time. Anyhow, such deviations in the animal world do not hinder the various races from forming one species. In man the difficulty is even less. For as the races are generally fertile, intermediate forms are everywhere possible, and these act as links and transmission agents. Blumenbach has pointed out that transitional forms grow more and more numerous. Humboldt considers that the many intermediate stages in skull formation, and in the color of the skin, are a strong plea for unity. The

transition of races is made still clearer by modern researches. The American stock is the connecting link between the Caucasian and the Mongolian; the Malay bridges over the Caucasian and the Negro.

6. Nor, again, is the distinction into higher and lower races justified by anatomy. The Caucasian has no claim to the highest place, for other races are equally complete, not to say adapted to their environment. The Negro can endure heat and cold, and withstand fatigue better than the Caucasian and American. And in this respect the Malay, climate notwithstanding, is superior to the European. In intellect, however, the case is altered. No one denies that the very lowest races are still human. But there is a widespread opinion that some races are, and have been, low, and will never rise. Darwin could hardly believe that the inhabitants of Terra del Fuego were men. Similar stories are told of Australians and Polynesians, and in the case of the Negroes have passed current as an axiom. Intellectual inferiority is regarded as a specific characteristic of the Negro race, especially of those stocks that are the typical representatives of the race. It is likewise pretended that the ape approximates to man in the formation of the brain. With the physical differences we have already dealt, but speech and reason clearly demonstrate that the intellectual difference between the ape and the Negro is specific; whereas there is a difference of degree only between the Negro and other races. The intellectual inferiority of the Negro and savage tribes has been grossly exaggerated. Even Darwin was subsequently obliged to reconsider his verdict on the people of Terra del Fuego. Owing to the praiseworthy efforts of missionaries notable results have

already been achieved. This proves that they possess a great capacity for education. The Indians often display great shrewdness and intelligence. Thanks to Jesuit influence, a new and able nation has sprung up in Paraguay, Colorado, and elsewhere. Negro children educated in America and Europe learn easily. All tribes are susceptible of education and culture; all are possessed with a greater or less intelligence. The animals, especially those of the superior species, are not wanting in a certain (animal) intelligence and memory, but all of them are devoid of reason, while there is not a single human race which has not the faculty of reasoning, abstracting and generalizing.

7. All men, even the most savage, are social. It is a long time since Aristotle defined man as a "political animal," that is, a social animal. Certain animal species are also social, especially the bees and the ants; but their organization is not the work of reason; it is not supple and flexible like ours; it has not the family as basis, and cannot accommodate itself to circumstances of time and place. Human association has the same end everywhere — security and mutual assistance, founded in part on the ties of friendship, in part on community of interests. It secures to the individual the means of existence, and special advantages which he could not possess in a state of isolation.

8. All human races are endowed with the gift of speech. From the comparative study of languages, we learn of developments that had taken place before history had dawned. Languages are in fact as numerous as independent peoples, and history tells us that language and customs were the great barrier that separated tribe from tribe. Some people have, indeed,

changed their language. One original language may not be an absolutely certain proof that the human race is one. Still, language is a sure-footed guide, and the original language is at least a negative proof, and affords a strong positive presumption in favor of unity. Whence comes it that languages differ? This question, though scarcely ever broached formerly, seems now to be coming to the front. Outside the Old Testament there is scarcely a record of any nation busying itself with the problem why languages should be many instead of one. The Indians of Central America, however, have a saying very much like the words of Scripture, that all men had one speech and one religion, but that when the town of Tulan worshipped false gods their speech was changed.

9. "Though languages," says Humboldt, "may at first sight appear very different, though their notions humors, peculiarities, may seem singular, nevertheless, they betray a certain analogy, and we shall understand their numerous relations better according as the philological history of nations, and the study of language become more perfect." The last twenty years have proved the correctness of this view to a great extent. The Mosaic account represents nations as related whose relationship antiquity was unable to recognize. The Romans and Greeks, in spite of their culture, never dreamed that they were nearer related to the Aryans and Germans than the Syrians and Tyrians. What Holy Writ had stated the science of the nineteenth century has confirmed: Ionians, Aryans, and Germans are of common origin. The study of language has proved that before the ancestors of the Hindoos and Persians emigrated toward the south, and before the

Greek, Roman, Celtic, Teutonic, and Slav colonies went to Europe, there was probably on the plains of Asia a tribe of Aryans who spoke a language, which was not Sanscrit, nor Greek, nor German, but which called the Giver of light and life by the same name which to-day may be heard in the temples of Benares, in the basilicas of Rome and in the cathedrals and churches of northern Germany. "All the Indo-Germanic languages," says Pott, "were identical before the separation; they exist in the germ in one original language, which disappeared when they were differentiated from it."

10. In conclusion, we can hold that the Mosaic account, which tells us that the division of languages took place a long time after the creation, and brings this division into immediate connection with the division of mankind into different nations at the building of the Tower of Babel, appears to be confirmed by the results of the science of language.

CHAPTER XI.

THE EARTHLY PARADISE AND ITS SITE.

OUR first parents were placed in a garden of pleasure, which we call "Earthly Paradise." Moses names the country where it was situated and calls it Eden (Gen. ii, 8; iv, 6), and the Paradise itself, in the Hebrew Bible is called Eden, i. e. joy or delight. We recover our word Paradise in the Hebrew under the form of *pardes* (Cant. iv, 13), Vulgate, *paradisus ;* Eccl. ii, 5, Vulgate, *pomaria ;* 2 Esd. ii, 8, Vulgate, *saltus*) to signify like in the ancient Persian (pairadueza) "park," garden planted with trees, enclosed.

The Sacred Text determines the situation of Paradise by stating that Eden was in the Orient, according to the original text (Gen. ii, 8), and that a river which flowed through the garden, divided afterwards into four streams, capita, called Phison, Gehon, Tigris, and Euphrates. The identification of the Tigris and the Euphrates offers no difficulty; these are the rivers which have been always known under these names; on the contrary, the identification of the Phison and of the Gehon is still undetermined. It is said of the Gehon that it flows around the land of Cush, which latter place, as translated by the Septuagint and the Vulgate, signifies Ethiopia, because Ethiopia has been inhabited, after the dispersion of the nations, by the Cushites; but the latter lived previously in Asia, and Cush designates here certainly a country of Asia.

The most of the commentators, down to the present day, have believed that the earthly paradise was situated in Occidental Asia. Some place Eden into Armenia, others near the Persian Gulf below the confluence of the Euphrates and the Tigris, where these two rivers form the Schat-el-Arab. A certain number of modern savants believe, on the contrary, that we must seek it in India or on the plateau of Pamir. According to them, Hevilath, the country which is watered by the Phison, and where gold, bdellium and onyx are found, is India, which was known to the ancient Jews as a country extending indefinitely towards the southeast. This explanation is not reconcilable with the Biblical text.

The Deluge and other disturbances which have

overthrown certain parts of the earth, may have modified notably the topography of the place where Paradise was situated, and thus rendered insolvable the question of its site. The opinion which seems the most probable is that which places it into Armenia, in the rich valleys of which still exists a territory as fertile as any in the world. The Euphrates and Tigris have their sources in this region; the Tigris rises about three miles from the Euphrates, in the north of Diarbekir. It is hereabouts that the first man was placed on earth. The Phison is either the Phase of the classical authors, which flows from east to west, and empties into the Black Sea, or the Kur, the Cyrus of the ancients, which has its source in the neighborhood of Kars, not far from the occidental source of the Euphrates, and thus empties into the Caspian Sea, after having mingled its waters with those of the Arax. Hevilath, watered by the Phison, is the Colchis, the country of precious metals, whither the Argonauts went to seek the Golden Fleece. As to the Gehon, it is the Aras of to-day, the ancient Arax, called by the Arabs *Djaichoum* (or Gehon) *er Ras*, which proceeds from the neighborhood of the occidental source of the Euphrates, and empties, as we have said, together with the Kur, into the Caspian Sea. The land of Cush which it crosses, according to Genesis, is the country of the Kosseans, Cassiotis, *regio Cossæorum*. "That the Eden . . . must be sought in the sources of the Euphrates and Tigris," says a learned German philologue, M. Ebers, "appears to us beyond all question; this is established by ethnography and geography, by the Hebrew history and the Armenian chronicles, and, in our days, by a particular authority, the compared philology."

THE EARTHLY PARADISE AND ITS SITE.

The traditions of the earthly Paradise have been preserved among a great number of nations. Several of them locate the cradle of humanity among the high mountains of Central Asia, where the great Asiatic rivers have their sources. According to the Hindoos, the four or five great rivers arose to the north of the sacred mountain, the Merou (Himalaya) or Pamir, to direct themselves towards different points of the world. The ancient Iranians placed it in the north, on Mount Hukairya, one of the peaks of the sacred mountain Hara-Bærezaiti, called also Albordj, whose summits reached until heaven, to the revivifying waters of Ardvi-Cura, which had its source in heaven itself, thus obtaining the power to fructify the earth. The Chinese describe the cradle of mankind thus: " It is a mountain situated in the middle of the central plateau of Asia, forming part of the chain of Kuen-Lun. In the midst of the mountain, there is a garden where a tender zephyr breathes constantly and moves the leaves of the beautiful Tong. This delightful garden is situated at the gates close to heaven. The waters which furrow it proceed from a fruitful yellow source, called the source of immortality; those who drink thereof do not die. It divides itself into four rivers flowing towards the northwest, the southwest, the southeast and the northeast. (Cf. Lüken, " Überlieferungen," vol. i, p. 100.)

CHAPTER XII.

THE CREATION OF EVE.

ACCORDING to the Rationalists the history of the creation of Eve is a fable, improbable and impossible. To this we answer that there is no absolute impossibility and improbability here. Certainly God could do all that is related in the Sacred Text (Gen. ii). He could form the first woman out of the rib of Adam. That those who pretend not to believe in the existence of God, refuse to believe this truth, we can very easily understand, but one must know that they reject this truth because they are atheists or deists, and all that we have to prove against them is that God could act as He pleased, that He could create the first woman as indicated in Holy Scripture.

In the very nature of the thing itself, the creation, and early existence of mankind must have been replete with extraordinary events; nearly everything in that time had to be produced, not as now in the natural order, but by means of a supernatural agency. Eve could not have a mother, hence she had to be born in an extraordinary manner. And why could the Creator not form her, in order to give us the grand lessons derived from her creation, in the manner related by Genesis?

The Church has not condemned the commentators who have refused to accept literally the Biblical narrative of the creation of the first woman. She has not censured the opinion of Origen and Cardinal Cajetan, who have explained in an allegorical sense the formation of Eve out of a rib of Adam; but, irrespective of very rare exceptions, the Fathers and Doctors accepted literally the Biblical statement, and in this they were right. It is not the supernatural character of the account that should here prevent an incredible feature. The creation of the first woman was necessarily miraculous and supernatural.

Why did God select that mode of creation which the sacred author reports rather than another? Were we unable to explain this, we could conclude nothing from our ignorance against the fact itself, but the reason is evident and palpable, so to say, as Lacordaire has very well demonstrated. "The creation of Eve," he says, "gives plurality to man without destroying his oneness. Taking as a standard of human society the eternal order of divine society, God knew that there would be no moral unity in the relations of man to man; therefore, He wished that these relations should take their source in a substantial unity, imitating as much as possible the tie which keeps together the three uncreated divine persons in an ineffable perfection. Humanity should be united by nature, by origin, by blood, and form in all its members, by means of this triple unity, only one soul and one body. This plan was conformable to the general ends of God, which were to create us after His image and likeness, in order to communicate His goods to us all. This was worthy of His wisdom and goodness, and when we remember that an impious infidel can scoff and ridicule this magnificently divine conception, we can feel only the greatest pity for such a man who considers his intelligence greater than that of his Maker." (Conferences de Notre Dame, no. 51, Paris 1848.)

CHAPTER XIII.

THE FALL AND ORIGINAL SIN.

WITH regard to the history of the temptation and of the Fall, as related in Genesis (iii). we must not be astonished when we find therein wonderful particulars.

Man, according to the first design of the Creator, should not have that unfortunate inner inclination towards evil which is our sad inheritance. And, nevertheless, God having created him free, wished to try his fidelity. How could He do this, since neither Adam nor Eve felt the sting of concupiscence? Only by permitting a foreign agent to tempt them. But how could the devil, who is a pure spirit, tempt them, if not clothing himself with a sensible form, or by making use of a corporeal body? And how, finally, could God try the fidelity of his free and reasonable creature in a more natural and logical manner, than by requiring an exterior act of obedience, easy in itself, consisting in not eating of a forbidden fruit, which the obedience due to the Creator should have restrained them from tasting, but which all the human passions, aroused by the tempter, pride, sensuality, curiosity, the spirit of independence caused the fall of both the man and the woman?

Hence, Catholic doctrine has not been unreasonable by taking, in the literal sense, the account of Genesis. With reason it has believed that, because what precedes and follows this account is historical, and not mythological, there was no good ground to believe that the account itself is a myth, but the pure and simple expression of truth.

One can say that the most ancient traditions of humanity justify the general interpretation of the Church, for the most ancient nations have preserved the tradition of a primitive golden age and of the first sin, which is but a remembrance of the Eden of Genesis. This remembrance is undoubtedly more or less vague, but on this account it is not less worthy to draw our attention. The Assyrian monuments, discovered at modern times, frequently represent to us a deity wrestling with a dragon, and the seduction of the first men often appears attributed to the dragon Tihamat. The role of the serpent itself is not unknown in the primitive traditions.

The infidels object, it is true, that all the primitive traditions of some peoples, are allegorical and mythological, and that the Hebrew people cannot form an exception to the general rule, but we ask: Why not? Because all the religions claim to be true, does it follow from this that they are all false, without exception? We maintain expressly that the Bible is not a book like the other books, just as the Christian religion is not a religion like the other religions. We believe that Genesis alone gives us the explanation of the real origin of evil upon earth, whilst all other explanations, conceived with great pains by the philosophers or invented spontaneously by the popular imagination, explain nothing.

Another accusation against Genesis is that it wounds the moral feeling in making us responsible for a fault which we have not personally committed. Certainly, we have to admit that, at first sight, there is something mysterious and terrible in this solidarity which renders us partially responsible, after so many past generations, for a fault which we have not committed. But the enemies of the Church, when they attack this wonderful chapter of Genesis which teaches us more about man and humanity than all the philosophers together, do not pay attention to the fact that Moses proclaims an incontestable truth, the law of solidarity, one of the greatest laws which govern the world.

The heavenly bodies attract and move themselves reciprocally according to the laws of universal gravitation. Men are neither independent nor isolate; they exercise naturally one upon another an efficacious influence, either for good or for evil. The entire universe is like a great organism, where everything is held connected and enchained, and just like every individual feels pain when one of his parts is attacked, so also a local disorder can engender a general disturbance, which often extends beyond the place where it took rise.

Hence, it is not only in this particular of original sin, but in a multitude of occasions and circumstances that we play an unpleasant part in the great scheme of the universe, and that the Creator makes us carry the weight of the sins of our fathers. We enjoy the fruits of their virtues, but we also suffer from their faults and vices. The parents transmit to their children their health or their diseases, sometimes something of their good or evil moral dispositions. The voice of the past has in the history of nations a continuous echo. In the family the glory and the honor are an inheritance like property and riches, and the infamy of a parent impresses itself like a stigma of shame upon the forehead of the children. In society, the prosperity of all depends upon the government of one or a few; good or bad laws made by a few men, or even by a single man, save or destroy the people; the faults of the chiefs result again in calamities to those whom they lead, and whole nations groan during centuries under the weight of ancient crimes. A victory or a defeat can effect for generations the fate of a nation. Those brilliant populations of Asia Minor, which were shining so brightly at the beginning of our era, have seen their civilization eclipsed, because they were wanting in power to resist the Crescent, and their degenerate descendants are to-day the shadow of what they formerly were. If Charles Martel had not crushed, in the fields of Poitiers, the Arabs of Spain, what would have become of the European nations? Would the Moslem invasion not have dried up in its source that great river of civilization which has since penetrated into the very heart of Europe, and nourished into being the magnificence of the continent.

Such is the law of solidarity, general and universal, which is limited neither by time nor by space, which applies itself to man, to the family, to society; which renders in a certain measure the children responsible for the faults of their fathers, the subjects responsible for the faults of their kings and rulers. Both are heirs of the merits and of the virtues of their ancestors, and of those who have governed them; it explains in part the degeneration as well as the ennobling of the races, the prosperity and the power of the nations, as well as their weaknesses and misfortunes.

With these principles, original sin explains itself. It is the consequence of the solidarity which God, Creator and Sovereign Master, was pleased to establish between the first man and his posterity. This conduct might present some difficulty, if the victims of the original solidarity had found themselves wronged in their strict and individual rights as creatures. But such was not the case: the goods of which mankind remains deprived on account of their own fault were not due to it. The Creator was free to refuse them purely and simply; with much more reason could He make depend their possession upon any condition He pleased.

CHAPTER XIV.

THE PATRIARCHAL RELIGION OR PRIMITIVE MONOTHEISM.

ONE of the most predominant errors of our days among the rationalistic exegetists is that the patriarchs of the Old Testament had no knowledge of the dogma of the unity of God. According to certain critics, the teaching of the Bible that the antediluvian patriarchs were monotheists, must be looked upon as fabulous and legendary. According to others, monotheism made its first appearance in the eighth, or even only in the seventh century before our era, that is in the epoch of the great prophets who are looked upon as the real originators of monotheism. This doctrine, they pretend, is a product of evolution and of the progress of ideas among the Hebrews. At first they had only one local, national religion, which became in time a universal religion, under the influence of prophetism.

The arguments certain Rationalists make use of to establish the above theory are derived from circumstances connected with the sanctuary at Bethel and Betyles; other critics find in the Teraphim, or small idols, which Rachel had stolen from her brother Laban, the evidence of patriarchal idolatry; the majority, however, support themselves especially on the laws of evolution.

Thus in the first place, according to the enemies of the Bible, there was a Chanaanite sanctuary at Bethel which the Hebrews adopted when they invaded Palestine, and of which they made a place of worship until the reform of Josias.

Apart from the answer we have given already in a preceding chapter in regard to this point, we will add: the precise indications of the Bible are in formal contradiction with this theory. Bethel was primitively called Luza (Gen. xviii, 19); Abraham had raised an altar there in honor of the true God (Gen. xii, 8); it received its name Bethel from Jacob, after the vision he had in this place, as we will evidence further on. In the time of the Judges we can see, indeed, the Ark of the Covenant established at Bethel, but only as a temporary institution, and undoubtedly on account of the war (Judg. xx, 27) then being waged. From this time until the schism of the kingdom, there is no further mention of a sanctuary erected at Bethel. True, after the schism, Jeroboam erected two golden calves and located one at Bethel, where he raises an altar and institutes a priesthood (3 Kings xii, 29 ff.) But this precisely proves that before Jeroboam, Bethel was not a sanctuary, but that it was selected for this purpose because of its having been the place of a sanctuary in a period more remote. Moreover, the action of Jeroboam cannot be looked upon as in accordance with the Hebrew religion; it was a schismatic and idolatrous action, and above all, a political measure intended to keep away the Israelites from Jerusalem, whither they considered themselves bound to go, because here was located the only legitimate sanctuary. The political system would have been of very short duration, had Jeroboam left his subjects free to go and sacrifice at Jerusalem, and had he not completed his work by a religious schism. Since that time we find Bethel mentioned as a sanctuary, but it is a schismatic sanctuary, which proves nothing more against monotheism and the unity of the sanctuary at the Hebrews, than the different schisms of Protestantism prove against the unity of the Catholic Church.

In regard to the "Teraphim," we have to observe that nobody knows exactly in what they consisted. Nothing proves that they were real idols, which they considered as real deities; perhaps they were only amulets, magic or superstitious objects, which implied in no manner the belief in the plurality of gods. But supposing that Rachel adored them as gods, what would result from this? That Rachel had not completely abandoned the polytheistic belief of Mesopotamia; not at all that Jacob, who proscribed the Teraphim (Gen. xxxv, 2, 4), himself was a polytheist.

When Jacob, the Rationalists argue, did not adore the Teraphim, he at least committed an idolatrous act in consecrating Betyles. It is sufficient to read Genesis in order to be convinced that there is nothing that savors idolatry or polytheism in the action of Jacob. Whilst going to his uncle Laban after having had the mysterious vision, " Jacob, arising in the morning, took the stone, which he had laid under his head, and set it up for a title, pouring oil upon the top of it, and he called the name of the place Bethel — house of God. (Gen. xviii, 18-19.) Later, God having appeared to the patriarch in the same place: " Jacob sets up a monument of stone in the place where God had spoken to him, pouring drink offerings upon it, and pouring oil thereon, and calling the name of that place Bethel." (Gen. xxxv, 14-15.) In these two passages, the stone (or stones, for in the second place there were perhaps several) is called, not *bétyles*, but *masêbâh*. This is an important point to be noted. The word *masêbâh* in Hebrew may signify column, stela, statue, monument, raised object in remembrance of an event; it is not an ærolite, and much less is it an idol. Consequently, it is impossible to draw any conclusion from the erection of these *masêbâh* by Jacob against the purity of his monotheistic belief; in his history, like in that of Abraham, Isaac, Joseph, Moses, Josue, Judges and of the first kings, we meet nothing that is in opposition with monotheism.

The God of the Hebrews is not a local God, but the universal God, the master of heaven and earth which He has created, the God of man whom He created after His image (Gen. i, 26-27), the "Judge of the entire world" (Gen. xviii-xix), the "God of the spirits of all flesh" (Num. xvi, 22; xxvii, 16). In the numerous oracles of the prophets against the foreign nations, Jehovah appears to us as God of Egypt, of Chaldea, of Assyria, of Phenicia, as well as of Palestine, but the prophets did not conceive the idea of monotheism. The God of the Pentateuch is no national God, He is also the sole God and the God of the whole world. The first eleven chapters of Genesis occupy themselves with humanity in general. The Decalogue is not a particular code, but a universal code. The love of the neighbor is not only the love of the Israelites, but the love of all men (Lev. xix, 18, 34). The Bible alone teaches us the unity of all mankind, and thus it alone teaches universal fraternity, by informing us that we all have one and the same Father who is God. As it is our Saviour who has taught us to say: Our Father who art in heaven, it is the first chapter of the Bible which teaches us the truth expressed by these words. It is also the Pentateuch which teaches us that the true God has no sensible form which can be represented by any image, because He is above all material forms and the Being par excellence the "One Who Is."

As a matter of fact, the avowed or concealed principle upon which the infidels support themselves, who deny the primitive monotheism of Israel, is the principle of Evolution. They refuse to admit a primitive revelation, and they pretend that the religious ideas have progressed as have the sciences and arts, the plants and animals, according to the Darwinian theory. But history gives the lie to their assertions. The first men have been monotheists, and their descendants, instead of progressing in religion, fell away more and more, until the coming of Christianity. George Rawlinson has devoted an entire work to the study of this important fact, and this is the conclusion he arrives at: "The historic review which has been here made lends no support to the theory that there is a uniform growth and progress of religions from fetichism to polytheism, from polytheism to monotheism, and from monotheism to positivism, as maintained by the followers of Comte. None of the religions here described shows any signs of having been developed out of fetichism, unless it be the shamanism of the Etruscans. In most of them the monotheistic idea is most prominent at first, and gradually becomes obscured and gives way before a polytheistic corruption. In all, there is one element at least, which appears to be traditional, viz., sacrifice, for it can scarcely have been by the exercise of his reason that man came so generally to believe that the superior powers, whatever they were, would be pleased by the violent death of one or more of their creatures. Altogether, the theory to which the facts appear on the whole point is the existence of the primitive religion, communicated to man from without, whereof monotheism and expiatory sacrifice were parts, and the gradual clouding of this primitive revelation everywhere, unless it were among the Hebrews." (G. Rawlinson, "Ancient Religion," p. 175.)

CHAPTER XV.

THE BOOK OF EXODUS.

A PORTION of the events related in Exodus and Numbers are miraculous and supernatural. For this reason negative criticism rejects them *a priori* without waiting to make an examination. Other events of this epoch do not offer the same objectionable feature, but the Rationalists refuse equally to admit them in order to be able more easily to deny the prodigies in the others, and to deprive Moses of the composition of the Pentateuch. What in their eyes is sufficient to destroy credence in the accounts of the sacred historian, is the improbability. According to them we cannot accept as veracious accounts which are shocking common sense on each page.

1. THE PERSECUTION OF THE HEBREWS IN EGYPT.

E. Reuss does not dare to deny openly that the Hebrews could not have been persecuted in Egypt, but many details, in the account of this event, appear to him very contestable. This is what he says: "The events contained in the Books of Exodus and Numbers are they related by a contemporary and eye witness? The account commences by stating that, after having passed through a period, more or less long, of prosperity, the Israelites established in Egypt found themselves exposed to attacks and persecution by the nationals who were afraid of them, and who by all kinds of means endeavored to weaken them, especially by employing them at hard labor on the public works. There is absolutely nothing improbable in this. We know from other sources that there have been in Egypt numerous dynastic revolutions, and that foreign rulers, probably Semitics, ended by being overpowered by native aspirants. We can understand that the colony which had come formerly from Canaan became involved in the defeat of those who had been their protectors. However, we have to admit that we find here only a partial evidence of such an event which, if proved, would have to be admitted as readily explaining the change of fortune of the Israelites in Egypt." ("Die heilige Geschichte und das Gesetz," vol. i.)

The Book of Exodus expressly states that the new king who persecuted the Hebrews "knew not Joseph" (Ex. i, 8). The author does not enter into details, precisely because all the readers at that time knew very well that the Hyksos or Shepherd Kings had been expelled by the native Pharaohs, and because it was sufficient for him to briefly indicate this revolution. The Hyksos were not simply the protectors of the Hebrews, as Reuss says, but they were of the same race, and both had in Egypt the same interests, consequently, they had to make united resistance to the native kings in the war which the latter had made against the conquerors of Lower Egypt; they had also to undergo the evil consequences of the defeat. The hatred of the Egyptians against the Asiatics who had held, during several centuries under their power, the most beautiful part of Egypt, is revealed by a very great number of monuments. It required not less than one hundred and fifty years of war for the Egyptian patriots to triumph completely over the power of the Hyksos. Yet the Pharaoh Ahmes, their conqueror, was obliged to grant to them, according to Manetho, a capitulation which permitted the rest of the hostile army to withdraw into the countries of Canaan and of Aram. It was quite natural for the Israelites to defend in the ranks of the Hyksos, the land which they had received from the munificence of the latter in the time of Joseph. Some of them must have accompanied their compatriots to places in Syria where they took refuge after their defeat. This is confirmed by a monument of Karnak. It proclaims that between the death of Joseph and the exodus, the Pharaoh Thotmes III had warred against other enemies in Palestine, those termed in the royal list as Jacobel and Josephel, that is, we believe, descendants of Jacob and Joseph. Indeed, we read in the list of the people or tribes, which comprised the allied army defeated by Thotmes III at Mageddo: *Jakobaal, Josepal* (Cf. I, Par. vii, 21-24).

The role which the Israelites must have played in the last war of the Hyksos explains easily how the conquering Pharaohs must have treated the Israelites, who had been conquered with the ancient invaders. They kept them in bondage, like many other prisoners of war of whom there is mention in the hieroglyphic monuments, because they were in need of them to assist in the erection of public works, and kept them under a strict surveillance to prevent them from increasing in too great a number, and from uniting with their former allies in the event of their return to Egypt with hostile intentions. Moses does not speak of these facts, because it was not his aim at all to make known the reasons the Pharaohs had to persecute his brethern; to attain his end, he had to dwell on the grievances of the Israelites against the Egyptians, not those of the Egyptians against the Israelites. Therefore, he speaks as he should speak, but the Egyptian history completes for us what he passed by in silence, and by revealing to us which did not enter into his plan to relate, it shows us how everything related in the Sacred Text agrees with the original monuments.

E. Reuss continues: "Moses is not sufficiently exact; he continually speaks of the King Pharaoh, but does not tell whether it is the one whose daughter found him in the river, or the one from whom he asked the deliverance of his people." Let us observe, in the first place, that it is false to state that Exodus names the King of Egypt "the King of Pharaoh;" never are these two names joined together, never is the title Pharaoh given as a proper name. When the text designates the Pharaoh by his title, and never otherwise, it is easy to discover the reason; it is because the Israelites called him always thus, and because the first consideration of Moses was to write for their understanding. To-day the governor of a State is almost always referred to as "the governor," and a great number of citizens trouble themselves very little to know his real name. It was the same in regard to the Pharaohs among the children of Jacob; they ignored for the most the list of the pompous and complicated names which the sovereigns displayed in their public acts, and Moses had no desire to enlighten his co-religionists on this subject; for them it was simply the Pharaoh.

Besides Reuss insinuates falsely that "the statements of Exodus are never precise in dealing with proper names." Just as Genesis makes known to us the names, when it is necessary, e. g., that of Putiphar master of Joseph, and of Asenath, his wife, daughter of another Putiphar, priest of On, so also Exodus names the two midwives, Sephora and Phua, who refused to execute the barbarous orders of the Egyptian sovereign, as well as the two cities at which the Hebrews were obliged to work — Ramses and Pithon.

When Moses "does not speak of the persecutor of the Hebrew except under the title of Pharaoh," he describes him in features and characteristics sufficiently distinct to recognize in him Ramses II, the conqueror so well known under the name of Seostris. This terrible monarch who persecuted so cruelly the Hebrews, and from whom Moses had to fly, we know well through the numerous monuments with which he has covered Egypt, and by means of his numerous statues, and even to-day the photograph of his mummy can be seen in the Museum of Boulak.

"The account of Exodus proves quite a very poor knowledge," says Reuss (*opus cit.*), "of the situation of the Israelites in Egypt, in the epoch when Moses came to be their leader. In telling that the new-born boys should be drowned immediately by the Egyptians, the narrator supposes that the Israelites were all established on the shores of the Nile. . . ." Moses does not suppose that the Israelites were all established on the shores of the Nile, but he supposes, and with good right, that there were all over Egypt canals fed by the Nile, which served to irrigate the lands, and which served also, in time of persecution, as convenient places to dispose of the newly born. If Reuss had studied the works on Egyptiology, in order to attack the Pentateuch, he would have read that Ramses II had caused the repairing, even in the Land of Gessen, of a canal of which the hieroglyphic texts speak, and the remains of which were discovered at a recent date. He connected the Nile with lake Timsah, and this canal traversed the center of the country which the Hebrews inhabited. The papyri describe the city of Ramses, *Pa-Ramessu áa-náht,* and they speak of the practice of fishing in the waters that watered it, although this city was not on the shore of the Nile.

"From where did the Hebrews get their meat in Egypt," asks Reuss. And he answers: "From their flocks undoubtedly." In this he deceives himself. Here, like in so many other places, the critic is not sufficiently schooled in the Egyptian customs, nor the customs of the nomad shepherd, and hence his error. The flesh which the Israelites regretted (Num. xi, 4, 13) whilst in the desert referred to the numberless birds which swarm on the shores of the Nile and its surrounding canals. We see them often figuring in the Egyptian monuments, which serve us here as illustrations and commentaries. All those who know the habits of the shepherd peoples, are well acquainted with the fact that they live chiefly on milk-food, and that they eat the meat of their sheep only under very exceptional circumstances. In Egypt the children of Jacob must have eaten very little of what we call butcher's meat, but if they wished to have a feast, they also indulged in various kinds of fowl and game. This is what they regretted in the desert, where their eyes, they say, beheld only manna. For the proof that their appetite did not crave beef or mutton is evidenced in the manner by which God ceased their murmuring: He sends them quail, not cattle.

Besides we must not forget that the Hebrews did not complain only for not having any longer pots full of fleshmeat like those of the Nile valley; they are equally afflicted for being deprived of the vegetables of Egypt, of the onion and leek, which were indeed the favorite nourishment of the Egyptians, as is evidenced by their figured monuments. The Israelites were deprived of both the meat and vegetables of their liking while in the desert. What is more natural than their regretting the foods to which they had long been accustomed? This feature, far from being improbable, as Reuss pretends, is, on the contrary, like so many others, a striking confirmation of the perfect knowledge which the author of the Pentateuch had of Egypt. How could an author, living in Palestine, several centuries after the events, have known so well the tastes of the inhabitants of the Nile valley? The figured monuments in this, as elsewhere, show us the exactitude of the geographic picture of Exodus, and we have certainly the right to conclude, from a description so accurately corroborated by hieroglyphics, that the writer has seen the places which he has so perfectly described, and that he has lived in the midst of the people whose customs and usages are so familiar to him. The progress of Egyptian archæology, far from revealing errors in the accounts of Moses, have caused, on the contrary, the disappearance forever of doubts which had no other foundation than ignorance. All the modern discoveries strikingly confirm the veracity of the sacred historian.

2. THE EXISTENCE OF THE TABERNACLE.

According to the infidel critic, the Tabernacle did never exist. The Temple of Jerusalem and the Tabernacle are one and the same thing. Behold what Renan says in regard to this subject: "The existence of the Tabernacle is only a childish imagination, worthy of the jokes of Voltaire, its conception supposes the absolute contempt of the reality, its implements are whimsical, the whole is contained in the mind of Ezechiel, the man of plans which cannot be realized, and of chimerical combinations." ("Les origines de la Bible.") But are these big words arguments? Will it be sufficient for the infidel, who does not wish to believe in the existence of the great pyramid, to affirm that this structure is the invention of a childish imagination, which counts reality as nothing? That it is evidently an idle fancy to suppose a mass of stones, 696 feet wide, 426 feet high, and consisting in all of about 78,000,000 of cubic feet and destined to serve as a tomb for one single man? The monument of Cheops will be, nevertheless, a reality always existing. The Tabernacle of Israel differs from it in this that it does not exist any longer, but it differs also from it in this that it was of much easier construction, and at the same time something more reasonable. Indeed, what could be more natural for a religious people like the children of Jacob than to desire a tent which served them as a temple, and which replaced in some measure those grand temples which they had seen in Egypt? What could be more easy than to satisfy their desire? Living themselves in tents, accustomed, like all nomads, to see their chief dwelling in a larger and more ornamental tent than those of the other members of the tribe, they were influenced by the very circumstances of their habits and customs to erect the Tabernacle in honor of Jehovah and to ornament it with all the magnificence they were capable of.

The doubters assure us, with a large supply of affirmations and without giving the least positive proof, that the temple of Solomon was the prototype of the Tabernacle attributed to Moses. But how does it come that all the Books of the Old Testament teach us the contrary? "The authors of the Pentateuch," they say, "have invented the Tabernacle in all its parts." But in fact if it had existed only in their imagination, how could they have ventured to make it play such an important role in the sacred history? The Pentateuch is, so to say, full of the Tabernacle from beginning of Exodus. It is not only once or twice that it is mentioned, it is a multitude of times. Before the erection of the definitive Tabernacle, there is a provisional Tabernacle (Exod. xxxiii, 7; cf. xxxv, 10-11). With what object could the latter have been imagined by the last Jewish writers? After the portable temple had been constructed it is connected with all the events, and its name appears on each page in Leviticus and Numbers, as in the last chapter of Exodus. Also in the Book of Josue, the Tabernacle occupies the same place as in the last Books of the Pentateuch.

The great argument furnished against the authenticity of the Tabernacle is that it was impossible to construct it in the desert of Sinai. Now, nothing is more contrary to the truth, and nothing shows better the veracity of the sacred historian than the details which he gives us of the building of the Tabernacle. These details indicate a perfect knowledge of Sinai and its means, and a Jewish writer, writing several centuries after the exodus, could not have imagined the construction of a Tabernacle like that of Moses.

The sacred narrator tells us that the solid part of

the Tabernacle, and the furniture destined for the worship, were built of *sittim* wood, that is, of seyal accacia. An author who would have written in Palestine would never have supposed this, for the reason that they did not use this wood in the interior of Canaan, where it could not be found. The peninsula of Sinai produces scarcely more than three kinds of trees: the palm tree, the tamarisk and the accacia. Of these three kinds, the first two are unfit for cabinet work; the seyal accacia possesses, on the contrary, all the properties which Moses could desire for the use he wished to make of it; its wood makes excellent planks; it is, moreover, very light, an invaluable quality for the Israelites who were obliged to carry along the Tabernacle with them, each time they changed camp; despite its little weight, this wood is very durable and preserves itself for a long time; finally, it becomes darker as it grows older, and takes on a kind of ebony hue; hence, it is fitted for the manufacture of very beautiful furniture, such as the Hebrews constructed in the desert for the usage of worship.

The employment of seyal accacia in the desert of Sinai confirms, therefore, the exactitude of the accounts of Exodus. We find another confirmation of the veracity of the sacred historian in an analogous detail which refers also to the Tabernacle. We read in Exodus that they covered the Tabernacle with skins of *tahas*, a word which is generally agreed to-day to mean the dugong. This large aquatic herbivorous mammal of the order of Sirenia is common in the Red Sea, where they are found in shoals. The Israelites, in a place bordering the sea, were easily enabled to obtain this fish, but in Palestine they could not have done so.

A final objection is made against the building of the Tabernacle. There are, it is claimed, works of art which it was impossible to manufacture in the desert. As for the metals used in the manufacture of the implements of the Tabernacle, the bronze was furnished partly by the women who possessed looking-glasses of polished metals, and who offered them for the manufacture of the brazen laver (Ex. xxxviii, 8); the gold and the silver were given in abundance by the Israelites of every condition who possessed precious jewelry, which, as our modern museums still evidence, was superabundant in Egypt. During their sojourn in the land of the Pharaohs the children of Jacob necessarily accumulated a vast amount of this jewelry, which they augmented, as Moses relates, during the preparations for the exodus (Ex. iii, 23; xi, 2; xii, 35-36). He states that the Israelites carried off many precious objects which they received from the Egyptians.

CHAPTER XVI.

THE TEN PLAGUES OF EGYPT.

THE children of Jacob having gone down to Egypt with their father, multiplied themselves in such a manner, that the Pharaoh, fearful of an uprising, and in order to prevent the Israelites from becoming too numerous, forced them to engage in the most severe labor that tyranny could devise. God wished to deliver His people from this bondage, and He sent to the

Pharaoh, Moses and Aaron to demand of him in His name that the Israelites be permitted to depart. The Pharaoh refused, notwithstanding the proofs which Moses furnished to prove the divinity of his mission. Moses then called on God for aid, and He descended on the Egyptians the series of afflictions which are termed the Ten Plagues of Egypt. Formerly, the Rationalists not wishing to admit the supernatural character of these plagues, were obliged to denounce the Mosaic account as a preposterous fiction. Modern research in the antiquities of Egypt, has established that what Moses related could have happened, and, moreover, some of the things he mentions are still noticeable in that land of marvel. Thus frustrated, the infidel attack was turned in another direction to arrive at the same result. They admit the plagues as historical, but deny their miraculous origin.

This assertion is as false as the first; undoubtedly some of the scourges mentioned in Exodus had already been experienced by the Egyptians, and under different circumstances were due to natural causes, but on this occasion everything goes to prove that they were supernatural; their sudden production and cessation on the order of Moses; their intensity, and especially the fact that the land of Gessen, inhabited by the Hebrews, experienced none of the horrors; add to this the astonishment of the Egyptians who, although accustomed to these scourges, on this occasion saw evidenced in them a proof of the divine power permitted to Moses; and, finally, compare these plagues with the testimony furnished by Egyptiology and the comparison will establish their authenticity, and also their supernatural origin.

FIRST PLAGUE.— " Moses," states the Book of Exodus (vii, 20), " lifting up the rod struck the water, and it was changed into blood." The Nile is annually subject to a phenomenon which resembles this scourge. At the period of overflow, the water becomes brackish, and the river takes on that appearance which has given it the designation of the " Green Nile; " while in this condition the water is not fit for drinking purposes. Then, at the end of three or four days the water changes in color to a dark red hue, " more similar " says Osborn, " to blood than to any other matter with which I should compare it." This is the phenomenon of the " Red Nile," during which period the water is very healthful and palatable when used for drink. When this phenomenon became known, the Rationalists cried out: " Behold the Mosaic scourge! It produces itself annually, and in the most natural manner." Some Catholic apologists maintain that the first plague of Egypt was the phenomenon of the Red Nile, but produced by Moses in a miraculous manner.

The opinion of these Catholics does not seem to be well founded, and we have the right to reject absolutely that of the Rationalists. In the first place, we say: You acknowledge, as we do, that it was not more difficult for God to have changed the Nile into blood, than to have given it only the appearance of blood. Let us, therefore, agree with the Fathers and Doctors of the Church, who have always seen in the first plague a transformation of the water of the Nile into real blood, and some of these Fathers and Doctors were well acquainted with Egypt and the phenomenon of the Red Nile.

In fact: 1. The effects of these plagues were noticed at Tamis, where the court was located, and where Moses was pleading for the deliverance of his people. Now, the phenomenon of the Red Nile does not occur on this site in the present day, and it is, therefore, evident that it did not do so in the time of Moses, at least, not in the natural manner of this annual event. 2. It is in July, generally, that the Nile becomes red; now, we know, through Exodus, that the tenth plague took place at the beginning of April (xii, 18), the seventh in March (ix, 31), and the second, seven days after the first (vii, 25). A comparison of the time between these three plagues indicates that the ten plagues were separated from one another only by intervals of about seven days, and that, consequently, the changing of the Nile took place in February, a month in which the phenomenon of the Red Nile never occurs. 3. "The fishes that were in the river died, and the river corrupted, and the Egyptians could not drink the waters of the river" (vii, 21). These are circumstances of the Mosaic miracle which the Rationalists cannot explain by their hypothesis, because the water of the Nile is never more healthful than at the period of the Red Nile. The red water or blood which the Nile became, under the stroke of the rod of Moses, cannot, therefore, be explained by natural causes, but by the admission of a miracle.

SECOND PLAGUE.—This plague was an invasion of frogs; a real scourge, peculiar to Egypt, which fact helps to establish the authenticity of the Mosaic account; but it was also a supernatural manifestation at the same time. In fact: 1. Egypt was never infested with these animals as it was in the time of the second Mosaic plague, on which occasion the frogs entered the apartments, covering the floors and furniture, and the utensils of household usage; all facts which suppose an immense number of these animals which behaved, moreover, in a manner entirely foreign to their instincts and habits. 2. The time of the year when frogs are most numerous in Egypt is that which follows the overflow of the Nile, whilst the invasion produced by Moses preceded the inundation. 3. The frogs appeared all on a sudden, when Aaron stretched forth his hand over the water (viii, 6), and they departed at the moment fixed by the Pharaoh himself, and besides, the supernatural character of the scourge was acknowledged by the Egyptians, as evidenced in the request of Pharaoh to Moses to rid the land of that pest.

THIRD PLAGUE. — At the stroke of Aaron's rod "there arose *sciniphs* (gnats and flies) on man and beast." The word *sciniphs* used in Exodus (viii, 13-17), apparently means various poisonous flies and insects. Origen considers *sciniphs* to refer to swarms of mosquitos (Hom. iv). The Greek Bible, translated by Jews who, like Origen, lived in Egypt, uses the word "*sciniphs*," which not only applies to comparatively harmless insects, but also to winged pests, which were fatal even to horses and cattle.

Whatever may be the meaning of *sciniphs*, one thing is certain that immense swarms infest Egypt, and Moses makes use of some kind of insects to compel the Pharaoh, always obstinate in his refusal, to permit the Hebrews to depart.

FOURTH PLAGUE. — The mosquitos were followed by flies not less insupportable (viii, 24). The foregoing observations apply also to this plague. The abundance of flies in Egypt confirms the historical character of the account; the fright of the Pharaoh, and the concessions which he commences to make to Moses, show very well that there was something supernatural in this plague, where they again witnessed the hand of God.

FIFTH PLAGUE. — Pharaoh having retracted his promises, after having been delivered from the scourge of the flies, God struck the animals of the Egyptians with a disease which caused them to perish in great numbers. Here again one cannot deny the supernatural character of this plague, although the epizoötics may be frequent in Egypt; the Biblical plague begins and ceases at the precise moment designated by Moses, and Pharaoh himself testifies that the animals belonging to the Hebrews were exempted from it (xi, 7). The land of Gessen was spared equally from the sixth plague.

SIXTH PLAGUE.—In the sixth plague the hand of God descended still more heavily upon the Egyptians, for now they themselves were smitten. The pest with which God miraculously inflicted the Egyptians in this scourge attacked all the Egyptians without exception, high and low, rich and poor. Even the magicians were not spared. Its miraculous character was evidenced by the fact that it arose at the precise moment when Moses, by the command of God, took ashes and threw them into the air, under the eyes of the heart-hardened Pharaoh.

SEVENTH PLAGUE.—All these afflictions were without effect in obtaining the release of the Israelites. Moses went to the king and addressed him thus: " Tomorrow at this same hour an exceedingly great hail shall take place, such as had not been in Egypt from the day that it was founded, until the present time; men and beasts and all things that shall be found abroad, and not gathered together out of the fields, which the hail falls upon, shall die " (ix, 18). The Pharaoh frightened promised to grant to Moses all he desires if he will stretch forth his hand and cease the plague.

EIGHTH PLAGUE.—The work of destruction began by the hail, was completed by an immense invasion of locusts. The ravages which an army of these innumerable and voracious insects create when they invade a fertile field, are summed up in the epigrammatic utterance of Vigouroux: " Before them a paradise; behind them a desert." The invasion which took place in this epoch was much more dreadful than any that had ever been experienced, and it arrived at the hour, and with the intensity foretold by Moses. The Egyptians were astounded; seldom had they felt this scourge, and never in so terrible a manner. The entire population felt the effect of this plague. Pharaoh was humbled and submitted, but only to become obstinate again.

NINTH PLAGUE.—The obstinacy of the king was punished by a ninth plague: darkness so thick that it could be felt, figuratively speaking, covered the land of Egypt (x, 21). The supernatural features of the ninth plague are: its instantaneous production, in accordance with the command of Moses, the exemption of the land of Gessen, and the duration of the scourge.

TENTH PLAGUE.—As Pharaoh seemed determined to resist the divine command, the Almighty finally, as it were, prepared a decisive stroke. The exterminating angel destroyed all the firstborn of the land of Egypt, from the firstborn of the Pharaoh, who sitteth on his throne, even to the firstborn of the handmaid that is at the mill, and all the firstborn of beasts (xi, 5). Here the supernatural character of the scourge cannot be questioned, even if the exterminating angel would have employed natural means, like pest for instance. With regard to the historical accuracy of the tenth plague, it is confirmed by the Egyptiological discoveries: the monuments reveal to us that Menephtah, the Pharaoh of the exodus, had associated with him on the throne his eldest son; but they also give us to understand that his son died before his father, because this firstborn called himself Menephtah, and the successor of the Pharaoh bore the name of Sethos.

From all we have related it is evident that the authenticity of the Pentateuch is clearly established, and that it is not in the history of the Plagues of Egypt that ammunition can be obtained to destroy its veracity. On the contrary, all research confirms the Biblical narrative, and we can say once more that the finger of God was there.

CHAPTER XVII.

THE CROSSING OF THE RED SEA.

THE route followed by the Hebrews when leaving Egypt, and the spot where they crossed the Red Sea, has given rise to many inquiries and controversies. From the apologetical point of view, the only one which occupies us here, we enter the discussion to refute the systems which tend to deprive this event of its miraculous character.

1. According to M. Brugsch, the Hebrews passed from Egypt into Asia, not by way of the Red Sea, but by the Isthmus of Suez; from here they passed along the Mediterranean Sea. Now, in this locality there are many lagoons called Serbonis, which are separated from the Mediterranean only by a long and narrow strip of land; it was upon this narrow road where the Hebrews found themselves, when the Egyptians wished to recapture them. During this attempt, that is, while the Egyptians were in pursuit of the Hebrews, a high sea arose and, engulfing this jetty or isthmus-like projection, swallowed up the enemies of the people of God.— We have to reject this theory for the following reasons: 1. In order to establish it, the author is forced to have recourse to descriptions and geographical identifications which are absolutely imaginary, as posterior voyages have proven. 2. Exodus does not speak of a passage on the shores of a sea, but of a crossing of the sea, which is something quite different; moreover, it does not speak of the Mediterranean, but of the Red Sea; it is true that Exodus designates this sea Yam Souf, " sea of weeds;" but it is thus that this sea is called in the Old Testament, and it is certain that this name is that of the sea called Red Sea by the Greeks. Lake Serbonis, whatever Brugsch may claim, cannot have been this " sea of weeds," for its waters are inimical, as are those of the Dead Sea, to all lacustral vegetation. 3. Finally, the result of this theory would be to destroy the miraculous character of the Biblical account: " The miracle," says Brugsch, " ceases then to be a miracle;" he adds, it is true, that Provi-

dence plays its role nevertheless therein, and that his theory is orthodox; but this is a declaration which his adherents themselves do not take as serious.

2. Thus, one of the reasons which compel us to reject the theory of Brugsch is that it destroys the miraculous character of the passage of the Yam Souf; indeed, this character is unquestionable, and hence, we must, in considering other theories, which have attempted to locate the place of the miraculous passage of the Red Sea, distinguish two things: the place and the character of the passage. As to the exact place, we do not need to discuss that here, but as to the supernatural character of the event we cannot say like Josephus: " Let each one think about it what seems best to him." Du Bois-Aymeé, Salvador, etc., wished to behold in this fact only a purely natural event. They suppose that the passage was effected by fording a sort of high ground which the low sea had left partially uncovered. The only evidence on which their theory is based, is that there still exists two fords at the extreme northern or northwestern point of the Red Sea. To overthrow this hypothesis two observations are sufficient: 1. " The water," says the Sacred Text, " was as a wall on the right and on the left hand of the Israelites;" now in the hypothesis of Salvador, it is quite the contrary; the water would have been below and not above the Hebrews. This detail is very important, for it is impossible to sensibly liken a wall to a ditch. 2. The Red Sea was crossed by more than two millions of men, encumbered with numerous herds; in supposing that they formed in files of a thousand men each, it would have required at least one full hour before the whole column could have entered the sea, and about four hours to

effect the crossing. Can any one sensibly maintain that this could be done within the space of the sea-tide? This is inventing one prodigy to reject another, and, moreover, it is torturing a text in order to make it state something that it does not contain.

CHAPTER XVIII.

MYTHIC SYSTEM.

ACCORDING to the Rationalistc criticism, all the personages of Genesis, and particularly Adam, Eve, and the antediluvian patriarchs, are only mythical. It would take too long to point out what the infidels have written on this subject, but fortunately it is not necessary to do so. It is useless to refute their fantastic hypotheses as to the myths; nothing is more convenient and easier. Certainly it requires the mind of a Rationalist to suppose that Noe or Abraham are solar myths, Sara and Agar lunar myths, but nobody in the world can refute the existence of Adam, Noe, Abraham and Sara. This is the actual powerless condition of the rationalistic criticism; an important fact to be borne in mind.

There are, however, timid or shallow minds, predisposed to doubt, who feel themselves troubled, or even shaken in their convictions, because they are told that Adam, the first man, is Zeus *kataibates*, that is, a Jupiter descending upon earth in the lightning, or a Hephæstos (Vulcan), a Dionysos (Bacchus) and a fugitive Hercules expelled from paradise and what not?

These minds, so easily affrighted, seem to forget that, on the one hand nothing is easier than to behold at leisure, in a real personage, images and types without number, and that on the other, these images, these types prove absolutely nothing against the historic reality of this personage. The only conclusion one may have the right to draw from this, is that the author or authors possess more or less ingenious imaginations; but to doubt that Adam has existed, because a rationalistic exegetist has imagined that the first man represented Apollo or the sun, is the same as if one, in the ages to come, were to doubt that Louis XIV ever reigned over France, because some mythologist would affirm that this great king, who was termed Le Grand, and to whom was given the sun as an emblem, was nought in fact but a personification of the sun, typifying by his early triumphs the victory of the rising day-orb over the darkness; representing in the acme of his glory the noonday acme, resplendent in the heavens; and symbolical in his declining years and death, of the expiring monarch day, at length overcome by his enemy night. The rationalistic exegesis is not a scientific free agent; it sways with the oscillations of the infidel philosophy; it undergoes its vicissitudes; one might say that it follows the caprices of infidel fashion. At the present hour the craze is mythology, and the rationalistic criticism, in accordance with its habitual custom, has transplanted the meteoric or solar explanations of the ancient fables into the domain of the Scriptures, and thus we are amazed to hear that the famous personages of the Old Testament have been transformed into myths, solar heroes, clouds, tempests, etc. But we must not mistake the appearance of science for its reality.

The mythomania is a real illness of our epoch, and many savants, whom one might expect to be above its influence, have not escaped contamination. Some have fallen into exaggerations which is not out of place to point out. Certainly the efforts to determine the origins of the polytheistic religions and their myths, is deserving of encomium; but here, like all over, the abuse is blameworthy. This mythomania has evolved from the discoveries made within the last fifty years in the linguistics, and in the comparative mythology. Formerly almost nothing was known of the origin of the myths which relate the adventures of pagan deities; they were merely considered as pagan follies. The study of the Vedas gives the key to many stories of the Greek, Germanic, Asiatic, etc., mythology; here we discover real myths in the full sense of the word, metaphorical pictures of the storm or of the action of the sun, of the light, etc. Immediately enthusiasm exaggerates the bearing of the discovery, and the sting of free thought entering into the subject, it is concluded that the myths were solely poetic fictions, and, moreover, that all religion, at least the supernatural portion, is founded on myth, and has no more substantial basis. At first this mythologic research was confined to the pagan religions, but audacity and desire to invent soon applied the system to the Old Testament, to the Gospel, and to all our sacred books. The Vedas of India became henceforth the first expression of religion; all else had been borrowed from India, all was founded on the myths pertaining to the sun, the clouds, and the other phenomena of light. Adam, Abraham and Samson, for instance, were ranked in the category of the solar heroes; the serpent of Genesis was looked upon as that of the stormy cloud of the Vedas. Christ himself became a mythic hero ; his death was the disappearance of the sun in the twilight, his resurrection the retun of the sun in the spring or in the aurora, etc.

The danger of this system, in such great favor at the present day, is very considerable. The claim of philosophy and of geology would still permit Christianity to exist, but the mystic system annihilates it. Christianity is for its followers only a phase of mythology ; a superior religion like some others, but inferior in several respects. The danger is so much the greater, because the mythic system parades before the eyes of many as a real conquest and striking discovery ; it opens the way to new ones, and invites one to display his perspicacity in discovering new myths. Among the mythological researches there is an inconceivable infatuation, a real mania. With them a faint analogy immediately establishes a myth. We will evidence this by quoting a few examples :

The Hindoo gods, which we find among the Greeks and Latins, seem to be in reality only personifications of the sun and of the planets. So, also, the great Egyptian god, Ra, as well as the Chanaanite deity par excellence, Baal, are both the sun. Now, because these orbs have been personified in the polytheism of India, Egypt, Chanaan, Greece, Rome or Gaul, the conclusion is deducted that the Biblical patriarchs, Isaac, Jacob, Esau, are also personifications of heavenly bodies. Where is the connection ? Where is the proof ?

The history of Samson and of Dalia is, it is claimed, also a solar myth : it is the sun disappearing before the night. Samson, the giant, is the sun ; his hair, which causes his strength, are its rays ; his name Shamshon is an alteration of the sun's name, Shemesh. Dalia, who attracts him, upon the bosom of whom he sleeps and who robs him of his hair, is the night into the bosom of which the sun disappears, and which robs him of his rays. Dalia is an altered form of Dah-leihah (the night). Finally, the temple of the Philistines overthrown by the blind hero, is the temple figured by the clouds stopped in the horizon, and penetrated by the setting of the sun. The sun withdrawing itself crumbles down and disappears. On account of these analogies, they refuse all historic reality to Samson.

CHAPTER XIX.

CAIN, CAINITES AND SETHITES.

Cain

THE polygenists, in order to deny the unity of mankind or human species, appeal to the account of Genesis (iv, 14), where it is said that Cain was afraid that every one that would find him might kill him. But, say the Rationalists, when there existed no other men but the Adamites, how could Cain, after having committed his fraticide, be afraid to be killed by those he would meet? We can answer that it was because Cain could not ignore that the men would become multiplied, and since the remorse of conscience renders man suspicious and uneasy, what is there astonishing of being afraid, whenever the children of Adam would have become more numerous.

But, continue the infidels, how could Cain build a city? What workmen did he have? What citizens to people it? Here one attaches to the word "city" a meaning which it does not possess in Genesis (iv, 17.) The translators render by "city" the Hebrew word *'ir*, because this is the meaning one generally attributes to it, but one is much mistaken when he understands by the *'ir* of Cain a city in the actual sense of the word. To show how the difficulties they wished to raise against this Biblical episode are without foundation, it is sufficient to inquire about the real meaning of the Hebrew word. Now, behold how Gesenius, a Rationalist himself, explains it. He derives *'ir* from the verb *'our*, "to watch, to oversee," and adds: "This word has a very extensive meaning, and applies itself also to fields, fortifications, watchtowers, places under guard. . . . In Genesis (iv, 17), we must not understand a whole city, no more than a cave, because a cave is not built, but a camp of nomads, protected by a ditch or trench against the attacks of wild beasts" ("Thesaurus linguæ hebracæ," p. 1005). Cain, therefore, did not build a city, properly speaking, but a "watch-place, or watch-house, a place of refuge," in which he believed himself secure against those that might seek his life. Such is the true explanation of this passage of Genesis, and it is only in abusing the ambiguity of the badly understood word "city" employed in our translations, that one can derive from it, either the existence of non-Adamic men, or the impossibility or improbability of the fact itself.

CAINITES AND SETHITES.

A great number of Rationalists maintain that the genealogy of the children of Seth and that of the children of Cain (Gen. iv, 17-24 and v, 1-31) are only one genealogy. They pretend that the two genealogical tables of the Sethites and of the Cainites had formed at first only one, which was divided into two parts, as now presented, at quite an early date. The alleged proof of this is, that two names are identical in both lists, and several more are similar to each other. It is also claimed that the Israelites inserted into their sacred writings two traditions of different origin relating to the antediluvian patriarchs, the one of which considers Elohim-Jehovah as God, and Adam as the first man; the other admitted, they say, the Babylonico-Egyptian god Seth, and as first man, Enos; the descendants attributed to Adam and to Enos were the same, so that the two lists, differing in their origin, were identical in their content.

The statements formulated against the two genealogical lists of Genesis have been refuted by several exegetists and Assyriologists. One thing in connection with these rationalistic assertions will occur to any thinker not blinded by prejudice, and that is that the resemblance which the negative criticism pretends to discover in the patriarchal genealogies is purely artificial. In that of Seth, from Adam to Noe, we have ten generations; in that of Cain we have only eight. To find the same number, Reuss, a Rationalist, suppresses Adam and Seth in the Sethite genealogy, although the text names them expressly. Hence, it is only by the help of an artifice, contrary to the testimony of Genesis, and we can add also, contrary to the Chaldean tradition which had equally preserved the list of ten antediluvian kings, that one has an equal number.

But the divergence is not only in the figure of the generations, it is also noticeable in the account.

Whatever the summary may be, the differences which exist between the two genealogies show that they have always been distinct. The one gives particular details of Henoch, the other of Lamech, that of the Cainites being that of the reprobated by God, does not contain the duration of their life ; while, on the other hand, that of the Sethites, the elected by God, denotes the duration of their life. Thus, there exist more differences than resemblances between the two lists : there are more names on the one side than on the other ; the arrangement is different, and the details are not the same in both ; the interpretations of the names, which are said to be identical, are distinct. What more is needed to establish that these genealogies are not the same ?

CHAPTER XX.

LONGEVITY OF THE FIRST MAN.

THE longevity of the first men, who attained until nine hundred and sixty-nine years, has furnished quite early material for objections against the historical character of Genesis.[1] In the first century of our era, Josephus makes the attempt in his " Jewish Antiqui-

---

[1] Adam lived 939 years; Seth, 912; Enos, 905; Cainan, 910; Malaleel, 895; Jared, 962 (according to the Samaritan text, 847); Mathusalem, 969 (Samaritan, 720); Lamech, 777 (Samaritan, 653; Septuagint, 753); Noe, 950. Beginning with Noe the duration of life becomes gradually shorter until the time of Moses.

ties" to justify the Biblical account. Several Fathers of the Church, among others St. Augustine, do the same during the centuries following.

In our days, all the infidels reject the long duration of life of the antediluvian men. "It is difficult to believe," says Winer, "that a man could have lived seven hundred to eight hundred years." And Winer refuses to accept, not only this longevity, but also the different explanations by which they have tried to reduce it to about ordinary proportions. Reuss does the same. The hypotheses to which he objects are the following: Hensler has admitted a year of three months from Adam until after the Deluge; of eight months from Adam until Joseph; of twelve months since Joseph. Rask has supposed that until Noe months and years were synonyms. According to Lesueur, the years of the Septuagint, since the creation of the world until Abraham, must be reduced to Chaldean sosses, each soss containing sixty days. Other savants have supposed that the figures of the genealogies of Genesis did not designate the duration of life of each patriarch, but a period of civilization. Thus, according to Bunsen, the numbers which indicate at what age the family chiefs had their eldest sons and how long they lived afterwards, are posterior additions, marking cycles; the primitive text marked only the duration of their life, and they personified an epoch, so that we must understand that they have lived from seven hundred to nine hundred years, not by themselves, but by their race, in which they survived. Gatterer has maintained an opinion which approaches that of Bunsen: he believes that the names of the patriarchs designate not persons but tribes.

All these hypothetical explanations are subject to many difficulties. It is possible, undoubtedly, that the primitive years were not years like ours, but we cannot reduce them to one or six months. St. Augustine had already observed with just reason, that Seth having engendered at the age of one hundred and five years, and Cainan at seventy years, if we were to take the years for simple months, would reduce them to the unacceptable number of ten or seven years.[1] The mention of the seventh and of the tenth month in the account of the Deluge[2] shows, besides, that the year was composed at least of ten months. The cyclic system, proposed by Bunsen, and accepted by some Catholics, does not cause the same objections, but one can hardly bring forward any proofs in its favor.

Hence, we can admit only, purely and simply, the account of Moses. In accord with him, all the ancient traditions attribute to the first men a longer life than to their descendants. Not only Manetho at the Egyptians, Berosus at the Chaldeans, Mochus at the Phœnicians, but Hesiod, Hecateus, Hellanicus, Acusilaus, Ephorus and others of the Greeks speak of the longevity of the first men. In the Hindoos and Chinese, we find traces of an analogous remembrance. The Zend-Avesta makes to live Yima, the first man, more than thrice three hundred years. It is the same in America, where the traditions of the aborigines relate that the ancient men lived until their members were used up.

They refuse to admit the longevity of the patriarchs in alleging that it is physiologically impossible. But

---

[1] De Civ. Dei xv, 12, 1 vol. xlv. col. 450.
[2] Gen. vii, 11, viii, 4-13.

is this so certain? Has actual biological science the necessary resources to solve the question with full knowledge? This is at least very doubtful. We ignore the constitution of the primitive men. So many changes in the human organism have produced themselves on account of the formation of the races, the influence of the surrounding, heredity and crossings, that these notable changes may have effectively modified the duration of life. A savant who has made a special study of the question has remarked: " Nothing in the organs, in the functions or properties of the bodies indicates what their duration is. . . . It would not be at all contrary to reason, nor to the laws of the organism that man, under cover from illnesses which trouble the harmony, or from exterior violences which break the mechanism, would live several centuries. The long life of the patriarchs was a more rational fact, more in relation with the laws of physiology than the short existence of man who peoples the earth to-day."[1]

CHAPTER XXI.

THE ANTEDILUVIAN GIANTS.

THE sixth chapter of Genesis relates that " after men began to be multiplied upon the earth, and daughters were born to them, the sons of God, *benê ha-Elohîm*, seeing the daughters of men, *bennot ha-âdam*, that they were fair, took to themselves wives of

---

[1] Dr. P. Foissac, " La Longevite humaine," Paris, 1873, p. 346-347.

all which they chose. And God said: My spirit shall not remain in man forever, because he is flesh. . . . Now, giants, nefêlêm, were upon the earth in those days. For after the sons of God went in to the daughters of men, and they brought forth children, these are mighty men of old, gibborêm, men of renown " (Gen. vi, 1-4).

This short passage has given rise to numerous objections. It contains obscure allusions. Who were the sons of God and the daughters of men? Who were the *nefêlêm* and the *gibborêm?*

The *nefêlêm*, according to the common interpretation, were giants, although the root of this word *náfal*, to fall, renders its etymology difficult to explain. Their name is, therefore, mysterious; as to their history, it is quite unknown. Scripture, which alone could give us an account of them, teaches us nothing except their name. It does not even tell us anything of their genealogy. It is repeatedly affirmed that they were offsprings from the union of the sons of God with the daughters of men, but the text does not say so. We read only therein that "there were giants upon the earth," and that after the sons of God had united themselves with the daughters of man, they brought forth gibborêm. This latter word has been rendered like *nefêlêm*,. as giants, in the version of the Septuagint; it is, however, very different from it, and implies solely the idea of force, not of high stature. The original text establishes no direct genealogy between *nefêlêm* and *gibborêm;* nothing proves that there existed two species of *nefêlêm* (giants), those which have preceded the marriage of the sons of God with the daughters of man, and those which have been the fruit thereof. Hence, the Rationalists may state whatever they please in regard to this subject; we are not called upon to defend the Bible in subjects of which it does not speak.

In regard to the existence of giants, many ancient traditions have preserved the remembrance thereof. The Assyrian monuments represent frequently the hero Izdubar. The Titans are famous in Greek mythology. India, Persia and Germania have traditions of primitive giants. The Mexicans relate that in the second age, Tlaltoniatuh, or age of the earth, giants were annihilated by a catastrophe which overwhelmed the world. According to the Peruvians, in ages past giants invaded their country who became guilty of all kinds of crimes, and who were punished by death on account of their immorality.

CHAPTER XXII.

THE SONS OF GOD AND THE DAUGHTERS OF MAN.

THE infidel critics, and a great number of Protestant writers, maintain that "the sons of God" who took into marriage the daughters of men, were no other than angels, and from this they conclude that we have to do here with a fable. They can allege in favor, not of their conclusion but of their interpretation, the testimony of a certain number of Fathers of the Church, and several did not fail to take advantage of them.

Indeed, we acknowledge that Jewish and Christian interpreters have believed that the sons of God were angels. But those Fathers and ancient ecclesiastical writers, who, by the sons of God, have understood the angels, have been led into error through the wrong opinion which they had about the nature of the celestial spirits, to whom they attributed a body like ours, and through the unjustified belief in the apocryphal Book of Henoch, which made them forget the saying of our Saviour that the angels do not marry (Matt. xxii, 30). The infidels pretend, it is true, that we must not be surprised when the first Christians have believed in the reveries of the Book of Henoch, because, according to them, the Apostle St. Jude also believed therein, and thereby taught the faithful in his Epistle to venerate this fabulous writing as the word of God. These consequences do not flow at all from the words of St. Jude, and it is even uncertain whether the Apostle knew of this apocryphal writing. But supposing that it was known to him, even supposing that he quoted the same, his quotation would prove in no manner that he believed that the sons of God were angels. Henoch has prophesied: " Behold, the Lord cometh with thousands of His saints to execute judgment upon all."[1] Such are the expressions of St. Jude. He may have borrowed this prophecy from tradition, not from a written text; but, however this may be, his language contains no allusion to the question we treat here, and in no manner can one allege his testimony in favor of Lactantius and Tertullian, who attributed to the angels a body like ours. Even supposing that he would have praised the

---

[1] Jude 14-15. Cf. Henoch, i, 9. The Book of Henoch relates that certain angels, sent by God to guard the earth, were smitten by the beauty of the daughters of men, taught them witchcraft and finery, *lumina lapillorum, circulos ex auro*, as Tertullian expresses himself, and, being banished from heaven, had sons three thousand cubits high and gave birth to a race of celestial and terrestrial demons.

Book of Henoch, because it contains a true fact, it would not follow at all that he approved all that is contained in this apocryphal writing.

Besides the pretended testimony of St. Jude, the infidels make appeal to another argument, which they borrow from philology. The *bene Elohim*, or sons of God, they tell us, designate the angels in Job and in the Psalms,[1] therefore, also the sons of God in Genesis are angels.

Because the expression *bene Elohim* signifies the angels in the poetic Books of Job and of the Psalms, it does not follow that it has also this meaning in the Pentateuch. Never, neither in the Pentateuch, nor in any other writing in prose of the Old Testament, are the angels called sons of God, although there is often question about them; but they are always named messengers of God, *male'ak*.[2] If, therefore, Moses would have wished to speak of angels in chapter six of Genesis, he would have designated them under the name of *male akûn*. By the sons of God he would understand those who have remained faithful to God, as also by the daughters of man, he understands those who abandoned themselves to human passions. The expression itself designates simply creatures of God, made to his image; hence, it does not become less to men than to the angels; also the men are called sons of the Most High, in the Psalms; sons of Jehovah, their Elohim, in Deuteronomy: sons of the living God, in the prophet Osee (Ps. 81).

Let us note one point more in ending these observa-

---

[1] Job. 1, 6; ii, 1; xxxvii, 7; Ps. xxix, 1; lxxix, 7 (Hebrew).

[2] Gen. xvi, 7; xix, 1; xxiv. 7, 40; xxviii, 12; xlviii, 16; E. xxiii, 20, etc.

tions. It is worthy of remark that Genesis does not reproach the antediluvian men with acts of idolatry, but only of their immorality. There is no trace of idolatry, nor of false gods before the Deluge, which is a mark of antiquity and of authenticity. The author of the Pentateuch and of the prophets would not have failed to reproach their impiety to the great criminals who perished in the Deluge, had they been guilty thereof, for their chastisement would have served as example to the inspired writers in their objurgations against the idolatry of their times.

CHAPTER XXIII.

THE NOACHIAN DELUGE.

1. THE sixth, seventh and eighth chapters of Genesis are occupied with the story of the great Flood which destroyed the whole human race, save only eight souls in Noe's family. The Flood, which is described as overstepping the highest mountains, is made to appear as an extraordinary manifestation of God's vengeance on the human race for its wickedness. The account is in some respects peculiar. It is surprisingly diffuse, and abounds in repetitions — the same fact being stated and restated in different words. In chapter six God's action is declared to be due to the universal wickedness of mankind, and Noe and his family are said to be spared in reward of their righteous conduct in the midst of universal corruption. Then Noe is

charged to build the ark, and to take into it two animales of each kind. In sixth chapter, Noe is ordered to enter the ark, and take therein seven pairs of clean, and two of unclean beasts, and also of the fowls of the air, seven and seven, male and female. The execution of the order is then related, and it is noteworthy that two pairs of both clean and unclean animals entered the ark. This fact of the animals and Noe entering the ark is again mentioned when the Flood burst forth. That this is an additional narrative, such as was usual with Semitic writers, appears from the use of the pluperfect. At length the waters of the swollen Flood rose to their full height, overtopping the highest mountains by fifteen yards, and destroying all living creatures under heaven. In forty days the Flood reached its height, and for one hundred and fifty days it so stood. Chapter eight describes the end of the Flood. One hundred and fifty days after the Flood began, the ark rested on Mt. Ararat, and seventy-three days later the tops of the mountains came in sight. Forty days after, Noe sent forth a raven, and on every seventh day he thrice sent forth a dove. On removing the covering from the ark, he saw that the surface of the earth was drying; but fifty-seven days more elapsed before it was quite dry. At length God bade him quit the ark, in which he had abode one year and ten days — whether a solar or lunar year is not clear, but probably, according to the latest Hebrew calculations, the latter. Absolute accuracy in regard to numbers is hardly possible.

2. Fortunately, as in the case of Creation and the Fall, we possess, independently of the Bible, an account of the Deluge in the cuneiform inscriptions, which shed a flood of light on Genesis. The lay tablets are, it is

true, only copies from the seventh century B. C.; but the originals are pronounced by competent critics to be as old as the year 2000 B. C. The two accounts are of such a kind that they must have been drawn from different sources. In the Chaldean story which Abraham had brought with him from his own home, Noe is wrongly represented to have been near the sea (Persian Gulf), whereas Genesis and the ark presuppose the mainland. The Chaldean, also, would seem to have been conversant with two narratives, for he records the two episodes in Genesis vii, 16, with the difference, that it is Hasisadra and not God who shuts the door of the ark (ship). The Chaldean legend also bears traces of two passages at the end of chapter eight, and the beginning of chapter nine. It also tells how Hasisadra, after landing from the ship, offered acceptable sacrifice to the gods; wherefore they loaded him with favors. Nor is mention wanting of the three birds sent out in succession. External confirmation such as this is more valuable than myriads of external arguments, such as Jeovistic and Elohistic passages pointed out by the Rationalists, and shows conclusively that the story told in Genesis is not a subsequent fortuitous compilation from unknown documents. Moses learned the points of the story, and handed them intact and unaltered. In reading the Biblical story we are struck, not by the blending into one of two narratives, but by the lofty design, the moral theology that pervades it. In this, indeed, the finger of God is manifest.

3. Other traditions concerning the Flood need not here occupy our attention. They are to be found in almost all nations, especially among the Americans. "The tradition concerning the Flood," says Lenor-

mant, " is the universal tradition par excellence among all nations that have preserved the memory of the history of the primitive man."

4. The question as to the universality of the Deluge may be regarded from three points of view: in relation to the earth, to animals, and to man. Nowadays there can be no manner of doubt that the Flood did not overspread the whole earth. The old view now numbers adherents only among those who willfully shut their eyes to all collateral knowledge, and blindly put their trust in the literal sense of the text. An inundation of the whole earth to the tops of the highest mountains would require a volume of water so immense as to defy calculation. First of all, imagine a zone of nine or ten thousand metres in diameter girding the earth; then compare it with the sea, which has a mean depth of from two to three thousand metres; this will give some idea of the mass and weight of water required. It would require some twenty figures to express the number of cubic metres. This mass would have collected as quickly as it dispersed. To exclude the peaks of the Himalayas and Cordilleras because, being covered with eternal snow, they could afford no shelter to the animals, is to abandon the letter and to concede in principle the right to explain the text otherwise. The physical difficulties involved in a partial inundation that covered Mt. Ararat, a height of five thousand metres (if this mount, and not the whole mountain chain, may be exegetically considered the resting place of the ark),are, considering the configuration of Central Asia, far less for the inundation of the whole earth. Modern palæontology supplies many instances of the sea covering mountain ranges, and depositing animal remains at

the height of four thousand or five thousand metres. Hence, a partial Flood presents no difficulties.

By the story as told in Genesis we are not irredeemably pledged to this universality. The waters, it is said, inundated the earth, destroyed all things on the earth's surface, and submerged all the high mountains under heaven. But it argues a very imperfect understanding of the manner of speech adopted in Holy Scripture, to imagine that the sense is bounded by the letter. Naturally this interpretation was upheld until the catastrophe was looked at from its physical side. But once the question is viewed from a scientific standpoint, it becomes imperatively necessary to examine how far this explanation is a necessity. A little study of the Holy Scripture soon makes it clear that the sacred writers understood by "the earth," "the whole earth," the country in which they or their informant happened to be (Deut. ii, 25; iv, 19). Palestine is the whole earth, and Jerusalem the center of the world. Semitic writers delight in rhetorical generalizations (Cf. Gen. xli. 54, 57; 3 Kings x, 23-24; Mat. xii, 42; Is. xiv, 7, 26; Jer. iv, 23 ff.; xv, 10; Acts ii, 5), in magnifying the part into the whole. *Many* is put for *all*, *all* stands for *many*. From the informant's standpoint all seemed inundated; and we are perfectly justified in viewing these expressions from his standpoint. Nor do we thereby detract from God's wonderful work. For the waters of the deep, and the floodgates of heaven (i. e. the waters of the ocean, on which the land rested, from the earth's cavities, and from the clouds above) form so immense a volume that their aggregation for the purpose of inundation cannot have been a mere natural event, even if terrific waterspouts and tempests, with earthquakes and volcanic phenomena to boot, be dragged in as auxiliary forces.

5. How does the case stand in regard to animals. As to their fate the Bible seems to leave no loophole for doubt. "Every beast according to its kind," says Genesis, "and all the earth in their kind, and everything that moveth upon the earth according to its kind; and every fowl according to its kind, all birds and all that fly, went in to Noe into the ark, two and two of all flesh."

This passage was understood to refer to all animals, known and unknown, instead of referring to the animals known at the time of the Deluge. Thus, it becomes very difficult to explain, without multiplying miracles, how Noe could gather into the ark animals which were separated from him by the immense ocean, and how animals living, perhaps, on islands could return there after the inundation. The Deluge being, according to the Bible, a punishment for the sins of mankind, it follows that all men should perish in order to atone for their sins; but this was not true of the animals; hence there was no reason why they also should perish. Now, just as it is conformable to the rules of good criticism to understand by the "whole earth" the earth known at the time, it is equally correct to understand by "all the animals" only those which were known to Noe and Moses. Hence, we must admit that only those animals perished which were known to him at that time. These which Noe did not know, did not exist for him. We have no reason to suppose that God revealed supernaturally to Noe the existence of animals which he never had occasion to see, and of which he had never heard. Neither does anything prove that God ordered him to gather others than those which lived in his own country.

6. A less confident tone is, perhaps, becoming in discussing the partial character of the Flood in its effects on the human race. Genesis declares over and over again that the eight souls in Noe's family were alone saved. The legends, too, attest its universality. The Fijians have a tradition that eight, the Aztecs, that one or two survived. Deucalion and Pyrrha, according to the Greek tradition, Manu, according to the Indian, were the sole survivors. The very claim of being autochtonous implies this version. Is it, then, permissible to look at this part of the story from the narrow standpoint of the eyewitness, which the narrator has made his own? From the partial destruction of the brute creation, may we infer a partial destruction of the human race? It seems to be a natural inference, since the animals were punished on man's account. Such a solution would greatly simplify the difficulties, on which we have already touched as to the age of the human race (See Chronology) and which we have studied already. The absence of all tradition in Africa concerning the Flood seems to give strength to this supposition. In our days there are ethnographers, philologists, and palæontologists who hold either that the Flood affected human life only in its center, or that the Negroes were exempt, or that some only, probably the descendants of Seth, were destroyed. Harlez is not unfavorably disposed to this opinion, and the Jesuits, Bellynck and Delsaux, consider it, to say the least, compatible with faith. In favor of this opinion it is claimed that, according to Moses, the Cainites had long since gone forth from the land of Nod to settle in more

distant countries; that only Noachians were enumerated in Moses' table of peoples; that there were none but Semitics at Babel; hence, that none but the Sethites were destroyed. But, even critical questions aside, these are caverns too darksome to be ever exposed to the full light of day. Nor do Acts xxvii, 26, and Romans v, 12, tell against this position. The Apostle is merely teaching that the human race is one in descent; the Deluge he does not even mention.—The question becomes more complicated in dealing with passages in the New Testament that contain a special reference to the Flood. In Luke xvii, 27, Jesus compares the time of His second coming with the time of Noe. Noe's contemporaries tossed all warnings to the winds, and lived jauntily and heedlessly until the Flood came and destroyed all. The same expression occurs in the parallel verse 29, which narrates the destruction of all the people of Sodom, save Loth. In both cases the "all" must, it seems, be constructed literally. In I Peter iii, 20, it is distinctly said that eight souls were saved by water: "In the ark (of Noe) few, eight souls, were saved by water." "God preserved Noe, the eighth person, the preacher of justice" (2 Peter ii, 5). The unanimous tradition and the universal teaching of the theologians, interpret these words of St. Peter in the sense that only eight persons were saved i. e.: Noe, his wife, his three sons, and their wives. No sufficient reason is given for departing from the interpretation accepted by the Church until at present. The formation of the various human races, and the numerous languages spoken upon earth in dim antiquity, the progress of civilization had made long before Abraham, we are told, are so many proofs that some races escaped the

Deluge and preserved their characteristic features, language and arts. The supporters of this opinion suppose that a relatively short time elapsed between the Deluge and Abraham, but in the treatise on Biblical Chronology it can be seen that very probably this time is longer than was generally supposed.

CHAPTER XXIV.

ETHNOGRAPHIC TABLE; OR, DISPERSION OF THE NATIONS.

BEFORE circumscribing definitely its historic structure, in order to speak only of his race, Moses casts a general glance on the families issued from Noe, and draws a great picture, which the Rationalists themselves cannot help admiring. The tenth chapter of Genesis is not only a geographical table of the nations; but it is also an ethnographic tableau, or more correctly "ethnogenic," because it contains a genealogical and linguistic tree. However, it is not complete in its details.

The world which it describes, when one considers only the nations mentioned, without paying attention to their ramifications, is bounded on the north by the Black Sea, and by the mountains of Armenia; to the east, it extends scarcely beyond the shores of the Tigris; to the south, it reaches the Persian Gulf, embracing Arabia and the Red Sea, and enters into Abyssinia in passing through Egypt; in the west, it embraces the oriental islands of the Mediterranean. Moses did not desire to give a complete picture of the universe, nor the genealogy of all the peoples issued from Noe; he has depicted only those which it was most important for the history of religion and of revelation.

The exactitude of the teachings contained in the tenth chapter of Genesis is generally admitted. The critics are divided only as to the time in which the events occurred. Francois Lenormant makes the following reflections on the subject: " It is the most ancient, the most precious and the most complete document about the distribution of the peoples in the world of the most remote antiquity. One has even the right to consider it anterior to the epoch of Moses, for it presents a state of nations which the Egyptian monuments show us already changed on several points in the epoch of the exodus. Moreover, the enumeration therein is made in a regular geographical order around a center which is Babylonia and Chaldea, not Egypt or Palestine. It is, therefore, probable that this tableau of the nations and of their origin forms part of the remembrances which the family of Abraham had brought along from Chaldea, and that it represents the distribution of the peoples known in the civilized world at the moment when the patriarch left the shores of the Euphrates, that is, two thousand years before the Christian era " (" Hist. ancienne de l'Orient," vol. iii, p. 15).

Objection is made to the exactitude of the ethnographic table of Genesis, where the Phœnicians are ranked among the Chamites, when they were, in reality, a Semitic people, spoke a purely Semitic idiom, and differed but little from the Hebrews. It is true that the Phœnicians spoke the Semitic language, but it cannot be concluded from this that they were not Chanaanites. There are peoples in Europe who speak a Romanish language, derived from the Latin language, who, nevertheless, do not descend from the Latins.

It is a known fact that the Phœnicians of Palestine came, as Herodotus expressly testifies (ii, 89), from the Erythrean Sea, and consequently from a Cushite country. When later on we behold them speaking a Semitic language, it proves that they, like other peoples coming in contact with greater or more numerous races, met and mingled with the Semitics, and ended in being absorbed by them.

As to the dispersion of the Semitics, the opinion most generally received until lately is that the Semitics, after the Deluge, dwelt first in Armenia. But in what place did they separate to form different nations? Genesis, according to the universal interpretation of the narrative of the Tower of Babel, tells us that it was in the plain of Sennaar. Some modern savants object, at least indirectly, to this assertion, which, they claim, places the cradle of the Semitics in Arabia. Although it can be maintained that this opinion is not absolutely in contradiction with Genesis, because the Semitics could have at first settled down in the Arabic peninsula, and because the family of Abraham might have gone up afterwards from here to Ur in Chaldea, the natural sense of the text is little in accord with this theory. For a long time it was believed that all mankind had been gathered in the plains of Sennaar, during the epoch of the building of the Tower of Babel. To-day the exegetists admit quite willingly that there were only the descendants of Sem, at least the majority of them. The posterity of Noe had, indeed, become too multiplied in this epoch since the time of the Deluge, as to be enabled to keep itself entirely in the Babylonian plain.

Egypt was peopled for too long a time before Abraham to make it possible to suppose that there were not yet many inhabitants in the Nile valley, a few generations previous to Abraham, etc. The most of the arguments produced in favor of the antiquity in regard to man may be applied in the present case. Finally, the language of Moses refers only to the race of Sem. Hence, it is only according to this interpretation that we have to justify it.

The historic documents in existence do not furnish direct proof that all the Semitics lived together in the Babylonian plain, but philological research furnishes the means by which this fact is indirectly established. Although the means may not always appear peremptory, they are of so much more value in the present question, since the adversaries cannot allege any others to controvert them: they contest the exactitude of the inspired account in the name of the linguistics; we will answer them in the name of this same science.

First let us remark, that we can divide the Semitics into two groups: the southern group, comprising the Arabs, the Himyarites and the Ethiopians or Abyssinians, and the northern group, to which belong the Chaldeo-Assyrians, the Chanaanites, the Israelites, and the Arameans or Syrians. They are distinguished from one another not only by location, but also by various peculiarities of language, and by certain religious traditions. From this it follows that the Chaldeo-Assyrians, the Hebrews and the Arameans descend from ancestors who, after having separated from the Arabs and the Ethiopians, have continued to live together until the present day. But anteriorly, the Semitics of the north and those of the south formed only one people. From the testimony of all the Orientalists without exception, all the so-called Semitic languages, the Hebrew, the Assyrian, the Aramean, the Ethiopian and the Arabic are only so many branches from the same stem; in fact, the vocabulary and the grammar are about the same; the triliteral roots and the principal grammatical flections are identical.

The most of the Semitists are also agreed that the Arab language approaches nearest the primitive language of the children of Sem; but some of these authorities, going still further, wish to conclude from this that the Arabs present the most pure type of the primitive Semitic, in their language, morals, customs and religious ideas. Following the same line of argument, the antiquity of the Arabic language proves that Arabia is the cradle of the Semitic race. It was from the north of Arabia, they say, or from Central Arabia, that all the Semitics spread: the Ethiopians and the Sabeans went towards the south, the Babylonians and the Arameans or Syrians towards the north.

They have recourse to more serious arguments than to such vague analogies. They maintain, in the first place, that the Chaldeans of Armenia are the same people as the Chalybes, and that they have nothing in common with the Semitics. This particular point matters little. The second part of their thesis, namely, that all the Semitics came from Arabia, is more important. The proof they give for this last assertion consists, as we have already remarked, in the claim that the Arabic language approaches most closely the Semitic mother tongue. It is there, they say, where the primitive type has best preserved itself, that we must seek the cradle of the race.

To this we answer that the conclusion is not legitimate. The Sanscrit and the Greek, among the Aryan languages, are those which approach nearest the primitive Indo-European language; nobody, however, thinks about concluding from this that India or Greece is the primitive cradle of the Aryans. The preservation of the Arab dictionary, and particularly of the grammar, in a relatively greater purity and integrity than those of the other Semitic idioms, explains itself easily through the geographical situation of Arabia. This peninsula, isolated from the rest of the world by surrounding seas and deserts, had little communication with the nations, so that the contact with foreign races was not sufficient to change its language.

Hence, it is logical to assert, from the peculiarity of the Arabian tongue, that the ancestors of those who speak it settled quite early in the peninsula, before the Semitic idioms had obtained the distinctive features which we remark in them to-day. On the other hand, the Babylonians and the Assyrians, modified their forms of speech, adopting the idioms of the foreign tongues, under the influence of the surrounding nations with whom they were in relation. The Arabs, living alone, faithfully retained their language like their morals and customs, so that the documents which we possess in language, although they date only from the sixth century of our era, approach more closely the language of the children of Sem than any other Semitic document and even more than the Assyrian documents, anterior to them by more than two thousand years.

Mr. Schrader has made an attempt, but without success, to dispute this explanation. If this were established, he says, the Arabs, in traveling from the cradle of their race into Arabia, should have modified their primitive characteristics, like the other Semitics, by coming into contact with the nations which they met on their route, in going towards the west or into the south.

We can show that this reasoning is not well founded. The Sabeans who established a great kingdom, had commercial relations with the other nations; the Ethiopians who passed from southern Arabia into Africa, modified themselves. indeed, and had a particular language. The Arabs of the north and of the center of the peninsula preserved intact their idiom and mode of life, imported from elsewhere, thanks to the little traveling they engaged in, and the isolation in which they lived. By immigrating from the shores of the Euphrates and Tigris into their new country, they had crossed a desert, and it is only necessary to refer to a map, to become convinced that they had only a short voyage to accomplish, and that they met too few strangers on their route to exercise upon them a sensible influence.

But it is not sufficient to refute the assertion of those who pretend to place the cradle of the Semitics into Arabia: we have to establish by positive arguments the fallacy of their statements.

With the help of philology we dispute the opinion which makes Arabia the cradle of the Semitics. By comparing the different Semitic languages, one can arrive to determine in the principal traits, the flora and fauna of the country which the Semitic race inhabited, before the separation of its different branches. In order that these could give to plants and animals the same name, they must have known these plants and animals in the countries where their fathers dwelled together. As to the names which differ in the diverse languages, they must be of posterior date: they have been borrowed in another time and in another country.

These philological premises presented are incontestable in the eyes of all the linguists. The Semitic languages, by comparative study, prove that Arabia is not the cradle of those who speak them. Indeed, all the languages give the same name to the camel, which consequently was known before the separation; on the contrary, they call the ostrich differently one from another. Therefore, the first Semitics did not live in Arabia, for the ostrich is a native of this country. The Arameans alone call the ostrich *ne'ama*, according to the Arab *na'am*, but they have borrowed this name from the Arabs, whose caravans coming from Mecca, brought feathers of this bird into their country.

The Arabic dictionary contains two other names of animals, that of the small jerboa, *yarbû*, to-day *jerboa*, and that of the lynx, *tuffah;* but these quadrupeds which belong particularly to Arabia, have no name in the other Semitic languages, whilst the ostrich is given another than its Arabic name, at least, in Hebrew, wherein this bird is called *yâ ên, ya'anah.* If the Hebrews had emerged primitively from the Arabic peninsula, as some suppose, they would never have forgotten the name of the winged animal which they had learned to know in their native country, nor would they have given it another name. The name of many other animals furnishes analogous arguments.

But when Arabia is not the cradle of the Semitics, where then was it? According to some Semitists, following the opinion current to-day, the race originated in Upper Asia, near to the cradle of the Aryans. To credit their statements, it was in the Upper-Hauran, in the west of Bolortag, on the plateau of Pamir, that the first Semitics lived in contact with the Aryans. Starting from here, and following the great water course, particularly the Oxus, they directed their path towards the west, passed to the southwest of the Caspian, and penetrated, by one of the narrow passes of the Elbouz, into the mountains of Media. From there they entered into Mesopotamia.

The first part of the route traced for the Semitic journeying is a pure hypothesis. Only one fact can be historically established: we first meet with the Semitics in Mesopotamia. To maintain the contrary, they appeal to the Semitic flora such as the dictionary of their language makes it known to us. According to them, the Semitic languages give diverse names to the palm and the date trees; the most ancient appellation, they say, to designate the date tree, *dikla*, is met among the Aramean tribes who lived in the plains of Babylonia. This affirmation is not exact. *Dikla* is not the most antique name of the date tree in Semitic, and the Arameans, in the primitive times, did not live in the plains of Babylonia; they spoke the Aramean in Babylonia, only after the Assyrian had become a dead language, a few centuries before Christ.

The primitive name of the date tree, in the Semitic language is *tamara*, as is proved by the Hebrew *tamar*, which we read in Exodus and Leviticus, and the Ethiopian *tamart*. The ordinary name of this tree in Arabic must be recognized in *nachl*, but tamar is used also, and designates especially the date, or in general, a fruit.

These facts proclaim the original country of the palm tree to have been situated in the lowland of the upper and middle course of the Euphrates and the Tigris, as it was there also where lived the animals the names of which we find in the Semitic language, and finally, it is in these places that the traditions of the Semitics themselves place their cradle, to the west of Holvan, in praise of whose palm trees the Persian poets have sung; it is there, indeed, that we must locate the primitive home of the descendants of Sem. It was there that they were all gathered before becoming dispersed to the south and west.

Besides, we must remark that all we know of the primitive flora of the Semitics confirms this conclusion. Chaldea does not abound in variegated plants, but those which we can consider as indigenous in the lowlands of the Euphrates and Tigris, namely, the many species of poplars, the tamarisk and the pomegranate, carry, as well as the palm tree, the same name in all the Semitic languages. On the contrary, the plants which grow in the temperate zones or on the mountains, the elm, the ash, the chestnut, the oak, the beech, the pine or cedar, either have diverse names in the different branches of the Semitic family, or have taken the same name only in a relatively recent epoch. Chaldea was a real granary of abundance, the barley and the wheat yielded wonderful crops. Also, the wheat, barley and corn are expressed in the same manner in all the idioms of the descendants of Sem, as are also the agricultural labors, the occupations of pastoral life, hunting and fishing. The same can be said of geographical situations, instruments, materials and metals.

CHAPTER XXV.

THE PATRIARCH ABRAHAM.

THE objections raised against the Biblical history of Abraham, can be reduced to three heads: 1. Origin: According to Genesis Abraham was born at Ur in Chaldea; emigrated to Haran, when God called him into the land of Chanaan by promising to him this land for his descendants.

Hitzig, a Rationalist, questions the Biblical record of the Patriarch Abraham. According to his statement the origin of Abraham is purely Hindoo. In order to convince ourselves of this it is sufficient to compare his name with that of Rama, the Hindoo god, and with the sanscrit Brahman. As to his wife Sara, her name reminds us of the nymph Saraju; therefore the Bible deceives itself in making Abraham a Semitic; consequently his history merits no belief; it is a myth.

This conclusion is not only a hasty, but an erroneous one. The name Abraham is so Assyrian or Chaldean, that we trace it in the list of the eponyms or magistrates of Ninive; furthermore, when we affirm that Abraham came from Chaldea, the language and customs which he brought with him must have left profound traces on his descendants. Now we are in a position to show that modern discoveries have established this to such a point that these coincidences cannot be attributed to chance, and sufficient to prove a common origin between the two peoples — the Hebrew and the Assyrian.

Let us briefly sum up these relations: 1. The Hebrew dictionary is almost the same as that of the Assyrian, at least for meaning of names which express ideas necessarily known in Abraham's time. God is called *Ilu* in Assyrian, and *El* in Hebrew. There are words in both languages almost identical, which designate the relations of family (father, mother, etc.); geographical terms (sea, river, star, etc.); members of the human body (head, eye, mouth, etc.); arms (arrow, lance, etc); metals, animals, etc. Moreover, we find other names, like those of fermented liquors, numbers, measures and calendar, which, by their similitude in both languages, show beyond doubt that the Hebrew civilization, outside its divine element, is only a detached branch of the Chaldic civilization. 2. The grammar of both languages is also the same. When Abraham left Mesopotamia the language had already arrived to its flectional period, and like all the Semitic languages had taken its definite imprint; consequently, we must be able to recover between the two grammars Assyrian and Hebrew features of resemblance numerous enough to permit a conclusion to a common origin. This has taken place in quite a remarkable manner.

We find here not only the general characters of the Assyrian are found in the Hebrew, but also the scarcity of abstract terms, poverty of the particles, poverty of the tenses and moods in the verbs, richness of form to explain in one verb the activity, passivity, causality, intensity, etc.; but we also discover therein ties of more direct relationship. We will mention a few examples: the personal, possessive or demonstrative pronouns are alike; rules of the formation of the gender, and the number of substantives are the same; similitude of the verbs and participles, seen in the verse recently recovered in Assyrian; the paralellism and even, certain rhym. Finally what completes the demonstration is that some Hebrew idioms, inexplicable for a long time, are now readily explained, thanks to the better knowledge of the Assyrian. Thus eleven is in Hebrew *aste'asar;* but when one knew that *'asarah* signified ten, we completely ignored the meaning of *aste.* Now the Assyrian explains the mystery: *'aste* or *es'tin* means one, and the Hebrew word signifies one and ten.

Although the close affinity of the two languages as exemplified here is not exclusive to both, for one can make a certain number with other Semitic idioms; it is certain, however, that no two languages are more intimately connected than the Assyrian and Hebrew. Besides this, when we compare the results obtained with the far-fetched etymology of Hitzig, one can easily see on which side the truth is. For more details see Guinie, " Lettres de quelques Juifs," 1827, vol. II., p. 346; Vigouroux, " La Bible et les Decouvertes Modernes," vol. I.; Delitzsch, " The Hebrew Language Viewed in the Light of Assyrian Research;" Opert. " Grammaire Assyrienne."

2. ABRAHAM'S JOURNEY TO EGYPT.

The twelfth chapter of Genesis relates that the famine caused Abraham to descend into Egypt. Almost all the circumstances of this account have been questioned by rationalists.

1. Before entering Egypt Abraham, fearing that his wife's beauty might cause his death, advised her to tell that she was his sister. This precaution has been made use of to calumniate the character of the patriarch, but

it is of itself proof that the episode is authentic, and has no foundation in myth. Moreover, it is true Sara was a near relative of Abraham, as Genesis relates (xx, 12). In the Oriental languages one employs the words brother and sister to indicate in a general sense near relationship; therefore, when Abraham did not tell the whole truth, he at least did not tell a lie.

2. Once in Egypt Sara is taken by Pharaoh. Abraham on her account was the recipient of marked favors. Pharaoh gave him numerous presents, among which were sheep, oxen, asses and camels. These gifts have served the rationalistic critic pretexts for attacks on the Bible, though modern research has verified the account.

There is nothing singular in this episode, as it is well known that the kings of Egypt, as well as those of other Oriental countries, have reserved the right to select or even force unmarried women to become inmates of their harems. Doubtless Pharaoh had many subordinate women in addition to his regular wives. A case in point has been brought to light by the evidence of an Egyptian papyrus which relates: A workingman had his ass taken away by an inspector; he reclaims it, and the case is taken before the Pharaoh who, after an investigation, decided in these terms: "He answers to nothing what one tells him. . . . Let them make a report to us by writing . . . his wife and children shall belong to the king. . . . Thou shalt give them bread." Is this not a case analogous to that of Abraham?

Again, it is asked: How could a Semitic like Abraham receive such a reception at the court of Pharaoh, and especially from a Chamite Pharaoh? This is another frivolous objection. Two Egyptian monuments have been brought to light which refute this and confirm the

Biblical record: 1. On a tomb is found represented the arrival into Egypt of Amu-nomads (of Arabia or Palestine), their chief calls himself Abschah (name analogous to that of Abraham); it is the famine that drove them into Egypt, and they are received with solemnity by the governor. 2. A papyrus preserved to us contains the curious history of Sineh: Amu or Egyptian, he enters the service of Pharaoh and was raised to high dignity; he fled, remains in Palestine for a long time, then returns, reenters into favor, and becomes counselor of the king with precedence over all courtiers. One can see the coincidence of the two accounts with the Biblical one.

But the chief points of attack are made on the presents which Abraham had received. "Behold," says Bohlen, "how the author of this account plays unfortunate; the horses were very abundant in Egypt, and he does not name them among the animals given to Abraham; in revenge the author quotes the sheep and the camels, very rare however in Egypt, and the asses one could not suffer there. How can we admit as authentic an account so full of errors?"

This is really a bold statement, independent of its recklessness, for the details of the sacred writer are borne out by historical facts. Sheep have already been represented on the monuments of the twelfth dynasty. We behold thereon, among other things, an inscription of three thousand two hundred and eight sheep, attributed to a sole proprietor. Of oxen, the geological diggings in the delta have brought to light from great depths their bones, and, according to the inscriptions, have served the same purposes as they do at present. From the times of the shepherd kings, the idolatry which the Egyptian priests taught the people was of a gross kind. Apis was worshipped in the form of an ox. Isis in that of a cow, and the history of the worship of the golden calf is familiar to every student. Asses are represented by herds on the tombs of the pyramids, the inscriptions attribute as many as seven hundred and sixty of these animals to one proprietor. Asses are also represented on the monuments of the fifth dynasty. About the camels — it is true, they are little represented on the monuments, but one cannot conclude from this that they were unknown to the early Egyptians. 1. Certain rules hindred the artists from representing certain animals, for instance, chickens and cats; a similar custom may have prevailed regarding camels. 2. It is certain camels were in Egypt at the time of the Ptolemies, though we do not see them on the monuments of that epoch. It might have been the same in preceding centuries. 3. The Arabs have employed camels from an early day, and surely their neighbors of Egypt must have known the use of these "ships of the desert," before the introduction of horses. 4. Some texts clearly prove that Egypt employed camels at an early epoch, and even taught them to dance. Salmanasar (in 857) quotes camels among the tributes paid by Egypt. 5. Finally, the geological diggings have unearthed bones from great depths, which belonged to dromedaries. The whole of these testimonies is so categorical that Chabas retracted his former attacks on the Bible.

The omission of horses which Bohlen criticises so triumphantly, is easily accounted for. Horses were introduced into Egypt only at the time of the invasion of the Hyksos, and appear in the hieroglyphics of that epoch — the eighteenth dynasty. It is generally conceded that Abraham's journey into Egypt took place during the twelfth dynasty.

3. ABRAHAM'S VICTORY OVER CHODORLAHOMOR.

Abraham returned to Palestine when Chodorlahomor, king of Elam, Amraphel, king of Senaar, Arioch, king of Ellassar, and Thadal, king of Guti, had conquered five Chanaamen kings, and led away among other prisoners, Loth, Abraham's nephew. At this news Abraham gathered three hundred and eighteen of his servants, pursued the conquerors, and delivered the captives. Such is in substance the account given in the fourteenth chapter of Genesis. This narrative also comes in for a share of rationalistic criticism by declaring it a fable. Knobel, however, in 1860, while acknowledging a historic tradition, found fault with the sacred author. He could not admit that the Elamites extended their empire so far in the time of Abraham, and must have been deceived by taking Assyrians for Elamites.

After Knobel, they even have denied all historical foundation to the Biblical account. Bohlen makes it appear that Amraphel is Sardanapel, Arioch, Arbaces and Chodorlahomor, Belesys. To believe Hitzig, the account of this campaign is taken from that of Sennacherib. Grotefend surpasses them all in cool assumption by stating that the Elamite invasion is merely an old Babylonian myth; supporting himself on the fantastic etymology which he draws from these names. He sees in Amraphel, the " spring," Arioch, the " summer," etc., and the five Chanaanean kings, only the five complimentary days of the Babylonian calendar. These statements, largely drawn from the imagination, are completely refuted by modern discoveries relating to the Elamite campaign.

The name Chodorlahomor or Kudur-Lagamar is perfectly Elamite. Kudur is met amongst all the names of Elam, and Lagamar is a deity, so that Chodorlahomor means "servant of Lagamar," and not "tie of the sheaf," as Grotefend renders it; as the country of Elam, subject to this king, its antique power is confirmed by discoveries made at Susa, the capital of the kingdom.

As to Arioch, king of Ellassar, Assyriology has furnished a most satisfactory result. We have recovered his name in that of Eri-Aku, king of Larsa; thus the name of the ancient king only found in Genesis, and treated as a myth by the critics, reappears to their astonished gaze inscribed on the monuments of a very high antiquity, in testimony of the historic character of the account in question. We add here that Arioch signifies "servant of the god moon," and not "lion," as Grotefend renders it, in order to make him a personification of the summer.

When the names of the other confederate kings have not yet been recovered, we are at least certain about their etymology. Grotefend translates Armaphel "great lamb," whilst this word means "the son is Emir." Thadal or better Thargal, signifies probably "great chief;" but in any case we cannot translate it "experience" or "setting of the sun," as Grotefend distorts it for the purpose of making Thadal the personification of winter. This far-fetched straining of versions, for the avowed purpose of fitting them to represent mythological or allegorical signs, and weaken Biblical history, cannot be upheld any longer in the face of facts acquired by science.

CHAPTER XXVI.

SODOM; THE ORIGIN OF THE DEAD SEA AND LOTH'S WIFE.

IT WAS in the time of Abraham that the catastrophe of Sodom took place. During a long time one did believe that this city, and the four other cities of the Pentapolis, had been submerged into the Dead Sea, and even that this sea dated only since this epoch. This is an error which is so much more important to point out, because the apologists of the eighteenth century have adopted and maintained it against the author of the "Questions sur l'Encyclopedie," who was right this time.

That what caused the commentators to believe that the Dead Sea deducted its origin from the catastrophe of Sodom, is because Moses tells us that Chodorlahomor defeated the king of Sodom in the valley of Siddim "which is the salt sea" or Dead Sea. From this they concluded that this sea did not yet exist in the epoch of the campaign of the confederate kings, but they interpreted the text in a wrong manner: they supposed that the valley of Siddim formed the whole actual bed of the Asphaltic lake. Now, this is not the case. This valley forms only a small part of the ground occupied to-day by the waters; the lake existed already before, and it became enlarged in the time of Abraham in submerging this valley.

It is generally admitted to-day, in spite of some contradictions, that the Jordan never emptied into the Red Sea, as it was believed in former times. However it may be in regard to this point, the Dead Sea existed already when Abraham arrived into Palestine. Genesis does not tell that the guilty cities were submerged into this sea; it assures us, on the contrary, that they were consumed by a rain of fire and brimstone, and thus destroyed; and the sacred writers teach us that the ruins of the cursed cities were visible on the shores of the Asphaltic lake. In what place were they situated? We do not know, and the opinions in regard to this subject are divided. To-day the most place them in the south. Besides, this is of little importance. It is sufficient to remark that the southern extremity of the Dead Sea is much less deep than the central and northern part, and that it is of more recent date. Therefore, one can admit that it goes back until to the epoch of the catastrophe. This is acknowledged by M. Lartch, one of the last savants who have studied the question on the site itself.

LOTH'S WIFE.

When the day had arrived that fire from heaven should destroy Sodom, the angels led away from the doomed city Loth and his family, giving them the following instructions: "Save thy life, look not back, neither stay thou in all the country about." But a rain of fire and brimstone having come to fall, the wife of Loth looking back was, in punishment for her disobedience, immediately turned into a pillar of salt (Gen. xix).

This history has furnished the pretext for many attacks against the Bible. The author of Wisdom tells us that in his time the pillar of salt still existed. "A standing pillar of salt is a monument of an incredulous soul" (x, 7). How could such an affirmation find grace before the Rationalists, especially Volney! The latter writing about the Dead Sea, the author of "Ruins" says: "We see there, at intervals, shapeless blocks which credulous eyes take for mutilated statues, and which the ignorant and superstitious pilgrims regard as a monument of the adventure of the wife of Loth, although it is not said that this woman was changed into a stone like Niobe, but into salt, which must have melted during the winter following."

Whatever Volney may say, we can without leaving ourselves open to either ignorance or superstition regard as authentic the episode related in the Book of Genesis. In the first place, we could explain by a miracle either the death of the wife of Loth, or the preservation of her transformed body until the epoch when the author of Wisdom lived. But it is not even necessary here to interject the miracle, properly speaking. In the neighborhood surrounding the Dead Sea, the atmosphere is as if saturated with salt, and this salt impregnates everything into which it can enter. The transformation of the wife of Loth into a statue must, therefore, be understood probably as a sort of saline petrifaction. It is not astonishing that such a statue could exist for a long time. "We came across," says Vigouroux, "near the Dead Sea, of masses of crystallized salt, having a height of from 40 to 50 feet, by 100 feet width at the base; among these blocks there is even one which the local tradition considers as the statue of which Genesis and the Book of Wisdom speak. When M. Lynch admits this tradition, without considering it as absolutely inadmissible, we can state that we are in no need to have recourse to it to justify the Biblical account; because this statue is no longer in existence to-day, it does not follow that it had disappeared when the author of Wisdom lived.

CHAPTER XXVII.

THE PATRIARCH JACOB AND THE MANDRAKES OF RUBEN.

THERE are two qualifications which are equally appreciated by the Orientals: force and cunning. He is not the less admired who triumphs over his enemies by the subtlety of his mind, than he who obtains the victory by the strength of his arm; and he who, being weak, triumphs through stratagem over the stronger, is praised not less than the brave who has struck down his antagonist with intrepidity. Among the nomadic people divided into small tribes, and often badly governed, where war is perpetual, and where murder and violence reign supreme, the smaller tribes, who are the most numerous, applaud rapturously the fox who carries the victory over the lion: it is the revenge of the oppressed against the oppressor. We find this sentiment among all nations of antiquity. Jacob is, as it were, the type of Oriental cunning. Weaker than Esau, his brother, or than Laban, his uncle, he triumphs over both by knowing how to bide his time, by watching for the opportunity to come, and when it does come, by knowing how to take advantage of it. The means which he employed to obtain his end were not always irreproachable; but when we judge his conduct, we must not lose sight of the fact that he made use of the artifices employed by those among whom he lived. Moses reports the whole with impartiality, and by making known to us the details of wisdom and virtue, he has not concealed the faults. While everything cannot be praised in the son of Isaac, the good, however, greatly outweighs the evil. Moreover, the critics least disposed to indulgence, as Stanley (" Lectures on the History of the Jewish Church," 7th ed. London, p. 45-46), after having judged Jacob severely, could not refrain from granting him justice in the end.

I. JACOB BUYS ESAU'S BIRTHRIGHT.

The first reproach made against Jacob, is for having taken advantage of Esau in a manner not at all praiseworthy and even unjust, in order to obtain from him his birthright. Esau, who could not withstand the cravings of his gluttonous appetite, when tempted by Jacob, who had in his possession a mess of pottage, exchanged his first birthright for this paltry pleasure, thus selling his right of inheritance, as related in Genesis (xxv). We are under no obligation whatever to uphold Jacob in this circumstance of his life, for he was not impeccable, and Holy Scripture, relating the whole with impartiality, does not approve the faults of the patriarchs, and of the saints of the Old Testament, because it reports them. The sacred historians are narrators, not judges. They do not directly laud the praiseworthy acts; neither do they blame the blamable acts; they limit themselves to a mere relation of the facts as they occurred without commenting good or bad. This is something to be borne in mind for a correct appreciation of the Sacred Books. "Generally," says St. Augustine, "the Scriptures neither approve nor disapprove; they leave it to us to criticise and to judge, by reconciling the justice and the law of God."

Besides, in the present case, the conduct of Jacob was as worthy of the attention as has been bestowed upon it. He had some reason to claim the first birthright, because Esau was his twin brother, and, moreover, we must do the justice to remark that he did not deprive his brother of his earthly possessions, deriving from the paternal heritage. Esau received from his father Isaac an equal share with Jacob, "the dew of heaven and the fat of the earth" (Gen. xxvii, 39), that is, the riches of this world; what Jacob particularly desired in his barter was only the spiritual blessing. Moreover, when Jacob on his return from Mesopotamia, desires to make presents to his brother, then Esau refuses to accept of his generosity, stating that he was quite rich enough himself, and we do not see that there had been any dispute between the sons of Isaac on the death of their father as to the subject of inheritance (Gen. xxxv, 9, 29).

2. THE BLESSING OF ISAAC.

What is more blameworthy in the life of Jacob, is the means he employed to surreptitiously obtain the blessing from Isaac. Listen to what Du Clot has to say

THE PATRIARCH JACOB. 299

on this subject: " Jacob, by the advice of his mother, deceives Isaac through a lie, in order to obtain the blessing intended for Esau. This was a fault on the part of both. We are not obliged to justify all the actions of the patriarchs, because the sacred writers who report them do not approve of them. Neither is it necessary to assert that these actions were types, figures, mysteries, which announced future events; this would not be sufficient to excuse them; as also, on the other hand, even unworthy actions and condemnable in themselves, could have, however, after having been committed and without having ever been approved, become figures of other future events. These unworthy actions of the patriarchs, could not have been committed in order to figure other events, but, after they had taken place against God's will who always condemns what is evil, they could have been designated to figure and to represent posterior events.

" According to these principles, we can understand that God, who had announced His designs regarding the two children of Isaac and Rebecca, did not wish to derogate from them to punish the two guilty ones. Isaac himself, after having learned of the lie of Jacob, did not revoke his blessing; he confirmed it. " because he remembers " the promise God had made to Rebecca; he says to Esau: " Thy brother has received the blessing which I had destined for thee; I have blessed him, and he shall be blessed, and thou shalt be subject to him " (Gen. xxvii, 33, etc.). When Jacob departed for Mesopotamia, Isaac renewed to him the blessing and the promises made to Abraham (xxxviii, 4). We must not conclude from this with the infidels that " God rewarded the deceit of Jacob;" there is no question here of a "reward," but of the execution of a promise which God made before Jacob was born. Also, Jacob was punished for his lie, through the fear with which, for a long time, the threats of Esau inspired him, and through the exile which he was obliged to undergo" (Du Clot, " La Sainte Bible vengée," vol. 2, p. 234-236).

3. CAUSES OF JACOB'S VOYAGE.

According to the Rationalists we have in the actual text of Genesis a flagrant contradiction in regard to the motives which determined Jacob to go into Mesopotamia: it is said, according to one narrator, in order to fly from the wrath of Esau, whom he had supplanted by obtaining the paternal blessing, that Jacob makes the journey; according to another, on the contrary, it is to marry a woman of his family, and not a Chanaanite (Gen. xxvii, 41-46; xxviii, 1-2).

The Rationalists have often made analogous objections against diverse parts of the Pentateuch and against the other Biblical books; but with how little foundation, only a little attention is necessary to weigh these assertions in their true value. Might not more than one motive influence only one action? Victor Hugo, in the preface of the " Roi s'Amuse " and in that of " Lucréce Borgia " gives two different explanations of the first of these pieces. Does it follow from this that the two explanations are not from the same author, and even that both are not true? So also in Genesis, the truth is that Jacob goes to Mesopotamia with a double motive: the first, to withdraw himself from the wrath of his brother Esau; the second, in order to take a wife from his family.

4. THE SHEEP OF JACOB AND THE MANNER HE OBTAINED THEM.

Genesis (xxx, 25, 43; Cf. xxxi, 7-12, 41) relates that Jacob, whilst he watched the flocks of Laban, obtained lambs of any color he wished, by throwing green rods of poplar, of almond, and of plane trees in the troughs, where the water was poured out, and where the sheep came to drink at the time when they were about to breed. This episode is related in a very obscure manner in the Sacred Text; St. Jerome, the translator of our Vulgate, has justly remarked this. The commentators are not agreed as to the meaning of the divers parts of this narrative. The following interpretation appears to be the most plausible:

Jacob, after having served Laban during fourteen years, without receiving any other reward than Lia and Rachel, after having even been deceived in his first marriage by his uncle, wishes now to leave him and raise flocks on his own account. As God, because of the upright character of Jacob, had blessed Laban, this greedy and avaricious man tries to retain him. On entreaties of his uncle, the son of Isaac consents to remain, but under the condition that he will be paid for his labors. His demand is too just to allow of its rejection; only, if we may employ the familiar and expressive figure, both play a fine game, and it is the son-in-law who beats the father-in-law.

In the Orient the most of the sheep are white (Cf. Ps. cxlvii, 16; Is. i, 18; Apoc. i, 14); the goats are generally black. The white fleece is highly esteemed, because it can be used without preparation, and because it can be more easily dyed; the skins of the black goats have a higher value, because they serve as covers for tents. Experience had taught the shepherd that in order to obtain white lambs, a process of quite natural selection was necessary wherein are joined the rams and the white sheep. In the bargain he had made with Laban, Jacob asks for his payment the speckled sheep and the white goats, namely, a small number which Laban already had, and the others which would be the result of breeding. The proposition is accepted, but as the brother of Rebecca is afraid that his nephew, when he has in charge the entire flock, might multiply the speckled lambs and the white goats, he leaves to him only the white sheep and the black goats, and intrusts the others to his own children. Thus he believed that Jacob would not have any profit, but he was very much deceived.

The spouse of Lia and Rachel obtains spotted lambs, thanks to the protection of God (Gen. xxxi, 9) and to his own industry (Gen. xxxi, 37-41). We learn by the sequel of the narrative of Genesis (xxxi, 7-8) that Laban, beholding himself deceived in his hopes, changed ten times, i. e., often, the agreements which he had accepted, asking for the speckled lambs when they were numerous, and the white lambs when they multiplied themselves more than the others.

Such are the main facts of the narrative. In whatever manner may be understood the different details, according to the interpretation rendered, the difficulty remains always the same. Does Jacob obtain through a miracle, or in a natural manner, the lambs of one or several colors? Voltaire and, following after him, the most of the Rationalists desire to behold in the means employed by Jacob only a recipe without value, which produces no result. According to the critics, the proceedings of Jacob are ridiculous. " If it were sufficient," they say, " to place colors before the eyes of the females to have young ones of the same color, all the cows would produce green calves; and all the lambs, whose mothers eat green grass, would be green also. All the women who would have seen rose bushes would have offsprings of a roseate hue."

These are pure pleasantries, without any serious foundation. When Jacob obtained through a miracle the lambs he desired, than all these assertions are false; if, on the other hand, the process he employed was naturally efficacious, it is not the red or the white color of calves that will prove the contrary. In fact, the solution of the question is doubtful. Jacob expressly attributes to divine protection the success of the means he has employed, but the text does not state formally that there had been a miracle, and he seems to present to us the use of the peeled rods in the watering-places, as a natural secret which has operated its effect without a special prodigy. Opinions may differ, therefore, in regard to what really occurred. The Greek Fathers have generally admitted the miracle. " It was not according to the laws of nature," says St. John Chrysostom (Hom. lvii, 2 in Gen.), " but wonderful and supernatural." On the contrary, the most of the Latin Fathers support themselves on the testimony of profane authors who attribute to the action exercised on the imagination of the mothers the color of their breed, the phenomenon produced would be conformable to the laws of nature. Such is the opinion of St. Jerome and of St. Augustine.

5. THE MANDRAKES OF RUBEN.

Genesis relates that one day the eldest son of Jacob, being yet a child, found in the field of Mesopotamia duadaïm and brought them to his mother Lia. Rachel having seen these dudaïm, wished for some and obtained them through her sister (xxx, 14-15). These dudaïm it is claimed, are the fruits of the vernal mandrake, to which antiquity attributed a prolific virtue: Rachel desired to eat them in order to have children. "It is thus," state the infidels, "that we find already in the first Book of Moses, a belief in superstition as evidenced in the powers attributed to this plant."

Indeed, it is generally believed that the dudaïm is the mandrake, the Hebrew word signifying "love-plant." The Arabs call it *toffa el djin*, or "apples of the devil," *yabrouh*, etc. There exists in no Semitic language, except in the Hebrew, a plant called dudaïm. The Arabs believe that the mandrake excites the senses even to madness, hence the name "apples of the devil," which they have given to it. According to Hesychius, the surname of Venus was Mandragoritis, and the fruit of the mandrake was called "love apples." Plato in his Republic speaks of the liquor drawn from the mandrake as intoxicating. Dioscorides identified the mandrake with the *kirkaia*, or plant of Circe, because it was believed that this famous enchantress effected her enchantments with the aid of this wonderful plant. It was made use of to compound philters. Josephus speaks it under the name of *baaras* as of a magical herb, endowed with power to expel the demon. This plant enjoyed great celebrity among the sorcerers of the Middle Ages, who attributed to it all manner of magical powers. Shakspeare has made allusion several times in his dramas to the properties they attributed to it. In the last century, the quack doctors and venders of extraordinary remedies sold on the markets, images of the mandrake which the credulous country folk considered possessed of magic properties.

The dudaïm are named only twice in the Bible, that is, in the episode of Genesis and in the Canticle of Canticles. The ancient translators have rendered this word into mandrake, but the modern commentators are far from agreeing that this interpretation is correct. Some believe that the dudaïm are a kind of small melon, called among the Persians *distembujch*. It is by this word that the Persian version of the Bible has rendered the dudaïm of Genesis. It grows in Syria and in Egypt, as well as in Persia. It is very odoriferous and juicy, and the women of the harem delight to hold it in their hands, like the lemon, on account of its agreeable odor.

We admit, nevertheless, because this opinion appears the most probable, that the dudaïm are mandrakes. But in accepting this interpretation, we except the marvelous properties attributed to these plants. These magical effects are purely imaginary; the mandrake is a narcotic, and travelers and naturalists are not in agreement as to the character of the peculiar odor the plant emits; it appears to be agreeable to some, and obnoxious to others. But, at least all serious observers acknowledge that it has not at all the power which popular credulity attributes to it.

Whatever the properties of the mandrake may be, one fact is certain, namely, that the Scripture does not attribute to it any property. The Scripture is not responsible for the controversy which has raged round this episode of Rachel. It is only necessary to read the sacred account, to become convinced that it is only through the most arbitrary and the most false interpretation that the writer can be accused of giving to the dudaïm any magical properties. St. Augustine, who had studied the plant out of curiosity on account of the mention made of it by Genesis, has correctly stated that the text does not attribute any particular property to the dudaïm, but merely states that Rachel had desired them. Why did she desire them? We do not know, Moses does not even state that Rachel ate of its fruit. The dudaïm might have been only a simple bouquet of mandrake flowers, the beauty of which charmed the sister of Lia. *Omnes flores amabiles* says a commentator as to this subject. It is believed that the Hebrew word signifies " love," and, perhaps, to this etymology has been attributed peculiar ideas which had been in vogue regarding the virtue of this plant.

CHAPTER XXVIII.

THE PATRIARCH JOSEPH.

1. The History of Joseph Confirmed by Scientific Discoveries.

THE history of Joseph is related in detail in the Book of Genesis. The subject which Moses treats therein gave occasion to him to relate the Egyptian customs with quite minute details. Now, as these customs are known to us to-day through the monuments recovered, and through the deciphering of the hieroglyphics, we can verify with perfect ease, all the assertions of the sacred author, and note whether they are conformable to science and history. This labor has been done mostly, not by friends of the Bible, but, on the contrary, by persons who had in view to discover what would prove inexactitudes of the Bible, and show, if at all possible, that Moses is not the author of the narrative. The result of these inquiries has been the most absolute confirmation of the Biblical narrative even in the smallest details. In order to be able to state what he did, it was not sufficient that the sacred author should merely have passed through Egypt, but he must have lived there for a long time, and even at the court, and he must have witnessed the operating of the mechanism of administration. Now, such precisely are the conditions which we see fulfilled by Moses, to whom we attribute this account. We do not need to prove in detail the exactitude of the Biblical text which to-day is admitted by all, but we content ourselves with authenticating certain particulars which have been the most often subject to disputation.

2. ANSWER TO OBJECTIONS.

Putiphar, the master of Joseph, is termed Eunuch of the Pharaoh.[1] Now, the Rationalists deny the existence of eunuchs in Egypt. The Bible, however, is correct. Since we meet with eunuchs everywhere in the Orient, from the most remote antiquity, why should there not have been any in Egypt? It is true that monogamy was the general rule there, but the Pharaohs had often several wives, the one a queen, the others simply favorites, and, consequently, the presence of eunuchs as keepers of the royal harem is not improba-

---
[1] Gen. xxxix.

ble. But there is more evidence on this point: the Egyptian monuments depict eunuchs, recognizable by the absence of the beard, the development of the chest, the obesity, and peculiar color of the skin. They accompany the women, play on musical instruments and occupy themselves with domestic labors.

But, it is said in answer, Putiphar to whom is given this title, was a married man. To this we reply: 1. The ancient writings, for example, the "Romance of the Two Brothers," make mention of married eunuchs, and we still meet to-day with such who possess harems. 2. The titles of dignity must not always be taken in their etymological sense; let us cite, for instance, the French "Chevaliers," which literally means horsemen, but in fact are knights and, as a rule, hold high positions at the royal court. In Chaldea all the court officers were called "eunuchs," and it may be that the Hebrews, originally of this country, had given this name to the dignitaries of the Egyptian court.

3. THE COLLAR GIVEN TO JOSEPH BY THE PHARAOH.

When Joseph became minister of the Pharaoh, the latter, among other insignia of power, gave him a golden collar.[1] "It is scarcely necessary," says Bohlen, "that the precious stones belong to a posterior epoch." Hence, he concludes that this history is not authentic. Now, the monuments give testimony absolutely contrary to his assertion; not only do they present the gods and the kings adorned with collars, not only does the stela in the Louvre of Paris show a Pharaoh investing his favorite with a collar, but we are in possession of collars and other Egyptian jewelry of a very remote

---
[1] Gen. xli, 42.

antiquity, and the workmanship of which is not inferior in any respect to the ornamented jewelry of our time, and yet behold the mention of these things in the story of Joseph, the Rationalists assert, is a proof that it is not veracious.

4. DIVINATION BY THE CUP.

Hated by his brethren and sold into slavery by them, Joseph wishes to know their sentiments in regard to Benjamin, and hardly had his brethren departed he pursues them as thieves, having first caused a valuable cup to be secreted in their possessions. The cup is recovered where the steward had placed it and he cries out: "The cup which you have stolen is that in which my Lord drinketh, and in which He is wont to divine."[1] As they did not discover until lately anywhere else this divination by means of a cup, the Rationalists profited by this to accuse Genesis of errors and superstition, and certain Catholic writers believed it best to suppose, in this passage, an alteration of the text. According to Aurivillius it would be necessary in order to admit that Genesis had made such a statement, to prove that the Egyptians employed, at the time of Joseph or later on, the mode of divination. The proof desired by Aurivillius has been obtained. The custom of divination by the cup has existed in Egypt even to the present day. Mr. Norden relates that, in his voyage to Egypt, a certain Baram received him very courteously and said to him: "I have consulted my cup and found therein that you are of those whom our prophet has said would come from the disguised Franks, etc." Another striking example was reported in the " Revue des deux

---

[1] Gen. xliv, 5.

Mondes" (August, 1833). It is, therefore, very probable that the use of the divination cup was not entirely unknown in ancient Egypt, and besides we find the use thereof in other countries, as, for instance, in Persia and Thibet.

But the words of the steward of Joseph give rise to another difficulty: can we not conclude from them that Joseph was addicted to magic? Certainly not. The overseer may have mentioned this particular on his own authority, being of the opinion, as were other Egyptians, that Joseph owed his great knowledge to magic. But even supposing the steward spoke thus in the name of Joseph, we could say, with St. Thomas, that Joseph could speak on this occasion, according to the common superstition which prevailed in Egypt, without affirming his own belief in it.

5. THE POSSESSION OF ALL THE EGYPTIAN SOIL BY THE PHARAOH.

In exchange for the grain which he distributed among the Egyptians, Joseph made the people give to him their silver; then their cattle, and finally their lands. Thus, the Pharaoh became proprietor of the whole soil of Egypt, except the domains of the priests, who, supported at the expense of the king, did not need to buy grain. This important act of the administration of Joseph has been attacked by the Rationalists who have contested both its reality and morality.

In contesting the reality of the fact one of them says: "It is a wonderful story which could be hatched out only in the imagination of an Ephramite. . . . The Egyptians since all the epochs known were proprietors of their goods." The assertion of Genesis is, nevertheless, correct; everything goes to prove this: (a) The importance of the fact is such that a writer would not have dared to invent it for fear of being contradicted by all the evidence which existed on the subject. " One does not trifle thus," says Eichthal, " with the history of a great people, who live alongside of him, and under his very eyes, so to say." (b) According to Diodor of Sicily, the Egyptian soil was divided into three parts, belonging to the king, to the priests and to the soldiers (the privilege of the latter may have been introduced posterior to Joseph); hence, the mass of the people could not possess the soil, and in fact the monuments never designate single individuals as land proprietors. (c) Egyptology establishes the existence, under the Ancient and Middle Empire, of quite a turbulent feudality, proprietors of nomes or hereditary principalities; under the new empire, after the Hyksos, contemporaries of Joseph, we find no longer any trace of this organization. May we not suppose that the legislation of Joseph had given the death blow to this landed feudality? Thus we see Ramses III. speaking as the proprietor of Egypt: " I planted trees and shrubs all over the country, and I permitted the people to sit in their shadow." (d) Herodotus relates that Seostris (contemporary of Moses) divided the soil of Egypt into equal portions among all the inhabitants: now, this division presupposes an anterior condition of proprietorship, such as that which resulted from the measure taken by Joseph.

Joseph's action from a moral standpoint has been severely condemned. He is charged with tyranny. But: (a) The proprietary right of the Pharaoh remained a purely nominal one; the Egyptians continued to cultivate their lands, paying a tax of the fifth part of the revenue; in fact, the measure taken by Joseph was equivalent to an increase in the tax rates. (b) The Hyksos or shepherd kings, who reigned at that time, were foreigners and conquerors; and there is nothing astonishing in the fact that they displayed less consideration for the people than did the native kings, or that they profited by the circumstances to more firmly establish their dominion. To-day every citizen of an annexed province remains the master of his land; formerly only a few were usually allowed this privilege. (c) The proprietorship could never be established in Egypt as elsewhere; the fertility of the land depends there upon the measures taken to regulate the inundation of the Nile, and these measures could not be taken except by permission of the highest ruling power; hence for the public usefulness the lands were held in trust, as it were, by the state. (d) In the Orient the territorial proprietorship has never been considered and respected in the same manner as common with us; nowhere do they look upon the products of the soil as belonging exclusively to the owner of the lands on which they grew; neither is the land so carefully cultivated, and consequently the soil is an object much less valued than it is in our countries. Thus, we see to-day the viceroy of Egypt buying from his subjects their lands, in order to obtain revenues; Mehemet-Ali did not take this trouble, he simply confiscated the land. Hence, when we consider the Oriental customs and the peculiar proprietary conditions of Egypt, it will be seen that Joseph, in the whole, acted as a wise administrator, and one will conclude with the Rationalist Ewald: " That it is nonsensical to reproach Joseph, for his conduct does not need any further proofs."

6. ANSWER TO OBJECTIONS MADE BY THE RATIONALISTS AGAINST THE AUTHENTICITY AND VERACITY OF THE HISTORY OF JOSEPH.

From all these difficulties the conclusion can be easily drawn. When the most skillful savants, in the enlightened nineteenth century, have deceived themselves so greatly on the conditions, customs and rule of ancient Egypt, it would have been impossible for any one one except Moses to give faithfully, several centuries after the facts, and in Palestine, an account so replete with minute details. This, however, is not the conclusion which some Rationalists draw. They acknowledge in general the perfect probability of the account, but they nevertheless endeavor to deny the existence of Joseph; for them this history is only a romance, invented after the separation of the tribes, by some Ephraemite, to praise the kingdom of Israel at the expense of Juda.

If the author had been an Ephraemite nothing would prove that he did not write his account from more ancient documents, and the exactitude of the details regarding the Egyptian customs should make the infidel suppose this. However, the system of our adversaries will not stand investigation at all; the author of the story of Joseph, instead of glorifying the fathers of the tribes of Israel, attributes to them great crimes, and it is particularly to Juda that he assigns an upright character when the writer relates how the son of Jacob saved the life of Joseph, and how he made the most devoted efforts to deliver Benjamin.

But, finally, what evidence do the Rationalists present in their system? They refer: 1. To the difficulties in regard to the eunuchs and the landed proprietors, difficulties we have refuted. 2. They behold in chapter xxxvii of Genesis two different accounts of the sale of Joseph: in the one it is Ruben who causes Joseph to be thrown into a cistern; in the other it is Juda who instigates the sale; in the one he is sold to Madianites (Gen. xxxvi, 37), in the other to Ismaelites (xxxvii, 20). It is sufficient to read this chapter to perceive that Ruben and Juda interfered successively, and the 28th verse gives to the purchasing merchants the two names of Madianites and Ismaelites. 3. Again, according to the infidel criticism, the evidence which establishes that the history of Joseph is a pure legend is found in the fact that the prophets do not speak of him. It is not expected that they should speak of him unless their subjects so demanded, as if, for instance, they had summarized the history of their people. Besides, it is false to say that they made no reference to him whatever. Isaias recalls the establishment of Israel in Egypt (Is. liii, 4); Ezechiel mentions a feature of the history of Joseph (Ezechiel xlvii, 13); so also Exodus (xiii, 19), Josue (xxiv, 32), and especially the Psalm civ, 16-23.

We see, therefore, that this system of the infidels cannot be maintained; besides, if the history of Joseph is eliminated from Genesis, how will the sojourn of the Hebrews in Egypt be explained, where we find their traces until the present time? How can we explain the singular privilege of the two sons of Joseph, who also received a share in the Promised Land, and became the fathers of two tribes? Indeed, to relate the history of Israel with Joseph left out would be as difficult and nonsensical as to write a history of America in which Washington played no part. We must conclude, therefore, that all the attacks of the Rationalists do not prevail against the authenticity and veracity of the history of Joseph: tradition, reason and the testimony of scientific research all unanimously point to Moses as the author of this history, and also evidence that no one else except him could have written it.

CHAPTER XXIX.

THE BOOK OF JOSUE AND GALILEO.

1. Antiquity of the Book of Josue.

THE Book of Josue shares the lot of the Pentateuch before the infidel criticism. It condemns both as being unworthy of belief. The first writing does not merit any more confidence than the second, we are told, because the latter is only a part of the whole, a member of the same body. The denomination Pentateuch is incorrect: Hexateuch, we must say, for the work placed at the head of our Bible is not composed of five books, but of six, and the Book of Josue forms the sixth: it is of the same age as the Pentateuch, compiled in the same manner, and its informations are derived from the same source.

At first the Rationalists pretended that the Book of Josue consisted of at least twelve different fragments. But the fragmentary hypothesis, having been weighed and found wanting, was abandoned for a new system, that of the complimentary hypothesis. They pretended that the pieces designed under the name of Elohists, in the Pentateuch and in Josue, had belonged primitively to one sole writing which embraced the whole time elapsed since the beginning of the world, not only until the death of Moses, but until that of Josue. A few critics adopted the foundation of this opinion. Thus arose the idea of the Hexateuch. The other Rationalists agreed neither with these few, nor among themselves, in regard to the numerous points of detail. They maintain, however, to-day, the existence of the Hexateuch. The Book of Josue presupposes that the Pentateuch is the work of Moses; now it is this that the infidels do not wish to admit at any consideration. Hence, it is especially the desire to negative the supernatural which makes them reject the antiquity and the authenticity of the Book of Josue. We have not to defend here the supernatural, but we will answer the special objections in a manner as follows:

Although the Greeks "invented the title of Pentateuch," as Reuss says, it is probable that they did not invent the distinction of the work into five books, and that this arrangement is more ancient than the translation of the Septuagint. It is certain, at any rate, that the distinction of the Books of Moses and of the Book of Josue did not originate with the Greeks, and this is the only point which is important to establish here. The most ancient tradition has always considered the two works completely distinct. As far back as we can go we see the Jews class the Pentateuch in an apart category; the Book of Josue is ranked in a different series, that of the first prophets, where it occupies the first place. It is, therefore, established that a tradition which had its birth in a very ancient epoch, and which has never been contradicted until at the close of the last century, certifies us the antiquity of the history which relates the conquest and the occupation of the Promised Land. The reasons brought forward by criticism against the traditional belief, do they shake its solidity? Not at all.

It is true the Book of Josue is intrinsically connected with the Pentateuch, inasmuch as it takes up the history of the Hebrew people at the conclusion of Deuteronomy. The tribes which Moses had led out of Egypt did not die with him; their history does not end with that of their liberator; they continued without him the work which they began with him; they were already on the shores of the Jordan; they but needed to cross it to undertake the conquest of the Promised Land, for so long a time the object of their vows and of their desires. The writing which bears the name of Josue relates to us the history of this conquest; it has, in consequence, a necessary relation to the books which precede it. But while relative to the writings of Moses, and a continuation of them, it is not identical with them.

"It is true," says Reuss, "that a writer who has commenced his writing with glowing promises made to the patriarchs has to conclude by showing us their fulfillment; at least he could not pass in silence the consummation thereof." What a singular deduction, and how very clearly it shows that rationalism is always blind with partisan spirit! Certainly Moses could not pass in silence the conquest of the Promised Land, provided he had not died before the end of his task. In order that the author of the Pentateuch could relate the fulfillment of the promises, they had first to be fulfilled; now, such had not happened when Moses, the author of these promises, died. They were fulfilled under Josue, and by Josue and a writer posterior to Moses has completed the account.

Besides, we must remark that the existence of Deuteronomy, placed between the Numbers and the Book of Josue, renders quite inadmissible the hypothesis that the six first writings of the Old Testament form only one whole or, as claimed, a Hexateuch. Deuteronomy is an abridgment and a summary of the Mosaic Law, it forms its conclusion; consequently, it ends and finishes it; what comes afterwards can be only a new work which resumes the thread of the history there where the preceding author had left it. If the Hexateuch had ever existed in the sense as the Rationalists understand it, Deuteronomy should form, not the fifth, but the sixth part of the Pentateuch or Hexateuch.

In its composition the Book of Josue has nothing in common with the Pentateuch; it forms a complete whole, and it has a plan which is peculiar to it. Its subject is the conquest and the division of the southern and northern Palestine; the second subdivision enumerates the possessions attributed to the tribes of Israel in the conquered country. Thus, we have not a kind of journal written day by day as is Exodus, Leviticus and Numbers, nor a series of discourses like in Deuteronomy; it is quite a new and different plan. The author makes known to us the history of Josue and the people which the successor of Moses led to victory, from the moment when he became its chief until his death. Never had a writing a more remarkable individuality. The adversaries of the Bible are themselves forced to acknowledge that the Book of Josue has a different character from that of the Pentateuch.

The Book of Josue is, therefore, a separate work, an independent work. It is connected with the Pentateuch like the Acts of the Apostles are connected with the Gospels, because it is the sequel of the same history; but it is, nevertheless, a complete, distinct writing. Undoubtedly the language is alike in many respects to that of the Books of Moses, but what is there astonishing in this, and how could it be otherwise? Its author is very probably Josue himself, because he speaks as an eye-witness of the events he relates; hence, he had lived with Moses, he served him more than once, as we may suppose, at least as secretary, therefore he should speak and write in a manner very much resembling that of Moses. The book which carries his name, did it emanate from another, as some maintain, certainly could not have been composed in an epoch posterior to David, because, as an examination of its contents show, when it was written Jerusalem was not yet the capital of Israel, but belonged still to the Jebusites (Jos. xv, 63). Hence, when this book was written it could not have been but a short time after the epoch of the exodus, and the Hebrew language could not have undergone a great change.

2. HISTORIC AND SCIENTIFIC DIFFICULTIES.

Besides the general accusation against the antiquity of the Book of Josue, the negative criticism attacks as contradictory and as inadmissible certain details contained in this book. It is hardly necessary to state that they reject as impossible the miraculous passage of the Jordan, and the not less miraculous taking of the city of Jericho (Jos. iii, vi). But we have not to discuss here the impossibility or improbability of miracles, we will give attention only to facts which, irrespective of their supernatural character, present some particular difficulty.

3. THE CIRCUMCISION AT GALGALA.

After having crossed the Jordan, Josue, by the order of God, caused the circumcision of all the children of Israel who had not yet received this sign of the Covenant between Jehovah and His people. Taking this incident as a basis, numerous objections have been raised against the historical character of the "Hexateuch" in general, and against the Book of Josue in particular. The critics have endeavored to discover contradictions in the different accounts concerning this practice of the Jews.

Nothing is more simple than the reconciliation of these "different facts." Far from contradicting themselves, on the contrary, they explain themselves, one perfectly substantiating the other. All that is related about the circumcision is founded upon the precept given to Abraham in Genesis. Josue formally identifies the ancient practice when we read in his account that those of the Israelites who had gone forth from Egypt without being circumcised "had disobeyed the order of God" (Jos. v, 6). An angel threatens to kill the son of Moses or Moses himself, when he returned into Egypt with his family, because the child was not circumcised. The menacing attitude of the angel can be explained only in the existence of the law of circumcision. Punishment can be justly inflicted only for the violation of a law. The account of Exodus is very laconic, and does not enter into any details, but sufficient is said to render it comprehensible as a whole. It is Sephora, the wife of Moses, who circumcises the child. The law did not exclude women from officiating in this rite. But it is evident that Sephora performs it with reluctance, and only because she has no other alternative. When, afterwards, she exclaims to Moses: "O bloody spouse art thou to me," her remark is equivalent to an admission that it was she that had delayed the circumcision of her son. Moses would have wished to observe on this point the customs of his race, but his wife had prevented the fulfillment of a ceremony which was repugnant to her because it was bloody. It was not expedient, however, that at the moment when Moses presented himself before the people to transmit to them the divine orders, that he should present in his own family an example of the violation of the bond concluded between God and his fathers; the Almighty command, therefore, compels Sephora, who had not complied with the vows of her husband, to consent finally to the fulfillment of the law, and, in spite of her disinclination, she resigns herself to the task, not, however, without complaining over its performance in the midst of a desert. The fact is nowhere "mentioned as something new and extraordinary," not one word insinuates this in the account which, on the contrary, we repeat, presupposes the existence of the rite of circumcision.

But, adds Reuss, the Israelites were not circumcised during the sojourn in the desert. Now, "a disobedience of this kind to a fundamental article of the theocratic covenant, under the very eyes, and with the toleration of the legislator is inexplicable." Nothing is nevertheless more easy to explain, and it is only necessary to read the account itself of Josue with unprejudiced eyes, without endeavoring to contort every statement into a contradiction, in order to see therein clearly the reason why this rite was not practiced in the desert. The Israelites in the solitudes of Sinai lived as nomads; hence, they often changed their encampments, and as they were surrounded by hostile tribes they had to be ready to depart at a moment's warning. Under such conditions circumcision was impracticable, because several days are required after the operation to allow the wounds to heal. Moses had, therefore decided that the circumstances dispensed the people from the law until the time when they would enjoy rest and security, which would enable them to resume the practice. Josue himself demanded an observance of the rite when the tribes of Israel had crossed the Jordan and only, after receiving the report which the spies sent to Jericho had made to him, he had the assurance that the people could rest in peace at Galgala without fear of disturbance. All this clearly corroborates the exact words of the sacred texts: " After they were all circumcised in the same place of the camp until they were healed " (Jos. v. 8).

Finally, what Mr. Reuss adds is also founded on an equally fallacious interpretation. "The circumcision," he says, "being practiced by the Egyptians and other nations, we cannot see how it could be a distinctive sign of the Israelites." Certainly one does not see it, but what should oblige us to see it? The professor of

Strasburg here makes the Bible tell something that it does not tell at all. He has such an ardent desire to fault-find, that he, himself, falls into the errors with which he wishes to charge the Sacred Scriptures. It is not the Bible that tells us that circumcision is "a distinctive sign of the Israelites;" it is Mr. Reuss who kindly makes this loan and gathers in the interest. God, in Genesis, says to Abraham that circumcision will be "a sign of the covenant" (Gen. xvii, 11), which they conclude together, but the word "distinctive," nor anything approaching to it is found in these words. Now, the error which the rationalistic commentator pretends to discover consists solely in the word, "distinctive," which he adds himself to the sacred text. Far, therefore, from being contradictory, the Biblical account is perfectly in harmony in all its parts, and the Book of Josue only confirms what the Pentateuch relates.

4. THE CONQUEST OF PALESTINE.

Many objections have been made against the conquest of Palestine by Josue. One has pretended that what we read in regard to this subject in the book which bears his name is full of contradictions and given the lie by the Book of Judges and the Books of Kings. When statements of this character are made, it comes from a false interpretation of the diverse passages of the text, which have been made with the purpose in view of so arranging the text that various passages are placed in opposition. One supposes that the sacred author affirms that the conqueror of the Promised Land took hold of "all" the cities, of "all" the strong places, in "all" the parts of Palestine. Now, Scripture does not affirm anything of the kind. Thus it is pretended that the Books of Kings contradict Josue because they say it was the Pharaoh of Egypt, who, under Solomon took Gazer, a city which should have been taken already by Josue. There is no contradiction here. The Book of Josue mentions the death of the king of Gazer, but says nothing about the capture of his capital. Besides, we must not be surprised that several cities, taken and burnt by the invaders, nevertheless remained or fell again into the possession of their first inhabitants. The latter could retake them or need never have abandoned them completely; for one would have a wrong notion of the wars of this epoch were he to suppose that the conqueror left a garrison in the conquered places to keep them under his obedience. The general custom, even of the most powerful monarchs, as the kings of Ninive, for a long time, was to devastate a city by pillage and the torch, in order to destroy its usefulness to the enemy; but generally the destruction was not complete, and when the conqueror had withdrawn with his troops, nobody prevented the inhabitants from repairing the disasters of war, a proceeding they hastened almost always to effect. This explains how cities besieged, taken and burnt by the Hebrews could be erected anew and flourishing some years afterwards, and in the possession of its ancient possessors. Such was the case with Hebron, Dabir (Jos. x, 36-37; xi, 21; xiv, 12-13; xv, 13-14; Judges i, 10).

The Rationalists arise also, in the name of morality, to denounce the war of extermination which the Israelities raged against the Chanaanites. What right, cried out already the Manicheans in the early ages; what right, repeat the enemies of the Bible in our days, had the descendants of Jacob to destroy this people and take their country? How could God, the Father and Creator of all men, ordain the massacre of these, His children?

Holy Scripture answers us that God chastised the Canaanites for their crimes (Gen. xv, 16; Lev. xviii, 20; Wisdom xii). Certainly He has the right to punish and cause to be punished at His pleasure the sins of His creatures; He can strike them with death if He so desires, either through a sickness or through accident, through plague, famine, pest or war; whatever the form of death may be, it is within the divine prerogative, and it is only through want of reflection that one who believes in the existence of God can contest His right, His power, or question His justice.

As to the part played by the Israelites in the extermination, without speaking here of the donation of the land of Canaan, which the Lord had made to their fathers, it is sufficient to remember that the oppression of Egypt had forced them to leave this inhospitable country, and that the conquest of Palestine was for them only a struggle for existence, an act which has been proclaimed in our days as one of the greatest laws which rule the world. They were in need of a place to lay their heads, of lands to give them food, of homes for the people; force alone was their recourse. Besides, their manner of warfare was not more bloody, nor more cruel than was usual to their day; they even treated the Canaanites more humanely than the latter treated their enemies.

5. THE MIRACLE OF JOSUE COMMANDING THE SUN TO STAND STILL AND THE CONDEMNATION OF GALILEO.

There is, perhaps, not a single passage of the

Scriptures which caused more controversy than that in which the Book of Josue relates how the battle of Bethoron ended. In this battle the Chanaanites of southern Palestine were completely routed with great slaughter. Here the objections multiply and accumulate. And it is not only the sacred text that is attacked, but also the commentators and the Church itself. By a strange phenomenon, wherein during long centuries was seen only a miracle which everyone accepted in making simply an act of faith, without question, to-day everything appears suspicious, obscure, doubtful and inacceptable, not only to the infidels, but also to orthodox Protestants, and even to some Catholics. The famous passage is found in Josue x, 12-14.

The first difficulty which the reading of this passage presents is to know in what sense we have to interpret it. All the ancient interpreters have taken it in the literal sense; they saw therein that the sun really revolved around the earth, that the earth was immovable, that the sun and the moon had really stopped in their course by order of Josue, and that the day of the battle of Bethoron had been thus the longest day that ever took place upon the earth. To-day multitudinous objections are raised against every particular of this exposition.

As to the first point, that is, the stopping of the sun, the ancient interpretation is universally abandoned, since astronomy has established that the sun is the center of our solar system, and that it is the earth which revolves around this planet. When the conqueror of the Canaanites commanded the sun to stand still, this does not imply that he admitted the system one has called since the system of Ptolemy, teaching the diurnal movement of the sun around the earth; he has enunciated the general belief, in judging the facts after the sensible appearances. There is no more question in the Book of Josue of the system of Ptolemy than of that of Copernicus. The Hebrew general beseeching a miracle employs the language used in his time and in his country, and God, granting his request, employs the means which he judges proper. Throughout the Scripture the sacred authors express themselves in an analogous manner, that is, conformably to the popular belief in regard to scientific questions, and the interpreters are unanimous in admitting this fact. Hence, one must not seek in their words scientific apophthegms which they never had the intention of formulating.

But in what sense have we to understand the account in the Book of Josue? The liberal Rationalists, and a certain number of Protestants, to whom we have to add a few Catholics, who are frightened at the mention of a miracle, maintain that neither the Hebrew poet nor the historian beheld any prodigy, strictly speaking, in that what we call improperly the standing still of the sun, and consequently, that the readers of to-day must not discover therein anything wonderful. But this interpretation appears to be quite forced, and it seems difficult to make it agree with the letter of the text of Josue. It is, moreover, in contradiction to what we read in Ecclesiasticus: "Was not the sun stopped in his anger? and one day made as two?" (Eccli. xlvi, 5).

It is true that several savants and critics maintain that the miracle of the stopping of the earth, in her diurnal rotation, would have brought on such a revolution in our planetary system, and would have been the cause of a catastrophe so immense that it is impossible to believe in so abnormal a disturbance, of which, besides, no trace remains. To this objection we can answer that the suspension of the movement of our globe would have changed nothing in the universe, outside of the prolongation of an earthly day, only in so far as the Master of the universe would have willed, for it depended upon His will to prevent all the catastrophes which would have naturally resulted from the miracle of Josue. Those who admit that our earth really stopped, and among these we must place Galileo himself (Cf. Alla Granduchessa, *Opere* Milan, 1811, vol. XIII, p. 62), suppose, or even affirm explicitly that this first miracle was accompanied and followed by numerous others, miracles which were necessary to remedy the disastrous effects which the temporary immobility of the terrestrial planet would have produced.

But we have to add that nothing obliges us to believe in this indefinite multiplication of prodigies. We can logically claim that the prolongation of the day beyond the ordinary day was only due to an optic and meteorological phenomenon, a local miracle proportioned for the end, and not an astronomical and universal miracle, and thus we overcome difficulties which seemingly appall and dismay so many. God could have heard Josue without disturbing the order of our planetary system, and, consequently, without the production of this general perturbation which would have revolutionized the entire universe.

This interpretation of Josue's command to the sun to stop in its course is universally admitted to-day by the commentators and theologians, but it gives rise to a new difficulty which we must overcome. This difficulty is not only raised by Rationalists, but also by the Protestants. They pretend that the Catholics are obliged to admit that the earth is immovable, and that the sun revolves around the earth, because the Church, infallible interpreter of the Scripture, according to our belief, has defined that this is the real meaning of the words of Josue. "All the Catholics," says Roberts, " are bound to conclude from the bull *Speculatores*, and from the decrees of Popes Paul V. and Urban VIII. that the heliocentric doctrine is false, and that this conclusion is infallibly certain" (William W. Roberts, "The Pontifical Decrees," etc., Oxford, 1885).

The decrees which Roberts attributes to Paul V. and to Urban VIII. are decisions of the Roman congregations against Galileo, the famous Florentine astronomer. No fact of Church history has been exploited with such persistency and bad faith as the condemnation of this astronomer. The Church, it is stated, has condemned itself in the person of this illustrious victim of the Inquisition: either one has to acknowledge that she denied herself, and in this case has proved that she can err in interpreting the Scriptures; or one has to maintain against all evidence that she has not failed, and then all Catholics are bound to believe in the immobility of the earth.

Journals and reviews repeat this accusation to satiety. One could furnish an entire library with the books that have been published on this subject. It is, therefore, necessary to establish that it is not the Church that has pronounced against Galileo, but a fallible congregation, and one subject to error, so that the infallible authority of the Sovereign Pontiff explaining the word of God is not in question at all, and that there is for the Catholics no law that prevents them from believing that the earth revolves around the sun. All the authentic documents in regard to the trial and condemnation of Galileo are in existence to-day, and nothing is more easy than to obtain the truth of this matter in its whole integrity and simplicity.

In the first place it is important to remark that Galileo was not the inventor of the system which has made him so famous, and that the Church before him did not oppose herself at all to the theories of which Galileo made himself the propagator and defender.

Before Galileo, in fact 500 years before our era, the Pythagoreans taught that the earth revolved around the sun. In the fifteenth century Nicholas of Cusa revived this opinion in Italy and upheld it publicly in his book, "De Docta Ignorantia," as the most proper hypothesis by which to explain the planetary system; not only did he not scandalize anybody, but he was raised to the dignity of a cardinal. About one century later a Polish canon, who had been professor at Rome, one of the creators of modern astronomy, Nicholas Copernicus (1473-1543), revived again and taught the same system in his book, "On the Revolutions of the Cœlestial Bodies," dedicated to Pope Paul III. "The orb of to-day, seated on his royal throne, in the center of our universe," he said therein, "governs the heavenly family in the space around him." He protested that it was only in abusing the Scripture, and by interpreting it falsely that one could form a weapon against his system. He died at the time when his work came into existence, but nobody took offense at his opinions until when Galileo appeared on the scene. Nearly seventy years had elapsed since the death of Copernicus when Galileo took possession of the chair of mathematics at Florence in 1610. The new professor taught in his course the mobility of the earth. The first writing in which he upheld publicly the system of Copernicus had for its title: " History and Explanation of the Solar Spots;" it appeared in 1613, but several years preceding he had been attacking, with all the force and energy of his excitable nature, the Peripatetician doctrines prevailing at that time, and thus he had created for himself many enemies. The storm which formed itself against him broke loose on February 5, 1615. It was on the occasion of his letter to the Grand Duchess Christina (Cf. Opere, Milan, 1811, vol. XIII. p. 17-18, 24). In this letter the author gives vent to some very correct statements. He does not speak otherwise than St. Augustine and St. Thomas; but unfortunately, after having promulgated correct principles, he makes a false application of them. Indeed, he wishes to make use of them to defend the system of Copernicus against the theologians, and he does not pay attention to the fact that this system, in this epoch, is far from being evident and demonstrated. The proofs which he gave thereof at that time, and later on, are very weak, as the savants of our days admit. They are only vain analogies, incapable of producing a reasonable conviction; hence, it is not astonishing that they did not satisfy men learned in the schools who opposed this system.

Another letter to the Archduchess, dated December 21, 1613, was not printed at first; only copies thereof were made; these circulated and produced soon in Florence and elsewhere a great agitation. The accusations made against Galileo were not directed to his astronomical opinions, but to his antiperipatetician propositions and his interpretations of the sacred text, which were judged as false and dangerous.

One of the errors of Galileo was certainly to enter into his discussions, either by his own initiative or that of bad advisers, questions of theology and of sacred exegesis. While Bergier has gone too far when he said that this savant had been pursued by the Inquisition, "not as a good astronomer, but as a bad theologian," it is not less certain that, if he had been more prudent and more conservative, and if he had not left his domain, he could have avoided the rancor of which he was the object. But all the friends of Galileo advised him in vain to content himself with scientific demonstrations, "without entering the domain of the Scriptures." While the Inquisition was wrong in condemning the opinion of Galileo, it was not so much on account of the new astronomical system he taught; but it was the conduct of the Florentine astronomer who rendered the judgment unavoidable.

Galileo was denounced in the year 1615, under the pontificate of Paul V. to the Congregation of the Inquisition and of the Index. Both, after having examined his doctrine and writings, gave February 26 and March 5, 1616, two decisions, the one dogmatical, declaring as false and contrary to Scripture the opinion with regard to the immobility of the sun and to the mobility of the earth; the other disciplinary, forbidding Galileo to teach this opinion either as absolute truth or as hypothesis. Out of regard for the author, the name of Galileo and the title of his works were not mentioned in the decree which condemned him; they required from him no formal retraction, and they imposed no penance upon him. Only they made him promise not to teach any longer his opinion either orally or by writing.

In the same time that they condemned Galileo, March 5, 1616, the Congregation of the Index rejected the book, "On the Revolutions of the Heavenly Spheres," of Copernicus, but only with the clause "donec corrigatur." By a new decree of May 15. 1620, the Congregation of the Index permitted expressly the acceptation of the system of Copernicus under the sole restraining clause that it should not be taught as an absolute truth, but as a scientific hypothesis, and it authorized the reading of the work of the Polish savant, in which they had made some few corrections bearing on the passages where this astronomer seemed to affirm too positively his doctrines. The Sovereign Pontiff neither signed nor approved explicitly any of these acts.

All appeared to be ended. Galileo had accepted his condemnation and promised without reclaim to submit himself to what they asked of him. However, in time he forgot his promises and, in diverse Memoirs which he published, he upheld his astronomical system in an indirect manner. Finally, sixteen years after his first condemnation, in 1632, he had published his famous "Dialogo dei due Massimi Systemi del Mondo." Although in the conclusion of his work the question was not decided, nevertheless, in the entire course of the Dialogue, a certain Simplicius defended the system of Ptolemy by ridiculous arguments, and it was impossible not to see in his writing an apology of the system of Copernicus. Indeed, this was patent.

The publication of the "Dialogo" was, therefore, a formal violation of the promises made by Galileo. The affair was carried to Rome, the work was examined and, by a decree of June 16, 1633, the Congregation of the Index condemned this writing. Moreover, it prohibited the author to further treat on this astronomical question in dispute. But this was not all. A few days later, on June 22, 1633, the Holy Office cited the Florentine astronomer before its tribunal. It declared him suspect of heresy in having violated the agreement made in 1616, it obliged him to abjure his opinion, and condemned him to an expiatory punishment, consisting of imprisonment, the conditions of which should be determined ultimately by the judges, and in the weekly recitation of the Penitential Psalms for a term of three years. Galileo submitted. Whatever the enemies of the Church may have said, he was never subjected to the torture nor confined in the dungeons of the Inquisition; he received even after his condemnation a pension from the Pope which continued until his death.

A month after the sentence rendered against Galileo by the Inquisition, August 23, 1634, the "Dialogue on the Two Systems of the World" was put on the Index purely and simply, that is, without indication of the motives. At the same time the judgment given against him by the Inquisition received, as well as his retraction, a great publicity. Thus ended the important affair. Since 1634 we find no trace of any new condemnation of the system of Copernicus. In 1757, under Benedict XIV., it was decided that the prohibition to teach otherwise except as a hypothesis the immobility of the sun, should be suppressed in the editions of the Index; nevertheless, the works anteriorly condemned were maintained therein, and we find them yet in the edition of 1819. Finally, a decree of the Inquisition of September 25, 1822, approved by Pope Pius VII. authorized, without restriction, that the mobility of the earth might be taught by astronomers, and all books which had been condemned for having sanctioned the ideas of Copernicus disappeared from the following edition of the Index, which was printed in 1835.

Such are the facts. Does it follow from this that Catholics are obliged to believe that the real meaning of the passage of Josue, commanding the sun to stand still, is in opposition to the system of Copernicus? Not at all. We know that the Congregations have condemned Galileo, but nothing forces us to accept as true their interpretation. The decree of 1616, considered in itself, lacks the characters required by the Vatican Council for the definitions to which the Church attributes the seal of infallibility.

CHAPTER XXX.

JEPHTE AND THE IMMOLATION OF HIS DAUGHTER.

ONE of the Biblical accounts most attacked is unquestionably the vow made by Jephte to sacrifice to the Lord the first living being he would meet, if he should be victorious over the Ammonites. We know that it was his only daughter that came to meet him, and the Bible tells that the unfortunate father executed the vow he had made.

It has been always a mooted question among theologians whether or not Jepthe really immolated his daughter. It does not enter into the plan of this work to venture a solution at the expense of the one or the other opinion; it is sufficient for us to show that the Bible is protected against all attacks, whatever the solution adopted may be.

Certain commentators have tried to justify Jepthe. Founding themselves upon the prohibition made by God of human sacrifices, upon the eulogy of Jepthe contained in the Epistle to the Hebrews, they refuse to suppose that the Judge of Israel, in order to obtain a divine favor, intended to make a vow contrary to the law. As to the formula itself of the vow: " The same will I offer a holocaust to the Lord " (Judges xi. 31), the one interpret it thus: " If it is a person, I consecrate her to the service of Jehovah, and if it is an animal which can be immolated, I offer it as a holocaust." The others, without removing themselves from the grammatical meaning adopted by St. Jerome, say that we must understand the vow of Jepthe in a figurative sense: To renounce, to give over to marriage, especially a daughter of a chief and conqueror, was a great sacrifice, which Jepthe expressed by the word holocaust.

Without endeavoring to justify these interpretations, which at best appear less plausible than the traditional interpretation, it is sufficient to state that rigorously they may be true, and that, consequently, nothing peremptory can be alleged against the Bible, in regard to the vow of Jepthe.

Let us suppose now that Jepthe really did promise and fulfill a human sacrifice, as the traditional voice, as well as the violent character of the Judge and the Biblical account itself, would seem to indicate. What can we conclude from this? Only one thing: that Jepthe committed a crime, or rather two crimes: an impious vow and the execution of this vow. But the enemies of faith have endeavored to deduce other conclusions from this account against God and the Bible. 1. They have pretended to prove thereby that God authorized human sacrifices among the Jews; but, on the contrary, it is absolutely certain that God formally decreed otherwise, and that the human sacrifices reported in some places in the Bible were criminal infractions of the law of God. To support one's self upon the vow of Jepthe, to pretend that these sacrifices were permitted, would be the same as if one would pretend that the American law permitted murder, because there are Americans who become murderers. 2. As to the Bible itself, it cannot be made responsible or considered an accomplice of the crime which it relates. It is true that it does not formally blame it, but it is not the custom of the sacred writers to express opinions on the facts they report. It is also true that St. Paul praises Jepthe, but he praises him solely on account of his faith, together with Solomon and David, without absolving any of these personages from their faults they might have committed.

CHAPTER XXXI.

GEDEON AND THE MADIANITES.

SINCE seven years were the Israelites sighing under the yoke of the Madianites, when an angel appeared to Gedeon to tell him to deliver Israel, and God gave him signs of his mission (Judges iv, 37-40). The hand of God appeared in such a visible manner in the history of Gedeon that the Rationalists, enemies of the miracle, did not hesitate to attack its authenticity, in spite of the numerous details into which the author enters, details which are all fully in accord with what science teaches of the topography and the customs of Palestine during this epoch. All that certain Rationalists wish to admit is the reality of a " signal defeat " undergone by the Madianites, and the honor of which is attributed to a powerful and rich sheik by the name of Yeroubabaal . . . designed by preference under the name of Giudeon." As to the rest, it is only a " legend, forged by additions, and rehandled successively." The sole reason which the infidel critic gives for his affirmation is that the two Madianite chiefs die in two different ways, in two different localities, where they are equally designated under two different names (vii. 24-25; viii, 10-12).

The objection answers itself: It would be astonishing, we admit, if the author had made these two personages die in two different manners with only the relation of a few events between the two deaths, if they had the same names, and if they were one and the same person. But because they do not carry the same name it is quite natural to suppose that the same chiefs are not meant and that Oreb and Zeb could not die in the same manner as Zebee and Salmana.

But when the Rationalists reject in the history of Gedeon everything that supposes a miracle, they are very careful to keep as history all that can serve them as pretext to attack the religion of the Israelites: 1. According to the Biblical account it was an angel of the Lord who came to tell Gedeon to take up arms against the Madianites, and who promises to him the victory (vi, 11-24). Now, according to this narrative, Gedeon offers to the angel a kid and azym bread, and the Vulgate calls this offering by the name of sacrifice. The Rationalists conclude from this that at the epoch of the Judges they did know neither the ceremonial rites, nor the Levitic priesthood, nor the unity of the sanctuary of which the Pentateuch speaks, and, hence, infer that this account is not authentic. But nothing hindered Gedeon to act as he did. The context requires that the word sacrifice must be taken here in the most general sense of offering. When Gedeon offered to the supernatural being that appeared to him a kid and bread, it was under the title of a gift, of a repast, and undoubtedly, to verify, to a certain extent, whether the apparition was a real one: "Give me a sign that it is thou that speakest to me" (vi, 17) he said to the angel, and it was then that he made this offering. When, later on, he offers a real sacrifice (vi, 27), he did this by order of the Lord, and, consequently, did not need to feel uneasy about the fact that he did not have the Levitical power to offer sacrifice. The ceremonial laws having God for author, He could very well dispense therefrom accordingly as He pleased.

2. Gedeon having received from his father the surname of Jerobaal (vi, 24-32), the Rationalists wish to behold in this name one of the numerous indications in which they pretend to find the traces of primitive polytheism of the Hebrews. In fact, it is sufficient to read the episode in question to see that this name indicates an aversion of the one who bore it to Baal.

3. After the victory, Gedeon causes all the golden earrings, taken from the enemies, to be delivered to him, and later on he makes an Ephod of them, which became an object of idolatry for the people. It was but natural for the infidels to grasp this fact, and to behold again therein a trace of the primitive idolatry of the Hebrews, but in the same passage it is said that the impious worship occasioned by the Ephod received its chastisement, which indicates very clearly that this was only an abnormal and accidental fall from grace. Moreover, nothing proves that Gedeon himself was guilty, and especially nothing proves that this ephod was an idol, a statue as the Rationalists claim, and not the sacerdotal vestment called Ephod.

The ephod was composed of two parts, of which one covered the breast and the upper part of the body, whilst the other was hanging back of the shoulders. The two parts were attached together on the top of the shoulders by two onyxes, upon each of which were engraved six of the names of the twelve tribes of Israel. The ephod was held together below by a golden, purple and linen cincture. On the ephod of the high priest was placed the pectoral, containing two precious stones, *urim* and *thumim*, of which he made use to consult the Lord. As to the manner this was done, we cannot accuse the Hebrews of idolatry, for the ephod was not a statue, but a sacerdotal garment (I Kings xiv; xxi; xxii); it said very clearly that the priests whom Saul put to death, "wore the linen ephod" (xxii, 18). Thus, Gedeon, in making his Ephod, might be accused of a wrongful action, which caused the people to commit acts of idolatry, but his action in itself was not idolatry.

CHAPTER XXXII.

THE BOOKS OF KINGS.

THE most punctilious critics cannot help but to acknowledge the historical value of the Books of Samuel or First and Second Books of Kings. "The events commence to become grouped and connected," writes Mr. Reuss, "the situations are sketched more neatly." The archæological studies made in the Orient, the deciphering of the Egyptian hieroglyphics, the discovery of the monuments of Ninive and of Chaldea, have confirmed the exactitude of the sacred account to such an extent that we are enabled to verify it by means of documents borrowed from foreign sources. Hence, infidelity is obliged to render justice to the historians of the kingdom of Juda and of Israel. They pretend, however, to find inaccuracies in their writings. Moreover, they incriminate the conduct, blacken the character of several personages praised by the sacred writers. Therefore, in the first place, we have to answer to the accusations made against certain accounts of the historians of the Books of Kings and justify, in the second place, against the attacks, the prophets and princes praised in this second part of the Sacred Scriptures.

Since all times the Books of Kings and of Paralipomenons have been accused of inaccuracies; one claim is that the different details do not appear to harmonize with one another, the other objections apply to certain figures or to certain assertions which seem exaggerated and improbable. Since all times, the commentators have tried to reconcile the divergencies of the text and to explain these figures. Negative criticism has hastened to collect the objections, without keeping account of the answers, in order to form weapons which they wield against the Sacred Writings.

The Rationalists pretend to conclude from the divergencies one can point out in the histories of the Kings that they are the work of unskillful compilers, who, having drawn from divers sources, did not have sufficient knowledge to separate, in the different accounts, the true from the false, that which they should have preserved and that which they should have rejected; and, consequently, they have given us a confused and rehashed amalgamation of matter obtained from anterior writings. In making these accusations against the historians of the kingdoms of Juda and of Israel, the objective point the infidels have is to bring them into discredit; they affirm that their work is wanting in unity, in order to maintain that it is unworthy of belief. All these accusations are without fcoundation as we are going to show. The history of the kings who have reigned over the people of God is related to us in three distinct writings, each forming a whole, which we shall study successively: 1. The two Books of Samuel or the First and Second Books of Kings; 2. The Third and Fourth Books of Kings; 3. The First and Second Books of Paralipomenons or Chronicles.

1. DIFFICULTIES DRAWN FROM THE BOOKS OF SAMUEL OR FIRST AND SECOND BOOKS OF KINGS.

It is especially in the two Books of Samuel or First and Second Books of Kings that apparent contradictions have been discovered. The developments which the historian gives to his account made him return several times to the same subject, and he has not always presented it in the same light, considering it now under one aspect, now under another, and writing, besides, according to the Oriental fashion, that is, without trying to follow a rigorous and logical order, and without believing himself obliged to unite and connect in a consecutive manner all the parts of his account. He has counted on straightforward readers of good faith like his own, and he did not foresee malicious and critical interpretation. In fact he was not writing for modern fault finders. When one is not predisposed to find the Israelitic writer in fault, nothing is ordinarily more easy than to reconcile what at first sight appears to be contradictory. We must never forget, in reading the Oriental authors, that they were not acquainted with what we call the art of composition, and, consequently, their writings are idiomatic and replete with omissions which were supposed to be understood, and which we must supply. To do this is, indeed, anything but difficult. Without entering here into minute and elaborate examination of all the so-called difficulties, it will be sufficient to quote some examples, selected among the principal ones, to show how insignificant are the divergencies of which the adversaries of the Bible would like to make manifest contradictions. One is even surprised that instructed men, who are acquainted with the peculiarities of the habits of Semitic writings, dare to allege in support of their thesis allegations so illogical as those which they present.

The first of these is directed against the Biblical statement of the causes which brought on the establishment of the kingdom of Israel. One of these causes was the old age of Samuel and the transgressions of his sons;[1] this was evidently not the most important motive of the institution of the monarchy. There had been several others, as is always the case in political revolutions. When the Israelites desired to have a king, because Samuel was unable to fulfill any longer his functions as judge, and when they had no confidence in his children, they desired him to anoint a king, so that they might be the better enabled to resist their enemies, and in particular the Ammonites,[2] with whom they were too weak to combat with success, as long as they were divided, but whom they could, on the contrary, conquer easily when all their forces were united under one chief. The Israelitic historian mentions this motive when his subject leads him to speak of the war; on another occasion he attributes the age of Samuel as a reason for the institution of the monarchy. In all this there is not the least contradiction; only the author has not enumerated together and in a methodical way. the diverse causes which occasioned the anointing of Saul as king.

---

[1] I Kings viii, 5.
[2] I Kings xii, 12.

The account of the election of Saul gives rise to a similar objection. He is at first anointed king by Samuel by the order of God,[1] then he is designated publicly by lot before the assembled people,[2] — the one does not exclude the other — finally, he is universally recognized by all Israel after his victory over the Ammonites,[3] because the deliverance of Jabes of Galaad and his triumph over the besiegers put an end to the partial opposition which had manifested itself until then against his elevation to the throne.

The contradictions which the critic attempts to discover in the history of David, after his victory over Goliath, do not exist in fact. The young hero carries the head of the Philistine to Jerusalem, although it was only later, when he had become king,[4] that he became possessed of the fortress of Mount Sinai; but we must remark that when the fortress belonged still, in this epoch, to the Jebuseans, the city itself belonged already to the Israelites.[5] David also, immediately after the combat, deposes in his tent, or in the house of his father, the arms of the fallen giant,[6] but David places aside the sword which he consecrates to God and which he recovers later on at Nobe.[7] Nothing is, therefore, more easy than to reconcile these different details and other similar ones. To conclude from these divergencies that the writer of the Books of Samuel was an ignorant compiler who did not know how to make use of the material

---
[1] I Kings x, 1.
[2] I Kings x, 21.
[3] I Kings xi, 15.
[4] II Kings v, 9.
[5] I Kings xvii, 54.
[6] I Kings xvii, 54.
[7] I Kings xxi, 1-9.

which he obtained from various sources of information, is to wish to obscure what is clear, to abuse and misunderstand the Oriental manner of writing.

The Rationalists claim to have discovered a more glaring contradiction which, according to them, can be accounted for in no other way, except by attributing stupidity and falsehood to the writer. This accusation applies to the account of the anointment by Samuel of the young David, and the statement of his arrival at the camp of Saul, preceding his combat with Goliath.[1] When Samuel arrives at Bethlehem, the historian makes us acquainted with the father and the brothers of David,[2] and a little further he presents them anew to the reader, as if he had never spoken of them.[3] Before the war Saul makes David, who is very brave, his armor-bearer,[4] and, when the war breaks out, we behold David watching his flock and going into the camp only by chance, in order to bring the necessaries of life to his brethren.[5] But what is more extraordinary still, Saul who, before going to combat the Philistines, had chosen David as his armor-bearer and knew him well, and also his father,[6] does not know the young man who felled Goliath.[7] Such is the objection.

We acknowledge quite willingly that a historian of our days would not have formulated his account as the Israelitic historian has done, but we must not forget that we have to judge a Semitic writer, and not a

---

[1] I Kings xvi, 1; xviii, 5.
[2] I Kings xvi, 1-13.
[3] I Kings xli, 12-16.
[4] I Kings xvi, 18, 21.
[5] I Kings xvii, 17.
[6] I Kings xvi, 18-22.
[7] I Kings xvii, 55-58.

modern writer. One of the most remarkable peculiarities of the Semitic writings, which distinguish them so greatly from our manner of narration, is the frequent repetition. The Orientals write as they speak. Now, all those who have traveled in the Orient know how the native narrators are given to repetition. We notice this peculiarity in all the Oriental books of these countries. The sons of Noe are enumerated four times in four consecutive chapters;[1] certain genealogies are repeated several times in the same book, for example, in the Paralipomenons;[2] hence, only those who are ignorant of this habit of the Oriental writers should be really surprised at these repetitions.

The two accounts in question are besides completely independent. The historian does not speak the second time of the brothers of David as if they were entirely unknown to us and, on the subject of David himself, he is careful to recall to mind that he has already made them known to his readers: "David," he says, "the son of that man of Ephrata (before mentioned, explains justly the Vulgate), of Bethlehem, Juda."[3]

But how, it is insisted, could Saul display ignorance of David when he had asked the latter's father to dedicate him to the royal service and be his armor-bearer?[4] And how does it come that Abner does not know him any more than his royal master?

The answer is plain, and it was given by St. Ephrem a long time since. The King knew sufficiently well the

---
[1] Gen. v, 32; vi, 10; ix, 18; x, 1.
[2] See I Par. vii, 6-7, and viii, 1-3; viii, 29-40, and ix, 35-44, etc.
[3] I Kings xvii, 12.
[4] I Kings xvi, 19-22.

shepherd of Bethlehem to attach him to his person, in the quality of armor-bearer and musician; but the courage of David astonishes him, and awakens anew the royal interest; moreover, having promised his daughter to the conqueror of Goliath, he desires, as a good father, more definite information on the character and family of the one who seeks to become his son-in-law, and with this object he charges Abner to question David.[1] Nothing could be more natural nor more legitimate. Perhaps, also, the king beheld in David the one who should supplant him, as Samuel had announced to him: this is also a commentary of St. Ephrem.[2] The persistence itself which Saul displays in making inquiries shows that the affair was to him one of no little importance, but of great moment, to which he attached great value. Hence, we have no real contradiction here, no more than in the other alleged inaccuracies in the First and Second Books of Kings.

2. DIFFICULTIES DRAWN FROM THE CHRONOLOGY OF THE THIRD AND FOURTH BOOKS OF KINGS.

The most of the difficulties which the Rationalistic critics bring forward against the Third and Fourth Books of Kings are so insignificant that they are not worthy of mention. One alone merits some attention. It applies to that drawn from chronology.

We have already given attention to the incertitude of the Biblical chronology[3] of the primitive times. The chronology of the Books of Kings is not less uncertain,

---

[1] I Kings xvii, 55-57.
[2] St. Ephrem, or I Kings xvii, 53. "Opera Syriaca," vol. i, p. 370.
[3] See Chapter ix.

although circumscribed naturally within a more limited sphere and for different reasons. Whilst there is question of centuries at the beginning of the world, there is question here of some years; whilst the synchronisms are wanting in Genesis, in the Books of Kings, on the contrary, they are abounding; but, as we shall see, they aggravate the difficulty instead of solving it. One sole point is common to the two problems, it is, that figures have been altered in both. They are established in Genesis by the comparison of the original text with the ancient versions; they are manifest in the history of the Kings by the simple comparison of passages parallel with the Books of Kings and Paralipomenons.

Already St. Jerome wrote to the priest Vitalis: " Read all the Books of the Old and New Testament and you will find such a discord as to the number of the years, such a confusion as to the duration of the reigns of the kings of Juda and of Israel, that to try to clear up this question will rather appear to be the occupation of an idle man than of a savant."[1] It will be sufficient to quote an example to prove this " confusion " and this " discord " of the figures. In the Fourth Book of Kings we read: " Ochozias was two and twenty years old when he began to reign," and in the Second Book of Paralipomenons, " Ochozias was forty-two years old when he began to reign."[2] The contradiction is flagrant. More or less ingenious explanations have been ventured to reconcile these contradictions, without admitting any alteration, but none of these explanations is satisfactory, and Cornelius a Lapide was right

---

[1] St. Jerome, *Ep.* lii, 5, vol. xxii, col. 675-676.
[2] IV Kings viii, 26; II Par. xxii, 2.

in saying that one of the numbers given is due to an error of the copyists.

All the analogous difficulties must, undoubtedly, be subject to this explanation. These alterations of the original figures may be easily accounted for. We find them in all the ancient authors, and they were unavoidable before the invention of printing — which has not done away with them completely — when each copy of a book was made by hand. St. Augustine remarked that the numbers were generally the most defective part in the transcriptions. A copyist is guided by the general meaning when he transcribes a phrase where he meets a word badly written, and thus he may guess the real meaning, but when he finds in the text which he copies one or more numerals nearly illegible, in many cases nothing can guide him to a positive knowledge of its or their determination. The transcribers of the works in question doubtless met with such a difficulty in the case of Ochozias who, according to one account, commenced to reign when he was twenty-two years of age, according to another not until he was forty-two years of age. Who is it of those accustomed to writing who has not been sometimes embarrassed to decipher or to transcribe a numeral which he himself has written, but which he has badly formed? The critic has the right to rectify them, when he can do so, but he has no right to draw any conclusion from them against the authority and exactitude of the Sacred Books. He could justly accuse of error the inspired writers only in so far if he would find false figures in their original work, such as it has gone forth from their pen. Now, nothing authorizes us, even without keeping account of the divine inspiration which guaranteed against all error the authors both of the Old and the New Testaments, to make ascend until them the actual alterations of their text.

A recent attempt has been made, it is true, to hold the sacred writers responsible for the contradictions of the dates which both the sacred and Assyrian history present. The Assyrian epigraphy, which has confirmed on so many points in a striking manner the sacred account, appears to disagree with the same on the subject of chronology. The synchronisms which the two sources offer to us are, at first sight, irreconcilable. The Assyrian chronology was exactly fixed in the document of Nineve by means of eponyms who gave their name to the year like the consuls at Rome. The original inscriptions having come down to us, they could not have been altered by any transcriptions; hence, they merit full confidence. Now they contradict the accounts of the Scripture. The harmony exists in both as to the taking of Samaria by the Assyrians in the year 721 B. C.; but, according to the Biblical chronology generally received, Achab, King of Israel, died in the year 898 or 897 B. C., and, according to the Assyrian chronology, he was defeated with the allied Kings at Karkar, by Salmanasar III., King of Ninive, in 854 B. C., that is, more than forty years after the date which we assign to his death.[1] Ozias, King of Israel, reigned from 809 to 758, and the inscriptions of Teglath Phalasar portray him engaged in war with this king about the year 742 or 740 B. C., or eighteen years after Ozias had died. Manahem, King of Israel,

---

[1] This event of the life of Achab is only known to us by the Assyrian documents; the Bible does not mention it.

reigned from 770 to 759 B. C. and twenty-one years after the end of his reign in 738. Teglath Phalasar II. counts him among his tributaries. Hence, there can be no more formal contradiction, say the enemies of the Bible.

Yes, apparently, we answer; in reality, no. The Assyrian chronology is in opposition to the artificial chronology manufactured from the Biblical texts by the commentators, but not with the Biblical texts themselves. Not only do the Ninevite documents and the Israelitic documents not contradict one another at all, but they are perfectly in accord as to the synchronisms; both state that Ozias, King of Juda, and Manahem, King of Israel, were contemporaries of Teglath Phalasar II., as Salmanasar IV., Sargon and Sennacherib were contemporaries of Ezechias, King of Juda. The Assyrian epigraphy confirms, therefore, the sacred account, instead of contradicting it, all over where the alterations of figures are out of question. The discord exists only in the calculations made by the chronologists.

To understand this discord it is sufficient for us to recall to mind what we have said above that, on account of the errors of the copyists, the reigning years of the Kings of Israel and of Juda, are unknown to us in a certain manner. In admitting the years of the kings of Juda on the one hand, and those of the kings of Israel on the other, instead of finding the same total sum for the two kingdoms in the two calculations, from the time of Jeroboam, first King of Israel, to the destruction of Samaria, about twenty years are wanting in the chronology of the kingdom of Israel. To fill up this gap many artifices have been employed, among others the supposition of two interreigns in Israel: the existence of these two interreigns does not rest upon any proof. Almost all the chronologists have admitted that we must lengthen the duration of the kingdom of Israel: the Assyrian chronological canons whose authority, contestable in some points of detail, are not so in their entirety, show that instead of adding years to the kingdom of Israel, we must substract the superfluous years from the kingdom of Juda. Achab and his successors, as well as the kings of Juda their contemporaries, are somewhat less ancient than supposed.

Hence, what is necessary to be rectified are the computations of the ancient chronologists. The text of the sacred authors does not enter into these controversies of the savants, except in one particular, which is within the province of critical objection, namely, that of the altered figures, which, however, do not affect the inspiration and veracity of the sacred authors, as we have already demonstrated. We do not need to inquire here what chronological system is to be preferred. It is the critic who should labor to discover, by means of the profane synchronisms, which are the figures that have been altered, and thus to restore the primitive numbers.

3. KING JOSIAS AND THE HIGH PRIEST HELICAS.

The Fourth Book of Kings and the Second of Paralipomenons (IV Kings xxii, 8-20; II Par. xxxiv. 14-33), relate that in the eighteenth year of the reign of King Josias, the high priest Helcias discovered the Book of Deuteronomy in the temple of Jerusalem. The Second Book of Paralipomenons, in relating the same facts, adds only certain details, among which we remark the following: "The Book of Law found by Helcias was the book written by Moses" (xxxv, 14). The Rationalists do not question the main facts of the account we are discussing. But when infidelity, according to its ordinary tactics, admits the exactitude of the sacred account, it is to pervert it and because they expect to derive from it some argument against the traditional belief. About the middle of the last century, an English deist, Samuel Parvish, enunciated the hypothesis that Deuteronomy had been written in the eighth century B. C., and that it was the work of the skillful forger, Helcias. Even he pretended to support his hypothesis on the passages of the Sacred Books which have been indicated above. His opinion was welcomed by the Rationalistic critics, and a great number of them to-day establish their theories concerning the origin of the Pentateuch upon the ideas of Parvish.

Thus the infidels accept the account of the Book of Kings, but only because they have an object in so doing, and to conclude from it that Deuteronomy was written in this epoch and had for its author Helcias or some contemporary. But by what right do they consider this passage partly true and partly false? Why do they accept the testimony of the sacred author reporting that the Book of Deuteronomy has been really presented to Josias, and why do they reject the testimony of the same writer, affirming that the Book of Moses was "found," and not invented and supposed by a forger? Solely to maintain their preconceived opinions and to deny the antiquity of the Pentateuch.

Every other consideration is subordinated to this object which to the infidels is all-important to establish. However, it is certain that the Pentateuch existed before Helcias and Josias, according to the account of Kings and of Paralipomenons. In order that a book may be "found," it must have existed before the finding; in order that this book found should be recognized as the "Book of the Law," this Book of the Law must have been known of before.

But say the objectors: If the Law of Moses was known, why did the discovery of this book produce such a commotion at court, and in the city of Jerusalem? Because then they read it with attention, after having neglected it for too long a time during which it had become lost sight of. We find an analogous fact several centuries later on. When Esdras had read the Law to the people (II Esd. viii), "the assembled Israelites shed tears. Esdras and the Levites console them and encourage them to rejoice. On the next day they seek to understand what Esdras had read to them on the previous day. They study the Thora which he read, as a text that was new and unknown to them." It is Mr. Renan who so states. However, they knew at least of Deuteronomy from a very early time. Very well! What occurred under Josias is not less surprising, nor less true than that which took place under Esdras. Besides it is impossible not to acknowledge that the Mosaic law and the history contained in the first books of the Pentateuch were known before Josias and Helcias.

A convincing proof that Deuteronomy was not composed under the Kings, at the time of Josias, is that it contains, not one law, but several laws which would have no meaning in this epoch. Thus, the Israelites receive the order to exterminate Amalek after their taking possession of the land of Canaan. Under Josias Amalek had disappeared from the scene of history since a long time (Deut. xxv, 17-19; Cf. I Kings xiv, 48; xv, 2; xxvii, 8; xxx, 1; etc.). — They were also commanded to destroy the Canaanites, who were at that time of no importance, and could not have been a menace to the Israelites (Deut. xx, 16-18).—A law is promulgated against Ammon and Moab in favor of Edom. It is the reverse of the dispositions which reigned in Israel in regard to the Idumeans during the last days of the kings, and the descendants of Esau were regarded as the most implacable enemies and the most deserving of hatred on the part of the children of Jacob (Deut. xxxiii, 3, 4, 7, 8; Cf. Jer. xlviii, 47; xlix, 6, 17, 18; Ps. cxxxvii, 7; etc.).—The legislator who gives counsels for the choice of a king, supposed that the people might desire some day to have such. How could counsels of this kind have been given several centuries after the election of Saul? (Deut. xvii, 17-20). What is said of the organization of the army could not have been written under the domination of a king (Deut. xx, 9). — Funeral practices and manners of mourning, which are interdicted by the Law, were, on the contrary, permitted at the time of Josias and later; hence, it is not in the epoch of Josias that they could formulate this interdiction (Deut. xiv, 1-2; Cf. Jer. vii, 27; xv, 6; xli, 5).

That Deuteronomy was composed only after the preceding books of the Pentateuch, we have also several proofs in Deuteronomy itself. We read therein that the Levites will not have heritage among their brethren, because Jehovah is their heritage, as " He had told them." Where had He told it to them? In the Book of Numbers, in that part of the Law which the actual critic calls Elohistic, and pretends to be posterior to the Captivity (Deut. xviii, 2; Cf. Num. xviii, 20-23).—

It is prescribed to the people to preserve in the treatment of the lepers all that the priests will teach them, as He had commanded to them. This ordinance we read in two chapters of Leviticus, and nowhere else (Deut. xxiv, 8-9; Lev. xiii; xiv).—The Numbers ordain the establishment of six cities of refuge in the land of Canaan. In Deuteronomy, Moses, in order to execute this command, chose three to the east of the Jordan, and he arranges to locate the three others to the west of this river after the conquest of the country (Num. xxxv; Deut. iv, 41; xix, 1-3).—What is said of the clean and unclean animals in Deuteronomy presupposes equally what is said thereof in Leviticus. All these facts are incontestable. Hence, it is supremely unjust to impute to the high priest Helcias, to Josias, or to other contemporaries, a fraud which they have not committed.

358 DIFFICULTIES OF THE BIBLE.

KINGS OF JUDA.	III KINGS.		KINGS OF ISRAEL.	III KINGS.	
Roboam	17 years.	xiv. 21.	Jeroboam i	22 years.	xiv. 20.
Abias	3 "	xv. 2.	Nadab	2 "	xv. 15.
Asa	41 "	xv. 20.	Baasa	24 "	xv. 33.
Josaphat	25 "	xii. 42.	Ela	2 "	xvi. 8.
Joram	8 "	viii. 17.	Zamri	(7 days.)	xvi. 15.
Ochozias	iv. Kl. 1 yr.	viii. 25.	Amri	12 years.	xvi. 23.
Athalia	6 years.	xi. and xii.	Achab	22 "	xvii. 20.
Joas	40 "	xii. 1.	Ochozias	iv. Kl. 12 yrs.	xxii. 52.
Amasias	29 "	xiv. 1.	Joram	28 years.	iii. 1.
Ozias	52 "	xv. 2.	Jehu	17 "	x. 34.
Joatham	16 "	xv. 33.	Joachaz	16 "	xv. 1.
Achaz	16 "	xvi. 2.	Joas	41 "	xiii. 10.
Ezechias, commencement	6 "	xviii. 10.	Jeroboam ii	(6 months.)	xiv. 23.
			Zacharias	1 year.	xv. 8.
Total	260 years, until the ruin of Samaria.		Sellum	10 years.	xv. 13.
			Manahem	2 "	xv. 17.
			Phacein	20 "	xv. 23.
			Phacee	9 "	xv. 27.
			Osee		xvii. 1.
			Total	241 years 6 months and 7 days, until the destruction of Samaria.	

There is therefore a difference of about twenty years between the total of the two chronologies.

CHAPTER XXXIII.

THE PARALIPOMENONS.

ALL the modern savants are agreed to acknowledge, in spite of some insignificant restrictions, the historical value of the Third and Fourth Books of Kings; they cannot refuse to them this justice, since the discovery of the Assyrian inscriptions has confirmed, in a manner both striking and unexpected, the exactitude of their accounts. But the infidels revenge themselves on the Paralipomenons for the admission they are forced to make in regard to the Books of Kings. It would seem that, according to their ideas, abuse falls short of expressing the contempt which this work deserves. At the beginning of this century they went so far as to deny the good faith of the author. In more modern times, they pretended that the author of the Paralipomenons invented everything, not only the genealogies and the accounts which we do not read in the other books of the Old Testament, but also the title of the writings which he cites as his sources of information. These accusations are so evidently false that many Rationalists of our days have refused to grant them their sanction. Wellhausen, however, has taken them up anew in his "Prolegomena zur Geschichte Israels" (1883, p. 178). In this work he declares that he takes De Wette for guide, and he revives all his objections, in spite of the decisive answers that had been made to them, because he desires by all means to deny the Mosaic origin of the Pentateuch, and because the authority of the Paralipomenons is sufficient to overthrow his thesis of predilection, as De Wette was forced to acknowledge. Hence, he finds no terms injurious and despising enough to characterize this work: " its author mixes and confounds everything he amplifies, falsifies and invents." Such an account is " a frightful example of the impudent imagination of the Jews." Such another is a " nonsense."

In spite of these accusations launched against the Paralipomenons, when we come to the details it will be found that the number of the incriminated facts is not so considerable. We are going to examine them successively; we will show that it is quite wrong to reproach with inaccuracies Esdras, the probable and well-informed author of this historical writing.

1. THE CAPTIVITY OF KING MANASSES.

The first and principal reproach made to the Book of the Paralipomenons is the account of the captivity at Babylon, of Manasses the King of Juda. It is affirmed that this is a mere fable, deserving of no credit whatever.

" Manasses seduced Juda and the inhabitants of Jerusalem to do evil beyond all the nations which the Lord had destroyed before the face of the children of Israel. And the Lord spoke to him and to his people, and they would not harken. Therefore He brought upon them the captains of the army of the King of the Assyrians, and they took Manasses and carried him bound with chains and fetters to Babylon. And after that he was in distress, he prayed to the Lord his God, and did penance exceedingly before the God of his fathers, and he entreated Him and besought Him earnestly, and He heard his prayer, and brought him again to Jerusalem into his kingdom, and Manasses knew that the Lord was God."[1]

The first objection to this account is derived from the silence of the Books of Kings, which do not speak of such an important event. This objection would have some foundation, if the Books of Kings contained a complete history of the kingdoms of Juda and Israel; but it is well known that these books often give but a summary of the events, and that they refer the reader to more elaborate writings, as the Chronicles of the Kings of Juda and Israel, for amplified details, and for omissions in their accounts. Hence, it is not astonishing that Esdras could relate events which he derived from other sources, which were known to or passed in silence by the writer of the Kings. The existence of omissions in the latter work is, moreover, unquestioned at present. The Assyrian inscriptions have revealed to us several incidents of the history of Israel which were totally unknown to us, as the defeat of Achab at Karkar, the paying of tribute by Jehu to the King of Assyria, and divers circumstances of the campaign of Sennacherib against Ezechias, King of Juda.

2. THE ANNALS OF ASSURBANIPAL.

The annals of Assurbanipal, King of Nineve, show us equally well how poorly founded are all the other objections which are raised against the Book of Parali-

---
[1] 2 Par. xxxiii, 9-13.

pomenons. The veracity of this account having been questioned, by a special permission of Providence, the cuneiform documents were brought to light to confirm it in every particular. It has been denied that a " King of Assur " invaded Palestine in the reign of Manasses. Assurbanipal, King of Assur, on one of his cylinders, states as follows:

> 69. Towards Egypt and Ethiopia I directed my march.
> 70. In the course of my expedition, twenty-two kings
> 71. from the shores of the (Mediterranea), all
> 72. tributaries, dependent upon me,
> 73. in my presence (came and kissed my feet).[1]

Another cylinder of the same monarch enumerates these twenty-two kings, and the second named is " Manasses, King of Juda, *Minasi, sar Yahudi*. The first statement objected to in the account of the Paralipomenons is, therefore, completely verified.

One has also denied that the King of Assur compelled a monarch to stoop over and receive his fetters in order to lead him away into captivity. Again Assurbanipal verifies this sacred narrative:

45. "Sardludari, King of Zihinu (in Egypt) and Nechao (King of Memphis), they (the soldiers of Assurbanipal) took and with iron chains and fetters they bound their hands and feet."[2]

Moreover, we can still see an ancient Assyrian bas-

---
[1] G. Smith, " History of Assurbanipal," p. 17-18.
[2] Vigouroux, " La Bible et les Decouvertes Modernes," 5 edit. vol. IV, p. 27.

relief which depicts these unfortunate monarchs bound hands and feet.

It is especially denied that Manasses could be led by an Assyrian king to Babylon, instead of being led to Nineve, capital of Assyria, but nothing proves better than this detail the exactitude of the sacred historian. A forger would have reasoned as do modern infidels, and he would never have imagined that Manasses was led to Babylon. But we know by the history of Assurbanipal that his brother, Samassumukin, whom he had established regent of Babylon, rebelled against him and dragged into his revolt a great number of tributaries of Assyria, among whom was, unquestionably, Manasses. Assurbanipal crushed the insurrection at Babylon itself, he took the title as king of this city, and stopped therein for some time. Hence, there is nothing surprising in the fact that Manasses was led into this capital, where his conqueror must have been well pleased to show to the Babylonians, in the person of the King of Juda, how he chastises those who throw off his yoke.

3. THE RESTORING OF MANASSES TO THE THRONE.

Finally, the infidels believe it incredible that the King of Assyria, after having treated Manasses so cruelly, should restore him to his throne. Assurbanipal again answers that he gave back to Nechao, King of Egypt, his kingdom, although he had inflicted upon him the same harsh treatment that he had inflicted upon the King of Juda:

> 61. In the place where the father had begotten me, at Sais. . . .

>62. had constituted upon him a kingdom. I re-established him.
>63. Good deeds and favors, beyond those of the father who has begotten me, I returned to and gave to him."[1]

Hence, there is not one single detail of the account of the Paralipomenons which is not verified by the annals themselves of the Assyrian king who lead away Manasses captive to Babylon.

CHAPTER XXXIV.

THE BOOK OF TOBIAS.

THE Book of Tobias presents itself to us under the form of a real history. The author writes like a historian, not as an inventor of fictions. He makes known to us the origin of Tobias and his genealogy; he gives us all the chronological and geographical details which the historians are accustomed to give. And, besides, it is within a recent period that this narrative has not been considered historical. What really prevents the Rationalistic critics from accepting the existence of the two Tobias, and the wonderful facts of their biography, is the wonderful character itself.

According to these critics, the facts related in the Book of Tobias are poetic fancies. For us, on the contrary, the miracle and the supernatural intercession of

---

[1] G. Smith, "History of Assurbanipal," p. 46.

God and His angels are no sufficient cause to deny or to question events which Providence had judged proper to surround with prodigious circumstances.

Irrespective of the miraculous role which the angel Raphael plays in the journey of the young Tobias, we cannot allege anything against the credibility of the whole book. The miracle once admitted, all the objections which are accumulated against the Biblical narrative solve themselves easily, provided it is remembered that the original text is lost, and that the versions which have arrived to us are more or less imperfect. Fortunately the diversity itself of the ancient traditions is a help here. It gives the means of easily overcoming the difficulties which have bothered the critics. The "Codex Sinaiticus," Greek manuscript of the Old and New Testament, dating from the fourth century, and found on Mount Sinai, contains in particular a version, the contents of which are very precious. It is according to the text which the manuscript of Sinai produces that the version of Tobias in the ancient Italic was formulated and used in the Latin Church before the adoption of our actual Vulgate.

FIRST DIFFICULTY.

One of the most embarrassing difficulties of the text of the Vulgate arises from the location of the home of Raguel, father of Sara and relative of Tobias, at Rages, a city of the Medes, and nevertheless it states that the angel Raphael departs from the city where Raguel dwelt to go to Rages, in order to reclaim from Gabelus the money the latter owes to Tobias (Tob. ix, 3, 6, 8). Hence, there is here a contradiction. To reconcile these statements, two cities of Rages, both situated in Media, have been imagined; but their existence does not rest upon any proof. Geography knows only one city of this name, that which at present is called Reii. It is situated at the foot of the chain of the Elbruz, not far from the actual site of Teheran, and we can still see there remains of ancient fortifications. To go from Assyria to Rages one has to pass Ecbatana. It is in this latter city, and not at Rages, that Raguel lived, as the Greek manuscripts teach us, and thus also correct with reason the faulty construction of the Vulgate.

Ecbatana, now called Hamadan, was the capital of Media. Founded by Dejoces and surrounded by seven walls of different heights and colors, it served as a summer residence to the Achemenide kings, and later on to the Parthian kings. Situated in the midst of high mountains, its climate is very cold; the altitude of the city is about five thousand four hundred feet.

FIRST OBJECTION.

All the texts are agreed that Gabelus, the debtor of Tobias, lived in the city of Rages, and it is thither that the angel Raphael went to collect the debt. It has been pretended that the sacred writer had committed an error, and that in the epoch in which he places Tobias, about 700 B. C., Rages had not yet come into existence, because Strabo reports that this city was built by Seleucus Nicator, a long time after the death of Tobias, that is, 300 years B. C. The objection is not well taken. Strabo expresses himself improperly, he means to say that Seleucus rebuilt and repaired the city of Rages. The proof that the Greek geographers understood it thus, is that he states that Seleucus substituted for the ancient name of Rages that of Europos (Strabo xi, 13). Besides we have positive assurances of the existence of Rages before the epoch of Seleucus. Alexander the Great sojourned therein five days in 331 B. C., about thirty years before Seleucus ascended the throne. The Zend-Avesta mentions it as a very ancient city, and Darius, son of Hystaspes, names it in his inscriptions.

The distance from Ecbatana to Rages is considerable. Arien states that Alexander, pursuing Darius, reached Rages on the eleventh day after his leaving Ecbatana. A traveler of our day who knows these localities well, Madame Dieulafoy, writes: " The distance from Teheran (Rages) to Hamadan (Ecbatana) is about sixty farsaks or parasangs, that is, about three hundred miles. A caravan composed of strong horses or mules, makes each day six farsaks; the camels, under the same conditions make from four to five forsaks. From Teheran to Saneh, on horseback, it required three days and a half for us to make the twenty-two farsaks which separate these two cities. If the beasts could have continued this gait, we would reach Hamadan in nine days, but there is no Persian camel which could have followed us. My impression is that Alexander, pursuing Darius, must have hastened his march with remarkable rapidity in order to have passed over the country embraced between Ecbatana and Rages in eleven days, the territory being very uneven and interspersed in places with high mountains. It may have been that the conqueror advanced with a selected troop, and left to his lieutenants the care of the main body of the army who were led onward by a less fatiguing route " (Letter of January 31, 1889).

SECOND OBJECTION.

The angel Raphael, traveling with camels and servants (Tob. ix, 6), must, therefore, have needed more than twenty days to go from Rages and to bring back Gabelus. They have made the attempt to draw from the length of this voyage another objection against the sacred account: they suppose that the writer ignored the distance between these two cities; but this supposition is without foundation, for the most of the texts, and in particular the Vulgate (Tob. ix. 6), do not indicate what was the duration of the journey. The critics have desired, it is true, to fix its length, indirectly, by stating that the marriage feasts continued only two weeks (Tob. viii, 23), that they had commenced before the departure for Rages, and that they were not yet ended on the arrival of Gabelus and, that, consequently, the voyage of the angel had taken less than fourteen days. Now, the Sacred Text does not prevent the supposition that the feasts were retarded in order that Raphael and Gabelus could participate in them, and it insinuates that the absence of Tobias lasted longer than it would have if he had gone to Rages (Tob. x, 1) without stopping for his marriage with the daughter of Raguel. His father-in-law did all he could to prolong his sojourn at Ecbatana, and they celebrated probably the solemn feasts only after the return of Raphael to Rages.

3. ANACHRONISM.

The Greek text, as published in the ordinary editions, furnishes matter for other objections, which are all answered by the "Codex Sinaiticus." We read in the conclusion of Tobias (Tob. xiv, 10) an allusion to the history of Esther and Aman. The old Tobias remembers as a past event the persecution which Achiacharus (Assuerus) waged against the Jews. This is clearly an anachronism, because the events reported in the Book of Esther occurred only long after the death of Tobias. The "Codex Sinaiticus," as also our Vulgate, does not speak of Aman; hence it is because of an error that we read his name in the Septuagint.

As for Achiacharus, in whom the critics pretend to behold Assuerus, King of the Persians, becaues he is named with Aman, it is in reality Cyaxares, King of Media, the conqueror and destroyer of Ninive. The text of Sinai is very precise and very exact on this point. It says in the final verse: "And (Tobias the son) before his death learned yet the ruin of Ninive, and he saw the prisoners who were led to Media, and who had been taken by Achiacharus, King of the Medes" (Tob. xiv, 15, Codex of Sinai).

The latter passage has been also altered in the printed form of the Septuagint. It gives rise to a new objection, in substituting wrongfully the better known name of Nabuchodonosor (Tob. xiv, 15, Septuagint) for that of Cyaxares. "And (Tobias) heard relating, before his death, the capture of Ninive which was effected by Nabuchodonosor and Asyerus."—Nabuchodonosor may have assisted in the ruin of Ninive, in the army of his father Nabopolassar, ally of Cyaxares, but the taking of the capital of Assyria cannot be attributed to him. The "Codex Sinaiticus" corrects this error which was entered into the printed texts of the Greek version.

4. THE DEMON ASMODEUS.

All the texts speak of the demon Asmodeus, and what they state of him appears incredible or even absurd to the Rationalistic critics. They say, in the first place, that it is a borrowing from Mazdeism.—It is possible that the name was borrowed, indeed, from the Mazdean belief, by the writer of Tobias who lived in Media, but "if this were the case, it was only the name that was interpolated, for the Biblical demon personifies impurity," which does not represent at all, "the *Ashmo dæva*, the deva Aeshma, of the Avesta." Besides, the borrowing is far from being demonstrated, and the similarity between Asmodeus and Ashmo dæva may be purely gratuitous, as this naming of the demon is readily explained in Hebrew, when it is understood as a derivation from the root *samad,* "the one who destroys," a terminology which is precisely equivalent to our familiar expression " the spirit of perdition."

But, whatever there may be as to the origin of the name of Asmodeus, that what is more important is the conduct of the demon. He, who is a spirit, loves a woman. He is expelled by the odor emitted from the burned liver of a fish, and is driven into a desert of Upper Egypt. How can anyone fail to recognize in all this anything more than a mere fable? ask the infidels.—In the first place the sacred writer does not state that Asmodeus loved Sara, daughter of Raguel: it is Tobias, the son, who, in the Greek text (the Vulgate does not mention it) comes to this conclusion, because he had learned that the demon had caused the death of the seven husbands of Sara. Now, this conclusion was not correct, for it follows clearly from the words of

Raphael to the young Tobias that the first husbands of the daughter of Raguel were stricken by the demon only on account of their incontinence (Tob. vi, 16-18).

In the second place, when it is said that Asmodeus is driven away by the smoke of the burning of a fish's liver (viii, 2), this signifies not that the liver had this virtue in itself, but that God contributed this virtue to this material object, as He has given to the baptismal water the power to drive away the demon. Finally, when it is said that Asmodeus is bound in the desert of Upper Egypt (viii, 3), this phraseology must be understood simply, according to the explanation given by St. Augustine, in the sense that " his power to do injury is taken away from him by the angel " Raphael, and that he was removed from the family of Tobias and Raguel, and banished to a place outside of which it is forbidden him to exercise his malevolent power.

CHAPTER XXXV.

THE BOOK OF JUDITH.

SINCE Luther, who declared that the Book of Judith was not historical, the Protestants, except a few, have adopted his opinion. A very small number of Catholics, notably Jahn, Movers and Scholz, have followed the opinion of Protestants.

According to Movers, the author of the Book of Judith desired to give to his brethren the following lesson: "As long as the Jewish people will remain faithful to God they will be capable of resisting the most powerful nations of the earth. In order to render this more sensible he had to represent a dreadful enemy of the Jews in an epoch when the people of Jehovah were still faithful and devoted to Him. Since the history of the past did not offer anything similar in his own country, he borrows, from the period anterior to the Captivity, the conquering Nabuchodonosor, such as the Book of Daniel depicts him, and he represented the Jewish people such as it had become at the return from Captivity."

A. Scholz, in a lecture delivered November 11, 1884, before the Historic-Philological Society of Wurzburg, denied also the historical character of Judith. According to him this book is certainly inspired, but it is not a history, it is a prophecy. The events which it relates are impossible, and, moreover, there is no moment of sacred history wherein we can place them; they cannot have fulfilled themselves either in Josias, under age, or during the captivity of Manasses. The confusion of personal and geographical names is such that one cannot help to believe that it was done intentionally on the part of the author, who otherwise appears to have been a well instructed man. Judith is the Israel of the New Testament, the Christian Church, widow and without children. Achior (brother of the light) is the converted Gentile; Bethulia, the house of God and the Holy Land; the return from Captivity is the conversion to the faith; the campaign of Holophernes is the campaign of Gog in Ezechiel; Israel-Judith triumphs, with the help of its God, over all its enemies. This prophecy was written in the time of Seleucid kings.

It is true that the Book of Judith, as Scholz maintains, might be inspired, even if it were no real history, but tradition considers this writing not only inspired, but regards it also as historical. This is the teaching of the Fathers. Until Luther, the unanimity has been complete and, in spite of the discordant voices since that time, the Catholic theologians of our days admit, like formerly, that Judith did really exist. Therefore, we can still say, with Richard Simon, that this " is the most general and the most approved opinion." It is certain that the author gives us his account as a real and true one, because, to quote only two characteristics, he assures us that the descendants of Achior lived in his time among the Jews[1] and that they also celebrated in his epoch an annual feast in commemoration of the victory of Judith. Consequently, one can contest his testimony only in so far as one would be capable of discovering in his account proofs of the fictive character one wishes to attribute to him. Let us now inquire whether the objections they bring forward against this book are sufficient to destroy the traditional belief.

I. PRETENDED HISTORICAL AND GEOGRAPHICAL ERRORS.

The main accusation made against the Book of Judith is that it is replete with historical and geographical errors.

It is certain, and acknowledged by all, that the text offers in this respect real difficulties, but we must remark that we meet with similar difficulties in all the ancient writings, where, as in this case, the proper names have been frequently disfigured and altered, so

---

[1] Judith xiv, 6 (Vulgate); xiv, 10 (Greek text).

that we cannot draw any legitimate conclusion against the reality of the facts which they relate. In the Book of Judith, the difficulties of this kind are quite numerous, because the quantity of the proper names, of both men and places, which are enumerated therein, is considerable. To recognize the primitive reading is sometimes, but not always possible. The original text, which, by general consent, was Chaldean or Hebrew, is lost. The different versions, Greek and Latin, which descended to us, all contain errors, and are not in accord with one another. More than once it happens that the correct name of a place is not given. Thus, the city of Tarsus, in Cilicia, has become in the Vulgate Tharsis, in Spain; in the Greek it is even less discernible, for here it has been transformed into Rassis[1]; the river Chaboras has transformed itself in the Greek into Abrona, and in the Vulgate into Mambre[2]; the river Eulæus, preserved exactly in the Syrian version, is known in the Vulgate under the name of Jadason, and in the Greek it takes a false name, that of another river, the Hydaspes.[3] Certainly, we can regard as errrors all these names changed or altered, but they are errors for which the copyists alone are responsible, and we have no right to impute them to the original author. Even the diversity of names in the different versions proves that the cause of these errors is the geographical ignorance of those who have transcribed them. All the false geographical denominations which we can point out in the Book of Judith detract, therefore, nothing from historical reality.

---

[1] Judith II, 13.
[2] Judith II, 24 (Greek text); II, 14 (Vulgate).
[3] Judith I, 6.

2. THE SITE OF BETHULIA.

It is claimed, it is true, that there is a geographical name, the most important of the account, that of Bethulia, which could not have been altered, and which alone is sufficient to establish that all is fictitious in Judith: both the personages and the facts, because this city itself, the site of which has never been discovered, is a pure fiction.

It is not at all demonstrated that Bethulia is a pure fiction. Several modern savants have identified it with Sanur, and this opinion has found a good deal of favor; but whether the identification be correct or not, it is incontestable that there were in Palestine other cities, the sites of which are completely unknown, but the existence of which is admitted beyond question. Bethulia, it is said, is named nowhere else in the Scripture. Undoubtedly, but neither are Nazareth, Capharnaum, Bethsaida and Corozain, named in the Old Testament, but appear only in the New. There are even localities like Bether, the mention of which we never read either in the Old nor in the New Testament. (According to Renan, Bether would be the Bethulia of the Book of Judith.)[1] The savants themselves are not in agreement as to the situation of this place; thus, some place Bether in Juda, southwest of Jerusalem; others place it in Samaria; nevertheless nobody maintains that Bether never existed and that the false Messias, Barkochebas, did not hold out there during three years, against the Roman legions, in the reign of Trajan (135). In reality, the geographical descriptions of the Book of Judith are

---

[1] E. Renan, "Les Evangiles" p. 26.

very correct, even for the most remote countries of Palestine, when the ancient documents furnish to us the means to verify them. It is thus that the description of Ecbatana, given by the Israelitic author is confirmed by that which we read in the Zend-Avesta:

"Arphaxad," the Book of Judith tells us, "surrounded Ecbatana with stone walls, the stones of which were three cubits wide and six cubits long, and he raised the walls to a height of seventy cubits, and their thickness was fifty cubits. He flanked the towered gates one hundred cubits high; their foundation was sixty cubits wide. He also constructed gates: they arose to a height of seventy cubits, for the exit of his troops and for putting his foot soldiers into battle order."[1]

Behold now the description of Ecbatana in the Zend-Avesta. Zemschid, it is said there, " raised a Var or fortress sufficiently large, built of hewn stones; here he gathered a numerous population and supplied the surroundings with troops for their use. From the large fortress he caused water to flow in abundance. In the Var or fortress he raised a magnificent palace, surrounded by walls, and divided into several distinct divisions; there was no elevated point therein, neither in the front nor back of it, which could command and dominate the fortress."[2] The two texts, while expressing themselves in quite a different manner, are agreed in substance.

3. HISTORICAL DIFFICULTIES.

The geographical difficulties alleged against the Book of Judith do not prove, as we have seen, that this

---
[1] Judith i, 2-4.
[2] Cf. De Harlez, "Avesta," vol. i, p. 96-98.

book is a fiction. The historical difficulties do not furnish a better proof. A first objection is made to the passage last quoted, in which it is said that Arphaxad, King of the Medes, surrounded Ecbatana with walls. Now, no king of the Medes seems to have borne this name.

Arphaxad is very probably Phraorte, whose name may be still recognized in its Hebrew dress. The kings of Media bore Turanian names, the pronunciation and formation of which were quite different from those of Semitic and Aryan languages; from this it followed that the transcriptions of the names in the foreign idioms have altered and changed them considerably. The Cyaxares of the Greeks is called in the Behistun inscription Uvakhsatara and, according to Ctesias, he called himself Astibaras. We see in this case that the modifications of the proper names in Scripture are not such an extraordinary fact as one might believe at first sight. The Persian form of the name of Phraorte was Fravartis. In the Babylonian (Semitic) text of the Behistun inscription, he is called Parruvartis, and in the Medic text Perruvartis. In Diodor of Sicily, he has become Artynes. The Semitics could not pronounce two initial consonants without the help of a vowel intercalated between these two consonants, like Parruvatis, or placed before the first consonant, as in *Ahasveros* (Assuerus), a name of Chschaarscha (Xerxes), which explains to us the a placed at the head of Arphaxad. The name of Arphaxad being known in the Hebrew language, the name of Phraorte under its Persian or Medic form of Fravartis or Parruvartis, could easily become Aphravartis, Arphavartis, Arphaxad, because we are naturally inclined to approach an unknown name to a known name, as we had already occasion to remark.

4. ASSURBANIPAL, THE NABUCHODONOSOR OF JUDITH.

Phraorte, successor of Dejoces on the throne of the Medes, reigned twenty-two years, from 657 to 635, before our era. Thus, he was contemporary with the King of Ninive, Assurbanipal, who reigned from 668 to 625. Assurbanipal is therefore the Nabuchodonosor of the Book of Judith, who sent his general Holofernes for the conquest of Occidental Asia. The campaigns of this Assyrian general are related in the first chapters of the Book of Judith. They have criticised these chapters from a literary standpoint, on the charge of irrelevancy and prolixity. This is of little importance. The author wrote a history, not a fiction; he describes the events as they took place without troubling himself to satisfy the impatience of the reader by eliminating the details, which, from a literary standpoint, are uninteresting; a romancist should consult only the art; a historian must seek above any other consideration to tell the truth.

It is true that all these wars attributed to Holofernes seem very improbable, and even incredible. It is easy, however, to show that this is a false judgment. We are in possession of the originals of the annals of the reign of Assurbanipal, the King of Assyria, who, according to all probability is, as we have seen, the Nabuchodonosor who placed Holofernes at the head of his army. Now, in his annals we recover the account of all the campaigns of which the Book of Judith speaks. Assurbanipal had combated the Medes in the first years of his reign. His dominion extended over the whole territory from Asia Minor to Egypt inclusively. This is attested by both his inscriptions and the Sacred Text. Manasses was then King of Juda, and one of the tributaries to the Assyrian monarch. Having revolted against him, Manasses is made prisoner and led away captive to Babylon, as related in a previous chapter.[1] But this prince was not the only one that had revolted. All those whom the King of Ninive had subdued, on from Lydia and Cilicia to the shores of the Nile, had thrown off the yoke of Nabuchodonosor. Assurbanipal's own brother, Samassumukin, who governed Babylonia, had kindled the fire of the revolt to gain his own independence. The Assyrian king, as he himself relates, and as we behold him in the Book of Judith, desires his former vassals to expiate their revolt, and he undertook to subdue in person, or through his generals, all the countries that had refused to pay him tribute: Cilicia, Lydia, Syria, and the neighboring countries of the Mediterranean. He made the conquered peoples undergo the same treatments as those which are mentioned in the Book of Judith. Finally, and this is a very important and significant detail, after having undertaken the war in order to reduce Egypt under his obedience, he speaks no longer of this kingdom: certain proof that he could not lead this enterprise to a triumphant conclusion, and indirect confirmation of what we read in the sacred author concerning the disaster which annihilated in Palestine the army of Holofernes, who had been ordered to reconquer Egypt. It is impossible not to be struck with the accord which exists between the Hebrew document and the cuneiform inscriptions. How many accounts are there whose historical value

---

[1] Cf. Chapter xxxii.

is not contested, that are less solidly established than that of the Book of Judith?

5. ANACHRONISMS.

However, we are not yet done with the objections raised against the history of the war of Holofernes. Many anachronisms, it is claimed, are found in the text; the author names the Sanhedrin (*gerousia*),[1] the vigils of the Sabbath, and the Neomeniæ.[2] Now, the institution of the Sanhedrin dates only from the third or fourth century B. C., and the vigils of the Sabbath and the Neomeniæ were regarded not as feasts until a much later period. Consequently the Sanhedrin and the vigils did not exist in the time of Judith.

Certainly, the Sanhedrin is posterior to the epoch in which this history takes place, but the text does not make any allusion to it. When it employs the word *gerousia*, one of the names which designate that assembly in the language of the Hellenist Jews, the sacred historian employs it in a different sense, namely, meaning the ancients of the people. This expression has often this sense in the version of the Septuagint, and it has also this meaning in Judith, as the Vulgate has rendered it.[3] As to the vigils of the Sabbath and the Neomeniæ, nobody can affirm that these were unknown in the time of Judith, because nobody knows in what epoch their observance originated. It is nevertheless probable that the original text did not speak thereof,

---

[1] Judith iv, 8; xi, 14; xv, 8 (Greek text).

[2] Judith viii, 6 (Greek text).

[3] Lev. ix, 3; Exod. iii, 16, 18; iv, 29; xii, 21; Num. xxii, 4; Deut. v, 23, etc.

for there is no mention made of them in our Latin translation, which enumerates only the Sabbaths and the Neomeniæ (Judith viii, 6).

6. DISCOURSE OF ACHIOR.

The final objection made against the Book of Judith is derived from a passage of the discourse of Achior, where it is said that the inhabitants of Juda have returned from Captivity, after having been led into a foreign land, and after their temple had been profaned.[1] This passage evidently refers, it is claimed, to the Babylonian Captivity, which, however, did not occur until after the events related in Judith had happened.

Nothing proves that the Sacred Text makes allusion to this. We have seen that King Manasses was led away captive into Babylon; certainly he was not the only one that was thus led away, but a certain number of his subjects were also transported, according to the invariable custom of the Assyrian kings as recorded by the inscriptions. Several of these captives could receive permission to return into their country, as it was granted to Manasses himself. As to the profanation of the temple, there is no reason to be surprised from what we know of the character of the King of Ninive; however, we must remark that the Latin translation states nothing of this; the expressions which the Greek translation employs are very obscure and, moreover, we cannot determine whether Achior had an exact knowledge of the events he relates, so that we have no assurance that his narrative is true in all its details.

---

[1] Judith v, 18-19 (Greek text); 22-23 (Vulgate).

7. THE HEROINE JUDITH.

We have only one more observation to make on the Book of Judith. This heroine was remarkable for her piety and chastity, as well as for her courage which was far beyond that usual to her sex. We must, however, admit that several of her acts were not at all praiseworthy. The means which she employed to deliver her people cannot be approved without reserve. She deceives Holofernes with falsehoods, and when these falsehoods may be justified by the good faith in the mouth of Judith, they are not inexcusable in themselves. As to the legitimacy of the murder of the Assyrian general it is difficult to render judgment from our point of view. According to the ideas of the time, it was certainly an heroic act. The employment of stratagem and violence to overcome an enemy is not considered demeaning in the eyes of the Orientals. Besides, the magnificent patriotism which inspired the courageous act of the widow of Bethulia, would command the greatest admiration among any people, in any land, in any epoch. Those souls who have imbrued their hands in blood always form an exception, and often we cannot help admiring them, although we cannot always approve of their acts. The infidels make it a cause of reproach to her historian in praising her without reserve. Divers Catholic interpreters, who justify it without restriction, have believed like them that the Sacred Text approved in everything the conduct of Judith. But the language of the Scripture is not so expressive as one has supposed sometimes. The praises given by St. Paul to Samson and to Jephte, for example, are no approbation of their lives, which have not been irreproachable in everything; what is said to the glory of Judith does not imply the justification of all the means which she employed to deliver her so hardly oppressed people. It is this what St. Thomas teaches expressly in his " Summa Theologica."[1] The sacred authors have praised the good intentions, and the acts worthy to be approved; from this, however, it does not follow at all that the precious metal did not contain some alloy.

CHAPTER XXXVI.

THE BOOK OF ESTHER.

THE Book of Esther finds no more grace in the eyes of the negative critic than Tobias and Judith. It is presented to us as an historical book: the events take place at the court of Xerxes, in his capital, the city of Susa; but this matters little in regard to the Rationalists. For them this book is a " parable, a superabundant testimony of the Jewish pageantry and arrogance." Mr. Noeldeke, after having affirmed that " this book is, in all its parts, void of any historical value," is forced to contradict himself and make the following avowal: " Does this account rest upon any historical foundation? We are unable to answer with certitude. The Ahasveros (Assuerus) would seem to indicate this; one is agreed to acknowledge him as identical with

---

[1] Cf. 2a 2, q, 110, a. 3, ad. 3 um.

Xerxes. It is quite possible that he admitted into his harem a Jewess, named Esther, and that she acted in favor of her people."[1]

When all this is possible, why deny the historical character of the book? One alleges the improbabilities. But a fact is not always true because it is probable, and it is not always false because it is improbable, or even incredible.

1. ESTHER, THE WIFE OF KING XERXES.

The objection which all the Rationalists produce is as to how " Esther, having become the wife of the king, could conceal for so long a time her origin from the court, the king and Aman himself." But wherever polygamy is practiced, they do not attach any great importance to the origin of a woman. How many inhabitants are there of harems whose birth and lineage are unknown, and even could not be ascertained if such were the desire. Besides Mardocheus had advised Esther not to reveal that she was a Jewess, and when Assuerus had the curiosity to inquire who she was, the young queen being orphaned quite early in life, having been born in Persia, speaking the language of the country, given a Persian name, and the tutor who had raised her, a Babylonian name, it was very easy for her to dissimilate her nationality and to answer without betraying her secret all the questions propounded by her royal husband.

2. THE DELAY OF AMAN'S VENGEANCE.

It is equally incredible, the Rationalists add, that Aman delayed his vengeance for eleven months; the

---

[1] Th. Noeldeke, "Literarische Geschichte des Alten Testamentes."

vindictive spirit is not so patient. "How can we believe that if the Persian despot, even gained by a favorite, had formed the project to annihilate all the Jews of his kingdom, he would have caused this to be announced publicly in all the provinces of his kingdom to all the peoples, and not secretly to his governors, twelve months before the execution?" The text gives us the explanation of this delay. The Persians were very superstitious; they believed in lucky and unlucky days— in our time there are many who believe the same. Aman, therefore, consulted the fate during the first month of the twelfth year of Xerxes (473), in order to know what would be the most propitious moment for the execution of his design, and the oracle designated to him the twelfth month. Hence, he was obliged to wait eleven months (Esther III, 7). It was thus that Providence permitted to reveal its protection to the chosen people.

But, they insist, in this case why did he publish the edict such a long time before? To prevent the king from revoking his word; to excite, undoubtedly, the cupidity of the nations subject to the Persians and to increase the antipathy of the enemies of the Jews, — finally, to render more easy the execution of the measure.

But this was, they say, providing the condemned with the means to escape the bloody measure taken against them. It was not so easy for them to leave the Persian Empire, which covered an immense territory; they could not take refuge in Palestine, because this was a province of the great king. If, besides, some succeeded in finding a refuge, Aman, perhaps, desired this, for they were obliged to abandon their goods and thus furnish to the favorite the means to pay Assuerus the ten thousand talents which he had promised him.

3. THE IMMENSE NUMBER OF THE DEAD.

It is not less incredible, again say the Rationalists, that when the king, repenting of his order and refusing nevertheless to withdraw it, had authorized the Jews by a second edict to defend themselves against the enemies who would attack them, this second edict could have for consequence to cause to perish in all the countries where there were Jews, seventy-five thousand men equally subjects of the king.

The number of the dead is not "incredible" for an empire which extended from India to Ethiopia. In a much smaller kingdom, Mithridates caused the killing of eighty thousand Romans in one day.

In supposing, they continue, that the royal governors through fear of the new royal favorite, Mardocheus, only protected the Jews, they could not assist them, however, in an efficacious manner, because the first edict had not been reported.

The effect of the second edict must have restrained all the chief citizens from attacking the Jews, in order not to incur the anger of the king and of Mardocheus. Nothing prevented the Persian satraps and officers from upholding secretly, or even publicly, those who were then in favor at the court. It is even difficult to explain a similar objection, for who does not know of the servility which an Oriental functionary is capable of in order to please those who can procure him advancement or, at least, have power to keep him in office? Personal interest removes all scruple, and it is not the first degree annulled by a second, which could have paralized official ambition and obsequiousness.

Again they say, it is contrary to nature, that, when the Jews had killed, on the day when the first royal edict ordained their death, five hundred of their enemies in the city of Susa, the king could listen to the prayer of Esther, who, insatiable for blood and vengeance, implored him to issue another edict authorizing to continue the massacre, since it was no longer permitted to attack the Jews.

It was no longer legally permitted to attack the Jews, but those of their enemies who had not perished undoubtedly formed the project to make them expiate on the following day, when they expected that they could strike them with impunity, for the murders committed on this day. It was in order to foil this calculation that Esther interceded anew at Assuerus. We are far from pretending that in this the queen acted with an evangelical kindness, but she was a woman of her time, she shared its ideas and habits and, as we have observed for Judith, while everything in her conduct is not praiseworthy, one cannot at least refuse to render homage to her patriotism, and admire her devotedness to her people. Thus, none of the alleged objections of the negative critic against the sacred account has any value.

4. THE FACTS JUSTIFIED BY HISTORY.

But not only are the objections of the Rationalists without force, but all the facts can be verified by history. All that is said about the ostentation and the magnificence of the Persian kings, of their palaces and their gardens, is confirmed by the ancient authors and by the excavations executed at Susa itself. All the depictures of the character of Assuerus or Xerxes (485-472 B. C.) are equally confirmed by the most unexceptionable historical testimonies. Herodotus and Plutarch present him to us in the same light as the sacred writer, that is, a whimsical, fantastic and extravagant monarch. He strikes with rods and ties with chains the Hellespont, because a storm had carried off the bridge of boats, which he had built over the sea.[1] He writes a letter to Mount Athos to forbid it from rolling stones upon his soldiers.[2] The one who has committed such acts of folly is very well capable of all that the Book of Esther attributes to him. This book does not ascribe to him such senseless actions. Herodotus tells us, moreover, like the Hebrew historian, that the empire of Assuerus extended from India to Persia,[3] and that in his army they counted over sixty different nations.[4] Finally, Herodotus indirectly confirms the Biblical account of the feasts which were celebrated at Susa, and which resulted in the repudiation of Vasthi, followed by the elevation of Esther to the dignity of Queen. In 482 B. C., after having conquered Egypt, Assuerus assembled at Susa all the principal chiefs of the empire and deliberated for a long time with them in regard to the expedition he projected against Greece.[5] The war against the Greeks commenced in 480 B. C. After his defeat, Xerxes returned to Persia in 479. It was then when they had gathered the young

---

[1] Herodotus, vii, 35.
[2] Plutarchus, De cohibenda ira, 5.
[3] Esther i, 1; Herodotus vii, 7, 9, 97, 98; viii, 65, 69.
[4] Herodotus vii, 61-95.
[5] Herodotus vii, 8, etc.

girls to be offered to the king, and it is this expedition against the Greeks which explains to us the long interval between the repudiation of Vasthi and the choice of Esther. The chronology of the history of Xerxes is therefore in perfect accord with the Scriptural narrative.

5. LIVING PROOFS OF THE REALITY OF THE HISTORY OF ESTHER.

Besides, there exists an always living proof of the reality of the history of Esther; it is the celebration of the Jewish feast of the Purim, which is the annual commemoration thereof. The children of Israel have never ceased to celebrate it with the greatest rejoicings. They have given it the name of "Day of Mardochai" as well as that of *Purim*.[1] Such an institution can be explained only by the reality of the occurrences it commemorates; its name which signifies "fates," is fixed and interpreted by the sacred account.[2] The Rationalists have no serious objection to offer against such a formal and explicit testimony. "The author," says Noeldeke, "had for his object a desire to acquaint all the Jews with the origin of the feast of Purim, and to recommend to them its observation. The establishment of this feast, unknown to the Pentateuch, does not seem to have any connection with the deliverance en masse of the Jews from the threatened death. (This manner of denying without proof by a "does not seem," an event related at great length and with much detail, is still more than strange.) This feast must have been borrowed from Persian rites. (Again an affirmation *a priori* without proof.) Even to this day, the Jews

---
[1] II. Mach. xv, 37.
[2] Esther ix, 24, 26, 31.

celebrate certain feasts derived from other religions. (Admitted, but show us the authorities that affix to such feasts a distinctive Jewish origin, like that of the Purim.) In every case we can maintain that the occasion of this joyful feast is not that which one attributes to it."[1] And why? One does not tell. It is difficult to see a more pitiful argument: it is denying in order to deny, without even a plausible pretext. This language, stripped of its equivocals, signifies: We have no proof, but we deny nevertheless.

The borrowing of the Purim feast from Persia is, however, admitted by the Rationalists, in spite of the absence of the least proof. Paul de Lagarde has even discovered the Persian feast which the Jews adopted: it is that of Fordigan or Pordigan, by which the Persians celebrate with great festivities the commemoration of their dead. Such, however, is not the object of the feast of Purim, as we have seen. The word Purim, in certain Greek manuscripts, is written *phourdia*, *phourmaia* or *phrouraiena*,[2] and behold how the Jewish feast becomes a feast of Persian origin! A *lapsus calami* of the scribes furnishes the demonstration. When recourse to such ill reasoning becomes necessary, it is equivalent to an admission that no good reasoning is possible.

6. ADDITIONS TO THE GREEK AND LATIN BIBLES.

It only remains for us to say a few words about the additions we notice in the Greek and Latin Bibles.

The Book of Esther, besides its pro-canonical part we have in Hebrew, contains a deutero-canonical part,

---

[1] Th. Noeldeke, "Literarisch Geschichte de A. T.," p. 124.
[2] P. de Lagarde, "Gesammelte Abhandlungen," p. 161-165.

which exists no longer in the versions. It contains a certain number of passages which we might call justifications, i. e., the edicts of the great king, and diverse parts which are so many supplements: the dream of Mardochai, his prayer to God, and that of Esther, etc. The authenticity of all the additions is naturally rejected by all the Rationalists as also by many Protestants who admit the historical character of the book, as it appears in the Hebrew Bible.

However, they have no particular objection to bring forward against these fragments. They were known and accepted by the historian Josephus Flavius, who made use of them in his "Jewish Antiquities:" consequently, their antiquity cannot be questioned; the Hebraisms we remark therein, as well as the existence of two different Greek translations, tend to prove that they are translated from a Hebrew original; all that we read therein is in harmony with the content of the proto-canonical part. Hence, there exists no reason to contest the veracity thereof.

CHAPTER XXXVII.

THE BOOKS OF THE MACHABEES.—BOOK I.

ALL the critics, even the Rationalists, are now agreed that the First Book of the Machabees is historically correct. However, four objections have been made against the same. They have reference to the Greco-Macedonian history and to the judgments passed on the Romans.

I. ALEXANDER THE FIRST THAT RULED OVER GREECE.

The history of the Machabees opens as follows: "Now it came to pass that Alexander, the son of Philip, the Macedonian, who first reigned in Greece, coming out of the land of Cethim (Europe), had overthrown Darius, King of the Persians and of the Medes, etc." (I. Mach. I, 1.) The Greek text adds that Alexander was the first who reigned in Greece "instead of Darius." Such is the passage which gives rise to the first objection.

The reading of the Vulgate offers no serious difficulty. The sacred author could say very well that Alexander the Great was the first that ruled over Greece. Alexander did not possess the title of King of Greece, although the monarchical power was invested in him. This is admitted even by our adversaries. The general assembly of the Greeks at Corinth conferred upon Alexander the dignity of general-in-chief, as previously upon his father, and thus he was in fact King of Greece. He, is, moreover, the first who adopted on his coins the title of king. However, it is not certain at all that the original text did qualify here Alexander the "first" King of Greece. According to the Syriac version, and several Greek manuscripts, it is simply said "that he was King of Greece before becoming master" of Asia, but since, further on,[1] the Sacred Text explicitly states that Alexander "was the first King of the Greeks," it matters little that the Syriac version and Greek manuscripts do not also make this assertion.

As for the statement of the Greek that Alexander, instead of Darius, reigned over Greece, it cannot be justified in the sense in which it is generally understood. It has been stated that Darius Codomanus attributed to himself the royalty over the Greeks, and by destroying his power the son of Philip had thus replaced him; but, besides that this explanation is hardly a natural one, it does not make Alexander the first of the Grecian monarchs. Then, again, we do not need to defend an expression which we read neither in the Vulgate nor in the Syriac version. The Greek text which we possess is only a translation of the original Hebrew which has been lost. Now, the version of the first verse leaves much to be desired. The phrasing is poorly constructed, and we must not understand it in the sense that Darius reigned over Greece, nor that Alexander became King of Greece instead of Darius, which would be not only contrary to history, but also to the language of the historian, as we said above. We

---

[1] I. Mach. vi, 2.

must translate, as the Syriac version has done: "Alexander reigned over Greece, and he became King (of Asia) instead of Darius."

2. THE DIVISION OF ALEXANDER'S KINGDOM AMONG HIS GENERALS.

The second objection is directed against what the sacred author states[1] of Alexander the Great: That before dying he divided his kingdom among his generals. Here the Biblical writer is accused of great ignorance.

In fact, however, the Jewish historian has not displayed any greater ignorance than the historians of Alexander themselves. These relate that the most conflicting rumors were circulated with regard to his last moments, and as to the nature of the will he had made; his biographers contradict one another. According to Arrien, "when they asked the conqueror to whom he would leave his kingdom, he answered: to the most worthy," but Arrien is careful to remark that this is simply the version of the historians, and he adds, "that they have written many other things about the death of Alexander."[2] Quintus Curcius states expressly that "several have written that Alexander had divided by will his provinces among his generals."[3] It is this what the author of the Second Book of the Machabees relates, except the important circumstances of the will of which he does not speak. Several Oriental writers are also in accord with him, such as Moses of Khoren and diverse Persian and Arabian Chroniclers.

---

[1] I Mach. I, 6-7.
[2] Arrien, "Exped. Alexand.," vii, 16, 27.
[3] Q. Curcius, "Histor. Alex.," x, 10.

According to all testimony, it is impossible to-day to tax as false the account of the sacred author, and, even taking a purely profane standpoint, by what right can one reject his testimony, when nothing is certain, because he is the most ancient writer that has made known to us the last moments of Alexander the Great? He wrote one century before our era, and Diodor of Sicily wrote only under the reign of Augustus, Quintus Curcius under that of Tiberius and Arrien under that of Hadrian.

3. JUDGMENT ON THE ROMANS.

The third objection against the First Book of the Machabees has reference to the following passage: " Now Judas heard of the fame of the Romans that they were powerful and strong, and willingly agreed to all things that are requested of them; and that whosoever has come to them they have made amity with them, and that they are mighty in power. And they heard of their battles and their noble acts, which they had done in Galatia, how they had conquered them and brought them under tribute; and how great things they had done in the land of Spain, and that they had brought under their power the mines of silver and of gold that are there, and had gotten possession of all the place by their counsel and patience. And had conquered places that were very far off from them, and kings that came against them from the ends of the earth, and had overthrown them with great slaughter; and the rest pay them tribute every year. And that they had defeated in battles Philip, and Persis the King of the Ceteans, and the rest that had borne arms against them, and had conquered them. And how

Antiochus the Great, King of Asia, who went to fight against them, having a hundred and twenty elephants, with horsemen and chariots and a very great army, was routed by them. And how they took him alive, and appointed to him that both he and they that should reign after him should pay a great tribute, and that he should give hostages, and that which was agreed upon. And the country of the Indians, and of the Medes, and of the Lydians, some of their best provinces; and those which they had taken from them, they gave to King Eumenes. And that they who were in Greece had a mind to go and destroy them, and they had knowledge thereof. And they sent a general against them and fought with them, and many of them were slain, and they carried away their wives and their children captives, and spoiled them, and took possession of their land and threw down their walls, and brought them to be their servants unto this day. And the other kingdoms, and islands, that at any time had resisted them, they had destroyed and brought under their power. But with their friends, and such as relied upon them, they kept amity, and had conquered kingdoms that were near and that were far off; for all that heard their name were afraid of them. That whom they had a mind to help to a kingdom, those reigned; and whom they would, they deposed from the kingdom; and they were greatly exalted. And none of all these wore a crown, or was clothed in purple, to be magnified thereby. And that they had made themselves a senate-house, and consulted daily three hundred and twenty men, that sat in counsel always for the people, that they might do the things that were right. And that they committed their government to one man every year, to rule over all their country, and they all obey one, and there is no envy nor jealousy among them."[1]

The above passage is given by the Rationalists as an example of the errors into which the sacred writer has fallen.

Certainly, we are far from pretending that the judgment passed on the Romans, and that all the facts enumerated in chapter eight of the First Book of Machabees, are entirely correct. The republic had two annual consuls and not only one; its disinterestedness was not such as Judas the Machabee believed; jealousy and envy were not evils unknown to the Romans; the number of senators was not three hundred and twenty, but only three hundred; they did not assemble every day, even this was forbidden to them, etc.

But whatever one may point out in the detail, one cannot accuse the sacred historian of any historical error. He states expressly that Judas " heard the account " of all these things;[2] he speaks in the name of rumor, and he relates current rumors, as then existing in Judea, in regard to the Romans; his exactitude in the present case must consist and really does consist, not in writing a chapter of the real history of Rome, but in being the faithful interpreter of the rumors which, being circulated in Judea, had come to the ears of Judas Machabeus, and they moved the Jewish hero, the more so because of the falsity they contained, to seek the Roman alliance. It is a principle admitted by all the theologians and by all the authors who have occupied themselves with sacred hermeneutic: the inspiration does not imply that all that we read in Scrip-

---

[1] I Mach. viii, 1-16.
[2] I Mach. viii, 1-2.

ture is true in itself. The discourses of the friends of Job are partly tainted with error. That what the Amalikite writes to David about the circumstances of the death of Saul is false and a lie;[1] nevertheless the sacred writer tells the truth in relating this falsehood, because this falsehood had been effectively committed by the Amalekite. So also the author of the First Book of the Machabees tells the truth in relating the inexact ideas they had of the politics and history of the Romans in Judea, because they were really the current ideas in this country. Hence, one may point out in the passage quoted as many errors as he pleases, but nothing of all this can furnish material for a solid objection against the inspiration of the sacred writer.

Besides, it is good to remark that they have often exaggerated these inexactitudes. Thus what is reported of Eumenus II., King of Pergamum, may be true. It is certain that the Romans, in order to reward him for his attachment and services he had rendered to them in the battle of Magnesia, gave him Lydia, as the Sacred Text says. When they did not give to him India and Media, to round off his kingdom, which was in the west of the Taurus, they gave to him Ionia and Mysia,[2] etc., and it is probable that we must read in our text the "Ionians and the Medes."

4. TIES OF RELATIONSHIP BETWEEN THE JEWS AND SPARTIATES.

The last exactitude with which the First Book of Machabees is charged is that it supposes ties of relationship between the Jews and the Spartiates. The sacred

---

[1] II Kings i, 2-10.
[2] Titus Livius, xxxvii, 55 and xxxviii, 39.

author reproduces a letter of Jonathas, the high priest, to the Spartiates, and a letter of Arius I., King of Sparta, to the high priest Onias. In both it is said that these two peoples have a common origin.[1] A good deal of discussion has been entered into in order to determine whether this opinion was maintainable. The majority believes it hardly probable, but, be this as it may, we do not need to occupy ourselves here with this question. Whether the Spartiates have been or not children of Abraham matters little, according to several Catholic commentators. The sacred writer limits himself to report two documents, the exactitude of which he has not to certify to, but the existence of which he has only to affirm. The insertion of these letters into the structure of his account proves that these letters are authentic, but not that what they contain is veracious. Hence, in this regard the reader may believe or not believe as he pleases.

Only we have to remark that, according to these letters, one cannot deny that Sparta and Judea were united by an alliance, for when the correspondents could be deceived on the obscure question of a remote origin, it is not the same in regard to a recent fact. Also, the Rationalists themselves generally admit the reality of the alliance, although it is unknown to us by any other documents. Palmer, who has carefully studied this passage of the First Book of Machabees, has supposed that this alliance ascended to the year three hundred and two before our era. In this epoch, Poliorcetus, having conquered the Peloponesus, his father, Antigonus, recalled him to Asia Minor in order to coöperate with him to combat Cassander, Lysimachus, Ptolemy

---
[1] I Mach. xii, 5-23.

and Seleucus, all confederates against him. The Spartiates neglected nothing to increase the number of the enemies of Antigonus and Demetrius: they sought to stir up against him different nations of Asia, and particularly the Jews. Arius I. was at that time King of Sparta and Onias I., son of Juddas, high priest, as our text indicates. The first reigned from 309 to 300 B. C. The synchronism is, therefore, perfectly exact. Later on, about the year 144 B. C., Jonathas being in need of allies naturally sought to renew the alliance which he had concluded at that time with the Spartiates.

They have pretended, it is true, that the independence of Greece having been annihilated by the Romans since the year 146 B. C., it was not very probable that the brother of Judas, the Machabee, had counted on the help of Sparta, but we know through Strabo[1] that this city, which was for the Romans *civitas fœderata*, preserved both its power and liberty, even after this catastrophe, and that it was only obliged to render some services towards Rome; therefore, it could still be useful to the Romans. Consequently, one can allege nothing serious against the fact of correspondence. Also Wernsdorf, one of the most vehement enemies of the Books of Machabees, cannot help saying: " In the letter of Jonathan, I find nothing that could not have been written by a Jewish high priest. . . . Certainly it appears to have been written by a pious, grave and prudent man, a man well versed in the civil affairs. I remark therein well-connected words and very correct thoughts. . . . I find nothing therein that is blameworthy, except that he speaks too often of the ancient alliance between Arius and Onias, and of

---
[1] Strabo viii, v. 5.

the supposed relationship between the two nations. But he was a man and may have been deceived."[1] Therefore, one cannot bring forward any serious argument against the authenticity of this letter, no more than against the other official documents contained in this history.

THE DESCRIPTION OF THE ARMY OF ANTIOCHUS IV. EUPATOR.

We will say a few words, in ending the examination of the First Book of Machabees, of a passage which cannot offer any real difficulty, but which merits, however, to be discussed. In describing the army of Antiochus IV. Eupator, the sacred author says that they counted therein thirty-two elephants, on whom they placed wooden towers, and that on each elephant there were fifty-two men.[2] The presence of the elephants in the armies of the Seleucides offers no difficulty. This is attested by both the profane historians and by the medals of the Syrian kings. What is embarrassing is the number of men placed on each of these animals. In India, in all times, elephants have been made use of in warfare, and even in the present time these massive quadrupeds are burdened with towers in this country; but it is impossible to place thirty-two men therein. According to Titus Livius, the towers of the elephants of the army of Antiochus the Great, contained four men, aside from the elephant driver; Pliny relates that, in the games given by Julius Cæsar, the elephants who took part in a fictitious com-

---

[1] G. Wernsdorf, "Commentatio Historico-Critica de Fide Historica Librorum Machabaicorum," p. 148 and 169-170.

[2] I. Mach. vi. 30-37.

bat carried three men; Elien indicates the same number for India; Munro says that in this country these animals carry to-day four or five persons. Besides, it is sufficient to look at an elephant and recognize that he cannot carry thirty warriors. How could one place on the back of a single one of these animals a tower large enough to contain so many armed men, who need to be free in their movements in order to face the enemy? Moreover, the average weight which an elephant is capable of carrying is about three thousand pounds, and we have to reduce this to about the half for long marches and combats. Now, they have figured that thirty-two soldiers would weigh at least six thousand four hundred pounds. Also, the most judicious interpreters are unanimously agreed to acknowledge that the reading of thirty-two is false, on account of an error of either the Greek translator or by a mistake of the copyists. The correction which is most favorably accepted by the critics is that proposed by Michaelis. He believes that the sacred author had written " two or three;" three, put into the plural in Hebrew, means thirty. When the elephants had disappeared, because the Romans had forbidden to the Seleucid kings to employ these animals in warfare, the copyists, not knowing them any longer, were inclined, according to the custom of the Orientals, to exaggerate the figures so that they read two and thirty or thirty-two instead of two or three.

BOOK II.

As much as the Rationalists render homage to the historical value of the First Book of Machabees, so much, according to them, the second of these books is unworthy of belief. In regard to a great part of its contents, they say it is replete with fiction, and in contradiction with itself and the writer of the first book. Behold how Noeldeke expresses himself as to this subject:

"The value of the Second Book of Machabees is much inferior to that of the First. Certainly it gives some more complete accounts, especially for the history anterior to the moment when the insurrection broke out. Josephus, who did not know this book, confirms its exactitude. Nevertheless we meet therein many errors from the standpoint of chronology and of the events. It is over only an exaggeration, rhetorical, and partisan spirit. The miracles, the apparition of angels, return on each page, and for the first time appear those histories of martyrs related in a measureless manner. The book is full of an exuberant patriotism, and of a bitter hatred against the stranger. The author was quite a slave of popular prejudices, and he wrote to strengthen them. In his opinions he approached the Pharisees a good deal. Thus, he strongly believes in the resurrection. In summary, his work forms about many points, a striking contrast with the First Book of Machabees."[1]

The critic, in reproaching the author of his miraculous accounts, reveals to us the reason for which the Rationalists are so badly disposed in his regard. But the miracles, as we had occasion to state repeatedly, are no sufficient motive to question the veracity of a writer. Heliodorus, in whose subject is related one of

---
[1] Th. Noeldeke, "Literarische Geschichte des Alten Testamentes."

the principal miracles, which had for end to hinder the sacking of the temple of Jerusalem (II. Mach. iii), is quite an historical personage. He was minister of Seleucus IV. Philopator, King of Syria (187-175 B. C.). Appien teaches us that he caused the perishment of his master in order to take hold of his throne.[1] They have recovered, in 1877 and 1879, on the island of Delos, two Greek inscriptions which have reference to him. They make known to us that his father called himself Eschylus and that he was Antiochus. One of these inscriptions gives to him the same title as the Book of Machabees and in the same terms.

I. LETTERS OF THE JEWS OF JERUSALEM TO THOSE OF EGYPT.

The objections which they have raised against the letters at the head of this book, and in which we read also miraculous facts, are not better founded. The infidels, like Noeldeke, reject them absolutely. He says: "The Second Book of the Machabees must be before all freed from the two letters which they have placed at the head of this work. It is pretended that they were written by the Jews of Palestine to recommend to their brethren of Egypt to take part in the feast of the consecration of the Temple. The first even carries, as inscription, a date which answers to the year 143 B.C.[2] Both letters are evidently unauthentic; the first, quite incomplete, contains a false chronological account; the second is full of fables and would be the most absurd, were it really the letter of a com-

---

[1] Appien, "De Rebus Syriacis," 45.
[2] II Mach. i, 10.

munity. These letters contain more than one contradiction with the very facts related in the Book of Machabees."[1]

Such are the objections. Behold the answer: "The first letter, they say, contains a false chronological account." There is nothing of the kind. In verse 7, of chapter 1, there is mention of the year 169 and, in verse 10, of the year 144 and of the year 124 before our era. They pretend to hold in this two contradictory dates of the letter, but without reason. The letter was written in 124, and what is said of 144 is reported as a past fact.

They claim, it is true that if the letter was written in 124, the Jews of Judea would have invited those of Egypt, as they do by this letter, to celebrate the feast of the purification of the Temple; established by Judas the Machabee, only forty years after its institution.

What is inadmissible in this? The Jews of Palestine might have had reasons, of which we have no knowledge, to have written at that time only to their coreligionists of Egypt; besides, nothing proves that this invitation was the first; it is possible that it was only the renewal of an invitation which had been previously extended.

The second letter placed at the head of the Second Book of Machabees is still more lively incriminated than the first. The facts which they refuse to regard as historical are in the number of three: The miracle of the sacred fire drawn from a dried up well, by order of Nehemias, and kindling itself.[2] The history of Jeremias hiding the Tabernacle and the Ark of the Covenant

---

[1] Noeldeke. Opus cit. p. 99.
[2] II Mach. i, 19-36.

upon Mount Nebo,[1] and finally the death of Antiochus which is related differently than in the history of Jason, source of the chapters following.[2]

2. THE SACRED FIRE.

Those who deny the supernatural and the miracle have to reject the account of the sacred fire miraculously kindling itself, but they refuse to admit it on philosophical and not historical grounds, just as they refuse to accept, in virtue of the same principles, the miracle of the fire from heaven burning the holocausts of Aaron,[3] of Solomon,[4] and of the prophet Elias.[5] All these facts are nevertheless historical. What the letter of the Jews relates could be well known to them by oral tradition; moreover, it was drawn from written sources lost to-day, to which they were careful to refer.[6]

3. THE ARK HIDDEN.

With regard to the history of the Ark and the Tabernacle hidden by Jeremias on Mount Nebo, one could hardly understand why the Rationalistic critics refuse to admit it, would it be unknown to us that they pretend that the Ark and the Tabernacle never existed. Since the account of the Book of Machabees contradicts their affirmations, they deny it, and since they cannot deny it without some pretext, they say that Jeremias was in prison at the moment when the city

---

[1] II Mach. ii, 4-8.
[2] II Mach. i, 13-16 and ix.
[3] II Mach. ix, 24.
[4] II Par. vii, 1.
[5] III Kings xviii, 38.
[6] II Mach. ii, 1, 4, 13.

was taken, and that it was impossible for one man to carry the Ark and the Tabernacle from Jerusalem beyond the Jordan to Mount Nebo.

Undoubtedly, Jeremias was in prison, but he was delivered by the Chaldean conquerors, and between the time he was set at liberty and the destruction of the Temple, one whole month had passed.[1] Hence, he had ample time to transport these sacred objects. As for the necessary help, what should have prevented the prophet from appealing to his friends for assistance? Nabuchodonosor had given orders to permit to Jeremias full liberty.[2]

4. THE DEATH OF ANTIOCHUS.

The third fact, that of the death of Antiochus, offers a real difficulty. The letter seems to relate the same event which we read a few chapters further on, and which is also reported in the First Book,[3] but the circumstances, either to the place where Antiochus learned the news of the defeat of his army, or to the nature of his illness, are so different that a reconciliation appears impossible. "One has remarked," says Cellerier, "that in both books of the Machabees, Antiochus dies in three different ways."[4]

We admit that Antiochus whose death is related in the First Book of Machabees and in the body of the account of the Second is the same, that is, Antiochus IV. Epiphanes. Further on we will inquire whether the one of whom the letter of the Jerusalem Jews speaks is not different.

---

[1] Jer. xxxviii, 28; xxxix, 2, 11-14; lii, 12-13.
[2] Jer. xxxix, 12.
[3] II Mach. i, 13-16 and ix; I Mach. vi.
[4] Cellerier, "Introduction a la Lecture des Livres Saints."

5. THE NAME OF THE TEMPLE PILLAGED BY ANTIOCHUS.

It is claimed, in the first place, that a contradiction exists in the meaning of the place where was located the Temple which Antiochus IV. Epiphanes wished to pillage. In the First Book of Machabees, according to the received reading and the translation of the Vulgate, it is Elymaïs, city of Persia;[1] in the Second it is Persepolis.[2]

It is easy to clear up both passages. The reading "Elymaïs," city of Persia, is false; the better Greek manuscripts read: "There is in Elymaïd, in Persia, a famous city." This reading is the only true one, for there never existed a city called Elymaïs. Therefore, the sacred author does not name the city the Temple of which Antiochus tried to pillage; he only says that it was situated in the province of Elymaïd, which formed a part of the kingdom of Persia. Polybius and Appien do the same.[3] The Second Book of Machabees designates the city by the name of Persepolis. As this city was situated in Persia, properly speaking, not in Media, it can be supposed that "Persepolis" signifies in this passage, not the city called by this name, but in translating the word, "the city or capital of the Persians," that is probably Susa, in Elymaïd, one of the principal royal residences of the King of Persia, and one of the best known by the Jews on account of the history of Esther and of Assuerus.

---

[1] I Mach. vi, 1.
[2] II Mach. ix, 3.
[3] Polybius, xxxi, 11; Appien, "De Rebus Syriacis," 66, p. 308.

After his attempt to pillage the Temple, Antiochus Epiphanes learns of the disaster which the Jews caused to his army; he learns this "in Persia," says the First Book of Machabees; "near Ecbatana," consequently in Media, says the Second.

There exists no contradiction between the two accounts; only the Second, as in the preceding case, is more precise and indicates in a more express manner where the Syrian king found himself, whilst the first indicates this only in a vague and general manner, understanding by Persia the whole of Ariana, which comprised Media, because this province formed a part of the kingdom of Persia. Antiochus, according to Polybius and St. Jerome,[1] died at Tabes, city of Persia, province of Parætacena, between Ecbatana and Persepolis.[2] The circumstances of his death are related more at length in the Second Book of Machabees than in the First, but both passages are in perfect accord; the second narrator completes only what the first had abridged.[3]

6. THE LETTER OF THE JERUSALEM JEWS.

The reconciliation of these two accounts offers, therefore, no serious difficulty. Is it the same for the narrative of the death of Antiochus contained in the letter of the Jews? According to this letter, Antiochus, wishing to pillage the Temple of Nanea, is introduced therein by the priests of the goddess with a small number of companions and is killed therein:[4] according

---

[1] Polybius, xxxi, 11, p. 72; St. Jerome. "Comm. in Dan." xi, 44-45.
[2] Quintus Curcius, v, 13.
[3] I Mach. vi, 8-16; II Mach. ix, 5-28.
[4] II Mach. i, 14-16.

to the narrative of the First and Second Books of Machabees inserted in the body of the work, Antiochus is repulsed from the Temple which he intended to pillage and dies in the road, at his return into Syria.[1]

These details appear absolutely irreconcilable, when we admit, as the Rationalistic interpreters, and even many Catholics do, that the Antiochus designated in all these places is the same. But the letter of the Jews does not say at all that the king of whom it speaks is Antiochus IV. Epiphanes, and because the one whose death it relates has perished in another manner than Antiochus IV., the natural conclusion is that another Antiochus was meant. Indeed, it is hard to admit that a writer, even not inspired, could contradict himself so formally in so few pages apart. Even if we had no means of explaining these two passages by extrinsic testimonies, on account of the scarcity of accounts arrived to us about these so remote epochs, we would have the right to affirm as follows: The king whom the writer, at the beginning of his work, makes to die a violent death, in a temple which he intends to pillage, is not the same king whose death he describes further on. The latter, he tells us, was obliged to flee at the moment when he also wished to pillage a temple:[2] the author gives us the most circumstantial details of his flight and of the last days of his life, on the nature of his

---

[1] I Mach vi, 1-16; II Mach. ix, 2-28.

[2] That two kings of the same name made the attempt to pillage a temple, must not surprise us, because this was nothing rare in antiquity. Strabo reports, for instance, that a Parthian king, Mithridates I., pillaged, and with more success than the Antiochus, in the same province of Elymaid, two temples, the one at Athens, the other at Artemis. Strabo xvi, i, iv, p. 634. See what Diodor of Sicily says, xxviii, 3 vol. ii, p. 473, of a Macedonian king.

bowel troubles which caused him great pain, on the accident on the road which aggravated his state, on the worms which gnawed at his body and which caused it to fall into putrefaction. Both pictures are different; therefore, they do not represent the death of the same personage.

We would be justified to draw this conclusion even then, if we could not bring forward any other proofs. But to corroborate it, to render it unassailable, we have other arguments. We know through the profane authors that two kings of Syria, both carrying the name of Antiochus, perished, the one in the manner as related in chapter six of the First Book of Machabees and in chapter nine of the Second, — this is Antiochus Epiphanes — the other in the manner as related by the letter of the Jews of Jerusalem — this is Antiochus III. the Great. A fragment of Polybius happily escaped the wreck of a part of his works, contains as follows: " In Syria, the King Antiochus, wishing to procure money, resolved to undertake an expedition against the temple of Diana in the Elymaïd. When he had arrived there, he was frustrated in his hopes, because the barbarians who lived in these places hindered him from executing such a great crime. During his return, he died at Tabes, city of Persia, attacked with madness, as some say, on account of the prodigies produced by the deity of the temple whom he had offended."[1] The accord, for the ensemble, between Polybius and that of the two Books of Machabees as to the death of Antiochus Epiphanes, leaves nothing to desire.

Behold now how various ancient writers relate the death of Antiochus III. the Great "Antiochus the

---

[1] Polybius, xxxi. 11.

Great," says Strabo, " desiring to pillage the Temple of Belus, the barbarians of the neighborhood attacked him without any other help and killed him."[1] "The King Antiochus," says Justin, " with his army attacked at night the temple of the Elymean Jupiter. The matter becoming known, he with his army was killed by the concourse of the inhabitants."[2] According to these accounts, Antiochus III. perished, therefore, as related by the letter of the Jews, that is, murdered whilst pillaging the temple of Belus.[3] Since the circumstances of the death related by both the letter and the profane authors are the same, and different from those of the death of Antiochus IV., how could we doubt that there is question here of Antiochus III.?

Against this explanation it is objected that the king in question had persecuted the Jews, and that Antiochus III. was no persecutor. But the text does not speak of a persecution properly speaking; it speaks only of combats,[4] and contains nothing against the king himself.[5] The letter even makes no allusion to the profanation of the temple, although it had for end to ask the Jews of Egypt to participate in the feast of the

---

[1] Strabo, xvi, l, 18.

[2] Justin xxxii, ii, 1.

[3] It is called temple of Belus or Elymean Jupiter, whilst the letter designates the temple of Nanea. Nanea was the espoused goddess of Bel. Therefore, they must have also honored her in the temple of Bel.

[4] II Mach. i, 12.

[5] At the end of the paragraph of the letter, II. Mach. i, 17, we read only the qualificative " impious " in the plural form, applied to both king Antiochus and his soldiers, but when they are designated thus, it is because they wished to pillage a temple, commit a sacrilegous work, not on account of their conduct towards the Jews.

temple. There is every reason to believe that the Jews of Jerusalem would have adopted quite a different tone, if there had been question of persecutions by Antiochus Epiphanes. When the First and Second Book of Machabees relate the death of the latter, their language is quite different.

Besides, the whole part of the letter with regard to the death of the King of Syria applies itself easily, when one admits that it has reference to Antiochus III., as is indicated by the details given by the Jews and by the profane writers. The news of his death must have been agreeable to the Egyptians, and also undoubtedly to a Jew who, like Aristobolus, lived at the court of the King of Egypt, because Antiochus III. had been almost his lifetime in war with the Egyptians. It is for this motive that the inhabitants of Jerusalem commence their letter with the narrative: " Having been delivered by God out of great dangers, we give Him great thanks, forasmuch as we have been in war with such a king."[1]

This king is the King of Egypt, of whom there is question in the preceding verse, and who was master of Palestine at the death of Antiochus III. The Jews had already fought against the King of Egypt. They subjected themselves willingly to Antiochus III., King of Syria, in joining his troops who besieged Scopas, general of Ptolemy, in the fortress of Jerusalem;[2] now they were expected to combat Egypt anew. Some time after the capture of the citadel of Jerusalem, the King of Syria had ceded Palestine, which had fallen again under his dominion, to the King of Egypt, in

---

[1] II Mach. i, 11.
[2] Josephus, " Jewish Antiquities " xii, iii, 3

giving it as a gift to his daughter Cleopatra.[1] He acted deceitfully, and he calculated on this marriage to realize his ambitious projects against the Ptolemys; he was deceived, his daughter took the interests of her husband against her own father,[2] and the Romans hindered him to take revenge on Egypt. Then he directed himself towards Asia Minor, where he had various success, passed into Greece, and by the advice of Hannibal, the famous Carthagenian general who had taken refuge to him, he entered into war with the Romans — an unfortunate undertaking. Stopped in his victorious course at the Thermophyles, in 191 B. C., he was, after different defeats, completely beaten at Magnesia of Lydia, in 190. The peace concluded in 188 was a hard one for him. The conquerors obliged him to give up all his possessions in the west of Mount Taurus, and to pay to them, in successive installments, the enormous sum of fifteen millions of Eubean talents.[3]

In order to fulfill this onerous condition, Antiochus desired to pillage the temple of Nanea where he perished. Had he succeeded in his undertaking, there is reason to believe that he would have made the attempt to take revenge on the Egyptians for the disgrace the Romans had heaped on him. After having been an enemy of Egypt all his lifetime, he certainly must have entertained evil designs against this country. Although the Jews could not personally complain against him during the latter years, they certainly

---

[1] Josephus, Op. cit. xii, iv, 1; Cf. Polybius xxviii, 17, part ii, p. 37.

[2] Dan. xi, 17 and St. Jerome, *in loc.*, vol. xxv, col. 564.

[3] Appien, "De Rebus Syriacis," 38. The Eubean talent amounts to about $1,100.

would have had to suffer by a war between the Seleucides and the Ptolemys. Whoever might have been the conqueror or conquered, they always would have been the victims. " Under the reign of Antiochus the Great, King of Asia," says Josephus, speaking of former wars, " it happened that the Jews, whose country was ravaged, . . . had a good deal to suffer. Whilst this prince waged war against Ptolemy Philopator and against his son,. surnamed Epiphanes, the Jews would have had to suffer, if Antiochus would have been the conqueror, and they would have had to suffer equally if he had been conquered, so that they appeared like a vessel which, in the midst of a storm, is tossed by the waves towards all sides, because they found themselves in the midst of the combatants, in the good as well as in the evil fortune of Antiochus."[1]

When Antiochus perished by assassination, Judea, we must not forget, belonged to the kings of Egypt, but, through Josephus, we know that Antiochus III. left nothing undone to gain the favor of the Jews, and all their sympathies were for this prince.[2] He had, therefore, a powerful party in the holy city and, as can be seen in the letter of the Jews, this party had risen its head, and the war was to break out at the moment when the news of the death of the King of Syria frustrated all the projects of his adherents.

Therefore everything concurs to establish that the Antiochus whose death the Jews relate is Antiochus III. the Great. They object, however, again, against this explanation, maintaining that this death was too old when the letter was written, in that it could be

---

[1] Josephus, Ant. Jud. xii, III, 3.
[2] Josephus, Ant. Jud. xii, III, 3.

announced as news to the Egyptians. But this objection supposes that we know the date of the letter. Now, the letter is not dated; therefore we can fix its date only according to its contents. Those who believe that Antiochus whose death is related is Epiphanes, say that it was written about 162, because Antiochus Epiphanes died in 163, and because Judas Machabeus, whom they suppose one of the authors of the letter, died in 161. According to this it would have been written twenty-five years after the death of Antiochus the Great (187). Certainly one does not announce an event of this kind twenty-five years after its fulfillment. But we cannot fix the date of the letter according to the date of the death of Antiochus, of whom it does not speak, as we have seen. The only thing which can serve to approximately determine the epoch when this writing was sent to Egypt, is the signature which teaches us that it was addressed to Aristobolus, " the teacher of King Ptolemy." It is generally admitted that this Aristobolus is the peripatetic philosopher of this name[1] who dedicated to Ptolemy Philometor his allegorical explanation of the Pentateuch.[2] This King Ptolemy is not distinguished by any first name. The Ptolemy who governed Egypt when Antiochus III. died was Ptolemy V. Epiphanes (204-181). Aristobolus, who dedicated his work on the Books of Moses to the son of Ptolemy V., that is, Ptolemy VI. Philometor (181-146), might very well have been the " counselor " of the father, as he was perhaps of the son. Hence, the letter must be dated from the year 187 or

---

[1] Euseb. *Praep. Ev.* viii, 9 vol. xxi, col. 636.

[2] They also explain the word "teacher" *didaskalos*, of King Ptolemy as meaning counselor.

186 B. C., shortly after the death of Antiochus III. the Great, and not from the year 162.

An apparently decisive objection is made against this date. The most of the critics maintain that the letter of the Jerusalem Jews had for end to invite those of Egypt to come and join them in the celebration of the feast of the purification of the temple, which had been profaned by Antiochus Epiphanes. This feast having been instituted only in 164 B. C., the letter cannot be anterior to this epoch.

Were the general opinion founded, were there really question here of the feast known under the name of Feast of Dedication,[1] the argument would be irrefutable; but whoever will read carefully, and with an unbiased mind, the letter of the Jews, will find that not one single word is said of the profanation of the temple by Antiochus Epiphanes and of the expiatory feasts which Judas Machabeus celebrated after having purified it. The feast to which the Jews of Egypt are invited to join, is, as is expressly stated by the letter, the feast of the discovery of the sacred fire by Nehemias: " Therefore, whereas we propose to keep the purification of the temple on the five and twentieth of the month of Casleu, we thought it necessary to signify it to you, that you also may keep the day of Scenopegia (Tabernacles) and the day of the fire that was given when Nehemias offered sacrifice, after the temple and the altar was built."[2] Can one desire anything more categorical and more conclusive? After the foregoing words, the letter relates at length the history of the discovery of the sacred fire by Nehemias and all that has

---

[1] I Mach. iv, 52-59; II Mach. x, 1-8; John x, 22.
[2] II Mach. I, 18.

reference to it, and it concludes saying: "As we are then about to celebrate the purification, we have written unto you and you shall do well to keep the same days (of the festival.)"¹ Consequently it follows from this that the feast they were about to celebrate in Jerusalem on the 25th of Casleu is not that which Judas the Machabee instituted in expiation of the profanation of the temple of which there is no question, but that of the discovery of the sacred fire. The text teaches us why it is called "purification," *katharismos:* it is because Jeremias had made use of water from the well where the sacred fire had been hidden "to purify what served for sacrifices,"² and because it had given to the place itself where the miracle of the sacred fire was effected the name of "Nephtar, which is interpreted: purification (*katharismos*)."³

Finally, a last objection they make against the explanation we have made, is that Judas the Machabee is one of the authors of the letter. Now, Judas the Machabee was at the head of the Jews only since the year 166 until the year 161. Consequently, the letter could have been written only between the year 166 and the year 161, and not about the year 186, as we said before.

This reasoning would be unanswerable were it proved that the name of Judas the Machabee is contained in the writing of the Jerusalem Jews, but this is not the case. We read in the signature of the letter: "The people. . . . the council, and Judas."⁴ It is

---

[1] II Mach. II, 16.
[2] II Mach. I, 33.
[3] II Mach. I, 36.
[4] II Mach. II, 14.

supposed that this Judas is the Machabee. At first sight this supposition is very plausible, for the personage of this name is best known in history and that most spoken of in the Second Book of Machabees. However, when it is well established, as we believe of having demonstrated, that Antiochus of whom the Jews and Judas speak is Antiochus the Great, it follows that the supposition is false, and that this Judas is not the Machabee, for a contestable hypothesis cannot overthrow a truth solidly proved. Besides, the author of the Second Book of Machabees seems to indicate himself that the Judas of whom it speaks is not the son of Mathathias: after having quoted the letter where the name of Judas is read,[1] a few lines further on it begins with his own account in saying: " Now as concerning Judas Machabeus."[2] This addition of the epithet of Machabeus seems to indicate that there is question of a Judas different from the one we come to speak of.

But who was this Judas they ask? In fact we are not obliged to know and to explain this. We have such meager accounts about this epoch that one does not need to be astonished when we ignore who was such or such a personage, when we know only of its name. These cases are not rare. If the ecclesiastical authors had not taught us that Aristobolus, named in the same verse as Judas,[3] had written on the Pentateuch, we would know nothing about him, for Josephus has not mentioned him in his works. Hence, there is nothing surprising in not knowing the history of this Judas, although he has played a certain role. The

---

[1] II Mach. II, 14.
[2] II Mach. II, 20.
[3] II Mach. I, 10.

ignorance of a fact cannot overthrow the rest of the thesis, and one has no right to conclude that a writer has committed grave historical errors because he speaks of a personage who, having lived about 200 years B. C., is not mentioned in his account. For many centuries we knew only the name of Sargon, King of Ninive, on account of a cursory word made by the prophet Isaias.[1] As this indication was an isolate one, several savants denied the existence of this monarch. They were wrong. We know to-day that this personage, unknown for a long time, has been one of the greatest kings of Assyria. Several other persons mentioned in the Books of Machabees are equally known to us only by name and by these books.

7. THE MARTYRDOM OF THE SEVEN MACHABEAN BROTHERS.

When we pass now to the objections made against the body of the account of the Second Book of Machabees, which is a summary of the history of Jason of Cyrene, the first we meet with has for object the martyrdom of the seven Machabean brothers. Antiochus Epiphanes was not so cruel as the account pretends, they tell us, and he could not be present at the execution of the seven brothers at Jerusalem, because he was at Antioch at that time.

The First Book of Machabees, the testimony of which is admitted by everybody, teaches us that Antiochus Epiphanes decreed the pain of death on all who would observe the Jewish law;[2] moreover, the orders which he gave to Lysias, in departing for Persia, to destroy and root out Israel, and to annihilate even its

---
[1] Is. xx, 1.
[2] I Mach. i, 52.

name, show his vehement exasperation against the Jews.[1] How can one pretend that the author of the Second Book of Machabees calumniates such a king in describing the torments which he inflicted on the seven martyrs.

But, it is added, the Seleucide king was then at Antioch, and consequently could not assist at their execution in the city of Jerusalem.

According to the most common opinion of the Churches of the Orient and Occident, the scene of the martyrdom took place at Antioch, and an ancient tradition alone can explain why they transported far from Judea an event which one would place naturally at Jerusalem. But when one refuses to admit this tradition, from this it does not follow that Antiochus was not at Jerusalem during the martyrdom of the seven Machabean brothers. Although the author had said before[2] that the king had returned to Antioch, it may be supposed that,[3] without telling this explicitly, he had come back. This manner of writing is frequent with all the authors.[4]

8. THE LETTERS OF ANTIOCHUS V. EUPATOR AND OF LYSIAS.

The second difficulty, and one of the most grievous which is offered by the Second Book of Machabees, is that which concerns the letters of Antiochus V. Eupator (163-162 B. C.) and of Lysias. We read in the First Book of Machabees: " So King Antiochus

---

[1] I Mah. iii, 34-36.
[2] II Mech. v, 21.
[3] II Mach. vii, 1.
[4] Cf. II Mach. vii, 1-42 and viii, 1-36; ix, 1.

(IV Epiphanes) died there in the year 163 B.C.). And Lysias understood that the king was dead and he set up Antiochus (V Eupator) his son to reign."[1] In the Second Book of Machabees,[2] they quote letters of Antiochus V., already reigning, after the death of his father, and of Lysias his tutor. Now, they are dated from the year 148 of the era of the Seleucides; that of Antiochus V. indicates moreover, as epoch of its authorship, the 15th of the so called xanthic month, that is, the sixth month of the Syro-Macedonian year, corresponding to the first month of the Jewish year called Nisan (March).

Various savants, and Froehlich in particular, have shown that the author of the Second Book of Machabees commences the year six months later than the author of the First Book, because the latter writing in Hebrew, follows the Jewish calendar, the first month of which corresponds to the sixth Macedonian month, whilst the former, writing in Greek, follows the Macedonian calendar, according to which the first month, *dios*, commences in October. This different manner to count produces a certain confusion in the minds of those who do not pay attention to this: but it explains the most of the chronological difficulties they have raised against the Second Book of Machabees, and in particular the apparent contradiction between the year of the death of Antiochus IV. which was the year 149, according to the First Book of Machabees, and the arrival of Antiochus V., which took place in the year 148, according to the Second Book. It results from the date of the letter of Antiochus V., dated from

---
[1] I Mach. vi, 17.
[2] II Mach. xi.

the xanthic month 148, that his father was dead at the commencement of this month, the Hebrew Nisan, or the sixth Macedonian month 148, according to the chronology of the First Book of Machabees which commences with this month the year 149 of the Seleucides. Hence, no serious objection can be made in regard to this subject.

But where the difficulty becomes aggravating, is when there is question of determining the date of the letter of Lysias. Chapter ten and the commencement of chapter eleven of the Second Book of Machabees relate, before reproducing the letters of Lysias and of Antiochus V., different victories carried by the Machabees against the generals of the new King Antiochus V. and against Lysias himself, victories so important that Lysias and his king write to the Jews for terms of peace. Now, the letter of Lysias, written under the reign of Antiochus V., is dated from the 24th of Dioscor, 148, that is, between October and November, and consequently, it seems to be anterior more than three months to the death of Antiochus IV., which cannot be the case.

Father Froehlich solves the objection in remarking that the Oriental histories do not always adhere in their exposition to the chronological order of facts. "Whoever will read carefully chapter eleven of the Second Book of Machabees will notice, I believe," he says "that we have here an inversion of this kind, and that the letter of Lysias and the two letters of Antiochus Eupator have not been written in the epoch in which they are placed in the account. In fact, the month of Dioscor of the year 148, date of the letter of Lysias, could not precede the xanthic month of this same year, which has been the first of the reign of Antiochus Eupator, and during which he wrote these two letters. Therefore, we must find in the xanthic month and in these two letters a place and an epoch which leave a sufficient interval for the fulfillment of the events related.

. . . (For this, it is sufficient to displace the letter of Lysias, and to admit that it is posterior of six months to the letters of Antiochus Eupator.) It is manifest, by the two Books of Machabees, that at the moment of the death of Antiochus IV. and of the arrival of Antiochus V. Eupator, the war had attained its full violence, and had been favorable to the Jews. Now, who ignores that the new princes, in mounting the throne, neglected nothing to enjoy peace at the commencement of their reign? This is the reason why Antiochus V. wrote to the victorious Jews, the 15th of the xanthic, at the beginning of his reign, to invite them to subscribe to a peace which would be advantageous to them, and to effect this he gave orders to Lysias, who was absent from court at that time. The very words which Antiochus addresses to Lysias prove the same thing: 'Our father being translated amongst the gods, we are desirous that they that are in our realm should live quietly,' etc.[1] Hence he made peace with the Jews at the commencement of his reign, in the xanthic month of the year 148. At this moment — the sacred historian relates the fact in the same place as the arrival of Antiochus V. — Ptolemy Macer or Macron, prefect of Judea and of Phœnicia, a just man, conducted himself peaceably in regard to the Jews. Peace, therefore, put an end to the recent combats. But this peace cannot have been of long duration on account of the criminal

---
[1] Mach. x, 10-16.

conduct of Lysias. The latter persecuted Ptolemy
Macer in such a manner that he forced him to poison
himself. Lysias, tutor of the king, succeeded him in
his commandment; he violated the peace and renewed
the war through the Gorgias.[1] These events probably
took place in the month of Artemisius (April). Since
the middle of the month of Artemisius until the 20th of
Dioscor, intercalated after the month of Hyperberety
(September), there is a space of time sufficient to place
the different combats delivered to the neighboring
nations. After the defeat of the other generals of
Antiochus Eupator, Lysias had time to come himself
with a select body of his army and be beaten. Hence,
it was during this half year, I believe, when those
glorious events for the Jews took place, and of which
there is question in the Second Book of Machabees,
chapters ten and eleven. And we can remove to about
the following year of the Greeks, 149, the military events
of which speaks the First Book of Machabees, in the
second part of chapter five, and the Second Book in
chapter twelve. Finally, Lysias, conquered anew by
the Jews at the commencement of autumn, the same
Syro-Macedonian year 148 nearing its end, that is, the
20th of the embolismic month of Dioscor, the last month
of the year, was obliged to ask for peace by his letter.
Thus, the whole seems to be in perfect accord and the
difficulty deriving from the different messages disappear
completely without that we are obliged to do violence
to the text.

"Thus, in summary, Antiochus IV. died in the
Syro-Macedonian year 148, the xanthic month or the
month of Nisan having commenced; this is why the

---

[1] II Mach. x, 10-16.

First Book of Machabees, according to its manner of counting, dates this event from the year 149. Antiochus V. surnamed Eupator, son of Antiochus IV., succeeded him immediately, and desirous to mark the beginning of his reign by peace, he wrote his letters on this subject to Lysias and to the Jews on the 15th of the xanthic month of the Syro-Macedonian year 148. Ptolemy Macer, partisan of the peace, poisoned himself shortly afterwards about the month of Artemius; Lysias succeeded him in the government of Phœnicia and Judea and behold the peace; the war lasted six months; Lysias, conquered after his generals, was forced to ask anew for peace by his letter to the Jews, dated from the 20th of the embolismic month of Dioscor, the last of the year 148 of the Syro-Macedonians."[1]

All the other objections they raise against the Second Book of Machabees are of little importance, and do not merit to be discussed: they are improbabilities or exaggerations, for example, they say, in number of enemies killed in the combat delivered by the Jews against the Syrian armies.[2] For the pretended improbable facts, criticism cannot prove in any manner that it has a right to reject them as aprocryphal facts. That the inhabitants of Joppe did drown Jews in the sea,[3] what is there impossible in this? That Razias rather killed himself than to fall into the hands of his enemies,[4] what is there incredible? As to the number of the dead who perished in the battles, one may admit, if he wishes, that the figures have been increased by the copyists in this book as in several others.

---
[1] E. Froelich, *Annales Compendiciarii regum Syriae*, p. 26-28.
[2] II Mach. viii, 24, 30; x, 23, 31; xi, 11; xii, 19, 26, 28; xv, 27.
[3] II Mach. xii, 3-4.
[4] II Mach. xiv, 37-46.

9. THE ANNIVERSARY OF THE BIRTH OF ANTIOCHUS EPIPHANES.

Finally, another objection made against the Second Book of Machabees is completely false. The sacred author reports that they forced the Jews to celebrate " every month "[1] the anniversary of the birth of Antiochus Epiphanes. As to this subject Mr. Grimm says: " Every month means that if the king, for example, was born on the 6th of xanthic, the sixth day of the eleven other months was also celebrated as his birthday. We find nowhere an example of a similar ordinance, and it can hardly be believed that such a decree was published by Antiochus Epiphanes. This also explains the omission " every month " by the Vulgate, although this reading is found in all the Greek manuscripts, in Theodoret and in the Syriac version. It seems to me that the sacred historian has mixed up and confounded that what concerned the annual celebration of the king's birthday with that what had reference to the sacrifice of the 25th of each month of which the First Book of Machabees speaks."[2]

In reality the author of the Second Book of Machabees has nothing mixed up and confounded; he was very well acquainted with the facts. The reproach made to the sacred author is, on the contrary, a proof of his exactitude. Examples of similar ordinances are existing, however extraordinary they may appear. Epigraphy establishes that the King of Syria did not content himself with an annual anniversary, but that he

---

[1] II Mach. vi. 7.

[2] I Mach. i. 59 (Vulgate, 62).—W. Grimm, " Handbuch zu den Apokryphen," vol. iv, p. 110–111.

prescribed a monthly anniversary. The custom of the monthly anniversary was, indeed, a constant one for all the successors of Alexander. We recover the same custom in Egypt,[1] at Pergamum,[2] finally at the last successors of the Seleucides, the Antiochus of Commagene.[3] Therefore, it cannot be questioned that the kings of Syria had also monthly anniversaries.

CHAPTER XXXVIII.

THE PSALMS.

THE attacks of the infidels against the Psalms regard either their origin, or the doctrine of these sacred chants.

1. The Council of Trent in its canon of the Sacred Books, calls the Book of the Psalms *Psalterium Davidis;* did it mean to tell thereby that all the Psalms are from David? Certainly not, for it is sufficient to read the Psalter to recognize, in the style, contents and title even of different Psalms, that they cannot be all attributed to David: some are anterior to him, others saw the light only a long time after him; but as the Vulgate attributes to the king-prophet eighty-eight Psalms, of which two only (Ps. xlii and cxxxvi) can be refused to him, the Fathers of the Council have added the name of David to the Psalter as that of the principal author, and this in virtue of the well known principle: *major*

---
[1] Decree of Canope, L. 26; Decree of Rosette, L. 52.
[2] Hermes, 1873, p. 115, L. 35.
[3] O. Hamdy-Bey, The tumulus of Nimrad, Dagh. col. iii, L. 115.

pars trahit ad se minorem. This being the case, one can hardly explain the pains which some infidels take to establish that the Catholics are deceived by attributing all the Psalms to David.

"Tradition," says Vernes, "pronounces the name of David with the same ignorant candor which makes it place the name of Moses at the head of the Pentateuch, and to place under the cover of Solomon the Proverbs, the Ecclesiastes and the Canticle of Canticles." In reality the tradition of which the critic speaks reduces itself to the opinion of a few Fathers, whose sentiments never found an authority in regard to this point, for St. Jerome said already in the fourth century: "Let it be known that one is deceived by attributing all the Psalms to David, and not to the authors whose name they carry." As to this point Reuss, a Rationalist, follows only Catholic tradition; but he goes further than this, let us say too far, in designating the epoch of the Machabees as that of the composition of the most of the Psalms. Undoubtedly, he is forced, in his system, to have recourse to this hypothesis, for one could hardly explain the existence of Psalms in an epoch in which the Rationalists show us the Hebrews as subject to all the errors of polytheism, to all the abuses of the inhuman worship of the false gods. But how must one torture the text to arrive at a similar result! The Psalms are the history of God's people related from day to day by the poets, they are great events of the Books of Kings, and even of the Pentateuch, related and commented upon by men, who certainly were eye-witnesses thereof, for one feels them under the stroke of the profound impressions which these events excited in their soul. But as this inconveniences the Rationalists, they are obliged to deny these events; there where tradition has always seen, for example, the anguishes of David persecuted by his enemies, the new criticism beholds nothing else but the anxieties of the Hebrew people oppressed by a foreign nationality, in the epoch of the Ptolemies or of the Seleucides, in the moment of the persecutions of Antiochus and the rising of the Machabees.

The reason for this change, we have seen, is the need of the cause; as to the pretext, behold it stated by Mr. Vernes: " It is against all probability," he says, " to make a book to preserve the reflection of circumstances peculiar to an individual; this book, on the contrary, is better understood when it expresses the anguishes, the fears and hopes of an entire people." It is Mr. Vernes himself who furnishes to us the refutation of this little serious reason, in quoting the following passage of Reuss: " Other (Psalms) expressed in the beginning, the individual and momentary sentiments of their authors, but in a manner that many other persons, placed in similar circumstances, could appropriate both the spirit and words of them." Behold, expressed by a Rationalist and repeated by Mr. Vernes, the usefulness of these Psalms which one can call *individual.*

We content ourselves with this general refutation; to render it more complete we would have to examine each Psalm one after another, which would lead us too far. However, let us observe that when Reuss, in order to justify his theory, has tried to apply it to each Psalm in particular, this attempt has been so unfortunate that Mr. Vernes cannot help saying: " In this regard we would have liked sometimes more rigor in the discussion."

2. As to the doctrine itself of the Psalms, it has been attacked also as well as their origin. 1. The Psalmist, they said, ignores a future life: "The dead will not praise Thee, O Lord," says the Psalms xciii. In regard to this subject we can refer only to another chapter "The Book of Ecclesiastes," where we sufficiently establish the belief of the Hebrews in the immortality of the soul. As to the words of the Psalm cxiii, they suppose in no manner the death of the soul, and are not a denial of the future life, but the authentication of the impotency in which were the saints of the Old Testament to praise God in Limbo; it is certain that before Jesus Christ had opened the gates of heaven to the just souls, the latter could not enjoy the intuitive vision, and, consequently, death had for them a particular horror. 2. Another reproach formulated against the Psalms concerns the imprecations, sometimes very violent, which are formulated therein against the enemies of God's people. To this we can answer that, the enemies of the Hebrew people being those of God himself, to desire their punishment was nothing else but taking into their hands the interests of the Lord. Besides, the so-called hatred manifested by the Psalmists has reference a good deal more to the sin than to the sinner; and when sometimes the sinner himself appears to be attacked, we must remember that the Jewish law was not perfect; the strict law of justice should be replaced by the more perfect law of charity. In summary, one objects nothing that is repugnant to the divine inspiration of the Psalms; now this inspiration is the only thing which the Church imposes for our belief in regard to these writings.

CHAPTER XXXIX.

THE BOOK OF PROVERBS.

A GENERAL accusation is made against the Book of Proverbs. Its contents are said to be of human conception, but vulgar and disedifying in purport. "The wise Solomon," said the Emperor Julian, "is he worthy to be compared to the Greek Proclydes, with Theognides or Socrates? Ah, why! If you compare the exhortations of Socrates with Proverbs, you will find, I am sure, the son of Theodore superior to the most wise of the kings." Voltaire is still more envenomed against the Proverbs. He says: "It is a collection of maxims, which appear to our refined minds sometimes trivial, low, incoherent, without taste, without choice, and without design. . . . Is it to a great king, to the wisest of the mortals, that one can dare to impute such follies?" All the men of good faith have at all times acknowledged the merits of the Book of Proverbs.

Thanks to the Old Testament, and especially to the New Testament, the doctrine taught by the Book of Proverbs has become familiar to us, and it has been perfected by Jesus Christ. But because the teachings of the Savior are much more beautiful and refined than the Proverbs of Solomon, it does not follow at all that the maxims of the son of David are neither noble nor worthy of the Holy Ghost. In a collection of this kind, which is general in its teaching, there are necessarily counsels which apply to all the conditions of life; there must be advice given within the intelligence of the ignorant as well as the learned, for the weak as well as for the strong; the wise king addresses himself to all, and speaks for all; hence, he cannot always embellish his language so as to indicate and not speak plainly his meaning and still be understood by everyone; the author addresses the mean as well as the mighty; he speaks to the children in the language of youthful understanding, and to the men, with the stern, rigorous voice of a man. But his language is always that of prudence and truth. Julian the apostate, compares him with the gnomic writers of antiquity, to belittle him by the comparison. His judgment is quite unjust. Nothing proves better the excellency of the Book of Proverbs than the comparison of his maxims with those of the pagan wisdom. From Phoclydes to Marcus Aurelius, although the latter had breathed somewhat of the Christian atmosphere, all are greatly inferior to the son of David. Who is the one among them sufficiently elevated in mind to have given us as a model of moral life, this principle which is the first precept of the Book of Proverbs: " The fear of God is the beginning of wisdom?" Human philosophy had seen very well that virtue consists in the happy medium between two extremes; but no pagan philosopher or Solon ever existed who occupied in his teachings this point of vantage. Errors of dogma and morals, excesses of so-called virtue and vice were ever present in the greatest of writers and teachers, while in Solomon, on the contrary, there is nothing to eliminate, nothing to change.

Theognides, the gnostic poet par excellence, who lived about 450 B. C., has left us in about 700 distiches which have escaped the ravages of time, a sort of moral code, but it is inspired by a defiant, bitter, and melancholy wisdom, which scarcely sees other than the evil side of man. Epictetes, the greatest of the pagan moralists, knows not how to advise man in his actions of life, but summarized his philosophy in the famous maxim: "Suffer, abstain." The most wise among the pagans have made only a vague acknowledgment of heavenly mercy and justice; and of the virtue of resignation. They advise the sufferer to consider his woes an illusion, and thus to obtain strength and comfort in self-deception; never did the idea enter their mind to invite us, as does Solomon, to seek in the thought of God a sweet occupation of the heart, to consider this thought a resting place, a refuge, a harbor for the storm-tossed ship of life. The doctrine of the author of the Proverbs is, therefore, much superior to that of the profane moralists. It is not yet the full day of the Gospel, but it is already its dawn. From that time God appears to us as a Father even in his chastisements: "Whom the Lord loveth, he chastiseth, as a father in the son he pleaseth himself." (Prov. III, 12.)

CHAPTER XL.

THE BOOK OF ECCLESIASTES.

THE infidels accuse the doctrine of Ecclesiastes of being impregnated with the most grievous philosophical errors: they pretend it to be in doctrine Epicurian, Sceptic, Materialistic and Pessimist.

1. EPICURIANISM.

What is the course man should follow in passing through the struggles of this life? The only answer which Ecclesiastes gives to this question, the Rationalist tells us, is that we must enjoy the passing hour. And this is the "sensual enjoyment, the pleasure of eating and drinking and the contemplation of beautiful things." The following passages especially are those which have given pretext to the accusations of the infidels: Ecc. II, 24; ix, 7, etc. These texts and similar ones do not prove at all that the author of Ecclesiastes was an Epicurian. Certainly, we do not find in Ecclesiastes a panegyric of penance and mortification on earth, but neither do we find this in the other books of the Old Testament. The Jews, without ignoring the future retribution, attached a greater value to the earthly goods than the Christians whose greatest earthly treasures were comprised in the promises made by God to His people. Hence, there is nothing astonishing in beholding *Cohelet* (Ecclesiastes) complacently engaged in earthly enjoyments; but to be Epicurean he would have to be obliged to consider these enjoyments as an end, as the end of man, and it is precisely this which he does not do, in fact, he condemns in a formal manner the abuse of the pleasures, repeatedly cautions that all this will be followed by death and judgment.

2. SCEPTICISM.

The author of Ecclesiastes is not a sceptic. The Rationalist, however, makes this accusation, when he says: "The dominating character of the author is scepticism. He has no firm conviction." The fact is, however, that he believes without hesitation in all the great fundamental truths; in the existence of God; in the obligation to live conformably to the moral law; he hopes for a just retribution for the actions of men, and acknowledges that God has disposed of all things. He does not even suggest these things as problematical; he asks only whether man can enjoy perfect happiness on earth and find in the enjoyments of study what he cannot find elsewhere (viii, 16-17), and he answers that our spirit is incapable, not to discover and know the truth, but, what is quite different, to search into the why and wherefore of things. Now, who to-day can deny that human intelligence is limited, or that nature is for us replete with enigmas and mysteries?

3. MATERIALISM.

But when the author of Ecclesiastes was not sceptic, was he at least materialistic? "This book," says one critic, "can be considered as the breviary of the most advanced modern materialism." Undoubtedly in several places (xii, 7, etc.), the author distinguishes explicitly the body from the soul; but, say the infidels, he denies or questions at least the immortality of the soul, the future life. Now, what reasons do they give for these assertions: 1. Faith in the immortality was not yet known, says one, consequently the Cohelet must, like his contemporaries, ignore the immortality of the soul. To this objection Renan himself answers: "In two or three places one might believe that the author sinks himself into pure materialism, but all on a sudden he rises with an elevated accent. . . . Cohelet does not forget God's judgment."[1] 2. To establish that Solomon did not believe in another life, the following text is quoted: "Therefore, the death of man, and of beasts, is one, and the condition of them both is equal; as man dieth, so they also die; all things breathe alike, and man hath nothing more than beast, all things are subject to vanity. And all things go to one place; of earth they were made, and into earth they return together. Who knoweth if the spirit of the children of Adam ascend upward, and if the spirit of the beasts descend downward?" (iii, 19-21). It is especially upon the interpretation of the last verse that the materialists claim is established. It can be explained in the sense that there are few who know exactly what becomes of the soul after death. The Hebrew Bible in the edition of the Massorets contains this verse: "Who knoweth the spirit of man which ascends upward and the spirit of the beast which descends downwards?" The massoretic meaning which is not difficult of interpretation, is much preferable. Hence, the

---

[1] E. Renan, "l'Ecclesiaste," p. 87-88.

sacred author means to say: How many men are there that dwell seriously on the future of the soul!

Besides, there are many passages wherein Ecclesiastes affirms explicitly his faith in an after life and in the final reward.[1] Therefore, the author of Ecclesiastes believed in another life, and a contrary assertion can only find support in a single verse of doubtful meaning.

4. PESSIMISM.

A final accusation against the author of Ecclesiastes is Pessimism. The Pessimists, since the invention of their system, have pretended to claim the author of this book as one of their own. It is true that Ecclesiastes describes the disenchantments of life with a melancholic eloquence, which produces the most profound impression. But the Pessimism of this book is much different from that of our contemporary philosophers. The latter are materialists and atheists, and the former believes firmly in vice and virtue; in a life beyond the grave; in a personal God (iii, 4-18), who will judge the good and the bad, these are so many irreconcilable beliefs repudiated by Pessimism which is one of the maladies of our century.

For the rest, to show how false are the accusations brought up against the Book of Ecclesiastes, it is only necessary to call the reader's attention to the following verses: Eccl. iii, 11 (13; ii, 24, 18; vi, 2; ix, 7); iii, 17, v, 3, 5; vii, 19, 30; viii, 2; 12-13; ix, 1; xi, 9; xii, 1; 13-14. " Fear God and keep His commandments: for this is all man, for God will bring into judgment whether it will

---

[1] Cf. Eccl. iii, 16-17, xii, 7; Ps. lxxxix, 49; xxxi, 18; lxxxviii, 6, 7, 13; xciv, 17; lxxxviii, 1; Job xxx, 23. The Psalms are quoted according to the Hebrew.

be good or evil," are the words of the last two verses, and indicate beyond question the true belief of the writer. An author who expresses such sentiments is far from being an Epicurian, Sceptic, Materialist or Pessimist. This is so manifestly true that the enemies of the Scripture, in order to incriminate the author of Ecclesiastes pretend that the epilogue was added afterwards and by another hand.

CHAPTER XLI.

THE CANTICLE OF CANTICLES.

THIS Biblical Book, when one adheres to the bark of the letter, is a nuptial song, under the form of a dialogue between groom and bride. But in reality of what nuptial is there question here? The Church has always believed that the covenant of which there is question in the Canticle was a quite spiritual alliance, as that of the Savior with His Church. Some, it is true, admit a double sense in the Canticle, the one literal, celebrating the union of Solomon with the daughter of the King of Egypt, and the other mystical, elevating itself above flesh and blood to consider only the divine alliance with Jesus Christ and the Church. But whilst Bossuet, Calmet, etc., ably defended this mystic sense, the most of the Catholics wished to behold in the Canticle only an allegory, a simple parable, having only a celestial meaning and no material meaning. One believes that the allegorical school is right, with Origen, St. Jerome, St. Bernard, etc., and that it is more true and respectful to behold in the Canticle only a parable as that of the mutual feasts, or that of the prudent and foolish virgins; but be this as it may, the two opinions we have exposed can be maintained, for both elevate themselves, although in different degrees, above the sensible love, and they acknowledge in the Canticle a useful aim, a divine end which justifies its canonicity.

There is a third interpretation, which is admissible; this consists in recognizing in the book in question only an exclusively literal sense. For the adherents of this system the Canticle is an epithalamium, a wedding song and nothing more. Did the author wish to celebrate the marriage with the Sulamite, or simply the union of a shepherd with a shepherdess? Have we before us a drama, as Renan wished, or a "collection of erotic poetries," according to the theory of Reuss? Behold the only questions which divide our contemporary Rationalistic critics; as to the question to know whether there is a mystic sense under the letter, there is nothing of the kind for the Rationalists; for them the Canticle is "the purely literary composition, without mixture of any religious element, that may have arrived to us from Jewish antiquity." It is Mr. Vernes that speaks thus.

Outside the authority of the Church two reasons are decisive to make us reject this literal theory: 1. Never would the Canticle have figured in the Canon of the Scriptures, if since the beginning one would not have known that it contained something else but a wedding song. The Jews inserted into their Canon only sacred books, and, for having introduced therein the Canticle, they must have seen a spiritual sense therein, a union more elevated and holier than that expressed by the letter of the text; also no Targumist beheld therein a purely literal meaning. After the synagogue the Church has always followed in the interpretation of the Canticle, the maxim of our Savior: " It is the spirit that quickens, the flesh serves to nothing." She has condemned the literal system since the year 553, for not our actual critics are the inventors thereof; finally, she has made such a usage thereof in her liturgy and in her teaching, that it is sufficient to read the offices in honor of Mary and the explanations of her doctors, for example, the letters of direction of Bossuet, to recognize the truth of the spiritual sense, and to be struck by its beauty. 2. It ought to cost so much less to recognize in the Canticle a mystic sense, as " nothing is more common in the Bible than the pictures of husband and wife, employed to render, under an expressive form, the union of the soul with God, of the chosen people with its master and king " (Mgr. Freppel). And, indeed, for the prophets, the Jewish nation is a bride chosen by God, sometimes faithful and sometimes adulterous (Jer. ii, 2; Ezech. xvi, 3 ff.); for St. Paul the Church is the spouse of Jesus Christ (Eph. v, 31); for St. John spiritual nuptials are prepared to the Lamb in heaven (Apoc. xix, 7); finally, Jesus Christ Himself compares the kingdom of heaven who go to meet the groom and the bride (Mat. xxv, 1). Therefore, there is nothing more natural than to admit, in the case that occupies us, an assimilation of the same kind, and to acknowledge that the inspired author has chosen the most beautiful and the most profound of human affections to give us a picture of the alliance of souls with God.

CHAPTER XLII.

THE BOOK OF JOB.

THE Book of Job is one of the most beautiful monuments of literature and an ideal of a Semitic poem. But is this magnificent poem a history or a fiction? The Church has always believed in the real existence of the Arab patriarch. Some ancient Rabbis have maintained, to the contrary, that the Book of Job is only a long parable, and the personage whose trials it relates was not a real man. In our days, a certain number of Rationalists also pretend that the poem of Job is a fiction, like the Iliad and Odyssey. They even imagine to recognize therein the work of several hands, like in the writings of Homer. To believe them the prologue and the conclusion are posterior additions. The discourses of Eliu, they say, are not authentic and form no part of the primitive poem.

It is generally admitted by the Catholic authors that the Book of Job has been embellished with poetic ornaments, but all are agreed in acknowledging its foundation as historic. It is this that Scripture itself teaches us when it gives us Job as a model of patience, in the prophet Ezechiel (xiv, 14, 20), in the Book of Tobias (ii, 12) and in the Epistle of St. James (v, 11). Nothing in the Biblical account authorizes us to deny the real existence of the holy patriarch of Idumea. A discussion of the subject will readily prove this point.

FIRST OBJECTION.

All the details of the history of Job have no probability it is stated. — That the misfortunes of Job are not within the usual province of human ills no one will deny. But " if the case of Job is most extraordinary, in whatever sense one may imagine it, the lesson it teaches will apply itself so much more easily to all other cases." It is M. Reuss, a Rationalist, who makes this remark. God permits that His servant is subjected quite on a sudden to the most distressing trials, in order that his example might justify more manifestly His Providence, and that the lesson might be more significant.

SECOND OBJECTION.

One wishes to behold contradictions between the Job of the prologue and the Job of the discussion. Inasmuch as the one is resigned, they assure us, so much is the other impatient, almost blasphemous, which evidences that the poet fashions the personage at will and does not even pretend to make him consistent with himself. These accusations are very unjust, and it is Reuss himself who again furnishes their refutation.

" Job the pious and just man is put on trial, and the history tells us that he sustained it. He is oppressed by pain; but he remains firm and faithful, not only in face of his personal misfortunes, but also, and what is greater, in face of the suspicions of his life-long friends who accuse him of hypocrisy and who treat him very uncharitably. From them and their unjust judgment, he always calls upon God; he does not cease to address himself to the One who alone can justify and console him. When doubt comes to assail him, he combats it and triumphs over it; and when momentarily he appears to give way to despair, it is solely because he believes God whom he seeks and whom he invokes does not wish to hear him. There is not in this, to tell the truth, any trace of incredulity, of an impious denial. On the contrary, at the same moment when the thought of his misery torments him most vividly, when he complains most bitterly of being abandoned, forgotten, despised by those who were his best friends, his faith shows itself most gloriously immovable, and he expresses the conviction that God will restore his name, were this even only after death. Hence, the really pious man will emerge victoriously from the trial, when he has to do with God alone, and when he does not permit the prejudiced utterances of others to disconcert and mislead him. He recognizes that God does not desire his misfortune, but that He permits it with the intention indicated. . . . Also, Job, towards the end, recovers his moral equilibrium, the tranquility of mind, as soon as his adversaries are silenced; and, in lamenting his lot, and in protesting his innocence, he expresses himself in a manner so touching that the reader, who might have been shocked at certain too vehement expressions, returns without difficulty to his first sentiments" (Reuss, Job, 24).

THIRD OBJECTION.

The friends of Job are not real personages, they are only fictitious they tell us. Reuss comes again to prove the contrary. "They are three," he says (Op. cit. p. 17-18), "but they do not represent three philosophic systems or three diverse solutions, even they do not place themselves in three different points of view, as is generally the case in our dramas, where each personage has his particular role. For the most, we can say that one of them speaks with more moderation, the others with passion and vehemence: in the main they say the same thing. . . . The discourses of the three friends are replete with repetitions. It is constantly the same topic: God punishes the wicked; misfortune is the punishment of sin; man is not wiser than God. . . . From his part, Job also returns continually to his protestation of innocence; he always affirms that he has not merited his lot. . . . The author describes this, not as a philosopher would do, producing thesis after thesis and demonstrating them by a logical and connected argumentation, so as to approach insensibly his end, and to finish by imposing conclusions upon his readers. He puts into the scene living personages; each one having his convictions and prejudices. They do not come at an understanding; what one affirms the other denies, and no decision is arrived at either as to the cause of Job's suffering or the means he should adopt to alleviate them."

FOURTH OBJECTION.

The improbability of the epilogue is especially insisted on, according to which God gives to the just Job double what he possessed before the trial: twice the number of sheep, camels, oxen, and asses, and twice as many sons and daughters. But what is there impossible in this? In all the epochs of histories we meet with singularities not less improbable. The descent of Hugo Capet has given successively to France three branches of kings; each one extinguished itself with three brothers who reigned one after another. Were we to meet a similar fact in sacred history, the critics would not fail to cry out that it was impossible and improbable, and the credulity and simplicity of people who believed such an assertion was to be pitied, etc., but the truth would be none the less incontestable. It is the same with the restoration of the fortune of Job.

FIFTH OBJECTION.

The critical spirit is so punctilious that it even finds fault with the names Job gives to his daughters after the return of his fortune. Because they are borrowed from graceful objects, it is concluded that they must have been "forged willfully by the poet." Who, however, does not know among those that are somewhat familiar with the Oriental customs, that similar names are there quite ordinary and common? Job calls his three daughters, the first "Jemimah," in Arabic, "the dove," on account of her dove-like eyes; the second "Qesiah," because she appears like wrapped up with the perfume of "cannell," and the third "Qerenhappuk," from the name of the principal cosmetic of feminine beauty, because her beauty must have become still greater by art (Job xlii, 14). The Greeks would have compared them to the Three Graces; Job compares them to the most beloved objects of the Orientals, and he names them accordingly. Even in the present day in Arabia and Persia, women are named from graceful animals, flowers, perfumes and precious stones, and it is not infrequently that one hears young girls named as they are in the "Thousand and One Nights": Garden Flower, Coral Branch, Sugar Cane, Day Light, Morning Star, etc.

Hence, the Book of Job is historical in its ensemble and principal points, in spite of the poetic frame in which it is placed, and the literary ornaments by which it is embellished. As to the date when it was written, this is a mere matter of discussion and we have not, consequently, any need to enter it into our inquiry.

6. AUTHENTICITY OF THE DIVERS PARTS OF THE BOOK OF JOB.

Let us establish now the authenticity of the parts of the Book of Job which are contested or denied by the infidels, that is, the prologue and the epilogue, the discourse of Eliu.

In regard to the parts in prose which serve as an introduction and conclusion to the work, the infidels themselves acknowledge that we cannot separate them from the body of the Book, and that, consequently, they have always been attached to it.

When the prologue and epilogue are authentic for the less extreme Rationalists, nearly all Rationalists denounce the discourses of Eliu as an interpolation of a much later date. " This portion," they say, " does not fit with the general plan; what God reproaches in Job is quite different from that which Eliu blames in him; Eliu is named neither in the prologue nor in the epilogue."

It is true that Eliu is named neither in the prologue nor in the epilogue, but the reason is simply because the author had no object in naming him. The rule which he follows is to mention nobody who is not directly interested in the part of the narrative under relation. It is thus that the brothers of Job are named accidentally in one of his discourses; his parents are mentioned for the first time in the last chapter. The poet speaks of the friends of Job at the beginning to show that they came to console him, and at the end to show that the reproaches which they made to the sufferer were without foundation in the judgment of God Himself; but Eliu was not an intimate friend of Job, he was simply an assistant to the discussion, whose presence one did not need to indicate, a young man who, in accordance with Oriental custom, remained in the background, observing silence while those older than he were speaking; when asked for his opinion he entered into the conversation. Moreover, Eliu, different in this respect from Eliphaz, Baldad and Sophar, states only what is just and true, and consequently in the conclusion, as Job has nothing to reproach him with, there is no need for the author to speak of him. He is the only one of the interlocutors named who does not err in his judgments of Job. The objections made against his role are European or American objections, which would never have occurred to the mind of an Oriental. The latter would not care about having the last word. As soon as he has nothing important any more to tell he keeps silence.

Very far from not fitting in with the "general plan," very far from being an outside work "without which the poem would remain not less complete," the discourses of Eliu round out the justification of Providence, such as it could be effectuated before the law of grace: they develop a new explanation which would be placed neither in the mouth of the friends of Job nor in the mouth of God, namely, the usefulness of suffering to purify man and to instruct him. The three friends of Job have maintained that, if he is afflicted it is because he has merited all suffering as a chastisement. Job protests against this accusation: he affirms his innocence with the greatest energy, and

the conclusion derived from his statements is, that he
does not know why God afflicts him, because he has
no fault to reproach himself with. God will not tell
him, for He will not demean Himself to justify His
conduct before man. It is enough that Job has to
bow down under the weight of God's majesty and the
spectacle of His magnificence. Pope justly reproached
Milton for having been wanting in respect towards God
and for having been guilty of bad taste in putting into
His mouth theses and arguments. The Book of Job
does not make this mistake. God speaks as a master,
and what should have been said by the friends of the
unhappy Job is said by Eliu. The latter reveals to the
holy patriarch the secret of his trials in showing to him
in the affliction a means to purify and perfect himself.
Thus the intervention of Eliu is far from being useless
and inexplicable. Without these discourses the justification of Providence, which is the object of the poem,
would be incomplete and imperfect. In showing how
God permits that afflictions are visited upon the just
to make him watchful against sin, when he has not
fallen, or when he has fallen, to excite to repentance, he exposes truths of the greatest imporance and of the greatest practical usefulness. It
is not true that all suffering is the chastisement
for crime, as the friends of Job maintained; but
we cannot agree with Job neither, when he says that
God is unjust when He visits afflictions upon the innocent, for it is for the good of the just that God permits
that the one who has not offended Him is afflicted.
The correct understanding of these discourses of Eliu
is, therefore, far from furnishing a proof that they are
not authentic.

CHAPTER XLIII.

THE PROPHET DAVID.

AMONG the personages of the Old Testament who are the object of universal veneration there is none that has been more abused by the modern infidels than King David. This great man has not always been a saint; there are stains in his life, but he has effaced them by his presence, and he is one of the most beautiful examples of God's mercy towards the "contrite and humble" sinners (Ps. li, 19). No matter; Rationalism cannot pardon him for having been one of the most illustrious faithful of the Old Testament and one of the chief instruments of which God made use to prepare, a long time beforehand, the advent of Christianity; infidelity seeks to lower and to degrade him. None has gone further in his hatred against David than Renan; he surpasses all his infidel friends by his violence, or by the brutality of his attacks against this holy man. The historic sympathies of the infidels are something remarkable. Renan has labored his whole lifetime, on the one hand, to reinstate Satan, Cain, Saul and Judas Iscariot, and on the other, to lower David, St. John and St. Paul. An irresistible penchant carried him towards the first and separated him from the second.

Ed. Reuss, although a Rationalist, points out with right, several characteristics which justify the glory of David, and thus condemns the excesses of Renan. But also this author is far from rendering complete justice to the founder of the Hebrew monarchy, to the pious king who conceived the project to raise a temple to Jehovah in Jerusalem, and who organized with such a splendor the liturgical chant and public worship, to the inspired poet who, in spite of all one may say against him, was "the exquisite chanter of Israel," the author of the most beautiful Psalms. To make the attempt to rob David of the glory of having composed a part of our sacred chants is one of the most foolish undertakings of modern infidelity. If David has not composed Psalms, there is not a single fact certain in the history of the past. Pindar has not written his Ode, and Virgil is not the author of the Eneid.

1. THE HOLINESS OF DAVID'S LIFE.

However, even supposing that David would not have left to us any poetical composition, the Church would not have a less right to consider him as a saint. Undoubtedly, these Psalms attest in a striking manner his sentiments of faith and piety, but his history alone is sufficient to show us in him a model worthy in several respects of our imitation. The first king of Jerusalem permitted himself, it is true, to fall into deplorable faults, he even commits great crimes, but he repairs them most generously; and just by his repentance, in bowing down under the hand of God, and in acknowledging that he was justly punished, he knew how to draw from his own fall a means to raise himself higher, and taught to all the future sinners the merit of penance and the value of an humble and sincere expiation. When one means to say that David did not merit the title of saint by a constantly irreproachable life, one has right; but the Church, which considers penance as a second innocence, and knows the extent of God's mercy as well as the frailty of man, grants the title of saint to the converted sinner as well as to the just who has never failed, to St. Paul, to St. Augustine and to David, as to St. Louis and to St. John; to Mary Magdalen as to St. Agnes. As to the Scripture, it calls David "the man according to the heart of God" (1 Kings xiii, 14), certainly not to approve of the faults which he might commit later on, but because he should nevertheless fulfill with fidelity the mission which Providence had assigned to him. Scripture blames quite clearly the sins of the son of Isaï, and we cannot behold in its words the eulogy of his whole conduct and the approbation of all his acts. The prophet Nathan announces to the guilty king that in punishment of his crime he will lose the son which Bethsabee had given to him and, a still harder chastisement, that his beloved son Absalom will revolt against him (II Kings xii, 10-12). God, on account of his repentance, pardons to him the sin committed, but the expiation thereof will be a public one, in order to repair the scandal (xii, 13-14). Is it possible to manifest in a more evident manner how God blames and condemns his servant when his conduct is reprehensible?

2. DAVID MERITS THE PRAISES OF SCRIPTURE.

Moreover, in spite of his violent passions and in spite of the most grievous faults, David did not less merit the eulogies which Scripture bestows on him and, in imitation thereof, the entire Jewish and Christian antiquity. God, who penetrates the hearts of men, beheld a vast difference between the dispositions of Saul and those of his successor. Both became unfaithful to Him, but whilst David returns to Him with generosity and sincerity, Saul never really repents for his faults, and even then when he asks pardon for them, it is only through egoism and self-interest. One must have lost all religious sense to confound Saul with David, and especially to place the son of Isai, as Renan does, below the son of Cis. Their history contains a characteristic feature which presents both to us in an analogous situation and makes to shine most brilliantly the difference of their dispositions.

When Saul had violated the order of God in sparing Agog, King of the Amalekites, the prophet Samuel reproaches him in the name of the Lord for his disobedience. When David had become guilty of adultery and homicide, the prophet comes to him in the name of God and exposes to him the horrible extent of his crimes. In these two circumstances, both kings answered with the same word: *Peccavi*, " I have sinned;" but this word had not the same meaning in their mouths. In the one it came from the heart, and he expressed a true and sincere contrition for the fault committed; in the other, it was only from his lips and had only one end in view, namely that to preserve to him his crown. David obeys to a movement of faith, to a supernatural motive; Saul has only human views and a self-interest. " I have sinned," says Saul to Samuel. . . . " but now bear, I beseech thee, my sin, and return with me. . . . Honor me now before the ancients of my people." (I Kings xv, 24-30.). Thus, in making his *mea culpa*, Saul thinks only about himself and his temporal interests.

How different are the sentiments of David! He only thinks about God whom he has offended, he humbles himself before Him: " I have sinned against the Lord," he says, and adds not another word (II Kings, xii, 13). Whilst Saul desires to do violence to Samuel, and tears away a part of his cloak in order to forcibly retain him, David accepts without complaint the terrible chastisements which Nathan came to announce to him in the name of God, and he acknowledges the justice of the expiation to which he is going to be subjected, in saying only the sole word: " I have sinned against the Lord." How can one be astonished that the Scripture and the religious men of all times had such a high idea of David and found just the reprobation of Saul? May they reproach, therefore, David of his faults and of his crimes of which he rendered himself guilty, in this he has been human and reprehensible; but let them also acknowledge his great qualities, and particularly that spirit of religion and faith, by which he so nobly raised himself from his fall.

3. ABISAG, THE CONCUBINE OF DAVID.

The Third Book of Kings ends with the episode of the Sunamite Abisag selected as a concubine of David, when this king was already well advanced in years. When the Rationalists arise against this fact, what do they pretend to attack? Is it the fact itself or only its account? When they show astonishment at the author of Kings relating this event, we observe: 1. That the fact related is told in sufficiently becoming terms. 2. That often certain persons are much more scrupulous, in regard to these matters, about words than about actions. 3. That the inspired writer had in view, in relating this account, to show in a striking manner the old, the exhausted condition of David.

When, on the contrary, the Rationalists attack the fact itself, we answer with the Abbé Clair: "We must appreciate facts of this king according to the ideas of the time, consider that polygamy in this epoch had entered the morals in general and the kings, in particular, seemed to have in this respect special privileges. Then again, that marriage had not yet been raised to the dignity of a sacrament, and the condition of the woman was not what it became in Christian society." What appears shocking to us did not so appear at that time, and, besides, the Sacred Text cuts short to all malicious interpretation.

4. DAVID AND THE PROPHECY OF NATHAN.

The Second Book of Kings (vii. 16) relates that God, in order to reward David for his faithfulness, promised to him that his house would always exercise the royal authority, and that his throne would be established forever. This prophecy, transmitted to David by Nathan, was a confirmation and development of that of Jacob. The latter had announced that the scepter would not be taken away from Juda until the arrival of the Messiah.[1] The prophet Nathan renders this prophecy more precise and, among all the families of Juda, he designates that of David to be the depositary of the Divine promise.

Now, the Rationalists say, this prophecy did not fulfill itself; the Captivity did away with the authority

---
[1] Gen. xlix, 10.

of the family of David and since that time this house did not resume its power. Esdras and Nehemias were not of the race of David; the Machabees were priests and children of Levi.

To this we answer: To interpret every prophecy we must examine both its spirit and letter. Thus, when Jacob foretells that the scepter would not be taken away from Juda, it would be wrong to say that this prophecy did not realize itself, because, from Jacob to David, the scepter was not in the possession of the tribe of Juda. So also would it be rash to pretend that the words *usque in sempiternum, jugitur, usque in aeternum* contained in the prophecy of Nathan, were expressed and accepted by David in the sense that the scepter would not be taken away from the family of the Hebrew king as long as the world would last. Therefore, we must interpret the prophecies not in a literal manner, but must keep account of the context, of the circumstances under which they were made, of the spiritual state of the one who received them, of the vague and more or less obscure conditions which ordinarily accompany a prediction, as long as the event has not come to clear it up and confirm it.

When we keep account of these rules, we will remark that nothing, in the prophecy of Nathan, authorizes to maintain that the royal power should never be eclipsed in the house of David. What the prophecy of Jacob had announced was the preëminence of Juda until the epoch of the Messiah; this prophecy fulfilled itself, because, even during the Babylonian Captivity, the tribe of Juda existed as a nation; the same was the case when it returned to retake possession of Palestine, whilst the other tribes always remained dispersed.

As to the particulars which the prophecy of Nathan added to that of Jacob, they can be summed up as follows: Whatever the events may have been, the race of David, for a long time, master of Juda, will again be the dominating power in the epoch of the Messiah. Now, this prophecy was fulfilled and even in a fuller manner than David could expect: his house effectively exercised the royal power over Juda; when afterwards there were eclipses, the race of David was always known as the one that had the right to the throne, always as the royal race, and when the Messiah came to found his kingdom, real kingdom, although not of this world, it was found that the Savior was of the race of David. Thus in the epoch of David, the house of David holds the scepter; in the epoch fixed for its fulfillment, it is again the house of David that holds the scepter, in the person of Jesus Christ and, finally, since the prophecy was made until the epoch of its fulfillment, it is always the family of David that is the royal family. For, although it does not in reality hold the scepter, we can always distinguish and recognize it as the one that should hold it. What more can one require? But there is more.

Nathan gave the promise to the family of David that it should reign *usque in aeternum.* Very well. This prophecy fulfills itself continually in a literal manner; the centuries which separate David from the end of the world behold the reign, at first temporal, then spiritual, of his offsprings; and from that time, in such a long series of years, the eclipse about which the Rationalists speak has only the value of a moment and proves nothing against the fulfillment of the promises made to David.

CHAPTER XLIV.

THE PROPHET ISAIAS.

1. THE AUTHENTICITY OF ISAIAS.

THE greatest of the prophets is Isaias. Of the collection of his oracles, divided into two parts, the most beautiful and the most important is the second, which comprises the last twenty-seven chapters. All the Rationalistic writers deny its authenticity. They suppose that the chapters forty to sixty-six of this prophet date from the Babylonian Captivity. A great number of Protestant theologians have followed in their footsteps. Since the time when supernatural prophecy became rejected, with the miracle, as an impossibility, it also became necessary to condemn writings wherein revelation is evident in the fact that they contained predictions. Hence, in reality, it is in order to deny the supernatural that the infidel critics deny the authenticity of the second part of Isaias. Several vehemently assert that Isaias could not have written the prophecies with regard to the Babylonian Captivity, because he lived during the Assyrian period, when the king of Ninive exercised the supremacy in Minor Asia, and, because Babylonia formed a part of this empire. It has been remarked with good judgment that, following this rule, the composition of the chapters fifty-two and fifty-five of Isaias could be carried on to the Christian era, and that it might be maintained that the one who has written them has read the Epistles of St. Paul. The negation of the prophetic revelation entails the negation of the authenticity of all the prophets of the Old Testament: Osee could not foretell the ruin of the kingdom of Israel and the return from the Captivity; Michaeus, the ruin of Samaria and of Jerusalem, the Babylonian Captivity and the birth of the Messiah at Bethlehem; Nahum, the destruction of Ninive and Habacuk, that of the Chaldeans. Nobody, however, dares to deny the authenticity of these prophecies. Besides, the Rationalists feel that the rejection *a priori* of prophecy is logically weak, so they all endeavor to discover positive proofs in favor of their conclusions.

2. The first argument they bring up in order to establish that Isaias is not the author of the prophecies concerning the Captivity, is the historic situation which they suppose. In other words, they find fault with the time given by the prophet, and hence deny the authenticity of the second part of Isaias, because the author speaks therein of the Captivity, not as of a future event, but as of a present fact, and because he describes it as if he were in Babylonia, not in Palestine.

To this we answer, in the first place, it is certain that Isaias lives in spirit in the midst of the captives, and it is thereby that he is a prophet, God unveiling to him the future. All, both Rationalists and faithful critics, must acknowledge that what characterizes the style of the prophets is that they cross the limits of time and to behold as if actually present. But since it is thus that the prophet Isaias speaks in many places as if he had lived in the midst of the captives, it does not follow at all that he did not prophesy before Nabuchodonsor.

However, it is true that the epoch in which the writer lived must manifest itself always by some features, for he writes for his contemporaries as well as for posterity. Also, we will prove against the Rationalists: (1) That he lived before the Captivity; (2) That the author of the second part of Isaias did live in Palestine.

In the first place he lived before the Babylonian Captivity. As it is "the servant of Jehovah," and not the prophet that speaks almost constantly in this part of Isaias, it is more easy for him to abstract himself in some way from his time and surroundings; however, the chronological indications are not wanting. And first the author speaks as prophet, like a man who writes a long time before the events which he announces (Is. xli, 21-29; xliii, 9; xlv, 21; xli, 9; xlviii, 5-16). "Who," he says among other things, "hath foretold these events beforehand? . . . It is I who have announced to you (the future). . . . I have announced to thee the future before the time. I have made it known to thee before it arrives. Assemble yourselves together, all you, and hear: who among them had declared these things? . . . Come ye near unto me and hear this: I have not spoken in secret from the beginning, from the time before it was done, I was there" (Is. xlv, 21; xlii, 12; xlviii, 5, 14, 16).

The great event which God had thus prophesied, is the deliverance of Israel by Cyrus. Now, if these words had been written only when the King of Persia had actually restored the liberty to the captives, how could the prophet have expressed himself thus by addressing himself to the captives themselves? These words suppose that the prophecies are known before hand, and consequently that they have been written before the events. They also throw the Rationalists into a great perplexity, and prevent them from agreeing among themselves as to the date of the second part of Isaias.

One cannot, therefore, deny that the author speaks of Cyrus as a prophet. How long before? "About twenty years," answers one of the infidel critics. We will show, by pursuing our inquiries, that these prophecies were made a good deal earlier. The fact established that the second part of Isaias is anterior to the events which it announces, because these events were foretold before they had occurred, we have not established how long was the time between the foretelling and the execution. Is it permissible to proceed farther and fix not a precise date, because the intrinsic examination of such a writing does not allow this, but an approximate epoch? Yes it is, and we are equipped also to establish that the writer composed his work before the Captivity. Indeed, he reproaches God's people for their idolatry, as a crime actually committed. These reproaches are renewed in a multitude of passages, he returns to them continually, with a persistency and vehemence which attest that idolatry was the curse of his time.

Now, the acts of idolatry of which the prophet reproaches the people of God could have taken place only before the Captivity? The Rationalists maintain, as they are obliged to do for their thesis, that the crimes with which the Jews are accused were committed in Chaldea, where they adored the local gods. This assertion is certainly false, as Juda is accused of violating the law by dwelling in tombs (Is. lxviii, 4), and by offering sacrifices to idols "on high mountains," *har gâbaôh*, all of which could not have occurred in Chaldea, where there are no mountains, nor tombs hewed out of rock, which might be used for habitations. Idolatrous worship was, consequently, rendered to the Canaanitish gods before the Captivity. The Captivity was the chastisement of their idolatry; consequently, these oracles were written before the Captivity, as were those of the first part of Isaias where the language is similar. If idolatry had been continued at Babylonia as in Judea, God could not have considered the captives repentant and would not reopen to them the gates of their country.

Moreover, the author of the second part of Isaias does not speak of the last years of the kingdom of Juda. This silence would be inexplicable, if these oracles had dated from the time of the Captivity, for what rich material would there not have been furnished to his eloquence derived from the chastisements inflicted upon Juda, because of its idolatry and its infidelity, by the arms of Nabuchodonosor! But God has not revealed these details to his prophet. He knows only of the impious worship rendered to the false gods at the time of Manasse, King of Juda. Here is his horizon. The nations which he knows best are not those who are the neighbors of Babylonia, but those with whom a resident of Jerusalem would be the most familiar in the epoch of Ezechias and Manasse, viz: the Egyptians, the Ethiopians, the Idumeans, the Madianites.

3. The intrinsic examination of the second part of Isaias leads us, therefore, in regard to its date, to the conclusions of tradition. The same holds good in

regard to the place where it must have been composed. When it really emanated from the first of the great prophets it could have been written only in Palestine, in the kingdom of Juda, because Isaias always lived in this country. According to the Rationalists, it was formulated in Chaldea, but this assertion is in contradiction with the language of the prophet. Indeed, he expresses himself in many places as only an inhabitant of the Holy Land could do, and what gives to this proof a particular value is, that the writer reveals to us unconsciously, through allusions to which he does not pay attention himself, the place in which he writes.

Not only does the prophet express himself as a man living in the country of Juda, but he speaks as an inhabitant of Jerusalem, such as Isaias was. He addresses himself to Sion and to Jerusalem, he tells that God places guards over the walls of this city (Is. lxii, 1, 16; xlii, 9); he speaks as living in the midst of it and, consequently, supposes that this capital of Juda is not ruined and destroyed (xl, 2, 9; lvi, 5, 7).

Whilst certain passages show that the author lives in Palestine, others prove that he does not write in Chaldea. Mentioning in one place (xli, 8-9), the vocation of Abraham, he says that God called him "from the extremities of the earth." One could express himself thus only in Jerusalem, where Chaldea, the country of Abraham, was considered as situated at the end of the world, but one could not speak in this manner at Babylonia and in Chaldea itself, where these expressions would not have had any meaning. The prophet also indicates to us very clearly that he is far from the shores of the Euphrates when he says in addressing himself to the Jews: "Depart, depart, go ye out from thence" (lii, 11).

Had he been in these places he would have said necessarily: "Depart from *here*." In the same passage he employs, indeed, the expression "here" (lii, 5) to designate the dwelling of God, the Temple of Jerusalem: "And now what have I here, said the Lord, for my people are taken away gratis." Finally, the allusions to Chaldea and to Babylonia are few and indefinite, as is natural for a writer who never saw this country.

4. The second of the more important accusations which have been brought against the authenticity of the second part of Isaias is derived from the style. But inasmuch as the Rationalists themselves are not agreed as to the real value of this argument, it certainly is not worthy of a place.

All the efforts of infidelity to rob Isaias of the greatest ornaments of his prophetic crown are therefore vain and futile. From all we come to tell we have sufficiently established that Isaias lived long before the Babylonish Captivity, and that he lived in Palestine and was an inhabitant of Jerusalem.

CHAPTER XLV.

THE PROPHETS JEREMIAS AND BARUCH.

I. THE PROPHECY AGAINST BABYLON.

THE prophecies of Jeremias have such a character of authenticity that they are universally accepted as the work of this prophet. But few critics assert that some other than Jeremias formulated his prophecies, except in the case of the prophecy he makes against Babylonia, which is considered unauthentic merely because he has the wrong, in the eyes of the infidels, to be too visibly prophetic. According to certain Rationalists this prediction was written about the end of the Captivity by a more recent writer, and fraudulently intercalated in the collection of the works of Jeremias. According to others, Jeremias was truly the author of it, but others have added to it and made many alterations.

"The author lived evidently in Babylonia," says Kuenen, "about the second half of the exile, in the epoch when Cyrus already gained great victories, and when he prepared himself for the decisive conquest of Chaldea. We do not need to state that this author could not have been Jeremias." Reuss is so convinced that the prophecy against Babylonia cannot have its origin from Jeremias that he has eliminated it from the book which contains the oracles of this prophet, and has placed it in a different volume of his translation of the Bible, as the work of an anonymous writer, who wrote "about the end of the exile." The principal reason which he gives in favor of his opinion is that Jeremias gave the prophecy to a person who went to Babylon to read it to the people, and then to tie a stone to it and throw it into the Euphrates, saying: "Behold how Babylonia shall be destroyed." "Besides this," says Reuss, "this prophecy is not according to the spirit of the time."

Why not according to the spirit of the time? The prophet should have promulgated his prophecy so solemnly and accompanied this promulgation by a prophetic action, in order that his prediction should be regarded as not in accordance with this spirit of time. He commanded that the manuscript containing it should be thrown into the Euphrates only with the object of attracting more attention, and for the purpose of engraving deeply on the minds of the captives the momentous prediction he had made. And, besides, was there anything to prevent the prophet and the other Jews from making a copy of the manuscript before it was consigned to the waters? And if so, could it not have been read in Babylonia in the same form as we read it to-day?

As to the contradictions which it is claimed exist between this prophecy and other oracles of Jeremias, they are imaginary. Jeremias had foretold that the Captivity would last seventy years (Jer. xxv, 12). The final prophecy is only the development and the complement of the first oracle. This is also admitted by several Rationalists.

2. LETTER OF JEREMIAS TO THE JEWS IN CAPTIVITY.

At the end of the Lamentations of Jeremias in the Greek version of the Septuagint, after the conclusion of the prophecy of Baruch in the Vulgate (Bar. vi), is placed a letter of Jeremias, the Hebrew original of which is lost. It is addressed to the Jews led away captives to Babylonia by Nabuchodonosor; it has for its object to warn them against the dangers of idolatry to which they were exposed in Chaldea, by proving to them that the idols are no real gods. According to the Rationalists, this letter is not from Jeremias. In the first place according to them, it is not his, "because if such were the case, we would have to suppose a Hebrew original; now, it is certain that if any of the apocryphal writings have been composed in Greek, it was this letter. The author of this writing must be a Hellenist Jew, living after Alexander the Great.

This affirmation is not founded. The letter of Jeremias, in spite of brevity, contains comparatively numerous Hebraisms and singular phrases, which cannot be explained except through a Hebrew original: it is thus that the author frequently employs the future instead of the present, according to the Hebrew custom, etc.

The second objection against the authenticity of the letter of Jeremias, is a pretended contradiction between this writing and certain prophecies of the priest of Anatoth. It is well known that the latter had announced that the Babylonian Captivity should last seventy years; now the author of the letter says that it will last as long "as seven generations" (Bar. vi, 2), that is, more than two hundred years, because it is calculated that each generation is equal on an average to a duration of thirty years. Thus the same prophet could not have contradicted himself in this manner, and the one who assigns such a considerable length of time to the

Captivity cannot be the same as the one who limits it to seventy years.

This reasoning would be conclusive if it were established that the word *dôr*, which was certainly here the original word, expressed in Hebrew a determined time, as does the word *genea* or generation in Greek, and in the history of Herodotus (ii, 142). *Dôr* signifies an indefinite time; the number "seven" is also employed in an indefinite manner, so that the expression " seven generations " signifies more or less time. Besides we have to remark that Jeremias alone could express himself thus in this letter, for the duration of seventy years of the Captivity was so well known that a forger, writing after the event, would not have failed to be precise in this passage.

Besides, the Assyro-Chaldaic archæology confirms in the most striking manner the letter of Jeremias.

3. BARUCH.

The prophecy of Baruch has come down to us only in Greek. It is considered by the majority of Protestants as apocryphal. But the objections against it are absolutely without foundation. The first is that it was, they say, written originally in Greek, and therefore long after the time of Baruch. This objection is so evidently false that certain Rationalists admit that only the first three chapters were written originally in Hebrew, while others maintain the entire book was so written. Origen was acquainted with the original Semitic text. Theodotion translated the same. Until the Greek version of the Septuagint the Semitic idioms are so clearly recognizable that the Rationalist Davidson justly ridiculed the vain attempt to deny it. The phraseology is Hebraic and not Greek, the different phrases being united among one another simply by the conjunction " and." Very many terms are plainly not of Greek origin. " We beg mercy in Thy sight, O Lord our God " (Baruch, ii, 19) is a Hebrew idiom. In several places we read " to make " instead of " to serve " the false gods or the Babylonian king, because *abád* signifies both to make and to serve (Bar. i, 22; ii, 21, 22, 24). Again the translator speaks of the " sackcloth of affliction," that is, the garment they wore as a sign of affliction. The word *enut* which is translated by *deésis*, as in the Psalms, certainly signifies affliction (Bar. iv, 20). " The merchants of Merrha," mean the " merchants of Madian," because the translator took a *d* for an *r*, on account of the resemblance of these two letters in Hebrew writing.

The second objection against the authenticity of the Book of Baruch is derived from the following sources. It is related therein that the prophet went to Babylonia five years after the ruin of Jerusalem, and that he read his prophecies in the presence of Jechonias, King of Juda. It is maintained that these details cannot be historical. Nothing, however, is offered to show that they are false; moreover, their truthfulness is evident from the fact that many who deny the authenticity of Baruch refuse to accept this argument. Baruch, who was the secretary of Jeremias, followed his master into Egypt, in the first or second year after the destruction of the Temple. Three or four years after this he went to Babylonia in order that he might console and exhort the captives. While there nothing prevented him from reading his prophecies to Jechonias, who was not confined as prisoners are with us, but who enjoyed a comparative liberty.

An incontestable proof, Rationalists declare, that the Book of Baruch is not genuine is found in the fact that the prophet names Joakim as the Jewish high priest, in the fifth year after the destruction of Jerusalem (Bar. i, 8). Now, some say "in the fifth year after the destruction of Jerusalem" Josedek was the high priest, according to others it was Saraias. — Whether it was Josedek or Saraias, matters very little. The actual text does not say Joakim was high priest, it merely mentions he was a priest. The reason he is particularly spoken of is because he was a more important person than the others, but from this fact it does not follow that he enjoyed the honors of the high priesthood. At the time of the destruction of Juda's capital the high priest was Seraias, who was slain at Reblatha (Jer. lii. 24-27). His son Josedek, who would have succeeded him, was carried off to Babylonia (Par. v, 41; Vulg. vi, 15). Hence, the captives could not send assistance to Josedek at Jerusalem, but they could easily have sent aid, as the text implies, to Joakim, who was, according to his own genealogy, a near relative of Josedek, who had undoubtedly replaced him as high priest at the capital (Cf. Bar. i, 7, with Par. vi, 13; v, 39).

It is further objected against the authenticity of the Book of Baruch two historical inaccuracies which is said it contains, namely, that the Jews offered at Jerusalem, at the time their prophet wrote, "sacrifices on the altar of the Lord" (Bar. i, 10), and that they read his prophecies "on the feast days, in the house of the Lord." At this date, they assure us, there was neither altar nor house of the Lord. Hence, only a falsifier could have imagined such an anachronism. As to the first point, we can grant that the altar of the true God was destroyed at the time of the destruction of the Temple, by the troops of King Nabuchodonosor, because their destruction although not mentioned is at least very probable, but we can hardly doubt but that the priests rebuilt the altar in order to offer to God the sacrifice of the law. In fact, nothing was easier, for we must not forget that the sacrifices were publicly offered in an open space, or yard, so that it would not require much labor to restore, at least, the altar of holocausts.—Since the victims were regularly immolated in honor of the true God, and this fact answers sufficiently the second objection, the Jews naturally assembled in the parvis of the Temple, as they were formerly accustomed to do, and where they could listen to the book, sent to them from Babylonia, being read to them. This place of reunion is called "the house" or "temple of the Lord," as our Vulgate translates, because this was the name they had been accustomed to give to that part of Mount Moriah where Solomon had built the Temple. But from this expression it does not follow that the building which the people of Israel called the "Temple of the Lord" was still erect. The proof that these words are to be taken in a broad sense is, that the public ceremonies were never performed in the Temple itself; there neither could anything be read to the people, as the people never entered it. The reading of the prophecies could only be held in the outside enclosure, which was also called "Temple," and by way of latitude of expression "Temple of the Lord," since it was here the victims were immolated to the Lord. These enclosures always existed, and, therefore, the people could assemble there just as they did before the destruction of the Temple proper by Nabuchodonosor. We have besides this, a formal proof of the oblation of victims about this time by the prophet Jeremias, who employs the same expression as Baruch. He relates that after the destruction of the Temple, twenty-four men from Sichem, Silo and Samaria came to Jerusalem, bringing gifts and incense " to offer them in the Temple to the Lord " (Jer. xl, 5; see also I Esd. ii, 68; iii, 2, 3, 6). This passage is conclusive. None of the objections, therefore, against the book of Baruch, gives us any fair grounds to question its authenticity.

CHAPTER XLVI.

THE PROPHECIES OF EZECHIEL AND THE VISION OF THE CHERUBIM.

1. THE authenticity of the prophecies of Ezechiel has never been seriously called into doubt. To contest them to-day is more impossible than ever: the modern discoveries in Assyria form the most eloquent commentary of this prophetic book, and proclaim both its incontestable authenticity and veracity.

2. The Rationalists, however, formulate not only objections of detail against the oracles of Ezechiel, but the infidels of the last century have often belittled him, and their sarcasms against this prophet are so well known that it is necessary to say a few words about them. Tindal considered inacceptable a portion of the

accounts contained in the book of this prophet, because they contain commands unworthy of God or of an impossible execution, such as, for example, the order to draw Jerusalem on tablets of clay to depict its seige. A brick recovered at Babylon and representing the plan of this city, crossed by the Euphrates, has shown that the fact was not only possible, but quite conformable to the customs of Chaldea.

The jokes of the same English infidel, elaborated by Voltaire, one that they have called the breakfast of Ezechiel (iv, 9-15), in order to show that the commandment given to the prophet was unworthy of the deity, are in bad form and manifest a great ignorance of the customs of the Orient. When God prescribed to His prophet to make use of dried human excrement for purpose of fuel, in order to mark the extreme scarcity to which one will be reduced, and when, on account of the repugnance Ezechiel displays, he is permitted to substitute for this animal excrement, this conduct of God may surprise us, but does not astonish at all the Orientals who are in the habit to prepare every day their bread with this combustible. In Egypt, in the neighborhood of Cairo, at Hubbah, and in Cairo itself, the Abbe Vigouroux relates that he saw women kneading cow dung with a little earth and straw, into the form of round cakes, to be used in place of wood fuel which is very scarce. Also at Nazareth, he saw women kneading cow dung for the same purpose, and an oven heated to bake therein the bread with the same fuel. Nothing is more common than this usage in a great part of Asia. In India it has even a kind of sacred character. The local customs explain, therefore, quite naturally the "breakfast of Ezechiel."

3. They have sought also to turn into ridicule the order given to Ezechiel to eat a book (iv, 4-6), to sleep three hundred and ninety days on the left side and forty days on the right side (xii, 3-7), to remove all the furniture from the house during the day and leave it himself in the evening through a hole pierced in the wall; but these are all symbols and prophecies of action, destined to strike more strongly than simple words the imagination of the people. Besides, nothing obliges us to accept them in the literal sense, particularly the eating of the book. Many commentators are of the opinion that all this took place only in vision. " Ezechiel," says Kuenen, " has often recourse to tableaux or to symbolic acts, which are ordinarily in relation with the prophetic visions. These symbolic acts are for the most of such a nature that the prophet can hardly be believed to have accomplished them." The Catholic interpreters do not believe different.

4. THE CHERUBIM OF EZECHIEL.

The vision of the Cherubim is one of the most celebrated in the Book of Ezechiel on account of its mystery and magnificence. Summarized, Ezechiel sees four animals with human countenances, each having four forms and four wings; their feet were those of a bull, their hands those of a man; their form, in front, was that of a man, at the right that of a lion, at the left that of a bull, and finally the wings gave them a fourth form, that of an eagle (Ez. I). In a second vision of these same beings, the prophet learned that they were Cherubim (20).

What could this strange vision mean? The image of the Cherubim carrying the throne of God was already a known figure and indicated the dominion of God over the most perfect beings. Such as the angels; but why did Ezechiel, employing this figure, give to the Cherubim such a mysterious, such an imaginable form? Both the Jewish and Christian interpreters, until lately, saw always therein an enigma the solution of which would probably never be arrived at. For the infidels this vision was not, as Ezechiel affirmed, a divine manifestation, but a product of fanatical imagination of the prophet; this alone could have conceived these " frightful Cherubim," with their stern features. Very well! there is no passage in the whole Bible which has been so wonderfully verified by the Assyriological discoveries, and to-day, although there remains still some obscurities, the key of the enigma has been found.

Ezechiel prophesied in the midst of the Jews captive at Babylon; now, among all the things which must have affected the imagination of the Jews transported into a country so different from their own, the most inclined to astonish them was the sight of those colossal idols, representing lions or winged bulls, specimens of which have been recovered in our days and may be seen in several European museums. The impression which these monsters, with an animal body and the head of a man make upon us is at first one of surprise, then of admiration; for they are equally remarkable by their dimensions, their imposing and grandiose aspect, the composition of the figure and the beauty of the work. But when we represent to ourselves twenty or more statues standing in a line in the midst of a city, the people of which venerated them, and to whom they attributed their victories, one will conceive the feeling the Jews must have experienced in beholding them. They must have made an immense impression upon the people, that was so much inclined to idolatry, and which found itself now captive among the adorers of these idols. They must have been tempted to believe the Chaldeans far above themselves, and the religion which had such a splendor could appear to them less despisable than they had imagined. Hence, it would not have been a difficult matter for them to have fallen into idolatry. But God resolved to put the Jews on their guard against this temptation: also, wishing to show to Ezechiel the Cherubim supporting the firmament which serves as His throne, He represented these angels, incorporeal by their nature, under the form of those mysterious beings which affected so greatly the imagination of the Jews, in order to show to them that these Chaldean gods were insignificant when compared with Him. Hence, there were two images united in the vision of Ezechiel: *God carried upon the wings of the angels, and God crushing with His foot the Chaldean idols;* both were well understood by the Jews, so much the more as the name of these winged beings was the same in whatever light one considered them: angels were Cherubim; idols also were Cherubim, for the Chaldeans called their winged bulls *kèrubè*.

The comparative and deeper study of the Biblical text and the Chaldean statues, shows that the system exposed above is not a singular hypothesis, but an incontestable reality. Both the Biblical and Chaldean Cherubim have features of human form upon an animal body, with the wings of an eagle. Undoubtedly, one can point out some differences, the principal of which is that each cherub of Ezechiel has the form of a bull and of a lion, whilst the Chaldean idols represented either bulls (kèrubè) or lions (nirgalli), and did not unite these two forms in the same individual; but, in summary, it is impossible in future not to see in the Chaldean *kèrubè* the reason for the strange form under which was manifested to the prophet the Cherubim who carried His throne; it is equally impossible to pretend that the Book of Ezechiel has been composed elsewhere than in Chaldea, in an epoch other than that of the splendor of Babylon.

CHAPTER XLVII.

THE PROPHET DANIEL.

THE Rationalists are in accord in rejecting the authenticity of the Book of Daniel. It contains very circumstantial predictions, hence it can have been composed, say the infidel critics, only *post eventum*, i. e., after the events of which it speaks had been fulfilled. The author of Daniel is inaccurately informed as to the events of the epoch in which the personage of this name lived; hence the Book is posterior to Daniel. On the one hand, the author is perfectly acquainted with the events which signalize the beginning of the war of independence under the Machabees, therefore, he must have lived in this epoch. This is the sort of reasoning of the infidels: prophecy is impossible, consequently, the so-called predictions which announce historic facts have been written only when the facts had already been fulfilled. Such is the argumentation of the Rationalists.

We acknowledge that Daniel knew very well the history of the Machabees, because God had revealed it to him, but we affirm that he did not less accurately know and describe the history of his time, that of Nabuchodonosor, and the fall of Babylon under the blows of Cyrus. Providence, to verify his prophet, has permitted the Assyriologic researches during late years, to resucitate a long buried past, in order to show to all the exactitude of the oracles contained in the Book of Daniel. Thanks to the Assyrio-Chaldaic discoveries, we can prove now that the pretended errors of this prophet were only the errors of his critics. To-day ignorance alone can make this reproach of a lack of historic truth. The negative criticism had the presumption to speak as the sole exponent of science, yet its own followers who make the science of the Scriptures a specialty, were ignorant of the modern discoveries, which confirm the veracity of Daniel in such a striking manner! Even the Assyriologues imbued with Rationalism, are careful to repeat the objections which the others never tire of repeating, while those who do not deny the supernatural render homage to the exactitude of the descriptions of the prophet.

2. The first difficulty the objectors raise against the account of Daniel is drawn from the history of the Jews. Namely, Daniel reports (i, 1-4), that in the third year of the reign of Joakim, Nabuchodonosor took Jerusalem, a part of the sacred vessels of the Temple, and led away to Babylon as captives some of the most considerable persons of the capital.

"Nothing of the kind took place under the reign of Joakim," say the Rationalists. Behold a very extraordinary affirmation. Without speaking of the formal testimony of the Paralipomenons, which have quite another weight than that of the negative criticism, we open the Books of Kings and read there: "In his days Nabuchodonosor, King of Babylon, came up, and Joakim became its servant three years, then again he rebelled against him. And the Lord sent against him the rovers of the Chaldeans and the rovers of Syria, and the rovers of Moab, and the rovers of the children of Ammon" (IV Kings, xxiv, 1-2), Nabuchodonosor made, therefore, war upon Joakim. About this war the Books of Paralipomenons give us more details than does the Book of Kings, but what we read in the text quoted is sufficient to explain what the Book of Daniel reports, for the kings of this epoch never made war, and never imposed any tribute without carrying off precious vessels and captives. All the cuneiform inscriptions attest to this, and to deny it would be denying the daylight.

But, they say, "we know from the Book of Jeremias that nothing of the kind has transpired under the reign of Joakim." This affirmation is not less false than the foregoing one. Jeremias expressly foretells the campaign of Nabuchodonosor, in which Daniel was led away captive; the most of the commentators are agreed in acknowledging this, and they accept with assurance a first transportation in this epoch, because it is at this date (606 B. C.) that the seventy years of the Babylonian Captivity begin, the prediction of which had become particularly famous among the prophet's contemporaries.

But how can we admit, continue the Rationalists, that Daniel and his three friends were received into the body of the Babylonian wisemen? Could they really have had access to their ranks? Yes, undoubtedly. We must not imagine that the Chaldeans had the same ideas and the same customs as ourselves. They were in the habit of providing themselves with slaves from the different nations, and when the captive children had been raised after the Babylonian fashion, they were regarded as Chaldeans. Besides, the kings needed to keep about them officers that had been born in the countries of which the Chaldeans had rendered themselves masters. This fact is attested by the cuneiform inscriptions. In one of them Sennacherib incidentally relates that a young Chaldean, named Belibni, had received a Chaldaic education in the palace at Ninive under the auspices of Sargon, and was afterwards placed by him on the throne of Babylon (Sennacherib, "Cylinder of Bellino," line 13; G. Smith, "History of Sennacherib," p. 27).

3. Another objection: During an idolatrous festival, related by Daniel, we find the enumeration of a certain number of musical instruments. Some of them bear Greek names. From this fact the Rationalists conclude that the book wherein we read these Greek words could have been written only under the Macedonian domination, a long time after the epoch of Daniel.

To explain how the Greek words find themselves in Daniel, it is well to remember, in the first place, that these instruments were known in Minor Asia since the epoch of Nabuchodonosor. The Assyrians and Chaldeans had a very pronounced taste for music; musicians are frequently represented on their monuments. On bas-reliefs we behold instruments of which Daniel speaks. Hence, there is no anachronism in his account as to those things. Is there in the words? Certainly one cannot prove this. To establish it one would have to be able to show that the Assyrio-Chaldeans had no relations with the Greeks, neither directly nor indirectly. The Phenicians were at first tributaries to the Assyrian kings, later to Nabuchodonosor. This commercial people spread through Asia the products of the Greeks, musical instruments, perfected by the Hellenists, who were great lovers of harmony. And, as it always happens in the importation of merchandises, the foreign name is introduced with the object itself, so the instrument kept its Greek name at the court of Nabuchodonosor.

4. The *miracle* which took place on the occasion of the festival in favor of the companions of Daniel, and an analogous miracle which later on saved the prophet in the lion's den, furnish other objections. To follow the infidels we have to believe that, according to the third and sixth chapter of Daniel, Nabuchodonosor and Darius had acknowledged without reserve, the absolute sovereignty of the God of Israel.

These two kings had not " acknowledged without reserve the absolute sovereignty of the God of Israel;" they had not abjured polytheism and their own religion; they had confessed only the power of Jehovah, the God of Israel, which in their thought reconciled itself easily with the religious beliefs, because according to these beliefs, each nation had its own god real and true. Nabuchodonosor in the proclamation to his people, makes express profession of paganism: he speaks of Daniel, who is called in the Chaldaic language Baltassar " after the name of my God "[1] (Bel), says he, " and three times he speaks expressly of the gods " (iv. 5,

---

[1] Dan. iv, 5.

6, 15). As to Darius praising the God of Israel, he did what Cyrus himself did with regard to the Babylonian deities as is attested by the inscriptions of this prince recently discovered. " In the work of the reparation of the sanctuary of Marduk, the great god, I occupied myself. To me (Cyrus) the king, his adorer, and to Cambyses, my son, the offspring from my heart, and to my faithful army (Marduk) granted graciously his favor. . . . And every day I prayed to Bel and Nebo, in order to prolong my days and increase my prosperity, and repeated to Marduk, my god, that adorer Cyrus, the king and his son Cambyses. . . ." (H. Rawlinson, " Clay Cylinder of Cyrus the Great," in the Journal of the Asiatic Society, 1880, p. 89.)

The conclusion to the above is wanting, but the passage proves sufficiently that when Cyrus, adorer of Ahurmazda, spoke in these terms of Marduk (Merodoch) and of Nebo, Darius could well speak as he did of the true God as related in the Book of Daniel.

5. As to the difficulties raised against the statue erected by Nabuchodonosor, they are also refuted by Assyriology. "That which we have to point out," says Menant, "with regard to the subject of this episode, is the erection of a colossal statue of gold in the plain of Babylon. Not only has this fact nothing of the impossible, but it has its reality. The gigantic sculptures of Ninive prove this. As to the metal employed in this work of art, we know that analogous statues existed; that of the sepulchre of Belus had forty cubits, and it was certainly not the only statue they had raised in this epoch. Finally, we have already pointed out the infidelity of a functionary who, charged with the execution of a golden statue, had stolen a portion of

this precious metal" ("Babylone et la Chaldée." p. 244).

We have to remark, however, that the Sacred Text does not say that the statue was of solid gold. Like many other statues it was probably only covered with, more or less thick, plates of gold.

6. With regard to the story of the lion's den into which Daniel was thrown, as well as that of the fiery furnace, they are strictly Babylonian. Assurbanipal tells us in his annals: "The rest of the people I threw alive amidst the bulls and lions, like Sennacherib, my father used to do."

7. As to the objection drawn from the silence of all the ancient authors about Balthazar, King of Babylon, it is to-day a well established fact that Balthazar was the son of Nabonidus, the last of the Babylonian kings. In a prayer addressed to the god Sin (Moon), this prince expresses himself thus: "In regard to Balthazar, my first-born son, the offspring of my heart, the fear of thy great deity, give that he may give himself up to Sin, and that he may not decline from justice" (Cuneiform Inscriptions). From the Book of Daniel it goes forth that Balthazar was commander at Babylon whilst this city was beseiged by Cyrus, and that he held, not the first, but the second rank, in the kingdom; for, desiring to give to the prophet the highest reward that was in his power, that is the first after him, he tells him that he will make him "the third" of the kingdom (Dan. v, 16), which proves that he himself is only the second. The inscriptions of Nabonidus explain and confirm all these details. This monarch was outside the city; he had left the commandery to his eldest son, who thus found himself charged with the defense of the

capital and fulfilled the functions as king. What the Book of Daniel relates of Balthazar is so much more remarkable and conclusive in favor of its authenticity, because no ancient historian had preserved to us the name of the son of Nabonidus, and it was known to us only through the writings of the Jewish prophet, before it had been discovered within the latter years in the cuneiform inscriptions of the king, his father. Hence, it can be seen how the accusations of the infidels are false, and how the details from which they draw their objections transform themselves into proofs.

8. THE CANTICLE OF THE THREE CHILDREN IN THE FIERY FURNACE.

When the companions of Daniel had been thrown into the fiery furnace, because they had refused to adore the golden idol of Nabuchodonosor, Azarias addressed to God a prayer in order to implore His mercy, and he thanked the Lord together with his two friends by a hymn of thanksgiving. This prayer and hymn are not found in the Hebrew Bible, but we read them in the Greek version and in our Vulgate (Dan. iii, 24-90). The Protestants reject both as apocryphal, and the infidels regard all the deuterocanonical parts of the Book of Daniel as fictions. " As to the legendary additions which the Greek version has joined to the Book of Daniel," says Kuenen, " these additions rest upon no tradition and are principally the invention of the translator or of somebody else." We will establish that the contested passages are authentic.

The Greek translator has joined these fragments, particularly the prayer and the canticle of the young men in the fiery furnace, to the account of Daniel, because he has found them in the original. The first proof which we can give for this, is that the prayer of Azarias and the canticle have been written primitively in Hebrew or in Aramaic. Although the most of the Protestants deny this, the fact is nevertheless so certain that several admit it, such as Bertholdt and Franz Delitzsch. The existence of the two Greek versions we have thereof, that of the Septuagint and that of Theodotion, can be explained only through one Semitic original. Even through the translations, the idioms can be easily recognized. Michælis, in his " Oriental Library," has pointed a certain number, so also Welte in his " Special Introduction to the Deuterocanonicals." The wind is called for instance, " spirit," *pneuma* (iii, 65), because the word *rouah* has the double meaning of spirit and wind in the original. In the enumeration of the material beings which are invited to praise God, the cold and the dew are named twice (iii, 64-69). The reason for this repetition can be only, as Bertholdt has remarked, the translation by one and the same word, of two expressions different from the original, for the manner of the composition of the canticle excludes the double mention of one and the same thing. The Babylonians are designated under the name of apostates (xiv, 9); this qualification is improper, for one can apply it only to those who have abandoned the true religion; now the inhabitants of Babylon had never adored the true God. But the employ of this Greek expression can be easily understood when one supposes a Semitic term in a multiple sense, such as *mordîm*, signifying at once rebel, apostate, enemy and stubborn. Hence, one cannot draw from the language in which the prayer and canticle have been written any objection against their authenticity.

To these philological reasons we can add that in the *Codex chisianus* the deuterocanonical part of chapter three of Daniel is marked with critical signs by which Origen, in his Hexaples, noted the differences between the Semitic original and Greek translations which prove that he had this original before him.

The context can be alleged neither to establish the apocryphal character of our piece, whatever the Rationalists may pretend. Bertholdt, quite admitting the Semitic original, says: "In the hymn all is wanting. Not a single word becomes those in whose mouth it is placed. Only in the conclusion; there are some expressions which agree to the situation, still they are very clumsy. The prayer of Azarias is more appropriate to the circumstances, and nevertheless is also wanting here and there." According to Eichhorn, we should understand the "sighs" of the companions of Daniel, "under the stroke of a mortal anguish." On the contrary, "all three pray as if they had prepared themselves and learned by heart before (I Dan. iii, 88-90).

9. THE HISTORY OF SUSANNA.

The Rationalists do not admit the authenticity of the history of Susanna (Dan. xiii). According to them it is one of the "moral legends." Since the time of Porphyrius, the word-play of Daniel in regard to the execution which awaits the aged calumniators of Susanna, is the principal source of accusation against the authenticity of this history. It cannot be denied, however, that the Greek text, in which we have the history of Susanna, is a translation of the Semitic original. Indeed, we have two different Greek versions, that of

Theodotion, which has been adopted by the Church, and that of the Septuagint. Moreover, both versions are replete with Hebraisms. The conjunction *and*, continually repeated, is one of the most characteristic features of the Hebrew style. The expression "as yesterday and the day before," meaning "as usually," is certainly not Greek. It may be said, it is true, that we meet with similar Hebraisms in the writings in Greek composed by the Hellenist Jews, but this has nothing to do with this case, as the Alexandrian version contains many less Hebraisms than the Theodotion, because the translator endeavored to write in pure Greek, and because the difference between the two texts is a proof of the Semitic original. It is acknowledged by all Biblicists that the version of the Septuagint is not an edition corrected from that of Theodotion: the latter in its date is even posterior to the former.

But how can we explain a purely Greek play on words with a Semitic original? It might be possible that the play on words did not exist at all in the primitive texts, but if it existed, which is the most probable, one can suppose, with Origen, who, in answering the difficulty which had been proposed to him by Julius Africanus, that the Semitic author had employed names of different trees, which lent themselves to a paromasia in Chaldaic or in Hebrew, and that the Greek translator had substituted for these names those of other trees, which permitted him to preserve the play on words (Cf. Origen, "Epist. ad Afric." 12, vol. xi, col. 77). This explanation appears to be the most probable.

When M. Reuss states that this "play on words cannot be conceived in a translation," we may ask, how it happened that he put it into his own translation, not very successfully, perhaps, but nevertheless really. If M. Reuss could play on French words from the Greek word play, why should the Greek translator not have been able to do the same from the Hebrew?

The other assertions of the infidels against the authenticity of the history of Susanna are scarcely worthy of mention. Susanna was not judged, they say, conformably to the law. Certainly the judges who condemned her were iniquitous, but the procedure which they followed was founded exteriorly on regular order and conformable to the Jewish customs, which the captives in Chaldea were permitted to follow.

How, the objectors add, could the people consent so easily to take up again the cause, at the demand of a young man? Because this young man was undoubtedly noted for wisdom, or, at any event, because he was a member of one of the first Jewish families and lived at the court of the King of Babylon, which gave to him an authority beyond his age.

"The social position," says Reuss, "of the husband of Susanna cannot be accounted for." And why should it be accounted for? The sacred historian stated only what was necessary to make his account clear; he tells that Susanna was the wife of an important personage among the Jews, and this was sufficient for him and must be sufficient for us.

10. BEL AND THE DRAGON.

The Book of Daniel relates in its deuterocanonical part, the history of the destruction of the idol of Bel. This deity had a statue to which they offered each day sheep, flour and wine; the priests entered each into the temple, appropriated for themselves these offerings and made the people believe that the idol had eaten them. Daniel uncovered to Darius the stratagem, and thus caused the destruction of the idol and its temple (xiv, 1-21). The authenticity of this episode has been lively attacked by both Rationalists and Protestants; but to-day one has to acknowledge that the author was a contemporary of the facts which he relates, and that his account offers all the characters of veracity, for the native monuments confirm all the details which make allusion to the Babylonian customs: the worship of Bel was in great honor at Babylon; they also offered there nourishment to idols, for Nabuchodonosor, in an inscription, mentions the presents which he daily deposited on the table of the gods Marduch and Zilbanit: an entire ox, fish, fowl, honey, wine, etc. Hence, the author must have been well acquainted with the Babylonian customs to describe this episode.

CHAPTER XLVIII.

THE PROPHET JONAS.

THE Book of Jonas, of all Biblical Books, has been one of the most attacked by the Rationalists. Since the end of the last century they have endeavored to eliminate from it the supernatural facts; the contemporary infidels consider it as a fiction. The real reason why the history of Jonas is thus treated is, because it contains too great a number of miracles for the rationalistic fancy. However, the infidels do not dare to condemn this writing solely because of the prodigies it relates, therefore, they seek to justify the sentence they pronounce against it in many ways. Behold their principal objections made to it: How can we believe, they say, that all the inhabitants of Ninive became converted to Jehovah, after having heard for one day the preaching of the Israelitic prophet? Admitting that he spoke their language, how could he have created so great a revolution in the religious opinion of a people. who had an established worship of their own, and who knew nothing of the worship of Jehovah? If really the Ninivites became converted, would one not have been careful to instruct them further in their new worship.

2. THESE OBJECTIONS ARE VERY WEAK.

They depict, on the part of the authors, a complete ignorance of the religion of Ninive. The Assyrians had been profoundly religious, as their inscriptions and their books denote. They had their national deities, but they believed that the other nations had equally their deities, not less real and not less endowed with power, although perhaps of an inferior power to their own. Moreover, they were very credulous and even superstitious, as is attested by the numerous magic writings discovered in the royal library of Assurbanipal. Hence, they were inclined to give heed to the prophets and to the oracles even of a foreign God. The idea of contesting the divinity of Jehovah, His power and His knowledge of coming events could never enter their mind, for they had no doubt about it. Consequently, the prediction of Jonas to Ninive is not so extraordinary as the Rationalists maintain. The prophet did not preach there only on one day, but during three days (Jonas iii, 3). The fact that he was a foreigner attracted only the more attention. The text tells us formally that the King of Assyria believed in his word (iii, 6), and that it was by order of this prince that the whole city did penance. The power of the king was so absolute that his order is sufficient to explain all that the Ninivites did. They fasted and " God saw their works, that they were turned from their evil way and had mercy with regard to the evil which He had said that He would do to them, and He did not " (iii, 10). The sacred writer does not tell at all that they became Jews and that they adopted the Jewish religion; the language he employs supposes even the contrary; he says merely that they did penance for their crimes. Hence, the prophet had no reason " to instruct them beforehand in the new worship," because they did not accept a new worship.

The infidel criticism further complains because Jonas did not relate his history more at length. But why should Jonas do this? No prophet has done so. Neither do we need " to know the name of the king of Ninive." It was probably Binnirar, called also Rammanirar. In every case we know for certain the approximate date of his reign, because we know by the Books of Kings that the prophet Jonas lived under Jeroboam II., King of Israel (824-809). When the Book of Jonas does not state who the king of Ninive was, it is because its author saw no necessity in telling us. The same silence is maintained, and for the same reason, in regard to the after conduct of the Ninivites and in regard to the prophet after his prediction. The author wished to write a historic account, but in doing so, he had also in view a useful and edifying object, and he composed a work "into the structure of which should enter, consequently, only the particularities which could further the end he had in view." It is a Rationalist who makes this admission.

3. JONAS IN THE WHALE'S BELLY.

The negative criticism attacks also the Book of Jonas in regard to the wonderful fact of the prophet's stay for three days in the belly of a fish. As to what character of fish it was that swallowed Jonas we do not know. We say generally that it was a whale, but this fish is seldom met with in the Mediterranean Sea, and besides, its narrow mouth would prevent the swallowing of a man. The Sacred Text defines no particular kind of fish; it simply says "a great fish." It is very probable that it was a large voracious shark, *squalus carcharias Linnei*, numerous in the Mediterranean, and which devours greedily all it can get hold off. A horse has been found in the belly of one of these fishes which weighed ten thousand pounds, and was caught on the Island St. Marguerite, France. In another they found a man with his armor on (See Làpide, "Historie des Poissons," vol. i, p. 189; Starck, "Animal Kingdom," p. 305).

A still more interesting fact is related as follows: "It happened in 1758 that, during a storm, a sailor fell overboard from a frigate, and as he was endeavoring to regain the vessel a shark appeared and seized him. Other sailors on the frigate, who had witnessed the catastrophe hastened into a small boat to render their companion assistance. They were too late, however, to be of service, the victim disappeared while still calling for help, into the capacious maw of the monster. At this moment the captain of the frigate, who had obtained a rifle, was sufficiently cool to aim it with precision at the shark, now rapidly swimming away with its victim. The captain fired and the fish, struck in a vital spot, released its captive, who was rescued by the sailors in the small boat, still alive and only slightly injured. The fish itself was caught by the sailors with harpoons and ropes, drawn aboard the frigate, and suspended there to dry. The captain afterward donated the shark to the sailor saved in such an extraordinary manner, and the latter exhibited it in nearly all the European cities (Cf. Des Ritter's Carl von Lenne, "Vollstændige Natur-System," Nüremberg, 1774. pp. 268-269).

We have to add, however, that whatever was the character of the fish which swallowed Jonas, it is quite evident that he could not have remained in its belly for three days only by means of a miracle.

CHAPTER XLIX.

THE PROPHET ZACHARIAS.

THE authenticity of the third section of the Book of Zacharias is denied in the present day by a certain number of critics. Condensed, their arguments are in the number of three: 1. St. Matthew attributes (xxvii, 9) a passage of this third section (Zach. xi, 12) not to Zacharias, but to Jeremias; consequently, at the time of our Lord chapters nine and fourteen of Zacharias were not entered among his prophecies. 2. The chapters nine and fourteen, according to their contents, must have been written before the Captivity. 3. The style of the chapters one and eight and nine and fourteen are totally different.

To these objections we can answer in the following manner: 1. Because St. Matthew attributes to Jeremias a prophetic text which we do not read as such either in Jeremias or in Zacharias, it does not follow by any means that the latter is not authentic. "I am afraid that they (the critics who deny the authenticity) undertake too much in wishing to contest three chapters of Zacharias in order to restore one single passage to Jeremias," justly remarks Calmet (in Matthew xvii, 9). The proof that the objection is without value is, that nobody does attribute to Jeremias the last part of Zacharias, as should follow if the Rationalists' argument was built on solid ground.

2. The objection against the authenticity of chapters nine and fourteen, derived from statements which they contain, would be decisive, if it were true. It is alleged that we find proofs therein that they have been written before the Captivity, but these proofs do not exist. The return from Captivity is pictured as a scene of rejoicing, and described in a like manner in both parts of Zacharias (Cf. Zach. ii, 10 and ix, 12; ii, 10 and ix, 9; ii, 14 and ix, 9, etc.). The author of chapters nine and fourteen is so little anterior to the taking of Jerusalem by Nabuchodonosor, that he has made use of the writings of the prophets who lived in this epoch. There is not one single word in the second part of Zacharias

which does not fit in with the time of the Persian domination.

3. The last objcetion derived from the difference of style which is noticeable in the first eight chapters from that in the six following, has this much of a foundation, that there is not a complete resemblance in the construction of the two parts; but the conclusion that they were written by different writers is not logical, because variation in structure and terminology is explained in the fact that the subject treated of is not the same in both places. The visions cannot be described in the same terms and in the same manner as the future glory of Jerusalem, which is unfolded in the final tableau; the wording of a narrator is not that of the orator or poet. Osee expresses himself quite differently (i-iii and iv-xiv; Ezechiel, vi-vii and iv). Besides we meet the same characteristic phraseology in the two parts of Zacharias (vii, 14 and ix, 8, transiens (euntes) et revertens); the eye of God for Providence (iii, 9; iv, 10; ix, 1, 8, etc.). The last chapters, as well as the first of Zacharias belong therefore to the prophet.

CHAPTER L.

AUTHENTICITY OF THE GOSPELS IN GENERAL.

TO judge about the historic value of an ancient book, it is necessary first, to know the person and the qualities of the writer; one must, moreover, have the certitude that the work of the writer has reached us without having undergone any notable changes; finally, it is necessary that it establishes the knowledge, the judgment and the probity of the author. Therefore, we have to treat successively: 1. Of the authenticity; 2. Of the integrity; 3. Of the veracity of our Sacred Gospels.

Since the most remote antiquity the Christian Church has acknowledged as portions of the Sacred Scriptures four Gospels, neither more nor less, and has attributed them to four determined authors, of whom two belonged to the apostolic college, namely Matthew and John, the two others, disciples of the apostles, Mark and Luke.

GENERAL PROOFS.

Since the second century of the Christian era, St. Irenæus (about 40 towards 202 A. D.) affirms with the greatest precision, that there are four canonical Gospels, and his testimony is so much more valuable and important because a native of Asia Minor, disciple of St. Polycarpus of Smyrna and bishop of Lyons, he is as the voice of the Churches of both the Orient and Occident: "The belief about the four Gospels," he says, "is so firmly established that the heretics themselves render testimony to them, and all those among them who separate themselves from us, try to confirm their own doctrine through the authority of the Gospels. The Ebionites, making use of the sole Gospel according to St. Matthew, are convinced by this Gospel that they do not think about the Lord with rectitude. Marcion, who cuts off a part of the Gospel of St. Luke, has shown himself a blasphemer against the only God through that which he preserves thereof. Those who separate Jesus Christ and say that Christ has remained impassible whilst Jesus has suffered, can correct themselves of their errors when they read with the love of truth the Gospel according to St. Mark which has their preferences. The sectarians of Valentinus who make abundant use of the Gospel according to St. John to establish their conjectures, can discover therein that they do not speak the truth. . . . Since, therefore, those who oppose themselves to us render such a testimony and make use of these books, the proof which we draw from them against them is well established and true. For there is neither a greater number nor a less number of Gospels. As there are four cardinal points in the world which we inhabit, and four principal winds (spirits), as the Church is spread over the whole earth, and as the Gospel with the Spirit of Life is the column and firmament of the Church, it is becoming that the Church should have four columns, breathing all over incorruptibility and vivifying men. Whence it is manifest that the Word, author of every creature, who is seated above the Cherubim and contains all things, having appeared in the midst of men, has given to us a quadruple Gospel, animated by the same spirit. . . . Therefore, things being thus, all those are vain, ignorant and audacious, who disfigure the beauty of the Gospel and admit more or less Gospels than those which have been enumerated."[1] St. Irenæus has written also the following remarkable words: " In spite of the diversity of languages spoken in the world, the power of tradition is all over the same. The churches of Germany have not in this respect a creed different from that which is received in Spain and by the Celts. The churches founded in the extremities of the Orient,

---
[1] St. Irenæus, Cont. Haer. III, xi, 7-9.

of Egypt, of Lybia, publish these same facts in the manner as the churches placed in the center of the world. And as one sole sun lightens the entire universe, one sole and the same light, a preaching perfectly uniform of the truth, lightens all men who desire to arrive at the knowledge of this truth."[1]

This testimony of St. Irenæus is categorical. Those of Clement of Alexandria and of Tertullian are not less this. In his "Stromata," the Egyptian doctor opposes to the false and apocryphal Gospels "the four Gospels which have been transmitted by tradition,"[2] and his "Hypotyposes," he reports the following words of an ancient: "He said," he wrote, "that the first Gospels which had been drawn up are those which contain the genealogies. That of Mark was composed on the occasion as follows: when Peter had preached publicly the Word at Rome and promulgated the Gospel, under the inspiration of the Spirit, many of his hearers exhorted Mark, who accompanied him since a long time and knew by heart what the Apostle had said, to consign by writing what he had heard. Having therefore written his Gospel, Mark gave it to those who had asked him for it. Peter, having learned of this did not encourage him publicly, but did not dissuade him either. As to John, the last of the Evangelists, as he saw that the other Gospels made known the corporal history of Christ, at the request of those who lived with him and inspired by the Holy Ghost, he wrote the Spiritual Gospel."[3]

Let us listen now to Tertullian: "The Gospels have

---
[1] St. Irenæus, Cont. Haer. l, x, 2.
[2] Clement of Alexandria, Strom. III, 13.
[3] Clement of Alexandria in Eusebius, H. E. vi, 14.

for authors the apostles, to whom the Lord Himself intrusted the mission to promulgate (His doctrine) and the apostolic men (who wrote them), not alone, but with the apostles and according to the apostles. . . . Among the apostles, John and Matthew communicate to us the faith, among the apostolic men, Luke and Mark renew it."[1]

The belief of the Church about the origin of our Gospels in Asia and in Gaul, in Egypt and in Africa, in the epoch when these ecclesiastical writers flourished is, therefore, incontestable. Strauss himself admits this: "About the end of the second century of our era," he says, "our four Gospels, as can be seen by the writings of three doctors of the Church, Irenæus, Clement of Alexandria and Tertullian, were known as deriving from the apostles and disciples of the apostles, among the orthodox, and in quality of authentic documents about Jesus, they had been separated from a number of other similar productions."[2] But, quite acknowledging these facts, which are clear as daylight, the rationalistic critics contest nevertheless the authenticity and veracity of our four Gospels. Therefore, we will establish against them that the canonical Gospels are from the authors whose name they bear, and that their accounts are worthy of faith.

---
[1] Tertullian, Adv. Marc. iv. 2.
[2] D. Strauss, "Leben Jesu."

CHAPTER LI.

AUTHENTICITY OF THE GOSPEL ACCORDING TO ST. MATTHEW.

1. FORMAL TESTIMONIES OF ANTIQUITY.

THE most important of all is that of St. Papias, bishop of Heirapolis, disciple of the Apostle St. John. In a passage, preserved to us by Eusebius, he says: "Matthew has written in Hebrew the discourses (logia) of the Saviour." This testimony is decisive. Attempts have been made to diminish its value, in pretending that Papias meant to speak only of a collection of discourses of Jesus, but this is not the meaning of his words. For what proves that the logia of St. Matthew did not exclude the narrative of the facts, is that Papias himself had entitled his work: "Commentary on the Logia of the Lord." Even Renan admits that the writing of Matthew of which Papias speaks, might very well contain accounts of the actions. This having been acquired, the supposition of the adversaries, who behold in this evangelical writing only a first foundation of the canonical Gospel, is absolutely false. It will be shown further on that it is inadmissible. Rationalism also tries to elude its probatory value, by declaring it not receivable, as being derived from another man destitute of judgment. Papias, according to Eusebius, was quite a learned mind. But to this we answer that:
1. This appreciation of Eusebius is full of exaggeration,

and seems to have no other foundation but the millenary opinion of Papias; in the words themselves of Papias quoted by Eusebius, this Father shows himself full of solicitude to collect from the mouth of the apostolic men the true traditions of the primitive Church; 2. A man of relatively limited mind, however, judged capable to govern as bishop an important Church, and an author of a work worthy of drawing the attention of a savant like Eusebius, had certainly intelligence enough to distinguish whether, yes or no, the Apostle Matthew had written in Hebrew a history of the Saviour. Had this history been another than our canonical Gospel, the writing of Matthew pointed out by Papias, would have left among the Fathers of the second century some trace of its existence. Now, these Fathers as we are going to see, knew no other writing of Matthew but our first Gospel. The testimony of St. Papias is therefore incontestable.

Besides it is supported by that of St. Irenæus, bishop of Lyons, in Gaul, about 178 A. D., whither he had emigrated from Minor Asia. He was a disciple of St. Polycarp, and according to St. Jerome, also of Papias. In his work against the heresies of his time, he states: " Matthew has published among the Hebrews, in their dialect, also a writ of the Gospel " (Haer. iii, 14, 3-4). A contemporary of St. Irenæus, the famous founder of the Catechetical School at Alexandria, St. Pantenus, having gone to preach the faith to the Hindoos, that is, to the Arabs of Arabia Felix, found among them, says Eusebius, the Gospel of St. Matthew, written in Hebrew characters, which had been brought to them through the Apostle St. Bartholomew. Titian, disciple of St. Justin, flourished in the second century, knew so well our Gospels that he composed a concordance about them entitled Diatesseron, that is, the work of the four. Clement of Alexandria, who was ordained priest in the year 195 A. D., states the same; and Tertullian, who was born in the year 163 A. D., and died in 242, calls St. Matthews the most faithful commentator of the Gospel.

We come to produce testimonies taken in the Churches of Asia, Gaul, Africa, Syria and Egypt. The Church of Rome, also possesses a monument of the second century, wherein mention is made of the Gospels: it is the fragmentary Canon, discovered by Muratori. The beginning thereof is lost. But since the part preserved mentions the third Gospel, as being from St. Luke, the fourth of St. John, no doubt the part lost makes mention of the Gospels of St. Matthew and of St. Mark.

2. INDIRECT TESTIMONIES.

We rank under this title the ancient manuscripts and the ancient versions of the New Testament, as well as the quotations of the writers of the first centuries. All the manuscripts bear at the head of the first Gospel the inscription: *According to Matthew.* Now, among the versions, there are two, the Latin and the Syriac, which go back to the first half of the second century. Among all the books of the New Testament, there is not one which the ancient Fathers and heretics of the primitive Church quote more often than the Gospel of St. Matthew. St. Clement of Rome (Cor. xiii), St. Polycarp (Phil. ii), St. Ignatius of Antioch (Polyc. ii and Smyrna i) report words of the Saviour, consigned in this Gospel. The book entitled "Doctrine of the Apostles," whose primitive text has been discovered quite recently, and which goes back perhaps to the first century (n. 1, 3, 7, 8, 15) also gives many sentences of our Lord, contained almost literally in our St. Matthew. It says among other things: "Do not pray as hypocrites; but pray as the Lord has ordained in his Gospel: Our Father, etc." Then the Lord's Prayer follows exactly according to the formula of the first Gospel. The works of St. Justin are full of quotations, almost textually, of our Gospel; and it is very gratuitously that the rationalistic authors pretend that this Father had in hand a primitive Gospel which served as a sketch to our synoptic Gospels. St. Justin is no more literal in his quotations of the Old Testament than in those of the Gospel. It is, besides, certain that this Father knew several canonical Gospels, because he attributes the composition of the Gospels to the apostles and to their disciples. We know through Origen that the pagan Celsus had also our Gospel. In his attacks against the Christians he speaks, among other things, of the arrival of the Magi, of the massacre of the Innocent Children, of the Flight into Egypt, all facts related by St. Matthew. Finally, when we pass to the Gnostics of this remote epoch, we learn through St. Epiphanes (Hær. xxiv, 5), that the Nazareans and the Ebionites had the Gospel of St. Matthew. Valentinus and Basilides often made use of it to support their errors, and a Gnostic book, found a few years ago, quotes in about twenty places texts from the same Gospel.

From all these documents it results that in the second century the Gospel of St. Matthew, such as we possess it to-day, was known and received all over, as the work of this apostle, not only by the Catholics, but even the heretics and infidels. From which we have to conclude that, since the first century, it must have been held as authentic in Palestine, where it was composed; without this, we cannot explain how all the Churches could have been, in so short a time, agreed to regard it as authentic. But, when since the first century it was attributed to St. Mathew in the very place where it was published, one cannot doubt that it was really from this apostle. A falsifier would not have succeeded in passing his work for that of an apostle, among the faithful who were the immediate disciples of the apostles.

3. INTRINSIC ARGUMENTS.

According to tradition, the first of our canonical Gospels was composed by St. Matthew, formerly a publican, and became one of the twelve privileged disciples of Jesus. The Book was addressed to the converted Jews, and had for principal end to confirm them in the faith by showing them, in Jesus of Nazareth, the fulfillment of the Messianic prophecies of the Old Testament. Our first Gospel answers perfectly to these traditional accounts. This Gospel alone teaches us that the Apostle Matthew was at first a publican, that he called himself Levi; he describes in detail the vocation of this apostle. He speaks constantly of the Jewish institutions as of things known by his readers, whilst the other Evangelists are careful to give an explanation thereof. He supposes his readers acquainted with the geography and the political divisions of the Holy Land. The Evangelist in following step by step the Saviour in His conception, birth, hidden life, and His public life, points out each halting place how Jesus realizes in His person the prophecies of the Old Law. This he shows at least in twenty places, without counting several allusions, perfectly clear, to these divine oracles. The prophetic quotations are ordinarily preceded by the formula: In order that may be fulfilled what the prophet says.

Both the extrinsic and intrinsic testimonies of the Gospel of St. Matthew establish, therefore, its authenticity.

CHAPTER LII.

AUTHENTICITY OF THE GOSPEL ACCORDING TO ST. MARK.

1. FORMAL TESTIMONIES OF ANTIQUITY.

FOR the second, as for the first Gospel, the most weighty testimony is that of St. Papias: "The priest (John)," he says, "related also that Mark, the interpreter of Peter, has written exactly that which has been said and done by Christ, as much as he retained it in his memory (from the preaching of Peter), yet not in order; for he has neither heard the Lord, nor followed him, but he had attached himself, as I have said, to the steps of Peter, who used to teach according to the circumstances and not as one who intended a regular composition of the works of the Lord. Hence, Mark committed no fault, writing a part of them so, as he remembered them: for of one thing he took care, that is, to omit nothing of what he had heard, and not to falsify anything in them." ("Hist. eccl.," iii, 39).

The modern critics, to escape the evidence of these words, pretend that this writing of Mark is not the Gospel which we read under his name, but an abridgement of the preaching of Peter, of which the second Evangelist has profited in making changes and additions to it. For, say they, the writing of Mark was a compilation without order, whilst our second Gospel offers well coördained accounts. We answer that the saying of Papias is sufficiently justified by the absence of chronological order, in the exposition of " some " of the things reported by Mark; for this characteristic is exactly found in our Gospel of Mark. Therefore, we have to understand the passage of Papias, as it has been understood by Eusebius, in regard to the canonical Gospel according to St. Mark. In understanding it thus, we will put the teaching of the Apostolic Father in perfect harmony with that of St. Irenæus, who reports the following incontestable testimony of the second century: " After the departure (death) of them (of Peter and Paul), Mark the disciple and interpreter of Peter, also has written the preaching of the Gospel, and bequeathed it to us " (Hær. iii, 1); a testimony whose meaning is completely precised by two others, about contemporaries, that of Clement of Alexandria and that of Origen, who explicitly tell us that Mark, in his Gospel (the second Gospel, says Origen) wrote down what he remembered from the teachings of Peter.

The Western Church has not remained dumb in regard to the fact that occupies us. Indeed the Scriptural catalogue of Muratori (Roman document of the second century) opens by these words, referring to the second Evangelist: *Quibus tamen interfuit et ita posuit*, which signifies, undoubtedly, that the author of the second Gospel was present at the preachings of Peter and consigning them by writ gave us a faithful account of them. Africanus tells us, in his turn, through the mouth of Tertullian: "The Gospel edited by Mark is affirmed to be that of Peter, whose interpreter Mark was (Adv. Marcion, iv, 5).

2. INDIRECT TESTIMONIES.

All the manuscripts and all the ancient versions contain our second Gospel with the inscription: *According to St. Mark*. We find it quoted much more rarely by the Fathers of the second and of the third centuries, which is due because it contains almost nothing that is not already related by Matthew or Luke. However, it can hardly be doubted, that St. Justin did only learn from this Gospel that the sons of Zebedee were called by the Lord, *Children of Thunder*, because Mark is the only evangelist that gives this detail. In fact, he says, this is written in the Commentaries of Peter; as if he were saying: in the Gospel of Peter, because he calls the Gospels Commentaries of the Apostles.

3. INTRINSIC ARGUMENTS.

Amongst the synoptic Evangelists, the second is the one who relates the facts with the most minute details and with characteristic circumstances so striking, that he could learn them only from an eye witness. Although this Gospel is the shortest, it is the most complete in teaching about the facts and actions of Peter, particularly about those which are not to the honor of the apostle, for example, his threefold denial. On the contrary, that which is to his credit seems to be purposely left in the shadow, for instance, the magnificent praise given to his faith by the Saviour, when Peter came to confess the Son of God before his colleagues in the apostolate. Mark, interpreter of Peter, answers to these indications. It is also manifest that the second Gospel was addressed, not to the inhabitants of Palestine, but especially to the Romans. The Hebrew words which he employs are carefully translated; the Jewish customs explained, and we find therein Latin technical terms, for example, in chapter twelve, verse forty-two, the word *quadrans*. Hence, everything corroborates the primitive tradition, attributing the authority of the second canonical Gospel to Mark, disciple of St. Peter, and places its composition at Rome, whilst the prince of the apostles was still alive. The Gospel of Mark gives us an abridgment of the preaching of Peter.

CHAPTER LIII.

AUTHENTICITY OF THE GOSPEL ACCORDING TO ST. LUKE.

1. FORMAL TESTIMONIES OF ANTIQUITY.

THE Catalogue of Muratori gives us an irrefutable testimony from the second century: "The third book of the Gospel according to Luke. This Luke, physician, whom Paul, after the ascension of the Lord, associated in his labors, . . . wrote in his own name according to the ideas of this (Paul). However, he did not see the Saviour in the flesh, and on account of this (he relates the facts), as he could inform himself about them. It is thus that he commences to speak of the birth of John." Tertullian reproaches Marcion for having altered the Gospel of Luke. This Gospel, he says, is received by all the churches; Marcion, on the contrary, is an unknown person. He claims in favor of this writing even the authority of the apostles, for he says, " the composition of Luke is generally attributed to Paul " (" Adv. Marcion," iv. 5). St. Irenæus reports the same tradition: " Luke, disciple of Paul, consigned into a book the Gospel preached by Paul " (Hær. iii, 11). He even gives of the Gospel of Luke a detailed analysis, answering exactly to our third canonical Gospel (Hær. iii, 14, 3, 4). Clement of Alexandria invokes in proof of one of his assertions, the Gospel according to Luke (Strom. i, 21), and Origen counts the Gospel according to Luke among the four, " which alone were admitted without contestation in the universal Church " (" Ap. Euseb. Hist" eccl. vi. 25).

2. INDIRECT TESTIMONIES.

All the ancient manuscripts and all the ancient versions give to the third Gospel the inscription: *According to Luke.* St. Justin, a Father of the second century, reports the history of the Annunciation; he gives about the birth of the Saviour details which are found only in St. Luke; he says that " the apostles, in their commentaries, called Gospels, have taught us that Jesus gave to them the order (to consecrate the bread and the wine); that Jesus, indeed, having taken bread and having rendered thanks, has said: " Do this in commemoration of me " (Apol. i, 66). Luke is the only Evangelist that reports these words. The letter of the Church of Vienne, document of the second century, applies to the martyrs of this city the eulogy which St. Luke awards to the priest Zacharias ("Ap. Euseb. Hist." eccl. v, 1). The Gnostics also render testimony to the authenticity of this Gospel. Basilides explains in a heretical sense the words of the angel Gabriel; Valentinus, according to the saying of St. Irenæus, employs several Sacred Texts which are only found in St. Luke; finally, Marcion, rejecting the other Gospels, admitted only that of St. Luke in making him undergo mutilations and interpolations. The pagan Celsus speaks of the double genealogy of Jesus, of the apparition of angels at the tomb of the Saviour, and finds the Evangelists in contradiction, because one speaks of two angels, and the other of one only, as having appeared to the women. It is, therefore, evident that, since the second century, the third Gospel was universally received as a Sacred Book, and attributed to St. Luke, disciple of St. Paul.

3. INTRINSIC ARGUMENTS.

In considering closely the third canonical Gospel, one easily discovers therein several indications that betray the influence of St. Paul, and thus answer to tradition, according to which the third Evangelist is a disciple of the great apostle, and whose special purpose it was to reproduce in his writing the teaching of his Divine Master. There is in the first place, between the third Gospel and the Epistles of St. Paul, a verbal concordance of the most striking facts. Several expressions, common to both, are hardly found under the pen of other writers of the New Testament. The words of the institution of the Blessed Eucharist are reported in the same manner by St. Paul, in the first

Epistle to the Corinthians (vi, 24-25), whilst they are different in St. Matthew and St. Mark. The order of the apparitions of Christ risen is the same in the third Gospel and in the first Epistle to the Corinthians (xv, 5-7). Let us add that the style of our Evangelist is purer and less Hebraist than that of the two other synoptics, a quality which answers very well to the Hellenic origin, and to the more careful instruction of St. Luke, physician, born at Antioch, the wealthy capital of Syria. Finally, the third Gospel is manifestly addressed to the converted Gentiles. Who other than a companion of St. Paul was more fit to fulfill a similar task?

CHAPTER LIV.

OBJECTIONS AGAINST THE AUTHENTICITY OF THE THREE SYNOPTIC GOSPELS.

BEFORE occupying ourselves with the authenticity of the fourth Gospel, we will examine first what one opposes to the authenticity of the first three. Their cause is about common, and differs notably from that of the fourth.

Everybody knows that there are among the first three Gospels a great resemblance, beginning with the account of the public life of Christ. We find therein related about the same facts, in the same order, and often considerable passages corresponding among one another almost word for word. But, aside from these resemblances, there are also very considerable differences, either for the details of facts, or for the order of accounts, or for the expressions. These resemblances and divergences require an explanation. In the rationalistic schools, this explanation is founded upon the negation of the authenticity of the three writings. The resemblances, they say, suppose a common foundation upon which the three authors or the three respective predecessors have labored; the divergences are the results of successive rehandlings, to which several unknown hands have contributed their contingent, and who answered to the unconscious evolution of the popular traditions, among the different surroundings where the Christian communities became established.

According to this system, our Gospels are personal compositions, so to say, escaping all responsibility, as well as all control. Eichhorn supposes the existence of a very elementary primitive Gospel, drawn up in Aramaic by the apostles in common, to serve to them as uniform catechetical formula. From this the common elements of the three Synoptics are derived: that what is common to two only owes its origin to a first rehandling of the primitive writing. As to that what is proper to one only, we have to attribute it, either to a common foundation, or to further rehandlings. They made answer to Eichhorn that a primitive Aramaic Gospel rendered a good enough account of the resemblances regarding the facts and the order of the accounts, but that it did not explain the *verbal* concordance of three Greek compositions: for one same Aramaic original would have been translated in different terms by three writers that had not planned together. Hence, the reason why this doctor modified afterwards his opinion, in supposing for common foundation a Greek version of the primitive Gospel. One generally believed to find this primitive Gospel in the *Logia*, attributed by Papias to the Apostle St. Matthew, or in the book which the same writer attributes to St. Mark. The idea of Eichhorn was worked in various manners by other critics. They subjected the three Gospels to a sort of an anatomic analysis, they classed by groups the different passages; each group received its place in a determined series of rehandlings; and from this fanatical genesis they made arise the three canonical books, such as we possess them to-day. Gratz, Ewald, Reville and Holzman distinguished themselves in these studies, wherein the ridiculous is in dispute with the arbitrary.

To overthrow with one stroke all these theories, it is sufficient to remark that this primitive Gospel, or at least the numerous rehandlings which one should have made it undergo, could not fail to leave in history some trace of their existence. Now, the adversaries themselves have to admit that not only all these rehandlings as well as this primitive Gospel have never been seen by any witness of the primitive Church, but we find nowhere the least mention thereof, and nowhere do we meet with the least allusion to them. The system tells us what might have taken place, but not what really took place.

The radical fault of the system of the primitively written Gospel did not remain unobserved by the more logical rationalistic doctors. In order to get rid of it Giesler and De Wette supposed a primitive non-written Gospel, but propagated orally only by the apostles in their catechetical preaching. The teaching of the apostles, constantly repeated about in the same terms, must have become engraved in the memory of the faithful, and expressed later on in an almost identical manner by those who undertook to teach them by writ. Parallelly to the apostolic teaching there arose also about the life of Jesus local traditions, more or less spread, whose formula, similarly fixed in the popular mind, passed into one or the other of the evangelical accounts. Hence, the resemblances common to two Gospels only, and the divergences of the one or the other.

This system of explanation gratuitously supposes that our Gospels contain about the life of our Lord legendary traditions, forming no part of the teaching of the apostles. This hypothesis is in contradiction with the most formal testimonies of antiquity. Always and everywhere the faithful have been persuaded that the Gospels taught them only the purest doctrine of the apostles. Always and everywhere the apocryphal Gospels have been rejected, because they substituted to this doctrine traditions without authority, or because they gave to the evangelical accounts developments of which the apostles had not spoken. Therefore, from this side the system of Giesler is inacceptable. It becomes, on the contrary, very plausible, when one admits that the apostles, accommodating themselves in their catechetical preachings to the very different surroundings where they made themselves heard, chose with preference certain facts of the life of Jesus, and varied in the manner of exposing them, according to the wants and dispositions of their hearers.

The Gospel of St. Matthew would be the abridged reproduction of the teaching of the apostles such as it was addressed to the faithful issued from Judaism; the Gospel of St. Luke would be the reflection of the apostolic preaching destined for the instruction of the converted Gentiles; the Gospel of St. Mark would represent the catechesis of St. Peter to the Christian community of Rome, mingled almost equally with the Jewish and pagan element. The system, thus modified, is actually in favor with several Catholic savants, and tends to supplant the system which wishes to explain the relations of resemblance of the Synoptic Evangelists, in admitting that St. Mark has known and employed in his work the Gospel of St. Matthew, and that St. Luke has made use of the works of his predecessors. This latter explanation seems little compatible with the simplicity of our Evangelists; it does not render sufficient account of the verbal divergencies which offer themselves all on a sudden in a passage which one supposes to be a transcription of a preëxisting copy. On the other hand, if the Gospels give to us the formula of the popular preachings of the apostles, one may ask with right why we find almost nothing of this formula in the numerous discourses of the apostles, which the Book of the Acts has preserved to us, nor in the letters which the apostles have written to the faithful; why do the apostles, in their discourses and letters, quote the text of the Old Testament differently than the Evangelists in their accounts; why, in addressing themselves to the Jews, have they recourse to other Messianic prophecies than St. Matthew in his Gospel, etc. Be this as it may with these difficulties, the Catholic systems to explain the mutual relations of the Synoptics, run against none of the impossibilities nor of the historic errors, against which the theories of the infidels miserably run aground.

We can omit here several objections of detail put forward by our adversaries against the authenticity of the Synoptics, which rather have reference to the veracity of these sacred authors. One pretends to point out in this book many improbabilities and contradictions of one Gospel in regard to the other. But these improbabilities appear only as such to minds that have formed a false idea of the supernatural Providence of God in the world, of the role which the miracle exercises in the execution of the divine decrees, etc.; the pretended contradictions, either have only reference about minute details, and then they are compatible, if not always with inspiration, with the authenticity and the subjective veracity of their authors (for even eye witnesses may be deceived about the minute details of a fact, or preserve imperfectly the remembrance thereof); or these contradictions are pointed out in the substance itself of the accounts, and then it is the duty of the orthodox critic to seek a reasonable reconciliation between the Evangelists. When, on account of the defect of documents arrived to us, criticism is unable to find an acceptable reconciliation, it has to confess only its ignorance, without that on this account it can question the authenticity of the Gospels which is based upon irrefragable proofs. In good logic, an insoluble difficulty is not sufficient to shake a thesis becomingly demonstrated by the arguments that are proper to it.

CHAPTER LV.

AUTHENTICITY OF THE GOSPEL ACCORDING TO ST. JOHN.

THE physiognomy of the fourth Gospel is quite different from that of the first three. It is an apart work, written with a special polemical end, to which all is subordinated in the choice of the acts of the life of Jesus which are related therein. The author wishes to establish the divinity of Jesus against the heretical sects who wished to deny this capital dogma. Ancient tradition also assigns another end in view to this Evangelist; the Synoptics having omitted almost entirely the facts of the first two years of the public life of Jesus, the author of the fourth Gospel proposes to supply this silence.

Whole antiquity is unanimous in proclaiming as author of this Gospel the Apostle St. John, the beloved disciple of Jesus. One points out, indeed, in this harmony the discordant voice of a heretical sect, that of the Alogeans, but we know that dogmatic reasons alone moved them not to acknowledge the hand of an apostle in a writing which so neatly affirmed the existence and the attributes of the Word of God. Analogous dogmatic reasons have pushed modern infidelity to cast a doubt on the authenticity of this apostolic document. Since one century they have been engaged in, and continue to pursue against this truth, a bitter war, whose stake is, they say, the dogma of the Divinity of Christ. Consequently, it is important to put this authenticity in its full light.

1. INTRINSIC ARGUMENTS—FORMAL TESTIMONIES OF ANTIQUITY.

None of these testimonies surpasses that of St. Irenæus, bishop of Lyons, born and raised in Asia, where he was the disciple of St. Polycarp, he himself a disciple of St. John. Behold what this illustrious doctor tells us: "Then John, the disciple who also rested on His bosom, has also brought forth the Gospel, whilst staying in Ephesus in Asia" (Hær. iii, 1). These words are so clear, the teaching is so complete, and of such a great authority, that, if we would possess only this sole testimony, we would have to hold the authenticity of the Gospel of St. John as unquestionable. But we are not reduced to this sole testimony, both the East and the West are united to corroborate it. The Church of Rome makes its thought known to us in the "Fragment of Muratori," where we read these words: "The author of the fourth Gospel is John, one of the disciples. As his fellow-disciples and the bishops exhorted him (to write), he says to them: From this day on fast with me during three days, and we will communicate mutually to one another that has been revealed to us. In that very night it was revealed to Andrew, that John should write the whole in his name, and cause his work to be revised by all the others." Whatever may be the historic value of this narrative, certainly it results from the words quoted that, about the year 170 A. D., the Church of Rome put out of the question the composition of the fourth Gospel by the Apostle John. The

African Church speaks in its turn through the mouth of Tertullian. This Father of the second century distinguishes neatly among the four Evangelists two apostles, John and Matthew. He affirms that before the appearance of the Gospel of Marcion, another Gospel makes known to us the incredulity of the brethren of the Lord, a detail which is given only by St. John (vii, 5). In Egypt we hear, about in the same time, Clement of Alexandria, teaching us that " according to the tradition of the ancients, John the last Evangelist, seeing that in the Gospels of the others were related facts concerning the body of Christ, wrote himself, under the breath of the Holy Ghost, and at the request of his companions, a Spiritual Gospel ("Ap. Euseb." H. E. vi, 14). Syria brings us the testimony of St. Theophus of Antioch, placing St. John among the inspired writers and reciting word for word the beginning of his Gospel.

The Clementine Homilies, in the midst of the second century, refer to them in terms which indicate the high esteem in which this Gospel was already regarded in this epoch.

Let us add here the testimony of the " Doctrine of the Twelve Apostles," known only since 1883. Herein we do not read textually any passage of the fourth Gospel, but as in several ancient writings, we can recognize in the language of the writer, a reminiscence of St. John. Let us quote in particular what the author of the Didache says of the Eucharist: " As to the Eucharist you shall render thanks thus. First for the chalice: we render thanks to Thee, our Father, for the holy vine of our servant David which Thou didst make known to us through Jesus, Thy Son. To Thee, be glory for ever and ever! For the broken bread: **we render thanks to Thee, our Father, for the life and the science which Thou didst make known to us through Jesus, Thy Son. To Thee be glory for ever and ever! Like (the grains of) this broken bread were sown on the mountains, and have united themselves to form one whole, that thus Thy Church may be united from the extremities of the earth in Thy kingdom, because to Thee belong the glory and power through Jesus Christ for ever and ever!"** This manner of speaking, which we also recover in the act of thanksgiving that ends the spiritual banquet, we find almost solely in the Gospel of St. John.

The formal testimonies do not go back beyond the second century; we do not need to be astonished at this, because St. John wrote only about the end of the first century, but, in more remote epochs, we can still collect precious indirect testimonies.

2. INDIRECT TESTIMONIES.

We find them in the ancient Italic and Syria versions which contain the fourth Gospel, *according to John*, and in the quotations of the Fathers.

St. Ignatius of Antioch, says of the Spirit of God, "that it knows whence it comes and whither it goes"; St. John says the same thing of the Holy Ghost (ad Philad. 7; Joann. iii. 8); the author of the "Letter to Diogenes," writer of the second century, speaks of the Word in the same terms as St. John in his prologue, and in the dialogue of Jesus with Nicodemus (Ep. ad Dignon. 7, 10); St. Polycarp certainly knew the fourth Gospel, because in his letter to the Philippians (vii.). he quotes a text from the first Epistle of St. John (iv,

2-3). We know that, according to the avowal of all the critics, this epistle is of the same author as the fourth Gospel, and, supposing its existence, St. Papias also makes use of the first Epistle of St. John ('' Ap. Euseb. H. E." iii, 39), therefore, he also knew the fourth Gospel. St. Justin quotes the words of Jesus Christ to Nicodemus in regard to the necessity of baptism (John iii, 5) and evidently makes an allusion to the objection which this doctor made to the Saviour (Tryph. 105); he reports exactly as St. John and otherwise as the Septuagint the prophecy of Zacharias: " They will look at the one which they have pierced " (Apol. i. 52). Tatian commences his *Diatessaron* with the prologue of St. John. Apollinarius, bishop of Hierapolis, can learn only from the fourth Evangelist that Jesus celebrated the Pasch on the fourteenth day of the moon, that His side was pierced upon the cross, and that water and blood came forth from the wound (Fragm. Pat. gr. V, 1297).

The quotations of the ancient Gnostics are not less striking. Basilides says that it is written in the Gospels: " He was the true light, which enlightened every man that cometh into the world " (Philosoph. 7, 22). Ptolemy quotes, as from the apostle, John i, 3 (Ad. Epiph. Hær. 33). Theodotus quotes John xvii, 11: " Father, keep them in my name." Heracleon wrote a commentary on the Gospel of St. John, the fragments of which Origen has preserved to us.

Conclusion.—St. John died about the end of the first century. Several of his disciples undoubtedly lived until the middle of the second century. Now, since the second century, the entire Church possessed the fourth Gospel, and attributed it without hesitation and without contestation to this apostle; it was used all over as an inspired work. How can one explain this phenonomen, if this Gospel, as Rationalism wishes, went forth only in the second century from the pen of a falsifier? Our adversaries have not even made the attempt to explain this; it is absolutely impossible to do so.

3. INTRINSIC ARGUMENTS.

The author of the fourth Gospel designates himself, without, however, giving his name. It is "the disciple whom Jesus loved," and this disciple, according to all tradition, was no other but St. John. There were in the college of the twelve apostles three men preferred by the Master—Peter, John and James. Moreover, Peter and John appear, in the Synoptic Gospels, frequently associated together in divers conjunctures of the life of Jesus. The author of the fourth Gospel names almost all the less important apostles; Peter plays a great role in his writings, he appears therein more than once associated with the beloved disciple of Jesus, but nowhere do we find designated by their names John and James, his brother. Once there is mention made of the sons of Zebedee, in the history of the apparition of the Saviour on the shores of Lake Tiberiades. The author often speaks of the Precursor, and nowhere does he add the surname of Baptist; he calls him John, without determining any more; in the Synoptics, only the apostle is designated by this name. The anomaly explains itself right away when John himself is the narrator. This narrator is, besides certainly a Jew of Palestine; anybody else would have been less acquainted with the Jewish customs and historical and geographical details. He speaks of Cana in Galilee, because he knows there exists another Cana in the tribe of Aser; he knows the exact site of Capharnaum; he knows that from the other side of the sea of Tiberiades arise mountains; that in this place the sea is only of a width that one can get around it on foot in one night, and arrive in the morning at Capharnaum; he describes in detail the pool of Bethsaida; he knows the fountain of Siloe, and estimates exactly the distance from Jerusalem to Bethania; he enumerates the great Jewish feasts, assigns the epoch when they are celebrated and remarks that the eighth day of the Scenopegia was especially solemn. Finally, he has been present at the crucifixion of Jesus, and has seen with his own eyes the water and the blood flow from His pierced side. Is there anything more needed to characterize the author, and to make us exclude any other person except the Apostle St. John.

4. OBJECTIONS OF THE RATIONALISTS AGAINST THE AUTHENTICITY OF THE GOSPEL OF ST. JOHN.

One pretends: 1. That the author of the fourth Gospel is not a Jew; 2. That this Gospel contains errors of fact which one cannot expect from an eye witness; 3. That he is in contradiction with the Synoptics and professes other religious doctrines than these; 4. That he puts in the mouth of Jesus discourses which Jesus has not pronounced; 5. That the day assigned by him for the celebration of the last Pasch is not in agreement with the tradition of St. John. Let us examine successively these difficulties:

1. The author of the fourth Gospel always speaks of the Jews in the third person, and puts himself in opposition with them. Therefore, they say, he was not a Jew. One forgets that St. John wrote at Ephesus for

Christians that had been formerly Gentiles, in an epoch when the Jews had lost their nationality. Besides, Jesus speaking to the Jews, does He not say to them: " Abraham, your father " (John viii, 56), which did not hinder him to be Himself from the race of Abraham?

2. They pretend that the author is deceived in placing Bethania beyond the Jordan (i, 28); in speaking of a city of Sichar, unknown in the history of Israel (iv, 5); in calling Caiphas high priest of that year, as if the sovereign pontificate had been an annual office, error so much more coarse as Caiphas occupied that dignity during ten consecutive years. — Answer: Instead of Bethania, we must probably read Bethabara. Besides, St. John speaks elsewhere explicitly of Bethania in Judea, neighboring borough of Jerusalem. Sichar was probably a corruption of Sichem, principal city of Samaria situated at the foot of the sacred mountain of the Samaritans. St. John says that Caiphas was high priest that year, without saying by that he was this neither before nor after.

3. The adversaries of the Gospel of St. John tax, as contradictory, accounts which mutually complete themselves. St. John knew the first three Gospels and supposed them to be known by his readers. He knew that his predecessors did not wish to give a complete biography of Jesus, that, on the contrary, each of them had chosen and disposed his accounts according to a determined plan. The Synoptics had pointed out only one voyage of Jesus to Jerusalem; John does not contradict them when he mentions five of them. He also could relate how Jesus, at the beginning of His public life, drove out the sellers from the Temple, although knowing very well that the Master had done a similar

thing three years later, according to the Synoptics. Besides, it is not impossible that the Synoptics, at the occasion of the account of the facts and acts of Jesus in the Temple, about the last Pasch of His life, had mentioned, in this place, the act of authority which the Master had exercised in the Temple three years previously. St. Matthew and St. Mark pay little attention to a chronological order; they prefer to follow the logical order of facts. Let us remark, moreover, that the precise duration of the public life of Jesus is not fixed by any of the four Evangelists. The Synoptics tell nowhere that all what they relate took place in one single year, and the fourth Gospel, although it speaks of three or four Paschs celebrated by Jesus, does not say that He did not celebrate any more after His baptism.

Rationalism claims that the Jesus of the Synoptics is quite a different personage from that which the fourth Gospel offers to us. The Master, at the Synoptics, is a simple and popular doctor; his teaching is almost exclusively a moral one; he proposes it in parables accessible to the popular understanding; when they call Him Son of God, He imposes silence upon the indiscreet tongues. On the contrary, the Christ of John is a philosopher, speaking through enigmatic sentences, an obscure and subtile dialectician; His teaching is dogmatic; always occupied with His own personality, He does not cease to inculcate belief in His superior nature. Behold what " criticism " has discovered, and what nobody had perceived during nearly nineteen centuries. Is it a professor of theology that speaks thus, when he addresses his scholars and when, getting down from his chair, he begins to catechize children or country people? The example applies very well to the case that occupies us. The Synoptics show us Jesus preaching to rural or commercial peoples of Galilee. John relates the disputes of the Saviour with the Scribes, the Pharisees and priests of Jerusalem, men instructed in the law and given up to all the subtleties of rabbinism. Let us remark, moreover, the difference of the end in view the Evangelists proposed to themselves. The Synoptics tried to make Jesus to be known as the Messiah, the great deliverer of Israel and of all the nations. John found himself in the presence of Gnostic dogmatizers, who attacked the divine character of the Saviour, he desired to oppose to them the affirmation and the demonstration which Jesus Himself gave of His divinity.

4. Finally, let us say that these discourses of Jesus must have made a deep impression upon the well-beloved disciple, who had rested on the bosom of the Saviour. Hence, there is nothing astonishing that these discourses have remained more present to his mind, dearer to his heart, and that he, in an opportune time, did communicate them by writing to the Church. When one replies that these discourses are too long, that no apostle could retain them and reproduce them after so many years, we can answer, that the Evangelist gives to us the meaning of the words of the Lord, and the substance of His discourses, rather than the development which the Master gave to them. No great effort of memory was needed, in order that the beloved disciple of Jesus could thus reproduce discourses to which dialogism gave sufficient relief and vivacity. Besides, we have to suppose that, in his preachings and catechetical instructions, the apostle had frequently commented on these divine words, and that he had become quite

familiar with them. Finally, when sometimes the memory of the writer was wanting in exactitude, he was guided by the Holy Ghost who reminded him on everything what the Master had said (John xiv. 26).

5. The fifth objection is drawn from the famous dispute that arose in the second century between Pope St. Victor and some bishops of Asia, in regard to the day of the celebration of Easter. Polycarp and his followers appealed to the tradition of St. John, to uphold their side to keep the feast on the fourteenth day of the month of Nisan. Now, say they, the fourth Gospel places the Last Supper of Jesus on the thirteenth day of this month. We can give a twofold answer. First, St. John might very well have adopted for the feast of the Pasch the fourteenth Nisan, even then, if he would have placed, in his Gospel, the Last Supper on the thirteenth. Then, can we deny the supposition of our adversaries. For it is much more probable that St. John places, in his account, the Last Supper on the evening of the fourteenth Nisan, according to the sense naturally presented by the narratives of the Synoptics. It is not here the place to enter into details of this question, one of the most complicated for the interpreters of the Gospels.

All these objections are drawn from elements intrinsical of the book itself. This is the usual proceeding of infidel criticism. It also has tried its strength on the ground of intrinsical testimonies. Incapable to bring forth against the authenticity of the fourth Gospel one single word of testimonies from antiquity, it has invoked their silence, to maintain that the apostle John had never sojourned in Asia. Otherwise, it says, Ignatius of Antioch, in his letters to the churches of Asia, would not have omitted to invoke, to reprimand them, the authority of this apostle. Now, St. John is mentioned nowhere therein. Paul, on the contrary, is named in the letter to the Ephesians. We answer: It is true that one might expect a similar mention in the letters of Ignatius, but one does not prove that we absolutely ought to find therein any mention. St. Paul had, as Ignatius, passed through Ephesus to go to martyrdom; and under this title his remembrance is invoked; St. John had not passed through this city, hence he must not, in this place of the letter, be associated with St. Paul. St. Polycarp in his letter left to us, speaks also of St. Paul, without mentioning St. John; but he writes to the Church of the Philippians, which had been founded by St. Paul, and which St. John never visited.

CHAPTER LVI.

INTEGRITY OF THE GOSPELS.

WHEN one admits, as we have shown in the preceding chapters, the authenticity of the four Gospels of Matthew, Mark, Luke and John, one can easily deduct from this their integral transmission, without substantial alteration.

In the first place, it seems that no alteration could have taken place whilst the apostles were alive. For if notable alterations would have taken place in their work, the apostles, dispersed all over the civilized world, would not have ignored this, and, knowing it, would not have tolerated it in silence. Besides, in this epoch, every corruption would have been right away established by the comparison of the autographs still existing. Neither could a corruption of the text have been executed after the death of the apostles, at the beginning of the second century. For, according to the testimony of Tertullian (Prax. 36), the autographs of the apostolic writings were still in existence at the beginning of the third century. In the second century, as we know through St. Justin (Apol. ad Ant. 65), the Gospels were publicly read during the celebration of the Liturgy. The text thereof became, so to say, notorious to the faithful, and all occult corruption was then impossible. Already in the second century they had composed and spread both the Latin and Syriac

versions of the Gospels, in which we find exactly our
entire text. Finally, since this epoch, there are in the
writings of the Fathers a great number of quotations
of the Gospels; all these quotations are found in our
actual copies. St. Irenæus, among others, gives the
analysis of the whole contents of the Gospel of St.
Luke. Everything therein corresponds exactly with
our actual text. Since the third and fourth centuries
the quotations from the Gospel are abounding at the
Fathers of the Church, and they are in conformity
with our texts. In the fourth century were drawn up
our most ancient manuscripts of the Gospels, which
are, in the present hour, the richest treasures of our
large libraries; once more, these precious documents
conspire to testify in favor of the integral preservation
of our Gospels. To prove our assertion, it is sufficient
to consult one of the critical editions of the New Testament, wherein are consigned all the different readings
of the text, and of which the most famous are those
of Tischendorf and of Tregelles. It would be senseless
to wish to explain this harmony in saying that in the
fourth century the corrupted text had become dominant. In fact, this would suppose that the Fathers and
the copyists of the third and fourth centuries had all
corrupted copies, and all corrupted in the same manner;
and that moreover, there has not been left any trace of
the different copies, corrupted or not corrupted, in any
other way, although, in the third and second centuries,
the evangelical text had been copied, translated and
quoted constantly and everywhere in the Church. Even
we would have to suppose that already in the time of St.
Augustine, every trace of a different text had disappeared. Behold, indeed, the words of the holy

doctor: "There cannot go forth from their mouth anything more impudent, or, to use more lenient terms, anything more thoughtless, anything weaker, than the affirmation saying that our divine Writings have been corrupted, because they cannot prove this by any of the manuscripts whose existence goes back to such recent recollections" ("Deutil. cred." 3, 7).

All we come to tell has reference to the substantial integrity of our Gospels. It would remain established even if criticism would succeed in proving the existence of some detailed interpolations. They have attempted this proof. To believe them, we would have to regard as apocryphal: 1. The first two chapters of St. Matthew; 2. The conclusion of the Gospel of St. Mark (xvi, 9-20); 3. The history of the bloody sweat of Jesus in the Garden of Olives (Luke xxii, 43-44); 4. The mention of the angel descending into the pool of Bethsaida (John v, 4); 5. The history of the adulterous woman (John vii, 53; viii, 11); 6. The last chapter of the Gospel of St. John. Let us briefly examine these contested places:

1. One has been led to question the apostolic production of the first two chapters of St. Matthew, on account of the difficulty one experiences in reconciling the accounts with other passages of the Bible. One was wrong, as we shall see. The first two chapters of the Gospel of St. Matthew are found in all the manuscripts and in all the ancient versions. There are only a few manuscripts which place the genealogy of Christ at the beginning of the book, outside the historical series of facts. The ancient Fathers quoted texts from these chapters. The pagan philosopher Celsus cites them when he treats on the double genealogy, and on

the adoration of the Magi. Julius Africanus published in the third century a dissertation on the harmony between the two genealogies.

2. Two manuscripts of the first order, that of Sinai and that of the Vatican, end the last chapter of St. Mark with the eight verse instead with the twentieth verse. The other *codices unciales* add the other twelve verses. All the manuscripts, even the Syriac evangelical fragments published by Cureton, have the conclusion complete. The minusculœ manuscripts have it also, some with a marginal note, saying that the final passage is wanting in the ancient copies and in the most exact (*accuratioribus*). The Fathers are greatly in favor of it. It is accepted by Irenæus, Aphraatus, Augustine, Cesarius of Constantinople, the so-called Synopsis of Athanasius, Eusebius and Jerome take notice of the divergence of the manuscripts. Victor of Antioch knew of the divergence, and nevertheless admits the entire text. Dionysius of Alexander says in his canonical letter that the Alexandrians, according to Matthew, broke the fast of Lent in the evening of Holy Saturday (Mat. xxviii, 1), whilst at Rome, according to Mark (xvi, 9), they fasted till in the morning of the next day. Is it, perhaps, this apparent contradiction that caused to suspect in the East the authenticity of the last words of Mark? This conjecture seems quite well founded; it would render account of all the different readings of the manuscripts in this place.

Dr. Davidson who upholds in England all the opinions of the negative criticism and who, consequently, rejects the authenticity of the last twelve verses of St. Mark, sets forth the reasons in favor of the authenticity in the following manner: " It is difficult to decide among the contradictory proofs. The fact that Irenæus had this paragraph before his eyes in his copy of the Gospel contributes against the authority of the numerous manuscripts which omit it. Beside the testimony of Irenæus on verse ten we have a still more ancient testimony for the verses fifteen to nineteen in the acts of Pilate, incorporated in the Gospel of Nicodemus. However, the relations of the now known Acts with the primitive work which Justin and Tertullian had in hands are too uncertain to furnish a solid argument. Celsus also shows that he knew this conclusion when he says: " Who has seen this? A mad woman, as you say," making allusion to Mary Magdalene, to whom Jesus had appeared first, and from whom He had chased seven demons. The language certainly differs from that of the rest of the Gospel, but this difference may be explained by the usage of another source, which the Evangelist chose here rather than St. Matthew. . . . It is difficult to believe that the writer could stop at the words *timebant enim*, " for they were afraid." The reason why this conclusion has been omitted in many copies is insinuated by St. Jerome, Eusebius,[1] etc."

Therefore, whatever may be the differences of the manuscripts, there are excellent and plenty of sufficient proofs in favor of the conclusion of the Gospel of St. Mark.

3. The two verses of St. Luke which relate the bloody sweat of Jesus are equally omitted in two manuscripts of first value, the Alexandrian (A) and the Vatican (B), but they are in the Sinatic, and in all the other *majusculæ*, except one. However, in many

---

[1] S. Davidson, "Introduction to the New Testament," vol. i, p. 575.

codices, the passage is pointed out by a mark or asterisk. St. Ambrose and St. Cyrillus of Alexandria do not give any commentary, St. Hilary is undecided. St. Jerome formerly admits the verses, by remarking "that they are found in some copies." A false fear of scandal might have caused the suppression of this history in the public readings, and thereby in copies destined for this reading. We know through St. Epiphanius that they acted in this way with a passage where there is question of the tears of the Savior.

4. We ignore why many manuscripts omit the verse of the angel of Bethsaida. The context, however, claims it: without this we cannot understand the words of the paralytic (v. 7): "Sir, I have no man, when the water is troubled, to put me into the pond. For, whilst I am coming, another goeth down before me." The Fathers of the different parts of the Church, Cyrillus of Alexandria, Chrysostom, Tertullian, Augustine, know and accept the verse. If it were not authentic how could one explain this harmony of the Fathers?

5. The most contested passage of the Gospel of St. John is the history of the adulterous woman. Many critics reject it as an interpolation, because we do not read it in a great number of important manuscripts, such as the Codex Sinaiticus, the Codex Vaticanus, the Codex Alexandrinus, and the Codex Regius of Paris, which are from the fourth or fifth centuries, and still many others. It is also wanting in the most of the versions, such as the Syriac of Cureton, the Peschito and the translation of Philomenus; in the Gothic version of Ulfilas, in the greater part of the Coptic manuscripts, and in the best manuscripts of the Italic. The Greek Fathers who have commented on the Gospel of

St. John omit this passage in their commentary: Origen, Apollinarius, Theodore of Mopsuesta, St. Cyril of Alexandria, St. John Chrysostom, St. Basil, etc. Among the Latin Fathers, Tertullian and St. Cyprian appear to have known it. Finally, the style of this portion differs from the style of St. John; we read, for instance, " all the people," instead of " multitude," etc., and is connected only with difficulty to what precedes and follows.

We have to admit that all these arguments have some weight; however, they are not sufficient to reject the authenticity of this evangelical passage. Several ancient manuscripts contain it, among others the manuscript of D. of Cambridge, which is only of the sixth century, it is true, but represents much more ancient copies, which we can make go back to the second century. We find it also in more than three hundred minusculæ manuscripts. Six Evangeliaries and other manuscripts indicate that we must read it on all the feasts of St. Pelagia, St. Theodora, St. Eudoxia and of St Mary of Egypt. As to the versions, the Latin Vulgate, the Arab, Ethiopian, Slavonic, Anglo-Saxon translations have the history of the adulterous woman, as well as the most of the Armenian manuscripts. The Apostolic Constitutions quote it in the third century, as does also the Synopsis of the Scripture which carries the name of St. Athanasius; St. Pacian in the fourth century; St. Ambrose, St. Augustine and many others. As to the Greek Fathers and writers who do not speak thereof: Origen, Theodore of Mopseustia and St. John Chrysostom, we must observe that the eighteenth volume of the commentaries of St. John by Origen, wherein this controverted passage should be found, is lost; and, moreover, we possess very incomplete fragments of the exegetical explanations of Theodore of Mopsuestia and of Apollinarius. St. John Chrysostom has not explained the fourth Gospel in a consecutive manner. No Greek Father positively rejects the passage. Euthymius, however, appears to be inclined to do so. The silence of St. Basil, of Tertullian and of St. Cyprian proves nothing, because they have not made any explanation of St. John.

As to the intrinsic arguments alleged against this account, they are far from being conclusive. Undoubtedly we read in this passage some words which we do not read elsewhere in the fourth Gospel; but it is the same in several other chapters; the style is in reality that of St. John, and it is false, moreover, that the episode does not belong to the place where it is found, as is admitted by the rationalistic Hilgenfeld: " This narrative cannot be separated from the context," he says. When one suppresses it, we cannot explain the Word of Jesus: " I judge not any man (viii, 15) and one cannot bring forth neither any reason for his presence in the Temple " (20).

6. St. John, they say, evidently ends his account with the twentieth chapter. Chapter twenty-one has been added by a foreign hand. — But why could not St. John himself, after having ended his work, add an appendix, which appeared useful to him? Should he have changed on this account the first authorship of the chapter by which he had at first the intention to finish? It is certain, according to the documents of antiquity, that the Gospel of St. John did never exist in the Church without this last chapter. Had it been even added by the disciples of this apostle to the work of

their master, we would have to accept it as an inspired writing. But no decisive reasons hinder us to regard it as having proceeded entirely from the pen of the Evangelist.

CHAPTER LVII.

VERACITY OF THE GOSPELS.

THE veracity of the Gospels proves itself by the following considerations. The veracity of a testimony is evident, when the testimonies offer all the desired guarantee as to the knowledge of the facts which they attest, and as to the probity which assures the sincerity of their account. The proof is complete when one can establish that, even had it been their desire to deceive their readers, this has been impossible for them. Now, all these guarantees exist from the part of the Evangelists.

The Evangelists had an exact knowledge of the facts which they relate. Two among them, St. Matthew and St. John, were apostles; as such they had lived during three years in intimacy with Jesus; they had been eye witnesses of the most of the events of the public life of their Master; as to the other facts of this time, they received the accounts from those of their colleagues who had been witnesses of them; finally, the facts of which no apostle had been witness, they knew them all through the testimony of persons worthy of belief who had been mingled with them, namely, the holy women, John the Baptist, Nicodemus, the Blessed

Virgin, etc. St. Mark, according to an incontestable tradition, received his teaching from St. Peter; St. Luke himself tells us in his prologue, that he gathered his information with the greatest care from those who were since the beginning eye witnesses, and from those who exercised the ministering of the Word. The latter words seem to refer especially to St. Paul who also saw the Lord, and received immediate revelations from Him. Testimonies so well informed might, for the most, be deceived in regard to some minute details, but indifferent as to the substance of the facts. If, moreover, as it is the case here, they have written under the inspiration of the Holy Ghost, they must have been guarded against all error. Let us note, however, that, the present discussion belonging to the preambles of faith, we must make abstraction from inspiration, and consider the Gospels only as historic documents.

The rationalistic criticism refuses to subscribe to these conclusions. All the testimonies of the evangelical facts were, they say, common people without instruction, simple and credulous, filled with prejudices as to the character of the Messiah, disposed beforehand to explain in a supernatural sense all the somewhat ordinary actions of their Master, whom they had taken for the Messiah.

The objection would have some value, if the testimony of the Evangelists, and of those who related to them what they had seen and heard, had a bearing on the explanation of the causes of these astonishing facts. It disappears when they attack the testimony bearing on the existence of these facts. The evangelical facts in question fall under the senses; to establish their existence with certitude, it is sufficient that the testimonies were neither deaf nor blind. Let us show this by an example. St. Matthew, St. Peter and St. John are with their Master in a desert place; a crowd of peoples has followed thither. Jesus puts among their hands five loaves of bread and two small fishes; with this slender provision they pass through groups each composed of five thousand persons; they behold the loaves of bread and fishes multiplying themselves among their hands. Five thousand men eat at will from these nourishments, which are distributed to them by the apostles; and, when they are satiated, the latter gather twelve baskets of what was left of this prodigious festival. Now, we ask, if the most subtile of the philosophers, and the most exacting of the Academicians had been present at this spectacle, would they have seen and established something else but these three men of the people, from whom we hold the threefold narrative of the miracle? Some adept of modern science might, perhaps, set up the hypothesis that Jesus had hypnotised His apostles, and that the latter, acting under the power of suggestion, imagined to perform all these acts among a crowd equally imaginary. But, had it been thus, the apostles, in leaving their state of hypnotism, would have remembered nothing of what they had done under the influence of the hallucination; and how could Jesus, on the next day, recall to the mind of the Capharnaites the prodigy which He had wrought in their favor? Infidel science may make every effort to deny the supernatural, it will never succeed in showing that, for this miracle and so many others equally easy to establish, the testimony of the apostles is less acceptable than that of the most cautious criticism. It is, therefore, manifest that the Evangelists are, in general, witnesses well informed about the events which they relate. As to the causes of these events, generally they do not seek to give an explanation of them; but content themselves in saying that Jesus Himself appealed to His works to confirm His divine mission.

The sincerity of the Evangelists is not less than their competency. This results from the moral qualities of the writers. They were simple and naive men, irreproachable in their conduct, who show themselves at every occasion full of candor and frankness. The spirit of man is made for truth; this is a moral law which he betrays only when he has an interest in lying. Now, what interest could the Evangelists have to deceive us in regard to the life and actions of their Divine Master? When, in their eyes, the facts which they relate were false, Jesus was not for them the Messiah, the Son of God; He was only a miserable impostor who had them shamefully seduced, and from whom they had nothing any more to expect. Besides, they beheld the powerful of the century breaking loose all over against the new doctrine and against its followers; hence, the lie could draw upon them only vexations and misfortunes of all kinds; and after a miserable life ended, perhaps among the most atrocious torments, they could expect only an eternity of punishment as price for their deceit. Except to be insane, man does not tell lies in similar conditions.

But let us admit for a moment that the Evangelists, contrary to all the laws that rule the free acts of men, had the desire to deceive their readers, it would have been impossible for them to execute their design; the lie would have been known very quickly. Indeed, let us not forget that the Evangelists are writers contemporary of the events which they relate; these events are facts of the greatest importance, which took place, for the most in public, before an audience partly sympathetic, partly hostile to the hero of the accounts. Mighty crowds heard the discourses of Jesus and saw His miracles. If, however, nobody had heard anything, seen anything similar, would the pretended witnesses not have discovered the imposture right away? From the time they would have been convinced of the lie, it would have been done forever with the belief in the Gospels. Let us remark, moreover, that, in the moment of the drawing up of the Gospels, the apostles had already preached in many places the discourses, the miracles of Christ, and especially His resurrection; all this had passed into the belief of the faithful. The narratives of the Evangelists could, therefore, be accepted only under the condition to be in accord with the preaching of the apostles. Consequently, if there had been fraud on their part, all the apostles would have been accomplices to this; all would have been agreed to tell a lie, and to lie in the same manner. Is it credible that so many men, otherwise recommendable on account of the holiness of their lives, had consented to such a criminal conspiracy, with such a stubbornness that all prefer to die in torments than to give the lie to their claims? Then again: had their hypocritical perversity even gone that far, how would they have succeeded by their coarse lies to persuade the Jews and Gentiles to renounce all that they had believed and practiced thus far, and to give credence to a new doctrine, offering to the mind unfathomable mysteries, and to the heart a moral opposed to all the instincts of sensual nature? Protests arose, it is true, in the bosom of Judaism and Paganism; but how were they produced? The magistrates of Israel prohibited to the apostles to preach in the name of Jesus of Nazareth; they wish to smother the voice of the witnesses, they do not even attempt to refute their words; the Gentiles turn the crucified Master into ridicule, and show a great despise towards His disciples; they come too late to throw doubt on the reality of the evangelical facts.

Let us conclude from all this that, if the evangelical facts were false, it would be the greatest of all miracles that the whole world had accepted them as true, and was resigned to conform its conduct to them, to bring the hardest sacrifices of both the intelligence and the heart.

Quite occupied to place in full light the impossibility of fraud of the Evangelists, we have said nothing of the seal of sincerity which these writers have imprinted upon their work. Never did a man of good faith, were he even a stranger or enemy to our belief, read our Gospels, without being profoundly impressed with the air of candor and truth which these wonderful books breathe. Here is no affection of human eloquence, no word of exaggeration in the accounts; nothing that has a taste of hatred, flattery and desire to please; all over the simplicity of the narrator, who has no other preoccupation but to communicate to others the things which he has learned. They do not conceal either the lowness of their origin or the uprightness of their ideas, they equally report the rebukes received from their Master, and the flattering words which He addressed to them. The most surprising facts are described without admiration; the most unjust and most cruel treatments inflicted upon their Master are reported without any expression of indignation. They take no precaution to be believed upon their word. St. John himself gives as supreme argument of the truth he advances, the assurance that he has been present, and that he tells the truth. Most often they insert into their accounts the most minute circumstances of time, place and persons with a tone of indifference which shows that they are fully assured that they will not be contradicted. Finally, among the things which they report, there are some so elevated, so mysterious, that the genius of the greatest philosophers could not imagine them, for example, the discourses of Jesus given by St. John. How could the limited mind of some common peoples have invented such sublime oracles?

OBJECTIONS.

Antichristian incredulity hardly occupies itself with the arguments we have brought forward in favor of the veracity of the Gospels. They go even so far as to avow that, if the authenticity of the Gospels were demonstrated, one ought, consequently, to admit their veracity. They retrench behind the supposition that these books are a kind of unconscious and impersonal work and, consequently, have not, from the side of their authors any title to our belief. Under cover of this arbitrary supposition they believe that all is permitted to them in regard to these writings. They refuse to treat them as one treats the profane historical works. Also, as soon as the least difficulty arises to bring into accord the writings of the Gospels with the accounts of some profane historian, were it the most obscure and the least exact, it is always the Gospel that is deceived, or which deceives its readers; all that, in the various Evangelists, has the air to contradict itself, is right away declared as irreconcilable; all that, from the rationalistic point of view, appears improbable, is proclaimed fabulous. Such or such a prodigy, related by its sacred authors, is, they say, unworthy of God; such other one is manifestly invented to render the account acceptable, etc. It would be too long and too tedious to inquire about all the places of the Gospels thus taxed with error by the rationalistic criticism, and to discuss the often futile arguments upon which one pretends to support his accusations. Many of these objections disappear by themselves, as soon as one acknowledges the Gospels as the authentic work of the apostles and their disciples; others have the reason of being only in the bad faith and partisan spirit of those who formulate them: a little good will in regard to the sacred authors is sufficient to dispel the clouds heaped up at pleasure.

We have only to occupy ourselves here with certain famous passages whose veracity has been attacked with some appearance of right, and which present serious difficulties even to a loyal exegetist.

I. THE DOUBLE GENEALOGY OF OUR LORD.

Among all the divergences of the Gospels, there is especially one that is very notable, namely, that of the two genealogies of Jesus as given by St. Matthew and St. Luke. The most ancient ecclesiastical authors occupied themselves with this divergence; the contemporary infidels are happy over it. The first explained the difference of the two genealogical tables; the second declare them irreconcilable. "When one reflects," says Strauss, "on the insurmountable difficulties in which all the attempts at reconciliation unavoidably involved themselves, one will despair with more liberal commentators, of the possibility to establish the harmony between the two genealogies, and one has to admit the reciprocal contradiction." Behold, according to this infidel critic, in what the disaccord consists:

"From David to Joseph, Luke counts forty-one generations, and Matthew only twenty-six. But the principal difficulty is that Luke gives to Jesus, for ancestors, for the most, quite other individuals than those which Matthew gives to him. It is not that they are not in accord to reduce the descent of Jesus through Joseph to David and to Abraham; it is not that they are not in accord also in the generations from Abraham until David, and later in the two names of Salathiel and Zorobabel; but the really desperate point is, that from David to the foster-father of Jesus, quite different names are found in Luke and in Matthew. According to Matthew, the father of Joseph was called Jacob; according to Luke, Eli. According to Matthew, the son of David, through whom Joseph descended from this king, was Solomon; according to Luke, Nathan. Hence, the genealogical tree of Matthew descends through the known royal line; that of Luke by an unknown collateral line. These two lines concur only in Salathiel and Zorobabel, so, however, that right away they differ about the father of Salathiel and about the son of Zorobabel."[1]

Such is the difficulty and discord. "This is," concludes Strauss, "a complete contradiction." But the

---
[1] D. Strauss, "Leben Jesu," vol. 1, p. 153-154.

infidels not only pretend that the two genealogies of the Gospels contradict themselves, also several among them maintain that both are manufactured and false documents. This is what, after the example of Strauss, Renan affirms. He says: " The inexactitude and contradictions of the genealogies tend to believe that they are the result of a popular labor. . . . The genealogy which we read in the Gospel called according to Matthew is certainly not the work of the author of this Gospel. He took it from an anterior document. . . . The tower of the genealogy of Matthew is Hebrew; the transcription of the proper names are not those of the Septuagint. . . . What is certain is, that this labor of genealogies was not executed with much unity or authority; for two quite discordant systems to connect Joseph with the last personages known of the Davidic line have arrived to us. It is not impossible that the name of the father and of the high priest of Joseph were known. The rest, from Zorobabel to Joseph is manufactured. As since the Captivity, the biblical writings furnish no longer any chronology, the author believes the space of time shorter than it is in reality, and puts too few steps in it. Luke even puts less therein. In general, the genealogy of Luke is the best studied. It appears that he seeks to correct that of Matthew according to his own views."[1]

All these affirmations of Renan, all these "it appears" are only pure hypotheses without the least foundation, except that in order to find fault with the Gospel. Even were we to admit that the two genealogies were irreconcilable, in good logic, it would follow only that one of them is not exact, not that both are

---
[1] E. Renan, "Les Evangiles," pp. 186-187.

false. The only thing true in the observations of the critics, is that there are omissions in the evangelical lists, but this is neither a new discovery — one has remarked these breaks at all times — nor an argument against their authenticity or their credibility, for the Hebrew historians did not believe themselves obliged at all to give in their catalogues all the names without exception.

The infidels try to deny the historical character of the evangelical genealogies, in saying, as Strauss does, "that it is very improbable that after the perturbations of the Exile, and of the times which followed, the obscure family of Joseph had preserved genealogies which ascended so far back." The infidel critic does not dare to say that it is impossible, but he draws the same conclusions as if he had established the impossibility. In order to make us believe that it is improbable, he treats as obscure the family of Joseph which descended from the kings of Juda! Undoubtedly, it had fallen from its ancient grandeur, but it must have held, nevertheless, to the preservation of its titles of nobility; the whole Biblical history shows us with what care the Jews preserved their genealogies. After the Captivity, since the return into Judea, Zorobabel occupies himself with genealogies.[1] Nehemias does the same.[2] The Books of Tobias, Esther, Judith, of the Machabees, furnish the proof of the care with which each guarded its genealogical tables.[3] The history of the census which took place in Judea at the epoch of

---

[1] 1 Par. ix; 2 Esd. xi; cf. 1 Par. iii, 19; 2 Esd. vii, 5, xii.

[2] 2 Esd. vii, 5; xii, 26; cf. 1 Esd. ii; 2 Esd. vii; xii, 22; 1 Par. iii.

[3] Tob. i, 1; Judith, viii, 1; I Mach. ii, 1-5; viii, 17; xiv. 29.

the birth of Jesus, what is said of Zacharias, of Elisabeth his wife, of Anna, daughter of Phanuel, are so many proofs of the same fact. Besides, the testimonies of the New Testament, Josephus, in the beginning of his "Life," makes known from whom he descended, and ends in saying: "Thus I have traced my genealogy as I have found it marked in the public tables."

The two evangelical lists, therefore, might have been drawn from authentic documents. It is true that they differ from one another, but they are not at all unreconcilable. One cannot assert positively, what the true solution of the difficulty is, because, as in many other facts of antiquity, the documents are wanting. However, to any mind, devoid of prejudice, the explanation which the Fathers of the Church have given, are sufficient evidence that St. Matthew and St. Luke, who show themselves otherwise well instructed and worthy of belief, are no less so in the matter of these genealogies. These explanations reduce themselves to two principal ones; the first of which is:

"How can it be that Joseph is at the same time the son of Jacob and the son of Eli, that he descends at the same time from David through Solomon and the kings (as St. Matthew says) and through Nathan and a branch which never has reigned (as St. Luke says)? The answer is readily given. If we had two genealogies of the second African, the one could give us the genealogy of the Scipions, the other that of the Emilians, both would be not less historical on account of this: the author of the one would be the genealogist of the natural father, the author of the other, of the adopted father of the heroes. It is thus that St. Augustine had already the idea to take the Jacob of Matthew for the natural father, the Eli of Luke for the adopted father of Joseph. And in order to prevent the extinction of the families, the Mosaic law prescribed that, when a husband came to die without children, but had a brother living the widow married this brother, and the first born of the widow and of the brother was inscribed to descend from the dead. A predecessor of St. Augustine, Julius Africanus, endeavored to reconcile the divergence in the two genealogies by supposing that the mother of Joseph married at first Eli, from whom she had no children, then, after the death of Eli, she married his brother Jacob, to whom she gave Joseph. From this it would follow that Matthew would be right in saying that Jacob had engendered Joseph of whom he was the natural father, and that Luke was not wrong to call Joseph son of Eli, because Joseph, in virtue of the law, had to be inscribed under the name of Eli."

The one who speaks thus and who exposes this explanation, is Strauss himself, in his "Neues Leben Jesu." We do not need to add that he does not consider it tenable. Imbued with a partisan spirit, he accepts nothing that favors the truthfulness of the Gospels, and the worst pretexts furnish sufficiently good grounds for him to find fault with the sacred writers. But in spite of what he says, he is obliged to agree that it can be admitted. "This is very ingenious, but not impossible," he says. We now come to the second explanation, also made by Strauss:

"One believes, lately," he says, "to be able to solve the difficulty in a much more simple way: it is pretended that we have, in one of the Evangelists, the genealogy of Joseph, and in the other that of Mary, and consequently the divergence of the two genealogies is not a contradiction. . . . The opinion that Mary also belonged to the race of David is already very ancient. . . . The opinion which promptly prevailed was that Mary descended from David. Several apocryphals express themselves in this sense; it is the same with Justin the Martyr, who says that the Virgin was born of the race of David, of Jacob, of Isaac, of Abraham, an assertion according to which one could even believe that he has referred to Mary one of our genealogical tables, which descend equally through David until Abraham. . . . The genealogy in Luke, iii, 23, would say: either Jesus was, conformably to the common opinion, son of Joseph, who himself, was a stepson of Eli, father of Mary, or Jesus was, as one believed, son of Joseph and by Mary grandson of Eli. . . . One cannot deny . . . that the genitive in Luke, being a case of dependence is not susceptible to signify all kinds of kindred, and consequently, that of son-in-law or grandson."[1]

This second explanation may be also true. However, the first appears preferable to us, because it is the traditional explanation, which the ancients have given; it was founded on the Jewish customs, and the Christians of pagan origin would have scarcely imagined of themselves a similar solution; also Julius Africanus teaches us that they obtained this explanation from the Desposyni or parents of the Saviour, which made him say: "It is not destitute of proofs and is no fiction." St. Matthew, writing for the Jews, has very probably reproduced, as Grotius assures us, the legal genealogy of Joseph, legitimate heir to the throne of David. St. Luke, writing

---

[1] D. Strauss, "Op. cit."

for the Gentiles, has inserted in his Gospel the real genealogy of the spouse of Mary. One can also admit, with a certain number of interpreters, that the Blessed Virgin was a cousin of St. Joseph and that, when the tables of the Gospel do not give us formally her genealogy, they give us, however, the same in fact, for she was also, like her spouse, of the tribe of Juda and of the race of David.

2. THE CENSUS OF QUIRINUS.

St. Luke relates, at the beginning of his Gospel, that Jesus Christ was born at Bethlehem at the same time when the census was taken in Judea, under the government of Quirinus, legate of Syria.[1] The enemies of revelation pretend that no such census was ever taken, and that it is through an anachronism that the Evangelists say that Quirinus was the legate of Syria at the time of the Saviour's birth.

The most of the Rationalists, and even a great number of ancient critics maintain that Quirinus became governor of Syria only after the year 5 of our era, that is, some years after the birth of Jesus Christ, who was born, as St. Matthew states, before the death of Herod, which occurred four years before our era.

However, no contradiction exists, and all that St. Luke states is exact and historical. In the first place, he teaches us that the Emperor Agustus published an edict ordaining a census of the whole Roman Empire. Now, Mr. Reuss maintains that this census took place only when Judea was incorporated into the empire, ten years, at least, after the birth of our Lord, and as

---

[1] Luke ii, 1-2.

this census referred particularly to the ancient kingdom of Herod, he denies that it had been taken in accordance with a general edict.

Several commentators, struck by the fact that Quirinus had proceeded to the enumeration related by Josephus,[1] in the year 6 of our era, and because we do not find in the ancient authors any trace of an analogous operation made by this same Quirinus under Herod, have believed that St. Luke wished to distinguish the census executed under Herod from that which had been made about ten years later on under Quirinus, and, according to them, it is on account of a false version of the text of the Evangelist that one has admitted a first census made by Quirinus, one must translate: "This census was made before Quirinus became legate of Syria;" and not: "The first enrolling was made by Quirinus, legate of Syria." The Greek word prôté has not in this passage of the Gospel, the positive meaning, but the comparative sense before. This is what we can call the philological interpretation. It is rejected in the name of grammar by different commentators and historians.— Although it may be correct rigorously speaking, we have to admit that it does not appear plausible; there is no good reason why St. Luke should have made allusion in this passage to the census of the year 6 of our era, if Quirinus did not play an important part in the facts which he relates. Besides, this interpretation is useless, for it is historically certain, against Mr. Reuss and those whose opinion he has reproduced, that Augustus had ordered a census to be made of the whole Roman Empire, in the epoch mentioned by St. Luke. This fact is attested by several

---

[1] Josephus, "Ant. Jud.," xvii, ii, 4.

VERACITY OF THE GOSPELS. 553

ancient authors, the most, it is true, little known, but whose testimony is not any the less incontestable.

The opposition has tried to attenuate the force of the arguments which establish that Augustus had ordained this census for the whole empire, in saying, that the imperial edict could not apply to Judea, during the reign of Herod, before it was incorporated to the empire. This objection is unfounded. Augustus, undoubtedly, did not wish to subject the Jews, under the reign of Herod, to a direct taxation, but he wished to prepare the way for the union of Judea, and to know exactly what were the resources, in men and money, of the kingdoms which were only his allies. Tacitus tells us expressly that the Emperor had drawn up a " Breviary of the Empire " which enumerated his allies.[1] He could have obtained this information only by means of a census. Hence, the enrolling was made in the allied kingdoms and consequently in Palestine.

It did not take place, at least, under the administration of Quirinus, retort the infidels, for this Roman functionary was placed at the head of the province of Syria only after the deposition of Archelaus, the successor of Herod. — A great number of orthodox commentators, even among those who acknowledge that a first census had been made in Judea some years before our era, have been so struck by the silence of the ancient authors, and in particular by that of Josephus, in regard to a first legation of Quirinus, that they have believed, indeed, that this personage had presided over the census only in the quality of extraordinary envoy of Augustus. But in future everybody has to admit with St. Luke the double legation of Quirinus in Syria, for it is proved by

---
[1] Tacitus, "Annales," I, II.

an epigraphic monument preserved in the Museum of the Lateran at Rome.

3. THE SITE OF EMMAUS.

"What Luke states in regard to Emmaus," says Renan, "cannot be justified by any typographical hypothesis." Here our ignorance is brought up as a proof of the pretended errors of St. Luke. We have no knowledge of the exact location of Emmaus; how, therefore, can we prove that St. Luke was in error, since we have only his own accounts to determine its site? Mr. Renan pretends that "what concerns Emmaus is not justifiable in any topographical hypothesis," and he expressly supposes that Kolonia occupies the site of the ancient Emmaus. "Kolonia," he says, "is about three and a half miles from Jerusalem." But, we repeat it, the situation from Emmaus is problematic and, it is even to-day, the subject of animated controversy. Hence, one cannot establish that St. Luke erred in fixing the distance from Jerusalem to Emmaus. The primitive local tradition located the latter place in Emmaus-Nicopolis, the actual Amouas, and the first Christians of Palestine should certainly have had some knowledge as to this point.

4. "Joanna is a feminine name and difficult to admit," continues Renan. How can a professor of Hebrew make this assertion? It is well known that the feminine proper name, Anna, exists in Hebrew, in both the Old and New Testaments, and all the Hebraists know that Anna and Joanna are the same name, because they differ only by the abridged element of the name of Jehovah, understood in the first case, and expressed in the second. Compare Nathan and Jonathan, Saphat

and Josaphat or Sephatya, which are different forms of the same name. Hence, here the error is not in St. Luke.

5. "In his account, Luke," Renan again pretends, "supposes on account of *distraction* the roof covered with tiles, *consequently inclined*. The flat roofs are always terraced." — The author of the "Evangiles" avows himself further on, that St. Luke knew the flat form of the roofs of Palestine. Moreover, in the supposed erroneous passage, the Evangelist does not state at all that the roof he speaks of was inclined. Renan makes him say this, in order to accuse him of error. St. Luke says that they led the sick down through the tiles,[1] which does not signify *tiles* properly speaking, but *bricks*. The locution is employed to designate a roof, because they made use of bricks to construct the roofs, and it is in this sense that it is employed, for example, by Aristophanes;[2] but in no manner can one conclude from this that St. Luke wished to speak about an inclined roof, nor of a roof made really of bricks, although the bricks could serve to form the terraces. To treat a metaphor of this kind as an error is not the work of a sincere critic. Besides, the text proves clearly that it was not a terrace upon which they ascended by an independent stairway. The stairway which leads up to the flat roofs of the houses, in the Orient, is ordinarily arranged in such a way that one has access to it without being obliged to pass through any apartment. At Jerusalem, where it frequently rains, the terraces on the houses are often paved, at least in the present day, to facilitate the flowing off of the water.

---

[1] Luke v, 19.
[2] Aristophanes, "Fragment," 129*d*.

Therefore, in olden times, they may have covered them with tiles. In order to make certain repairs or improvements, they uncovered a part of the terraces (Mark ii, 4), through the opening of which they hoisted different objects. Therefore, all the details which the Evangelist gives in regard to the episode of the paralytic are protected against criticism.

6. CHRIST'S PUBLIC LIFE; THE PORTRAYAL OF JESUS GIVEN BY THE SYNOPTICS.

The principal objection which is brought up against the veracity of St. John is based upon the essential difference which the critics pretend to discover between the portrayal of Jesus traced by the Synoptics and that of St. John. M. Renan, summing up all the rationalistic arguments, writes: " On the one hand, this Gospel (of St. John) presents to us a picture of the life of Jesus which notably differs from that of the Synoptics. On the other hand, John puts into the mouth of Jesus discourses whose tone, style, behavior and doctrines have nothing common with the Logia reported by the Synoptics. Under the second respect, the difference is such that one must make his choice in a decided manner. When Jesus spoke as Matthew claims, he could not speak as John pretends. Between the two authorities, no critic has hesitated. . . . This does not mean that there are not in the discourses of St. John wonderful explanations, traits which are really derived from Jesus. But the mystic tone of these discourses corresponds in nothing to the character of eloquence of Jesus such as we imagine it according to the Synoptics. A new spirit has breathed, the gnosis has already commenced; the Galilean era of the kingdom of God is finished; the hope of the near coming of the Messiah is removed; one enters the aridities of metaphysics, the darkness of abstract dogma. The spirit of Jesus is there no longer, and when the son of Zebedee did really trace these pages, we have to suppose that he had forgotten in writing them the lake of Genesareth and the charming entertainments which he had heard on its shores."[1]

To answer to these objections we have to remark in the first place that the differences one pretends to discover between the last Gospel and the three Synoptics, would they be as grave as it is pretended, the Rationalists would not have on this account the right to conclude that St. John is not the author of the fourth Gospel, as Mr. Reuss has correctly observed when he says: " Is it necessary, when there is question of different authors, to conclude from the diversity of ideas, from the shades of the conception of a theory, to an absolute priority of the one? Is it possible that in one and the same epoch, and especially in the same surroundings, different conceptions could produce themselves, the one more advanced, more elevated, and newer than the others? Have there never been men who were ahead of their contemporaries, and who adhered to more antiquated theories or popular beliefs? . . . Hence, the theology of the fourth Gospel is not sufficient in itself to determine the epoch of its composition."

7. THE BEGINNING OF THE PUBLIC MINISTRY OF JESUS.

According to Dr. Strauss, one account makes the public ministry of Jesus commence after the arrest of

---
[1] E. Renan, "Vie de Jesus," p. lix-lx.

John, the other before this. "John says (iii, 24) that when Jesus began his public life, John (the Baptist) was not yet cast into prison; now Matthew (iv, 12) depicts the return of Jesus into Galilee only after the arrest of John the Baptist." — Where is the contradiction? St. Matthew does not state that Jesus commenced to preach only after the imprisonment of the precursor. Even Paulus, a Rationalist, has remarked that St. Matthew relates here the return into Galilee which followed, not the baptism of Jesus by John, but the first feast of the Pasch.

8. PLACE OF RESIDENCE OF THE HOLY FAMILY.

St. Luke explains to us quite at length why Joseph and Mary had gone to Bethlehem. St. Matthew tells us, like St. Luke, that Jesus was born at Bethlehem, and he teaches us, moreover, that on their return from Egypt, the Holy Family went to Nazareth, where St. Luke had shown us the same settled at the moment when the angel Gabriel came to announce to Mary the great mystery of the Incarnation, and no critical historian of Jesus will behold here any contradiction, but, on the contrary, perfect harmony. For further particulars see objection fourteen.

9. THE NAME LEVI.

Dr. Strauss also sees a contradiction in the fact that St. Matthew is called Levi by two Evangelists,[1] in the history of his vocation.—Strauss might as well discover a contradiction in the double name of Simon Peter.

---

[1] Mat. ix, 9; Mark ii, 14; Luke v, 27.

10. THE DEMONIACS OF GADARA.

"Mark and Luke," says Strauss, "name only one, . . . Matthew names two."[1]—This is true, but from this it does not follow that St. Matthew is deceived. The rule we have to follow in explaining the divergent accounts, is that the most circumstantiated and most precise must be accepted literally, whilst the other accounts ought to be understood in a general manner. In the case in question, two demoniacs come forth from tombs, which in this country often served as dwelling places for entire families; St. Matthew mentions both; St. Mark and St. Luke are less precise and speak only of the one whose riddance of the affliction was most important to mention.

11. ANOTHER PRETENDED CONTRADICTION.

"According to one historian," says Strauss, "the John the Baptist acknowledged Jesus the Messiah destined to suffer; according to the other, he is surprised at His suffering state."— But we also acknowledge Jesus as the Messiah, and we are nevertheless surprised that He wished to suffer as He has suffered.

12. THE HISTORY OF THE VOCATION OF THE APOSTLES.

The critical historian of Jesus sees also a contradiction in the history of the vocation of the apostles. "According to one account," says he, "it is on the shores of the lake of Galilee that Jesus told his first disciples to leave their nets and follow Him; according to another account, gained them to His doctrine in Judea, and when He went into Galilee. — Both are true

---

[1] Mat. viii, 28; Mark v, 2; Luke viii, 27.

The Saviour had already called them to Him in Judea, and He made them leave later on their nets in Galilee to remain with Him, and to follow Him in His apostolic travels.

13. FINALLY.

Strauss declares as *suspicious the similar events* which took place twice, the discourses which have been repeated on different occasions, the facts which are omitted by some of the Evangelists, and are mentioned only by one.—There is, however, nothing extraordinary that the same man should repeat several similar actions; for a painter to paint twice the same picture, for a professor to repeat the same lesson to two classes of different scholars, for a preacher to preach the same sermon to two distinct audiences, for a thaumaturgus to heal successively persons afflicted with the same illness: all this is evident. As to the silence, Strauss is right in saying that " such an argument is of no value " of itself. He adds that " there is much therein when one can prove that the second narrator would have spoken of the thing if he had known it, and would have known it if it had taken place "; but he does not prove that this rule finds its application in the accounts of the Evangelists.

14. THE MAGI AND THE FLIGHT INTO EGYPT.

The Gospel tells us that the Magi did not return from Bethlehem to Herod, but went back another way into their own country. Then, according to Matthew, Joseph, warned by an angel in sleep, took the Child and His Mother, and retired into Egypt, and he was there until the death of Herod. Against these statements, a great difficulty is raised from the second chapter of St. Luke; for he says that after the days of His purification, according to the law of Moses, were accomplished (Mary and Joseph) carried Him to Jerusalem, to present Him to the Lord. The day appointed for the presentation was the fortieth after the birth. And then St. Luke continues: "And after they had performed all things according to the laws of the Lord, they returned into Galilee, to their city Nazareth." According to the first Gospel, the birth of Jesus, the coming of the Magi, their return and the flight of Joseph with the Child and His mother, seem to have taken place in the immediate succession, before Joseph had left Bethlehem; but how could St. Luke say without coming into contradiction with St. Matthew that the Child was presented to the Lord in the Temple on the fortieth day after His birth, and that Joseph returned after the presentation from Jerusalem to Nazareth? To evade this difficulty, some authors assert that the coming of the Magi did not take place, as it is the common opinion, a few days after the birth of the Lord, but much later. Joseph, they say, had returned in the meantime to Nazareth, not to stay there permanently, but with the intention to arrange all his affairs in such a manner as to leave Nazareth entirely, and to take his future abode in Bethlehem. At the time when the Magi came, perhaps a year after the birth of the Child, he had already returned to Bethlehem; the flight to Egypt followed then also about a year after the birth of Jesus. Yet this conjecture seems to be somewhat against the text of St. Matthew who connects the coming of the Magi most intimately with the nativity of the Lord, saying: "When, therefore, Jesus was born in Bethlehem of Judea, in the days of King Herod, behold there came Magi from the east to Jerusalem. Moreover, it is a very ancient and constant tradition that the Magi came thirteen days after the birth of the Lord.

Schegg in his commentary to St. Luke offers, therefore, another combination of the stated evangelical facts; he supposes that the whole that St. Matthew and St. Luke relate, took place in a very short time. The Magi came a few days after the birth of the Lord, and returned immediately; Herod, seeing himself deceived, did not delay the execution of his design; hence the flight into Egypt succeeded immediately after the return of the Magi; but as the death of Herod occurred not long after, the Holy Family could have returned to Jerusalem, perhaps, two months after the birth of the Lord; the Child was then presented to the Lord in the Temple of Jerusalem, and from thence brought to Nazareth according to the statement of St. Luke. But this combination is in direct contradiction with St. Matthew (ii, 22), where we read that Joseph, hearing that Archelaus reigned in Judea, instead of Herod, his father, was afraid to go *thither*, that is, to Judea. Hence, we adopt with Kenrick (on Luke ii, 39), the solution of the difficulty offered by St. Augustine; he places first the return of the Magi, then the presentation in the Temple, after this immediately the apparition of the angel to Joseph and the flight to Egypt; and from thence the return to Nazareth. To the difficulty, how it can be accounted for, according to this combination, that Herod seeing himself deceived, waited so long to take his cruel measures, the same Father answers: " Herod may have believed that the Magi having been deceived by a delusive appearance of the star, and not finding the Child, were ashamed to return to him; therefore, he laid aside all fear. But when the Child had been carried to the Temple and all that occurred at His presentation, according to Luke, had reached the ears of Herod, he was roused once more to fury; Joseph, perhaps, already on his way to Nazareth, was then warned to retire to Egypt, the more so, as the Child was neither safe in Nazareth, this place belonging to the territory of which Herod was king. Tillmont remarks, no better answer than this can be given; and though he feels himself not perfectly satisfied by it, Benedict XIV, in his work "De Festis Domini," considers it more wise to acquiesce in the judgment of so great a Doctor of the Church.

15. CONCLUSION.

It is a well known fact that we meet with divergencies, not only in various authors, but we even find that the same author relates the same facts. The same may be said of repetitions or omission of things which have been related by others. Therefore, it is entirely wrong to reproach the evangelical authors of having related several times one sole fact as distinct events, under pretext that this fact should have been brought forward but once. For in doing so, the character of the history is not changed in Scripture. It is very necessary not to form a false idea of the inspiration of the sacred writers when one wishes to understand the Gospels. The inspiration does not change the nature. God moves the inspired authors to write what He intends to make known to man, and He prevents the writers from falling into error; but He does not dictate to them the words of which they should make use. According to the majority of theologians the inspiration is not verbal; the inspired writer preserves the use of his faculties, he writes in his own manner, with more or less accuracy and according to his capacity; his style reflects his peculiarities and ability; he impresses upon his writings the mark of his personality in the same manner as any other writer. Hence, he makes use of both his intelligence and memory when he relates events which he has witnessed or which he has learned through the medium of others. God does not ordinarily manifest them to him through a revelation properly speaking; He limits Himself in preserving the writer from all error and mistake in his writings. Hence, the reason why there exists in both the Old and New Testaments a divine element which is not found in any other book; but there is also in it necessarily a human element, because Providence, in order to speak to men, makes use of human instruments, who enjoy the human faculties and speak the human language. Consequently, the inspiration leaves to the authors of the Gospels their personal seal, their peculiar aptitudes, their distinctive faculties, and it is this, when we join with it the particular object which each has in mind, the explanation of the divergencies which we remark in their works, and which we must necessarily find therein. These differences are unavoidable, we repeat it, in the writers of all countries; they are more apt to occur in the work of an Oriental writer who, by temperament, is little inclined to write with order and method, and who cares less than a writer of the Occident to acquire, so to say, that mathematical exactitude, exacted from the Evangelists by certain critics of our day. Now, although St.

Matthew, St. Mark, St. Luke and St. John have always been veracious in the biography which they have left us of the Divine Master, they have nevertheless remained Orientals, and they have written conformably to the genius of their nation; they relate the facts and reproduce the discourses, without attaching more importance than necessary to the form which they give to their thought. They have not, as is common with modern writers, entered into minute details, but believed themselves sufficiently exact in reporting the main facts, and precise enough for all purposes intended. Thus they are all exact, as to the substance, in reporting the inscription of the cross, but only one, St. John, has reported it word for word:

> *This is Jesus, King of the Jews*, says St. Matthew.
> *The King of the Jews*, says St. Mark.
> *This is the King of the Jews*, says St. Luke.
> *Jesus of Nazareth, King of the Jews*, says St. John.[1]

Therefore, the Evangelists had not the remotest idea of writing a history, so to say, according to the modern formula. There is none of the whimsicalities of Rationalism which pronounces judgments against the Gospels from the standpoint of a history of the Saviour such as Rationalists would have written. The historians of Jesus Christ, according to these irresistible fault-finders, should have conceived their subject and formed the structure of their narrative according to the requirements of actual criticism. Since they deviate from this, they do not merit any confidence; they contradict the reality, as they contradict themselves. Since they have not fixed chronologically the time and the date, as exact historians never fail to

---

[1] Mat. xxvii, 37; Mark xv, 26; Luke xxiii, 38; John xix, 19.

do in the present day, and since they contented themselves to indicate in an indefinite manner in what epoch the facts they relate took place, it is concluded from this that they were not well instructed about the facts themselves. Thus, according to the rationalistic method, the history of the foundation of the monastery of Carmel, written by the foundress herself, St. Theresa, is unworthy of credit, because she does not give the year of foundation.

This manner of judging our Sacred Books, becomes so much the more unjust, as it becomes more certain that the Evangelists had less the desire to write a history of our Lord than to make known His doctrine. His teaching is much more important in their eyes than all the rest. The facts are only there to serve as a frame for the lessons, and to show that He is the Messiah, the Son of God. We must never forget these things when we attempt to criticise the Gospels.

Neither must we forget that when the Evangelists had a common end in view, that to preserve the teaching of their Master, they had also each one a particular end. St. Matthew has written for the Jews, and he desired to show them in Jesus the Messiah announced by the prophets; St. Mark and St. Luke have written for the Gentiles and had not, consequently, to attach the same importance to the predictions of the prophets. St. John's purpose was to complete the work of his predecessors, and he has related certain facts by them omitted, or not given in sufficient fulness, and he has called attention to certain teachings which had an important bearing on the rising heresies in the early Church. This diversity in the objects intended resulted in a different exposition of the facts, because none could tell everything, and because, in the selection one is obliged to make, in the midst of the circumstances and the details of the events, they had to prefer those that were proper to the end they wished to attain. Hence, this became another abundant source of divergencies.

Finally, the end in view of the Evangelists would it have been identical, the divergencies in their accounts would have been, nevertheless, unavoidable, because four men, considering the same object or the same fact, see and expose it in a different manner, according to their faculties and impressions that are made upon them. The same personage painted by several painters of ability is differently depicted in many particulars by each. In history the same phenomenon produces itself: the eye witnesses of an event report it always with divergencies; there is never an absolute accord among the historians who relate the history of a man or of an epoch.

One does not conclude from this that these historians are unworthy of belief. One does not deny that a battle has been delivered, a city taken, because Titus-Livius, Polybius and Tacitus relate the battle or siege with different details. Why then have two weights and two measures? One has not the right, because he claims to be a Rationalist, to demand more from the sacred writers than from the profane writers.

The divergencies between the accounts of the Evangelists were, therefore, unavoidable; they should not surprise us; even if there were real contradictions between the four Gospels, the infidels could not legitimately deny their authority; they might only pretend that the historians of the Saviour were deceived in some points of detail.

CHAPTER LVIII.

DEMONIACS AND DEMONIACAL POSSESSION.

I. THE WORD DEMON.

DEMONIACAL possession is often disputed. St. Matthew, St. Mark and St. Luke, in the three first Gospels relate that the Saviour cured a great number of these unfortunates. To-day, the reality and even the possibility of the demoniacal possessions are denied in principle by the Rationalists, and according to certain infidel physicians, the sick, which the Scriptures call demoniacs and possessed, were only nevropaths. The descriptions in the New Testament of demoniacs are sufficient, it is claimed, to establish that these imagined possessions were simply insane or paralytic demonstrations. Now, those afflicted in this manner can be cured through exaltation of the imagination, for it is established by numerous authenticated experiments that the imagination sometimes cures the nevropaths where they excite themselves in a manner that give to their nerves a lively and sudden shock.

Let us see first, in answer to these critics, what Scripture teaches about the demons and the possessed; then we shall compare the possessed of the Gospel with the sick of our infidel physicians.

Both the Old and the New Testaments teach us that evil spirits exist, hardened in evil, wishing evil to man, and ever tempting him to evil. These evil spirits receive two different names, demons and devils; the latter name, in Scripture, is given only to the chief of the fallen angels.

The word "demon" appears to signify "knowing" or "dividing." The sacred writers have borrowed it from the profane writers, but attach to it a more precise and determined sense. In Homer, demon is about synonymous with deity: the old poet employs both words to express the same meaning (Iliad, xix, 188; xvii, 98; iii, 420, etc.). It is not thus in Hesiod: the chanter of the *Days* distinguishes the deities from the demons; the latter are the souls of men who lived during the Golden Age. They are the good genii (" Opera et dies," 121-122, edit. Didot, p. 33). However, as can be seen that neither in the one nor in the other, has the name of demon an evil definition. The Jew Philo employs it to designate the angels, both good and bad. Josephus, on the contrary, speaks of demons in the same sense as the Gospels (Antiq. viii, 2, 5; War, vii, 41, 3). This change in the meaning from a good to the evil genius was effected in great part among the pagans themselves. The *daimôn* of the Greek tragedians is often an evil genius, the bad genius of a family, for instance, like that of the family of Agamemnon. Man, dominated by a furious passion, which precipitates him into crime and misfortune, is represented as under the power of a *daimôn*.

From the ancient word *daimôn*, the Hellenists, in a more recent epoch, formed the neutral adjective *daimônion*, employed substantially to signify something more vague than *daimôn*. Plato makes of the term, in his "Banquet," to designate intermediary beings between God and men, "messengers" from the one to the other. The *daimón* of Socrates is familiar. Authorities differ as to the nature of this *daimónion*. Did the philosopher consider thus an advising spirit or a sort of inner oracle whose orders he obeyed? We venture no opinion. What is certain is, that the illustrious Athenian was accused of introducing the worship of a new daimónion, not acknowledged by the Republic. It is equally certain that the demon of Socrates was a good genius.

Such were the diverse significations attached to the word demon, when the Septuagint undertook the Greek translation of the Old Testament. They never applied the name to the true God, but they made use of it three times to name or qualify the false gods or idols, once in Deuteronomy (xxxii, 17) and twice in the Psalms (cx, 37; xcv, 5). In Deuteronomy and in Psalm cv, the corresponding Hebrew word is *sedim*, primitive meaning of which appears to be that of "masters" and by which the Rabbis understand the demons in the modern sense. In Psalm xcv, the word of the Hebrew original is *'elilim*, "the haughty," that is, the idols. The Septuagint have also translated by "demon" in the prophet Isaias the name of *gad*, the deified "fortune" (Is. lxv, 11) and the name of *'se irim*, by the "hairy" the roebucks (Is. xiii, 21). Finally, in Psalm xc, 6: *Qui habitat in adjurtorio Altissimi*, the Greek translators have transformed the verb "to devastate" into a name of agent "to exercise power" and they have rendered it "noonday devil." In all these passages the Jewish interpreters have designated demons what they considered as idols or false gods.

The study of the Greek of the Septuagint has a very great bearing on the correct intelligence of the original text of the New Testament, because their language is that of the Hellenist Jews, and, consequently, that of the deuterocanonical books of the Old Testament as well as that of the apostles in the New Testament. The translators of the protocanonicals had called the false gods demons ; the translators or authors of the deuterocanonical books received from them this appellation and gave it an evil meaning, in applying it not only to the false gods, but in general to the fallen angels. It is with the same signification we give it to-day that the term demon is employed in Tobias (vi, 7) and in Baruch (iv, 35); however, the Book of Tobias determines its nature in several passages by adding the epithet of "evil" (iii, 8, 17; vi, 7). For the writers of the New Testament, demon simply means an evil spirit (Mat. xi, 12, 43, etc.). He is represented as a pure spirit, originally, of the same nature as the good angels, but revolted against God, under the leadership of a chief, whom the people called Beelzebub, like the ancient deity of Accaron, and who is none other than Satan (Mat. xii, 24-27; Luke x, 17-18). He is forever plunged in evil; the enemy of God and man, and seeks only to injure man, by tempting him to sin (I Tim. iv, 1), and even by inflicting the body with physical ills.

It is this evil tendency of the demon which gained for him the other name by which he is known among the Christians, that of devil *diabolos*. This term, which signifies calumniator, detractor and accuser, and which is always employed as common substantive in the classic writings of Greece, has become in the New Testament a sort of proper name of the evil spirit. The apostles borrowed it from the Septuagint. In their version the word *diabolos* is the translation of "Satan," of which we read in the Hebrew text of the Book of Job (i. 11), of the Paralipomenons (xxi, 1), and of Zacharias (iii. 1-2), to designate the chief of the demons, the author of evil, who persecutes man and seeks to injure God. Hence it comes that this name, in the Gospels and in the Epistles, does not apply to the evil spirits in general, but only to their chief, called also in many passages by his Hebrew name Satan or "enemy" (Mat. iv, 10; Mark iii, 26; Luke x, 18, etc.).

The prince of the demon or the demons themselves being evil spirits, and inclined towards evil, have sought since the beginning of the world to injure men, like roaring lions in pursuit of prey (Gen. iii; Job i-ii; Wisd. ii, 24; I Pet. v, 8). They are the enemies of God, but as they cannot harm Him, they attack Him indirectly through his creation, man. To rob the soul, the most precious part of our being, from its maker is their special object, but sometimes they also torment the body as was quite frequently the case in the time of our Saviour.

2. DEMONIACAL POSSESSIONS.

The victims of the furies of the demon are known under the name of demoniacs, or possessed of a demon. The Gospels describe what these unfortunates had to suffer. Even the word *possessed* indicates that they were no longer their own masters, but that they had fallen under the power of evil spirits, to whom they served as instruments and organs. Besides, the New Testament does not employ the word possessed; the term by which it designates those whom the demon had taken hold of, has the same meaning, but expresses more strongly their subjection to the spirit of evil, in whom they seem to be transformed, hence they were called *endemonized*.

Later, the ecclesiastical language of the Greeks, termed the demoniacs "energumens." However, the words "possessed by the demon" or, by ellipsis, possessed and possession, became the ordinary terminology of the Christians. The Arabic language also designates the demoniac possessed, *maskûm, malbûs, m'amûr*, thing understood, *li-l-djinn*, possessed by a djinn (genius) or a demon. We must remember that the Talmud has no term to signify, either the possessed or the possession : It speaks of the evil spirit persecuting man, but it never says that he enters into him, and that he takes possession of him. The New Testament, on the contrary, reveals the demon as the master of the one of whom he took possession, and in whom he dwells. The words which proceed from the mouths of the possessed are accordingly not their own, but those of the evil spirits ; their strength is often on this account extraordinary and superhuman.

However, the possession, or the effects of possession, such as the Gospels speak of were not continuous : the unfortunate demoniac became master of himself at intervals; the spirit which tormented him left him some moments of rest; but soon he felt anew the whole weight of the burden, his intelligence and will vanished, and, powerless to control his faculties, physical evils of all kinds augmented his torments: almost always the possession is accompanied with infirmities, such as blindness (Mat. xii, 22), dumbness (Mat. ix, 32), or bodily disorders, principally nervous troubles, insanity (Mark i, 5) epilepsy (Mark x, 16-26).

It is the concomitant of illness to this extraordinary state which has furnished pretext to the modern infidels to deny the truth of possession: they only see in those whom the Gospels call demoniacs victims of diseases — insanity, epilepsy, dumbness, etc. In the language of the New Testament, "to have a demon," according to infidel reasoning, simply means to be demented (John vii, 20; viii, 48; x, 20); there exists, in the descriptions of the cases of possession, no feature, no detail which characterizes a specific and particular state; on the contrary, modern medicine discovers in the possessed all the peculiar symptoms in the natural diseases which it studies, and which it tries to cure: nevroses, hallucinations, hysterics, epilepsy. Who does not recognize, for instance, a case of ordinary epilepsy in the pretended possessed whom St. Matthew and St. Mark represent to us falling now in the water and then in the fire, gnashing with his teeth and throwing scum from his mouth? (Mat. xvii, 14; Mark ix, 17, 19, 21). How can one help recognizing a furious madman in the so-called demoniac of Gadara, who lives in tombs, gives vent to frightful shrieks, disfigures himself with stones, breaks the cords by which they wish to fetter him, and becomes the terror of the country? (Mark v, 3-5). It is the same with all the other cases of possession say the Rationalists.

One cannot doubt that the possessed of the Gospels had diseases, the symptoms of which agree in general with known natural diseases, according to the descriptions given by the three Synoptics. Also, a certain number of Protestant critics, even among those who admit the supernatural, believe in our days that they can deny the reality of the possessions. According to them the credibility of the evangelical account has nothing to suffer from their opinion, they assure us. Our Lord and the apostles in speaking of the demoniacs, adopted the language of that time but did not accept its superstitions and errors. When Jesus Christ speaks of possession by the demon, in order to be understood by those whom he addresses, he borrows the terminology of which they made use to designate certain extraordinary illnesses, such as insanity and epilepsy, which, by their singular character and phenomenal nature, have always appealed to the superstition of the masses. Even to this day, in the Orient, an insane person is looked upon as afflicted by an evil spirit. In healing the sick, it was not necessary for the Saviour to discuss the false or varied notions of the multitude, he conformed his speech to the understanding of the people.

Such is the argument of the Rationalists. It is untenable. Undoubtedly, we admit that Scripture very often makes use of popular locutions, although taken literally, they may be fallacious, the usage had familiarized a certain terminology among the people and its employ was sufficiently justified. We meet examples in the Sacred Books where the text seemingly contradicts scientific truths or things indifferent in religious matters, for instance, in the familiar miracle of Josue, when the successor of Moses commanded the sun to stop. But a like interpretation cannot be made where the Saviour and the apostles speak of the possessions. That the people, always inclined to exaggerate, sometimes imagined possessions where only ordinary diseases existed, certainly is possible; but that certain persons from whom the Saviour expelled the demons were not really possessed, is irreconcilable with the language of the Gospels.

Our Lord did not speak of the possessed only before the masses, but also to his disciples in the instructions which He gave them, and His language is always such that leaves no doubt of the reality of demoniacal possessions (Mat. xvii, 17-20; Luke x, 17-20). One of His discourses has entirely for subject the contradiction which would exist between Satan and the demons, his minions, if He, Jesus, expelled the demons from the bodies of the possessed by the power of the prince of the demons (Mat. xii, 25-29; Luke xi, 15-26). How could He have thus reasoned if He did not really expel the demons? Therefore, He did not speak according to popular belief, but according to truth.

Note also, on the authority of Josephus, that there existed in regard to this subject a popular idea which was erroneous, and of which no trace in the New Testament can be discovered. The current belief insisted on, was that the souls of the wicked entered into the possessed; the wicked, after their death, came also to torment the living (*Antq.* vi, 11, 2; vi, 7, 2; viii, 5; *War.* vii, 6, 3). We read nothing of this in the Gospels.

We must, therefore, admit that the possessed were really under the power of the demons. Their victims, it is true, were often attacked with nervous or other diseases, the symptoms of which were ordinary symptoms of natural disorders, but even in such complicated cases it is not difficult to designate some specific characteristics of the possession. The sacred writers do not confound the demoniacs with merely ill persons or infirm (Mat. iv, 24; Mark i, 32, 34; Luke v, 17-18). For them, every mute was not possessed (Cf. Mat. ix, 32 and Mark vii, 32). St. Matthew expressly distinguishes the demoniacs from the lunatics, the insane and the paralytics (Mat. iv, 24). That which, in their accounts, is the most important or distinguishing feature of possession, is that the demon speaks through the mouth of the possessed, who manifests a supernatural knowledge, by proclaiming that Jesus is not only the Son of David, as the Jews called Him, but the Son of God and the Messiah (Mat. viii, 29; Mark i, 24, 34; v, 7; Luke iv, 41; Cf. Acts xix, 15). The possessed are cured, when the demons leave their bodies. To demonstrate to us the reality of the possession, Jesus Christ permits the demons who leave the bodies of the possessed of Gadara to enter into swines who throw themselves into Lake Tiberiades (I Mat. viii, 30-32; Mark v, 9-13).

The proper and distinctive character of the possession is, therefore, the total or partial loss of reason and will, produced through the habitation of the demon in the body of the possessed. The actions of the unfortunate, his words and, to a certain point, his thoughts, are those of the evil spirit and not his own; he has in some manner lost his personality, or at least he has in him a real duality; he is under the power, under the tyranny of the demon; he may struggle against this odious burden and temporarily succeed in ridding himself of it, but soon he falls again under the dreadful influence in spite of all his efforts to reconquer his independence from the control of his oppressor; it is the wicked spirit that speaks through his mouth, he is the instrument and organ; this lamentable state ceases only when the Saviour has miraculously expelled the demon (Mat. viii, 29-31; Mark i, 24; v, 7, 9, 12; Luke iv, 41; viii, 27-39; Acts x, 38).

Objection is urged against the reality of demoniacal possession, because we find no mention of them in the Old Testament; St. John does not speak of them in his

Gospel, and finally, because they are unknown in our days, or rather are known to be only simple and natural pathological states.

The illnesses which the contemporary physicians identify with the ancient possessions are different from them, as one can determine by the characters we have indicated. Exaltation of the imagination could not have effected a cure of the disorders attested to by the Gospels in the cases of some of those possessed: thus, the demoniacs of Gadara, who were neither epileptics nor hysterics, but furiously insane persons (Mark v, 2-5). Imagination could never have cured these furious hallucinations. All the miraculous cures of the New Testament, and in particular those of the possessed, are entirely different from subjects remedied by hypnotism — another explanation of the driving out of the demons. That to this day there are people possessed of demons is attested on the authority of missionaries in pagan countries who not infrequently meet with them. And who can affirm that there are none such among us?

But, however this may be, the actual ceasing of the possessions would not prove that they did not exist in the time of our Lord, nor the non-existence before Christ. God could have given this power to the demon during the stay of Christ on earth, and neither before nor afterwards, just as He has permitted the frequency of certain miracles in the early days of the Church, which ceased to occur afterwards. Moreover, the possessions could have existed without history mentioning them. But the records of the Church testify that they have been frequently noted after Christ, although they were more common during the Apostolic Age because God wished to attest in this way how great in that time was the sway of Satan, and the magnitudinous power of the Son of God over the prince of demons. The curing of the possessed commanded the attention of the pagans, and the authors of the Apologies in favor of the Christian religion, did not hesitate to draw attention to the power of the Exorcist over these victims of the evil spirit (Cf. St. Justin, Apol. i, 6 vol. vi, col. 453-456). As to St. John, the Evangelist, when he has not related expressly curings of demoniacs, it is because one of the objects of the Gospel was to complete the account of the three Synoptics, and hence it was not necessary for him to report their testimony in this particular. However, he did speak of demoniacs (John x, 21.)

The possessions, therefore, are well evidenced facts, however extraordinary they may appear and, indeed, science in our days does not explain them at all; their curing remains a miracle, which a divine power alone is capable of producing.

CHAPTER LIX.

THE SO-CALLED BRETHREN OF OUR LORD.

ABOUT the end of the fourth century, a certain Helvidius, obscure man, who is known to us only by the refutation which St. Jerome has left us of his errors, dared to maintain that the Blessed Virgin Mary, after the birth of her divine Son, had from her marriage with St. Joseph other children, called in the Gospel brothers and sisters of Jesus. This monstrous doctrine which overthrew the dogma of perpetual virginity of the Mother of God, excited all over a great horror and indignation. St. Jerome wrote against it his "Libellus adversus Helvidium."

Helvidius pretended to support his opinion on numerous testimonies of the Holy Scripture. First, he quoted in his favor the text of St. Matthew (i, 18): "Before they came together she was found with child, of the Holy Ghost." Therefore, he said, they came together later on; why, besides, the marriage of St. Joseph and Mary, if they had not the intention to consummate their union? St. Jerome opposes to the alleged text several places of Scripture, where a *priusquam* does not suppose the ulterior realization of the thing which one says to have not yet arrived. He adds the argument *ad hominem:* "If I would say: Helvidius was surprised by death before having done penance, would it follow from this that he did penance after the decease?"— Besides the honor of Jesus and his mother required that the latter was acknowledged as the legitimate spouse of Joseph.

Another not less futile argument of the innovator was drawn because in St. Luke Jesus is called the "firstborn" of Mary (Luke ii, 7). Therefore, said Helvidius, Mary had several children; if not, why to speak of her firstborn? One should have said *only son.* This sophism rests upon a confusion of ideas. Every only child is a firstborn; every firstborn is not an only child, but may be this. Do we not say every day that a mother died in bringing forth her first child? Also, the law of Moses (Exod. xxxiv, 19-20), ordaining to offer to the Lord every firstborn of the male sex, found its application when the mother had given birth to a son; one did not need to wait for the birth of the second child.

The third argument is still less solid. St. Matthew says of St. Joseph (i, 25): "He knew her not (matrimonially) till she brought forth her firstborn." Therefore, he says, Joseph knew his spouse after this event. The falsity of a similar conclusion is set off right away when we compare these words with a parallel text (Deut. xxxiv, 6): "And no man hath known of his sepulchre until this present day." Now, it is well known that the tomb of Moses was never discovered.

The last argument upon which this insultor of the Mother of God insists the most is the frequent mention in the New Testament of brothers and sisters of Jesus. To show that this term must be taken in its strictest sense, and to designate maternal brethren of the Saviour, Helvidius alleges the testimony of St. Matthew and of St. Mark, who make assist at the agony of Jesus upon the cross, Mary, mother of James and of Joseph, and Salome, the mother of the two sons of Zebedee. He pretends that the Mary, mother of James and Joseph, is the Mother of Jesus and that, consequently, James the Minor and Joseph are the children of the Mother of Jesus, and the maternal brethren of the latter. He pretends to prove his assertion as follows: "We know through St. John that Mary, Mother of Jesus, was standing near the cross. Matthew and Mark could not omit this. Hence, the woman whom they call Mary, mother of James and of Joseph, is none other than the Mother of Jesus."

But, we ask in our turn, when these two narrators wished to tell us that the Mother of Jesus was there, how could it enter their mind to designate her by the name of mother of James and of Joseph? Why did they not call her simply: *the Mother of Jesus?* When the silence which they keep about this has something surprising, the supposition of the adversary is quite simply absurd. One might, in this regard, also ask him how St. John in the enumeration which he makes of the holy women standing near the cross, could omit his own mother Salome? All can be explained without great difficulty, when one admits that all the women named by the different Evangelists, did not remain constantly upon Calvary, gathered in the same group during the whole time when Jesus remained on the cross, but that they exchanged places. Were they all there already at the moment when Jesus spoke to His mother and John? Were there not some that came only after the death of Christ? The Synoptics speak only about them after having related the death of Jesus. As to the Mary, mother of James and of Joseph, she is designated by St. John under the name of Mary of Cleophas. In fact, we shall prove further on that Cleophas was the father of James the Minor.

The Evangelists designate nominally as brothers of Jesus four personages: James, Joseph or Joses, Simon and Jude (Mat. xiii, 55; Mark vi, 3). Mary, mother of James and of Joses (Vulgate Joseph) which, according to St. Matthew, kept herself near the cross upon Calvary, is called by St. Mark (xv, 40), Mary, mother of James the Minor. This James the Minor, called thus to distinguish him from another more aged namesake, James the Major, son of Zebedee, can be only James, son of Alpheus, also a disciple of Jesus, and one of the twelve apostles. This conclusion could be shaken only if among the disciples of the Saviour there had been a third James, as some really pretend, but without any solid foundation. Be this as it may, to establish accord between St. John and the first two Evangelists in the description of the scenes upon Calvary, nothing is more natural to identify Mary, mother of James the Minor with Mary of Cleophas, sister of the Mother of Jesus. When this genitive relates the relation of wife to husband, Clepohas would be the husband of the sister of the Blessed Virgin. Therefore, he would be the father of James the Minor, and the latter would be the nephew of the Blessed Virgin, or at least a near relative of hers. James the Minor and James, son of Alpheus, would be one and the same personage, if Alpheus and Cleophas are themselves one and the same individual. Now this appears out of doubt. For Alpheus is the Aramaic name for *Cholphai*, whence by a metathesis *Klopai* or *Klopa*, which is the Greek name of Cleophas.

Now, uniting the accounts of Hegesippus with those of the Evangelists, we arrive at the following conclusions: When the term *soror matris ejus* must be taken in the strict sense, Joseph and his brother Cleophas or Alpheus would have married two sisters called Mary; and James the Minor would be the first cousin of Jesus under a double title, as son of the sister of the Blessed Virgin, and as son of the brother of St. Joseph, foster-father of Jesus and real husband of His mother. The relationship would be less intimate from the side of the Blessed Virgin, if the latter were not the proper sister of the wife of Cleophas. This latter point remains doubtful, especially because one hardly admits that in one and the same family two sisters did carry the same name Mary.

Having thus established the relationship of James the Minor in regard to Jesus, one will admit, consequently, that Joses, also the son of Mary of Cleophas, is like James, his brother and first cousin of the Lord. It will be the same with Jude, called by St. Luke Judas Jacobi (Luke vi, 14-16; Acts 1, 13), that is, **Jude, brother of James**; for St. Jude, in the inscription of his Catholic Epistle, calls himself brother of James. Finally, the fourth first cousin of Jesus will be the Simon named in the Gospels, that is, Simeon, son of Cleophas, who succeeded St. James on the see of Jerusalem and suffered martyrdom in this city.

All the above leads us to count at least two of these brothers of the Lord among the twelve apostles, namely James and Jude. One may even ask whether the apostle Simon must not be identified with St. Simeon, the second bishop of Jerusalem. Antiquity tells us nothing about this identity, which the Biblical accounts render, however, very probable. The fourth, Joses, never belonged to the apostolic college. Had Jesus still other near relations, whose names are unknown to us, and to whom the Scriptures make allusion? This is quite probable. For in the Acts, St. Luke, enumerating the persons who withdrew into the Cenacle after the ascension of the Lord, names first all the apostles, then he adds: with the women and Mary the Mother of Jesus and His brethren. Jesus counted, therefore, several relatives outside the college of the apostles. Among these one will easily find those brethren of the Lord who, according to St. John, did not yet believe in Jesus, whilst the college of the Twelve was already constituted and had openly professed its faith in the divine mission of the Master (John vii, 3; Cf. John vi, 68-71).

It does not enter our plan to inquire whether there were really any of these cousins of our Lord among the apostles: this question is of little importance from the apologetical point of view.

CHAPTER LX.

THE ACTS OF THE APOSTLES.

THE Book of the Acts of the Apostles by its common allusions to the facts of the life of the Saviour, is a striking confirmation of the Evangelical accounts. It contains in itself an explanation of the events manifestly miraculous and of public notoriety; it touches with the finger, as it were, the supernatural intervention of heaven in the organization and propagation of the Church of Jesus Christ. Under these diverse titles this book becomes, no less than the Gospels, a shining mark for rationalistic attack. The veracity of the writing no fair minded person is willing to question, and no unbiased Biblical scholar will deny it as the Book of St. Luke. Unfortunately, however, men have been found in every age sceptical of established truths, and in the face of incontrovertible testimony. There are some who allege that the Acts of the Apostles is not the work of St. Luke, nor of his time, and base their doubt on the following reasons:

According to the Tübingen school, this book was the principal instrument designed to unify the two parties which had divided the Church of Christ. Indeed, nothing is more efficacious, in order to reconcile the Petrinians and Paulinians than to put into scene the two apostles, Peter and Paul, laboring in harmony at the organization of the work of Jesus. Peter receiving into the Church the first-fruits of the Gentiles, Paul practicing the Mosaic observances and collecting alms for the converted Jews, etc.

This is both a flimsy and false statement of facts, unsupported by any evidence or allusion in the Acts themselves, or by any unquestionable authority. However, it is our duty to prove the authenticity, integrity and veracity of this history of the primitive Church, and from sources too that will hardly be questioned by the adherents of the Tübingen school.

1. THE ACTS OF THE APOSTLES — THEIR AUTHENTICITY.

The Book of the Acts of the Apostles bears the imprint of authenticity. "The efforts they have made to prove that the third Gospel and the Acts are not from the same author, have remained quite fruitless," says Renan ("Les Evangeles," p. 436). The Acts are expressly quoted for the first time in the letter of the Churches of Lyons and Vienne to the Churches of Asia and Phrygia, in A. D. 177. We find them afterwards mentioned by most of the Fathers and Doctors: St. Irenæus, Clement of Alexandria, Tertullian, Origen. In the famous passage where he enumerates the writings of the New Testament Eusebius in his "Church History" (iii, 25, vol. xx, 269), ranks the Acts of the Apostles amongst those which are admitted authentic by the whole Christian world.

Evidently, the Book of the Acts carries the mark of the epoch in which it was composed. "The gaiety, the youthfulness of heart which these Odyssies breathe," says Renan "was something new, original and charming. The Acts of the Apostles, expression of the first movement of the Christian conscience, is a book of joy, of serene order. Since the Homeric poems they had not seen a work so full of fresh sensations. An early breeze, a sea of odor, if I may express myself thus, inspiring of something cheerful and strong, penetrates the whole book and makes an excellent travelling companion; the exquisite breviary of the one who pursues antique traces about the southern seas. It was the second poetry of Christianism. Lake Tiberias and its fishing barges had furnished the first. The prefaces which are at the head of both writings (the third Gospel and the Acts), the dedication of the two to Theophilus, the perfect resemblance of style and ideas furnish, . . . abundant proofs" (Renan "Les Apotres," p. 10), that St. Luke did compile the history of the foundation of the Church, like he did the history of its founder, and it is too apparent to need further proof.

2. ACTS OF THE APOSTLES — THEIR INTEGRITY.

Regarding the integrity of the Acts, they have alleged that the change one remarks in the second part of the book, where the author speaks in the first person, " that the passages where the pronoun *us* is found, have been copied by the last writer of the Acts in an anterior writing; in the original memoirs of the writings of St. Paul, of Timothy for instance, and that the writer, by an oversight, would have forgotten to substitute to us, the name of the narrator."

"This explanation," says Renan, "is hardly admissible. Such a negligence one would understand for the most in a rough compilation. But the third Gospel and the Acts forms a work very well drawn up, composed with reflection, and even with art, written by the same hand, and after a followed plan. The two books form an absolute whole of the same style, presenting the same favorite locations and the same manner to quote the Scripture. Such a shocking fault as that in question would be inexplicable. Hence, we are invincibly moved to conclude that the one who wrote the end of the work wrote also its beginning, and that the narrator of the whole is the one in the above quoted passage." (Renan, "Les Apotres," p. 11-12). Hence, we have every assurance, even from the infidel Renan, that the integrity of the Acts is as firmly established as is their authenticity.

3. ACTS OF THE APOSTLES — THEIR VERACITY.

A notable point in the author of the Acts is his familiarity of the subjects which he relates. Of all the Books of Holy Writ, none covers such a vast field, or is more familiar to the Jews. St. Luke leads us into Syria, Cyprus, Asia Minor, Greece and Italy. His accounts are full of allusions to the history, morals, customs and religions of the peoples who inhabit these countries, even the customs of navigation of his time, subjects so varied, and in the midst of the mass of details he moves with the greatest ease, and expresses himself with absolute confidence about persons, places and things; also with an exactitude which only a witness — an ocular, intelligent, attentive and conscientious one could possess. However, when it is possible to control his narrative by profane sources, and this is quite often the case, the trial is much in his favor. The most persistent and exacting Rationalist has only found three points of small consequence to question in the Acts, and by a curious singularity, they have reference to Jewish, and not to foreign history.

Outside these episodes, Rationalism can discover nothing in a book so full of facts, to contest its historical value. It is reduced to the sheer necessity of maintaining that the author did knowingly alter the events he reports for the purpose of giving them a meaning which they have not in reality. We propose to discuss these objections consecutively, and show wherein they are wanting in veracity.

4. ACTS OF THE APOSTLES — ANSWERS TO PRETENDED ERRORS.

The errors which Rationalists pretend to discover in the Acts are the following: The author has deceived himself as to the date of Theudas, and about the circumstances of the insurrection caused by an Egyptian; moreover, it is incredible, as St. Luke pretends, that St. Paul, when asked for the high priest at Jerusalem, ignored what was the dignity of the one before whom he had to answer.

Renan, speaking of St. Luke and the subject of the first objection, affirms without hesitation: "He commits errors of chronology. Before Judas, the Gaulonite, the Acts place another agitator, called Theudas; but this is an anachronism; the movement of Theudas took place in the year 44 A. D."

Thus, according to Renan, St. Luke was certainly deceived. But behold the truth: Gamaliel, member of the Sanhedrim, in the discourse which he pronounced in favor of the apostles brought before the great Jewish council, says among other things, when referring to the different revolters: "Before these days there has been a Theudas who believed himself something, and who had as followers about four hundred men; he was killed, and all those who had believed in him became dispersed, and were reduced to nothing. After him arose Judas, the Galilean" (Acts v. 36-37). The latter is mentioned by Josephus in the same epoch as by Gamaliel (Jos. Jew. Anti., xviii, 1); hence, one does not raise any objection to this point, but it is not the same in the case of Theudas, of whom also the Pharisean orator speaks, according to the rationalistic critics. The Theudas mentioned by Gamaliel has lived at a date anterior to that of Judas the Galilean, for the revolter of this name, of whom there is question in the "Jewish Antiquities," and who must be one and the same person, as alleged by infidels, revolted only about ten years after the discourse of Gamaliel, under Cuspius Fadus. Hence, there is an anachronism in the account of the Acts.

If there is a contradiction here between the two historians on the date of a certain revolter, nothing obliges us to prefer Josephus to St. Luke. The former has often been found in error, and numerous inaccuracies have been established against him—even formal contradictions between his "Jewish Antiquities" and "War of the Jews," whilst the author of the Acts proves a wonderful exactitude in all parts of his account, which could be verified. In the present case, his testimony merits the fullest confidence, because he was the companion of St.

Paul, who had been himself a disciple of Gamaliel, orator of the Sanhedrim. But the point is not established at all that the Theudas of Josephus is the Theudas of St. Luke; and we can without much difficulty, admit both accounts true. The name alone is common to both writers. Now, two revolters of the same name could very easily have raised disturbances within a few years. Even Josephus, since the death of Herod I, till the taking of Jerusalem by Titus, mentions five conspirators by the name of Simon, and three by the name of Judas: Judas the Galilean, also called Gaulonite, of whom Gamaliel speaks; Judas son of Ezechias and Judas, son of Saphore. In spite of the considerable number of rebels, the remembrance of which the Jewish historian has preserved, it is quite probable he failed to enumerate all; therefore, in the present case, we have a perfect right to reject the account of Josephus and accept that of St. Luke. But this conclusion may be further strengthened by referring to the epoch of which Gamaliel speaks, and of which Josephus places the revolt of a certain Matthias (Anti. xvii, 6, 4). This Matthias might have been the Theudas or Theodas of St. Luke, for the names Matthias in Hebrew and Theodas (abridged from Theodoros) in the Greek, have the same meaning (Gift of God); therefore, the same person may have assumed both names, as it was quite customary among the Jews.

Again, what is further said about an Egyptian is not erroneous. When St. Paul was led before the tribunal of Lysias, at Jerusalem, this person asked him: "Art thou not the Egyptian who before these days raised a revolt, and didst lead forth into the desert four thousand men that were murderers?" (Acts xxi, 1-38). When

St. Luke could have been exactly informed about the facts he relates, this was certainly the case with regard to the captivity of his master St. Paul. But Josephus fails to report this event in the same manner, whence it follows according to the critics, that the author of the Acts was certainly deceived. Unfortunately for their part, Josephus has twice related the revolt of the Egyptian, and both accounts widely differ. According to the "War of the Jews" (ii, 8, 5), this foreigner making himself pass for a prophet, gathered 30,000 men and led them from the desert on Mount Olives, from where he threatened Jerusalem. The inhabitants of this city joined the Romans to combat him; the most of his followers perished or were captured; the others became dispersed; the leader himself took to flight. We find in the "Jewish Antiquities" (xx, 8-16), the Egyptian seduced the multitude and drew them along on Mount of Olives, with the promise that the walls of Jerusalem would fall before him. The Procurator Felix unmasked the false prophet, attacked him on Mount of Olives, killed four hundred of the rebels and made two hundred prisoners; their seducer succeeded in escaping. Here we find that the thirty thousand men led from the desert in one account have dwindled down to four hundred in the other account, and furthermore, that most of the thirty thousand perished or were made prisoners.

The third objection which they find against the veracity of the Acts is made quite serious. When the high priest Ananias caused St. Paul to be beaten before the Sanhedrim, the apostle complained of being beaten contrary to law. The assistants cried out that he was wanting in respect to the high priest: "I know not" answered St. Paul "that he is the high priest" (Acts xxiii, 2-5). This is incredible! exclaim the infidels, St. Paul not knowing the high priest. Nothing, however, is more easy to explain: Ananias, son of Zebedee, exercised the sovereign priesthood of the council about the time St. Paul was arraigned, but he was deposed shortly afterward and sent a prisoner to Rome by Quadratus, legate of Syria (Anti. xx, 5-2). Claudius granted right to Ananias, consequently, they had to give him his liberty, but during his absence one was put in his place; Jonathan, his successor, was killed by order of Felix, before the revolt of the Egyptian, and before the arrest of St. Paul. At the moment when the apostle was brought before him, the sovereign pontiff was without title (Anti. viii, 5-8). Ananias in the quality of ancient high priest, fulfilled certain functions of the priesthood during the vacancy, which explains to us why he presided over the Sanhedrim, and also why the apostle ignored he was high priest. Indeed, he was not the high priest, properly speaking. St. Paul, without discussing his title, had a perfect right to say he did not know he was speaking to the pontiff.

To explain in a natural manner the origin of Christianity, infidels assert that the Acts are partial writings, composed with the view of reconciling and uniting the two opposed factions, which sprung up among the disciples of Christ regarding Peter and Paul.

In answer to this charge we can say that the author of the Acts did not seek to alter the truth in order to reconcile the followers of Peter with those of Paul. So little did he think of setting off the apostolate of St. Paul at the expense of historic exactitude, that he himself furnishes the strongest argument one could allege against his mission, if it had been "contested," as modern infidels affirm. Indeed, St. Luke relates that immediately after the Ascension, when there was a question to complete the Apostolic College, and to choose a new member to replace Judas Iscariot, St. Peter indicated beforehand, as a condition of the choice to be made, that the elected must have accompanied the Saviour since the baptism of John until the Ascension (Acts i, 21). St. Paul did not fulfill this condition. Later on, after his conversion, the Acts report again that Peter, in another discourse, calls "preordained witnesses of the Resurrection of Christ," those who did eat and drink with Jesus risen, a necessary condition for election. Surely, nothing obliged St. Luke to record these words in his writings; manifestly a desire to relate the truth in all its details was the motive which prompted him.

It was far from St. Luke's thoughts to flatter the Judaizers with the view of reconciling them with the other followers, or to bring them to an understanding with one another. He reminds us continually of the stubborness of the Jews, which he certainly would have avoided if he had at heart these sentiments, falsely attributed to him. Already St. Peter, in his first discourses, reproaches the Jews for what they had done against the Saviour (Acts ii, 23). St. Stephen treats them as stiff-necked, uncircumcised in heart, and ears that always resist the Holy Ghost (Acts vii, 51, 53). St. Paul himself applies to them the words of Isaias: "The heart of this people is grown gross, and with their ears have heard heavily, and their eyes they have shut, lest perhaps they should see with their eyes and hear with their ears, and understand with their heart, and should be converted" (Acts xxviii, 27).

How can one maintain that a writing which has so little consideration for the Jews, and which reproaches them for their obstinacy and prejudice, is a book of reconciliation, an instrument designed to bring on the Judaizers to the ideas of St. Paul?

CHAPTER LXI.

ST. PAUL'S EPISTLE TO THE GALATIANS.

THE authenticity of the Epistle of St. Paul to the Galatians is not questioned by anybody, but the rationalistic criticism seeks to exploit it in order to break down the Acts of the Apostles. We will show that there exists no contradiction between the Acts of the Apostles and the Epistle to the Galatians, after having established first that the Cephas, whom St. Paul resists, according to the account he makes to the Galatians, is really the Apostle St. Peter, although some Catholic commentators maintain the contrary.

1. THE CEPHAS OF THE EPISTLE TO THE GALATIANS.

St. Paul, in speaking of a personage whom he calls Cephas, relates in the Epistle to the Galatians that he "withstood him to his face" Gal. ii, 11). This Cephus must have had a real importance, because the apostle of the nations, whose zeal knew no obstacles, quoted as an example of energy the fact of his having resisted him. Also, the most of the Fathers and commentators have believed at all times that this personage was no other than St. Peter, whose Aramean name was, indeed, Cephas. Nevertheless, since St. Paul writes that he not only "withstood him to the face," but that he resisted to him "because he was to be blamed," there have been for a long time interpreters who cannot believe that the Cephas was the chief of the Church, and they maintain that he is one of the seventy-two disciples. The Rationalists, in agreement this time with the majority of Catholics, on the contrary, do not doubt that Cephas is Peter. In our opinion it is the only interpretation which can be defended, and we do not hesitate to acknowledge it. During the first six centuries of the Church, all the writers who occupied themselves with this question have recognized St. Peter in the Cephas of the Epistle to the Galatians, with the exception of Clement of Alexandria in a work without historical value, and the falsifier who has manufactured, under the name of Dorotheus of Tyre, the apocryphal catalogue of the disciples of the Saviour. The scholastics have not believed otherwise than the Fathers. During the whole Middle Age, we do not meet with one single writer who does not identify with St. Peter the Cephas of the Epistle to the Galatians.

The disciple Cephas finds only adherents after the rise of Protestantism. The Catholics then had to defend against the new heretics the infallibility and the dignity of St. Peter. Several among them believed that the best means to justify the chief of the Church in this circumstance was to maintain that there was not question of St. Peter; but the most prudent and most circumspect were very careful to claim for their opinions only a pure probability.

As to the infallibility of the Pope, it does not enter more into question than the veracity of the Acts of the Apostles. There was no discord of doctrine, but only of conduct between St. Peter and St. Paul. The Council of Jerusalem had decided that the converted pagans were not obliged to submit to circumcision, and to legal observances; it prescribed nothing as to the subject of the Jewish-Christians. Hence, these preserved their freedom. They were free to continue the observance of the law, because it was difficult to break all at once with long established customs, and those among them who lived in Judea believed it expedient to follow the social, religious and civil customs. It was with this motive that St. Paul caused his disciple Timothy to be circumcised. The synagogue should be buried with honor. But although it was permitted to the Jewish-Christians to submit themselves to the legal prescriptions, they were not obliged to do so. Where the Hellenist element dominated in the new Church, the result of the Council of Jerusalem must have been the prompt abandonment of the Mosaic observances. It was this that took place at Antioch. As the pagan converts here formed the majority, the Jewish-Christians among them soon abandoned the Jewish customs.

In this state of things it is quite natural that St. Peter, on his arrival at the capital of Syria, lived there with the Christians, who, contrary to the Jewish customs, had not been circumcised, and had with them the relations which he had already formed with the centurion Cornelius. That he did this is evidenced in the Epistle to the Galatians. St. Paul lived like the Jews at Jerusalem (I Cor. ix. 20, etc.). St. Peter lived like the Gentiles at Antioch. But an unforeseen incident came to trouble the harmony. Jewish-Christians having arrived from Palestine in Antioch, St. Peter found himself in great embarrassment. There are situations where it is very difficult to determine immediately which is the best course to follow. No question of principles was at stake; faith was not at all interested, and nevertheless to decide what action to take was very difficult. The newcomers, accustomed to observe the law in Palestine, did not wish, according to the Jewish custom, to eat with the noncircumcised Christians, and, as we have seen, they had a right to act thus. If St. Peter did not imitate them, he offended his brethren of Jerusalem; if he ceased to eat with the noncircumcised, he wounded the new Christians of pagan origin. What alternative was the better? How remedy the difficulty? Both sides had claims which must be respected. St. Peter was charged with the Gospel of the circumcision. In the fear undoubtedly that the Jewish-Christians would deny him in all Palestine, and cause him to lose, by accusing him to be lacking of respect for the law, the esteem he stood in need of in order to establish the faith with success among his brethren, the chief of the apostles decided to separate himself from his noncircumcised brethren and to live anew as a Jew, i. e., as a Jewish-Christian. Did he thus commit an error of doctrine? Certainly not. No point of faith was endangered. Had he the right to act as he did? Unquestionably, because the Council of Jerusalem had not affirmed, in this regard, any line of conduct. Jew by birth, he was authorized to observe the law, as St. Paul did himself when he was at Jerusalem. He merely followed the course which presented the least inconvenience. But by choosing thus, was it the best course, to avoid scandalizing the Jewish-Christians?

St. Paul did not think so. Every converted Jew had the right to observe the law, but St. Peter was the chief of the Church and, on account of the high dignity, his example had particular weight. His conduct would give the impression that the legal ceremonies of the Jews were always rigorously obligatory and not simply optional. These consequences followed immediately. All the converted Jews of the capital of Syria, Barnabas himself, the companion of St. Paul, considered it their duty to imitate St. Peter. The importance attached to his conduct, the influence which it exerted, proclaims very well that it was not the act of an unknown disciple, but of the prince of the apostles. Hence its great importance. If Cephas were merely a disciple he would not have commanded this attention. But being St. Peter, the consequences were pernicious: he disturbed the harmony which reigned in the Christian community of Antioch. The converted pagans who were the most numerous, found themselves as if excommunicated, and by their own bishop. St. Peter did not dare any longer to have relations with them. They complained and blamed St. Peter: this is the meaning of the Greek text, which has not, like the Vulgate, that Cephas was "blamable," but that he was "blamed." Then St. Paul undertook their defence publicly, "to the face," not in secret, because it was only a public act that could cease the division introduced at Antioch. In his Epistle, he designates the conduct of the chief of the apostles with "dissimulation," wishing to show thereby that St. Peter, although he knew he could have relations with noncircumcised, deprived himself thereof as if he had no right to do so. However, St. Paul did not contest that the Jewish-Christians could legitimately live as Jews, but he demanded that the converted Gentiles be not rejected and oppressed. The chief of the Church recognized the justness of the claim. He beheld the consequences of his conduct and, undoubtedly, proclaimed openly that it was permitted to all to have relations with the Hellenist-Christians.

Such is the episode of Antioch; such is the explanation of the account of the Epistle to the Galatians. St. Peter did not err at all in the doctrine; his pontifical infallibility does not enter the question; only he adopted a line of conduct which led to irregularities; the mistake was pointed out by St. Paul and humbly acknowledged by St. Peter. The humility of the prince of the apostles had its good results; it was decisive; it put an end to all the difficulties which, without the circumstance would have often been renewed. The ensemble and the details of the conflict, far from being irreconcilable with the dignity of the Head of the Church, on the contrary, increased his authority and power. They show the importance of his position. All is explained easily, when there is question of the first Pope; all is unintelligible, when applied to an obscure disciple, called Cephas. St. Paul considers his action as one of courage; he has presumed to advise his hierarchical superior, as St. Bernard will, later on in his book "On Consideration," give advice to Pope Eugen III; but even St. Paul's language implies the primacy of Peter, instead of denying it as the Protestants deny. The former has said, in advance of the passage in discussion (Gal. i, 18), that he went to Jerusalem to see Peter, or, as the Greek text has it, Cephas, whom he thus considers as his chief. When

St. Paul resists him, it is not to disown his authority. On the contrary, the language of St. Paul, understood correctly, precious in proportion to its indirectness, is an homage rendered to the primacy of the Holy See. The Epistle to the Galatians does not contain, therefore, any attack on the power of St. Peter. We will now show that it is not at all in contradiction with the Acts of the Apostles.

CONFORMITY OF THE EPISTLE TO THE GALATIANS WITH THE ACTS OF THE APOSTLES.

Objection is made, in the first place, to the exactitude of the narrative of the Acts, where St. Paul in his Epistle to the Galatians relates the dissent that took place between the Christians of Jewish origin and those of Pagan origin in quite another manner than St. Luke. We have two versions, it is said, of the same fact, and these two versions are in contradiction. Which is the true one? Evidently that of St. Paul who has been so intimately connected with the quarrel, and who played the chief role therein.

It is certain that St. Paul, in the second chapter of his Epistle to the Galatians, alludes to several facts which St. Luke relates in the Acts, but there exists no contradiction between the two sacred writers. Only St. Luke, writing a history, presents the events as an historian, stating the origin of the quarrel, its diverse peripetiæ and its conclusion, while the apostle of the nations, addressing a letter to the Galatians with a quite determined object, refers to these events only in so far as it is necessary and useful to his purpose. In both accounts, Peter and James maintain the right of St. Paul (Acts xv, 7-10; 13-21; Gal. ii, 9): this is the fundamental feature. The rest is accessory and without consequence. St. Paul writes to the Galatians that he had gone to Jerusalem " by revelation " (Gal. ii, 2), that is, by order of God, whilst, according to St. Luke, this apostle was sent on a mission (Acts xv, 2) into the capital of Judea by the faithful of Antioch. They desire to see in this a contradiction. In reality there is none. Whatever the precise sense may be of the Greek original, interpreters are not agreed, but it is certain that St. Paul means to say that he went to Jerusalem in obedience to the will of God, which does not contradict at all the account of the Acts. The latter, speaking of the council, enters into details which St. Paul omits, because he does not need to speak of them, but both affirm in the same way that the Apostles gave right to the preacher of the nations, and this is the sole essential point.

The rationalistic critic pretends to discover another contradiction between the Acts and the Epistle of St. Paul. St. Luke says that the apostle passed only through Galatia (Acts xvi, 6; xviii, 23); the apostle himself, by his letter, proves that he sojourned for a long time in these countries.

The contradiction is only an apparent one. Renan himself ("St. Paul," p. 51) has proved that it is only in the terminology, and that both accounts agree perfectly in meaning. " Paul," he says, " was in the habit of designating each country by the administrative name. Asia, Macedonia, Achaia, in his terminology refer to the provinces which were so called, and not the countries thus named before. The countries which he had evangelized from Antioch in Pisidia until Derbe, was called by him Galatia; the Christians of this country were for him the Galatians. By this we can explain that unique peculiarity of the Epistle to the Galatians, that it is not addressed to a particular Church. By this, we can also explain one of the apparent singularities of the life of St. Paul. The Epistle to the Galatians supposes that St. Paul makes among those to whom this letter is addressed a long sojourn; that he had with them intimate relations, at least was as intimate with them as with the Corinthians and Thessalonians. Now, properly speaking, the Acts do not mention the evangelization of Galatia. In a second voyage, Paul *passes through the country of Galatia.* St. Luke understands by this Galatia a distinct place, which he distinguishes from Pisidia (Acts xvi, 6; xiv, 23) and from Lycaonia (xiv, 6), whilst St. Paul understood by the name Galatia "an artificial agglomeration, corresponding to the transient reunion of provinces which had been formed by the Galatian King Amyntas. This personage after the battle of the Phillipians and the death of Dejotar, received from Antonius, Pisidia, then Galatia, with a portion of Lyconia and Pamphylia. . . . All these countries, at his death, formed one sole Roman province. The province which bore the name of Galatia in the official nomenclature, at least under the Greek Cæsars, comprised therefore, certainly: 1. Galatia properly speaking; 2. Lycaonia; 3. Pisidia, etc." (Renan, "St. Paul" pp. 48-49). St. Luke and St. Paul do not, therefore, contradict themselves; their apparent divergency is even a proof of the perfect exactitude of both, because both express themselves in a very correct manner, although in a different way.

CHAPTER LXII.

ST. PAUL'S EPISTLES TO THE THESSALONIANS.

THE authenticity of St. Paul's Epistles to the Thessalonians had never been contested until Christian Schmid came to the fore with objections in 1804. His attacks, however, were unnoticed until the epoch when his opinion was embraced by Bauer's school. Bauer rejected the two Epistles to the Thessalonians. However, not all his disciples did follow him on this ground; the most even admitted the authenticity of the first letter to the Thessalonians, and to-day they limit themselves to a denial of the second. But the Paulinian origin of neither can be seriously contested. The Muratorian Canon expressly names the two Epistles to the Thessalonians. St. Irenæus often quotes them in Gaul, Tertullian in Africa, and Clement of Alexandria in Egypt, so that at the end of the second century the belief of the entire Church was unanimous in regard to these letters.

The two Epistles to the Thessalonians are attacked *for doctrinal* reasons. "The sole serious objection which had been raised against the Epistle to the Thessalonians," says Renan, "derives itself from the theory of the "Antichrist" exposed in the second chapter of the second letter to the Thessalonians, . . . but this objection can be answered." The ideas here developed by St. Paul are found indeed in his other letters. The two Epistles to the Thessalonians are the most ancient in date. They were written before the Epistles to the Corinthians and to the Galatians. The subject treated therein by the apostle, is among others the resurrection of the dead. He returns to this in writing to the Corinthians (I Cor. xv.). Hence this thought was familiar to him. Several features we meet in the Epistles to the Thessalonians are also met in the pictures, which St. Luke, his Evangelist, forms in describing the last arrival of the Saviour. The second Epistle to the Thessalonians adds another particular, that of the apostasy which will take place at the end of time, but the same idea is found in St. Luke (xvii, 8); hence we can find no evidence in this against the authenticity of the epistle.

We must remark, however, that which St. Paul writes about the coming of our Lord furnishes grounds for a difficulty not so easily answered; not in regard to the authenticity of his letters, but as to the idea which the apostle had of the coming of the Saviour. This difficulty applies itself particularly to the Epistle to the Thessalonians; it is also found in other epistles. But, say the Rationalists, the apostles and Jesus Christ Himself, at least by intervals, believed that the events of the Last Judgment would be near. "The words of Jesus," says Renan, "could not give rise to any difficulty." But our Saviour expressly declared that His Father alone knew the hour of the Last Judgment. — What He had announced as near at hand, and that would occur before the present generation had passed away, was the ruin of Jerusalem, which was accomplished as He had foretold.

But had the apostles not misunderstood the Master? Jesus having spoken after the fashion of the prophets who did not distinguish the epochs in their oracles of the future, and who did not mark with precision the chronological succession of time, did His disciples not suppose that what should take place long afterwards was really at hand? Did not St. Paul in particular believe that he would see with his mortal eyes, before his death, the triumphal arrival of the Saviour, when he wrote to the Thessalonians: " This we say unto you in the words of the Lord, that we who are alive, who remain unto the coming of our Lord shall not prevent them who have slept?" (Thess. iv, 14.) These words so similar to many others we read in the New Testament, have appeared so decisive to a great number of Protestants, that they believed St. Paul was in error in regard to the epoch of the second coming of Jesus Christ, and that he really believed the end of all things earthly was at hand.

We have to admit that the expressions of St. Paul can be understood in this sense, and the proof for this is that, among the Thessalonians, there were many who so understood him, because the apostle explains to them in his second epistle, and declares that another meaning must be attached to his words (Cf. ii, Thess. ii, 1-2). But we have to add that it was by taking these words detached, without keeping account of the context, that the Thessalonians interpreted falsely the first epistle, on account of the natural fear which the thought of the approachment of the judgment of God has always produced. The human mind easily adopts the interpretations of this kind. But what the apostle said, a little further on, clearly proclaims that he did not believe the second coming of the Saviour at hand. "But of the times and moments, brethren, you need not that we should write to you, for yourselves know perfectly that the day of the Lord shall come, as a thief in the night" (I Thess. v, 1-2). Thus he recalls to their mind the same words of our Lord, as given in the Gospels (Mat. xxiv, 43; Luke xii, 49). Hence, St. Paul does not retract in the second Epistle to the Thessalonians what he had written in the first. It was only by not paying attention to what he had said of the incertitude of the moment when the Lord will come that one could misunderstand him. In several of his epistles he supposes that he will not live until the return of the Saviour: "I desire to be dissolved, and to be with Christ," he writes to the Phillipians (Phil. i, 23). In the first Epistle to the Thessalonians, we read nothing of the contrary. It is only in taking the pronoun "we" at the foot of the letter that one can attach to it a false meaning. The most of the Fathers of the Church have seen with right in this expression a change of mode of person; he does not designate himself by this word, but the faithful who will live in the epoch of the coming of our Lord. "He does not say *we* of himself," remarks St. John Chrysostom, "for he should not live until the resurrection, but he understands thereby the faithful." (Hom. vii, 2, in I Thess. vol. lxii).

CHAPTER LXIII.

PASTORAL EPISTLES OF ST. PAUL.

THE authenticity of the Pastoral Epistles of St. Paul, that is of his two letters to Timothy and that to Titus, has been universally accepted until our century. At the beginning of this century some rejected the first Epistle to Timothy, under pretext that it was in part manufactured from, and was an imitation of, the other pastoral epistles which they admitted as authentic. In our days the Rationalists have gone further: they have rejected the three letters entire.

According to these the Epistles to Titus and Timothy are not and cannot be authentic, because they speak of the ecclesiastical hierarchy which could not yet have existed in the time of the apostle of the Gentiles. Their whole system attempts to place the origin of Christianity within the course of a progressive and natural solution; the organization of the Church was the work of time and not that of Jesus Christ and the apostles. As these epistles demolish the rationalistic thesis, Bauer and his followers are under the necessity of relegating them to the second century. However, history will not conform itself to rationalistic systems *a priori;* it is for the systems not to contradict history. Eusebius of Cæsarea counts the three Pastoral Epistles among the writings of the New Testament, which are accepted by all without dispute. Before him Pope

Clement, contemporary of St. Paul, had made about twenty allusions to them in his first letter to the Corinthians. St. Ignatius, martyr, and St. Polycarp knew them equally well. It is useless to quote further — these names are sufficient guarantee of the antiquity of the Pastoral Epistles.

As to the objections alleged against their authenticity, they consist in picking out from them pretended historical errors. The principal grounds for objection are thus stated: " The organization of the Churches, the hierarchy, the presbyterial and episcopal power are much more developed than it is possible to suppose them in the last years of St. Paul's life." — It is easy to answer this assertion: It is true that the Pastoral Epistles suppose that there are, in the Christian communities, bishops, priests and deacons; it is true that one of the chief injunctions in the letters to Timothy and Titus recommends them to intrust to worthy pastors the care of souls, and to instruct the pastors as to their duties, but this can be easily understood. The apostles could not be without help and colaborers. They also needed successors. Timothy and Titus were the auxiliaries of the first disciples of the Saviour; they were in need of help in their turn, and as the choice of the ministers of the Church is of the highest importance, St. Paul counsels them on this grave matter. What is more natural? Even if no testimony had made known to us the existence of this organization, it is indispensable, so evident, that it must result from the necessity which Christianity had for chiefs to thrive and perpetuate itself. — But besides this reason, drawn from the very nature of things, we have positive evidence which confirms the truth of all that is stated in the Pastoral Letters. In the Epistle to Titus the establishment of the priesthood is especially recommended for the city of Crete (I Tit. i, 5, 7). It is the same thing we read in the Acts of the Apostles, namely, that St. Paul established priests (bishops) in each Church (Acts xiv, 22). The author of the first Epistle to Timothy writes: "Neglect not the grace that is in thee which was given thee with imposition of the hands of the priesthood" (I Tim. iv, 14). One cannot pretend the imposition of the hands was unknown in the Apostolic Age, because in the Acts of the Apostles, we also behold an assembly of prophets and doctors who impose the hands on Paul and Barnabas (Acts xiii, 1-3).

The Pastoral Epistles mention also the deacons. The institution of the deacons is expressly mentioned in the Acts; hence, it cannot offer, and does not offer, indeed, any difficulty of correct interpretation. The epistle was written, therefore, in the time of the apostles, when deacons, priests, and bishops had been established, and whatever may be said to the contrary, the ecclesiastical body is of apostolic origin. This is a demonstrated historical fact. It is undeniable that in the second century the ecclesiastical hierarchy was solidly established in Asia, Italy, Greece, Gaul, and Africa. In all these countries, at the head of the churches, are priests placed under the government of a bishop: all the ancient monuments unanimously attest to this. Thus we find the sacred hierarchy established everywhere; we do not see its rise anywhere. When one seeks to discover where, and in what epoch, this organization originated, and what were the conditions of its early progress, he will find his efforts barren of results. This proves that it is as old as the Church itself, and that it is the work of the apostles. Nobody dare deny that St. James, the brother of St. Jude, was bishop of Jerusalem.

The Epistles of St. Paul least objected to allude to the origin concerning the ecclesiastical hierarchy. The apostle does not forget the gift of government in the enumeration of the gifts of the Holy Ghost (I Cor. xii, 7-10). The Epistle to the Ephesians speaks expressly of "pastors," in the same time when it speaks of the apostles and doctors (Ephes. iv, 11). The consecration of bread and wine mentioned in the first Epistle to the Corinthians (I Cor. xi, 23-26; Cf. x, 16-17), implies the existence of a consecrator, that is, of a priesthood. The Epistle to the Hebrews, which is certainly anterior to the Pastoral Epistles, speaks of the Christian priesthood (Heb. iv, 11).

The Apocalypse which dates from the last years of the first century (95), and which, even according to the infidels, embraces the year 68, shows us seven bishops presiding over the seven churches of Asia Minor of which it speaks. Therefore, the ecclesiastical hierarchy existed at that time. The letter of St. Clement to the Corinthians, composed undoubtedly about the end of the first century, between the years 91 and 110, clearly supposes the existence of the hierarchy, and it speaks of it as of an institution known by all the Christians and, consequently, already ancient. St. Clement, twenty years at most, after the death of St. Paul, reproaches the Corinthians for having driven away their bishop to replace him by another, and he says in distinctive terms that the bishops have been established by the apostles. The one who expresses himself thus is a Pope. Hence, we have here all the degrees of the hierarchical order in the first century of the Church.

The rationalistic critics also pretend that the widows of which there is mention in the first Epistle to Timothy (I Tim. v, 9-16) did not become ecclesiastical auxiliaries until the second century. This assertion is false. The first Epistle to the Corinthians speaks of certain women who exercised in the Church a ministry of charity (I Cor. ix, 5). St. Paul names Phebe, deaconess of the Church of Cenchrea. The institution, already established in 56 or 57, naturally developed itself, and, about 64 or 66, in his first Epistle to Timothy, the apostle speaks of Christian widows, forming a kind of charitable association (I Tim. v, 9-16). Such progress was conformable to the nature of things. The existence in the first age of the Church, of the organization which the Pastoral Epistles refer to is therefore historically established.

Diverse critics, contending against the authenticity of these writings, assert that the letters to Timothy and Titus contain many passages which are discordant with the doctrine and character of St. Paul. This allegation is false. The Apostle St. Paul speaks of Jesus Christ (Tit. iii, 11-14) in the same manner in the Epistles to the Corinthians, to the Galatians, and to the Romans, and there do not exist, in regard to this most important subject, any contradictory passages in the different letters of the great apostle.

They object in particular against the Epistle to Titus in regard to what it contains on the subject of heresies. This language, they say, is suspicious. But why? Is it because the heresies did not yet begin to raise their head? The proof that they are almost as ancient as the Church itself, is that the first Epistle to the Corinthians mentions them already.

Finally, the Rationalists attack the Pastoral Letters by affirming that they contain falsehoods. The apostle has not done, and even he could not do, what they suppose. — What is impossible or apocryphal in their content? Let us examine them. The second letter to Timothy speaks of different voyages of St. Paul: they are quite in agreement with what we know of him. Neither do we read anything in his Pastoral Letters that is in contradiction with his character.

They raise against the Pastoral Epistles a last difficulty drawn from the epoch of their composition. The first to Timothy and that to Titus have been written between the first and second captivity of St. Paul; the second to Timothy was written during the imprisonment which preceded the martyrdom of the apostle; none of them can be anterior to the first imprisonment. From this the criticism concludes that they are all apocryphal, because, according to this, St. Paul was a prisoner only once, when he was brought from Palestine to Rome, as the Acts relate.

This objection has something surprising. One must have colossal audacity to deny a fact so well authenticated by history as that of the double captivity of St. Paul. Pope St. Clement, who was his disciple, distinctly affirms that the apostle had carried the Gospel unto the extremities of the Occident, which he could have done only after having been liberated from his first imprisonment. The fragment of Muratori equally relates that St. Paul went to preach in Spain: "After having pleaded his cause (Paul) departed anew for the ministry of preaching as related, and after a second visit to the same city (of Rome), he ended there his life by martyrdom." Therefore, the apostle could write to Timothy, when he was imprisoned for the second time in Rome. All that we read in the Pastoral Epistles is so befitting to St. Paul that even those who deny their authenticity are compelled to admit that "the Paulinian tradition affirms itself with vigor, and this is a point acknowledged by everybody," says A. Sabatier.

CHAPTER LXIV.

THE EPISTLES OF ST. JOHN.

THE first Epistle of St. John is similar to the preface of his Gospel. The relations between these two writings are so intimate that they would be sufficient to establish the authenticity of the latter, even if tradition was dumb on the subject. Tradition is, however, anything but silent in its testimony: Papias, St. Polycarp, St. Irenæus, Clement of Alexandria, Tertullian, St. Cyprian, leave us no doubt as to the authenticity of this letter, and in antiquity not one contrary opinion existed. In our days certain adventurous minds tried nevertheless to raise some doubts, by supporting themselves upon intrinsic evidence. They accuse it of having neither a personal nor local character, and they suppose that it might have been written by a writer who had tried to imitate the style of the fourth Gospel; but this accusation, had it any foundation, would prove nothing, for the epistle is not addressed to any church nor to a definite person, as are the

Epistles of St. Paul. It is generally admitted that the objections formulated against the first Epistle of St. John are insignificant and without value.

The second and third epistles have not in favor of their authenticity such decisive intrinsic proofs as the first, which can be understood without difficulty, on account of their brevity and of their subject; the testimonies are nevertheless more than sufficient to establish their origin. In the fifth century, there was scarcely any doubt on this subject. In the fourth century, St. Ephrem attributes them to St. John. Aurelius does the same in 256, at the Council of Carthage, as well as St. Irenæus about the year 200, in his refutation of the heresies. About 250, Dionysius and about 300 Alexander of Alexandria, acknowledge them also as being of St. John.

The intrinsic examination of the two last letters of St. John is conclusively in favor of their authenticity. The title is not that which a forger would have invented. The general tone, style, and thoughts are the same as in the first epistle. Of the thirteen verses of which the second is composed, there are eight of them which are found about the same as in the first. "The identity of the author is generally admitted; they form an intimate family, an original group, in the bosom of the apostolic literature. Christianity appears therein elevated . . . to a height, where all the contrasts confound themselves in the unity of one spiritualism . . . of an incomparable serenity" (A. Sabatier, in the "Encyclopedie des Sciences," vol. vii, p. 177). In reading these epistles, the mind reverts to the paintings of the Catacombs, which breathe only peace and tranquility, the ideas of which were derived in part from the

Gospel of St. John. The faithful are represented there under the form of doves who are nourished by the gifts of the Lord with joy and love. The beloved apostle appears to us in his letters, as well as in the picture he has traced of the Divine Master, the type of these sweet doves, so dear to our fathers in faith.

CHAPTER LXV.

THE EPISTLE OF ST. JAMES.

IN THE famous passage where he enumerates the writings of the New Testament, Eusebius of Cæsarea ranks the Epistle of St. James in the category of those which are "contested" (H. E. iii, 25). "The first of the epistles called Catholic," he says, "is attributed to St. James. One must know that it is looked upon as doubtful, because few ancients make mention thereof, just as that which is attributed to St. Jude, and which is also one of the seven Catholic Epistles. We know nevertheless that these two letters are read in most of the Churches with the others" (H. E. ii, 23). Luther termed the Epistle of St. James a "Straw Epistle." We do not need to tell that the Rationalists of our day deny its authenticity.

In spite of the doubts of Eusebius and the negations of the contemporary critics, the ancient tradition is in favor of the canonicity, and of the authenticity of the Epistle of St. James. Everybody acknowledges that Pope St. Clement has repeatedly made allusion to it, at the end of the first century, in his letter to the Corinthians. Hermas in the "Pastor," reproduces from it almost word for word five verses and inspired himself with about ten others. The Syriac version known under the name of Peshito, which omits the short Catholic Epistles, has preserved nevertheless that of St. James, and assigns to it the name of this apostle. Now, this version goes back to the most remote antiquity.

The intrinsic examination of the letter confirms the testimony of tradition. "Everything agrees," says Mgr. Ginouilhiac, "with the state of the Christianity of Jerusalem in the last years of St. James. As St. James was much respected by the Jews, the faithful were left in peace. But, in the bosom of the Church, the minds became agitated; two sorts of false doctors had arisen therein; the one who exalted beyond measure the importance of the law, the others who, under pretext of evangelical liberty, despised not only the legal observations, but counted for little the duties of the moral law, especially those who had for object the fraternal charity and its works. Among the latter, as at the first, the greatest number were proud and haughty men, and this was considered as wisdom. It was against these vices that the epistle is directed. It has for object to unmask these false doctors and to give an idea of the true Christian wisdom" (Ginoulhiac, "Les Origines du Christianisme," 1878, vol. i, p. 145).

"The Epistle of St. James," says Renan, "is by far the best written work of the New Testament; the Greek thereof is pure and almost classic. . . . The production agrees perfectly with the character of St. James.

The author is a Jewish rabbi; he holds strongly to the law; to designate the reunion of the faithful, he makes use of the word synagogue; his epistle resembles by the text, the Synoptic Gospels which we behold later on going forth from the Christian family of which James had been the chief. . . . When he speaks of humility, patience, mercy, etc., James seems to have kept in memory the correct words of Jesus" (E. Renan, "L'Antichrist," p. 47). The contents of the letter are, therefore, in accord with the general doctrine, which attributes it to the first bishop of Jerusalem.

According to the Rationalists this epistle is directed partly against Paul and in contradiction with the doctrine of the great apostle. "He is an adversary of St. Paul," says Renan, in speaking of St. James. . . . One feels that he held a good deal on the law. An entire paragraph of his epistle (ii, 14, etc.) is devoted to warn the faithful against the doctrine of Paul, in regard to the uselessness of the good works and the salvation by faith. A phrase of James (ii, 24) is the direct negation of a phrase in the Epistle to the Romans (iii, 28). In opposition with the Apostle of the Gentiles, the Apostle of Jerusalem maintains that Abraham was saved by his good works, that faith without good works is a dead faith. The demons have faith and apparently are not saved. Discarding here his habitual moderation, James calls his adversary a "vain man" (ii, 20, E. Renan Op. cit. p. 47, 55).

The vain man of which James speaks is neither St. Paul nor another determined person, it is in general the one who is devoid of good works. The antagonism and the contradiction one supposes between the two apostles are imaginary. St. Paul, in the Epistle to the

Romans and in the Epistle to the Galatians insists a good deal on the truth that faith saves, and not the good works. St. James, on the contrary, says that faith alone, without good works, does not save. Both are right and do not contradict themselves. The works of which St. James speaks are not, indeed, those of which St. Paul speaks. The latter speaks of the works of the law, of the legal practices of the Jews, and he speaks very justly that the observance of the Jewish prescriptions does not justify without faith. St. James does not occupy himself with legal works, but with Christian works, which is quite different. The true religion, he says, does not consist only in believing, but in conforming his conduct to his faith, not in observing the law of Moses, but the law of God and of Jesus Christ. This doctrine is identical with that of St. Paul. St. James does not mention, among the obligatory works, the circumcision, the observance of the ritual prescriptions, etc., he enumerates exclusively the works of charity and of mercy (James i, 27). His epistle, addressed to the converted Jews, has for chief end, not to make them observe the Mosiac law, but, on the contrary, to detach them from it in order to occupy themselves exclusively with the observation of the moral precepts of the Gospel.

CHAPTER LXVI.

ST. PAUL'S EPISTLE TO THE HEBREWS.

THE AUTHOR OF THE EPISTLE TO THE HEBREWS.

THE authenticity of the thirteen Epistles of St. Paul was universally admitted during the eighteen centuries of the Church. It is not the same with the fourteenth and last, which is addressed to the Hebrews. Its Paulinian origin has been a subject of discussion among the ancient ecclesiastical writers, and naturally the rationalistic criticism does not hesitate to maintain that the Epistle to the Hebrews is not of St. Paul. We will explain why the authority of this letter has been considered doubtful, and show at the same time that our Vulgate had reason to rank it among the epistles of this apostle.

Each of the other thirteen Epistles of St. Paul bears his name. But the present epistle is without either name or address, and it omits also at the beginning the usual salutation. Thus it commences in the form of an essay though it closes in that of an epistle. These circumstances in connection with its peculiar style and diction, and the peculiar range of the topics discussed in it, have produced a diversity of opinion on the question whether St. Paul was its author. For the full discussion of the arguments on both sides the reader must be referred to the commentaries, some of which are accessible to all.

Our limits will permit us to indicate certain facts and principles which have a bearing on the authorship of the epistle and its canonical authority.

TESTIMONIES OR EXTRINSIC PROOF.

We will not invoke here, as a great number of authors do, the words of St. Peter: " As also our most dear brother Paul . . . hath written to you " (2 Pet. iii, 15), because these words do not appear to have this epistle for object. But inspired texts being wanting, we can quote the testimony of the principal Churches of the Orient and Occident: 1. In the Orient, we will quote first the opinion of the three patriarchal churches of Jerusalem, Antioch, and of Alexandria. That of the Church of Jerusalem is revealed to us by St. Cyril in a passage wherein he remarks that St. Paul alone has left fourteen epistles, that is, that he has written twice more than the other apostles together. To this testimony we can add that of Origen who belonged to the Church of Palestine as well as to that of Alexandria. At Antioch, the tradition was the same as that at Jerusalem. Besides, St. Crysostom who places the Epistle to the Hebrews in the same rank as the thirteen others who explains it to the faithful in the same manner, we can quote in its favor a letter addressed (264) to Paul of Samosata, bishop of Antioch, through a certain number of bishops assembled in his episcopal city in order to judge him. In this letter the Epistle to the Hebrews is expressly attributed to St. Paul.

At Alexandria, where the science of the Scriptures was zealously cultivated by both the Jews and the Christians, we behold a Doctor of the second century, probably St. Pantenus (Euseb. H. E. vi, 14), explaining why the apostle did not put his name to the Epistle to the Hebrews. About the end of the same century Clement of Alexandria seeks to explain the peculiarities which he remarks in its composition; but the embarrassments he experiences in this regard do not hinder his quoting it under the name of St. Paul in eight places (Strom. vi, 8, 62, etc.). A little later, Origen discusses anew the same problem, without succeeding any better in the solution in regard to the authenticity of this epistle: *non temere*, he says, *majores hanc epistolam Pauli dixerunt* (Euseb. H. E. vi, 25). In another place, he says that, if the fact were contested, it would be easy to prove it (Orig. Ep. ad Afric. 9). Thus, in spite of the difficulties they beheld in saying that this epistle had the same author as the thirteen others, they did not fail to firmly adhere to tradition, and their conviction was immovable. For this reason, St. Athanasius, drawing up, in 360, the list of the unquestionably inspired books, in order to distinguish them from the apocryphal writings, which they tried to spread, enumerates among the first the fourteen epistles of St. Paul, in placing that to the Hebrews, not at the end, but before the pastoral epistles. The most ancient manuscripts we have, especially of Alexandrian origin, contain it equally.

In order to appreciate this testimony of the Church of the Orient, it is good to observe: (a) That we could join to the patriarchal Churches other Churches of a great authority, for example, that of Cæsarea represented by Eusebius, St. Basil, and St. Gregory of Nazianz; and all those of Mesopotamia, whose opinion is known to us through St. James of Nisibis (Serm. ii,

13; viii, 3; xii, 7), St. Ephrem, and by the Peshito, the Syrian version, which always contained the Epistle to the Hebrews. (b) That all the Churches which we have quoted were not very distant from Judea, consequently, better able to know than many others the truth in regard to the Epistle to the Hebrews. (c) That they had in their midst men who were well known for both their knowledge and zeal for the purity of the faith; that several held opposite opinions in regard to certain points, and consequently to watch one another; and that all beheld before them numerous Arians interested to combat and to reject this epistle.

When one keeps account of these observations, one will not hesitate to acknowledge as incontestable what is expressly affirmed by Eusebius (H. E. iii, 38 and vi. 25) and St. Jerome (Ep. cxxix, 3), both the most learned men, and the best critics of Christian antiquity, that there is only one voice in the Orient to attest that the Epistle to the Hebrews is the work of St. Paul.

2. In the Occident, the accord was not so complete or at least not so constant. In the first century, St. Clement had quoted this epistle as an inspired writing in several places in his Epistle to the Corinthians, and one could hardly question that it had an apostle for author. In the second century St. Irenæus quoted it in a treatise which has not come to us, but yet without naming its author. In the third century, it was attributed by Tertullian to St. Barnabas (Euseb. H. E. vi, 20). The Muratorian canon attributes to the apostle only thirteen epistles; and Cajus, priest of Rome (d. 220) counts no more in his writing against Proclus. But since the middle of the fourth century, which is the epoch of the great Doctors, they established that

the doubts in regard to the authorship of this epistle were not founded, and all hesitation disappeared. After this we see the Epistle to the Hebrews quoted like the others. From the time of the letter of St. Innocent I to St. Exuperus (405), and even since the Council of Hippo (395), one draws no longer any difference between this epistle and the others written by St. Paul. St. Jerome (d. 420) acknowledges that it is universally received in the Roman Church.

CHARACTERS OF THE EPISTLE OR INTRINSIC PROOF.

All the indications which this epistle furnishes refer its origin in the time of the apostles and designate St. Paul as its author.

1. In the first place one recognizes that the author is a Jew, converted to Christianity, who wrote before the year 70 A. D. He gives himself out as compatriot and contemporary of the Saviour (i, 1-2; xi, 2 etc.), and the picture he traces of the worship and of the legal ceremonies shows that in his time the Temple was yet erect, the sacrifices practiced and the ancient priesthood in honor (Cf. vii, 23, 27; viii, 3-5, 13; 1-10, 25; x, 1-3; xiii, 11-13). A little later the most of these considerations would have been superfluous: even they would not have presented themselves to the mind. How could the Christians have been tempted to return to Judaism? Why should they be afraid of being misled out of human respect? Why should they seek to detach themselves from their terrestrial country? To what use would it have been to refer to allegories and to mystic senses in order to justify the arrival of a new law and of a new priesthood? (xiii, 14; vii, 12; viii, 13). What should be the meaning, saying that there are

no carnal sacrifices any longer, no more family of Aaron, no more Levitical tribe; finally, that the hour has arrived to offer all over to the Lord a spiritual worship and worthy of Him? The Fathers have not failed to dwell on these considerations. It is, therefore, manifest that the epistle is anterior to the year 70, as it is evident that the "Apologetic," and the treatises "De Lapsis," have been written before the end of the persecutions.

The uniform tenor of the epistle indicates, moreover, that those to whom it was addressed were Jewish Christians without any mixture of a Gentile element. The salutations at the end further imply that the epistle addresses no Hebrew Christians in general, but some particular community of them, which is most naturally to be sought in Palestine, perhaps in Jerusalem.

All these indications, which we could multiply, have certainly a great force. It seems incredible that an author of the first century, capable of composing such a writing, should have appropriated to such a point the doctrine and the manner of the Apostle of St. Paul, that he could have made himself pass for him or to be confounded with him.

D. B.—40

CHAPTER LXVII.

THE APOCALYPSE.

THE Rationalists of our day are quite generally agreed on the authenticity of the Apocalypse, and attribute the same to the Apostle St. John. However, they are not satisfied with the Book of Revelations, and endeavor to discredit its inspiration. Among the most plausible of the rationalistic critics, Renan adduces the following theories in his "Antichrist:"

At the time the Apocalypse was composed there remained only John of the apostles whom St. Paul called "pillars" (Gal. ii, 9). "It is certain that the two apostles, Peter and Paul, had died in 70. . . . James had died in 62." — These two affirmations are incorrect, but the error does not delay to show itself. To prepare the reader for the conclusions one wishes to make him accept, St. John, contrary to all testimony of tradition, is represented to us as "violent and fanatic, the most hateful against Paul, extremely intolerant, etc." (see "Antichrist," p. 327-329. Such is the picture which Renan has drawn of the author. Behold how he manipulates the facts.

St. John accompanied probably St. Peter in his voyage to Rome in the year 62. In 67, during the martyrdom of Peter and Paul, John was condemned, after an ancient tradition, to be plunged alive into a kettle of boiling oil, on the spot which was called since Latin-Gate. He escaped death, and shortly afterwards he left Rome with several Christians and fled into Asia, to Ephesus.

Renan admits for the need of his cause, some accounts of tradition as to St. John the Evangelist, but disfigures them after his usual custom. To explain some passages of the Apocalypse, Renan intimates that the author of the book must have seen with his own eyes, since the time of Nero, Pozzuoli, Solfatara, and the corruption which reigned in these places of pleasure, frequented by the noble youth of the world's capital. Most of the testimonies refer the tortures of St. John to a much posterior date, but let us not insist on this. One is quite generally agreed that it took place in Asia about the year 65.

According to Renan, the Apocalypse was written in Asia Minor between the 10th and the 14th of January in the year 69, and at the end of the month it was already known by seven churches. Indeed, St. John tells us that he composed the Revelations at Patmos (Apoc. i, 9), but the author of "Antichrist" does not admit this. Tradition also assures us that the apostle was exiled to this small island. This point is equally denied, because the Island of Patmos does not form part of the places of deportation which are known to us through the classical authors. But no one has left us a complete and official list of the islands of banishment, and what Suetonius (Tit. viii) tells of the motives which made them to be chosen in *asperimas insularum*, agrees perfectly with the Island of Patmos. Renan's affirmation that the Apocalypse was written at Ephesus rests upon no foundation.

That what Renan writes of the date of the prophecy of St. John, and about the circumstances which caused him to publish it, is no less exact than that what he says about the place where it was composed. To him the Apocalypse rests upon an error of fact, namely, that Nero had not yet died in the year 68; it foretells an event which did never realize itself, for it announces that Nero would reappear and resume the reins of the empire. False prophecy, for Nero had died indeed and did not reappear.

The Apocalypse was not composed in the year 68 or 69. No ancient author attributes to it this date; and what is more, Renan is unable to bring forward a single authority in his favor. All historic testimony is equally against him. "The date of the Apocalypse," says M. Bullock, "is fixed by the great majority of the critics between the years 95 and 97. The imposing testimony of St. Irenæus (disciple of Papias and of St. Polycarp, disciples themselves of St. John the Evangelist), is almost alone sufficient to reject every other date. Eusebius reports also a tradition which he does not question at all, and according to which, under the persecution of Domitian, St. John, Apostle and Evangelist, lived yet, and was exiled on the island of Patmos, on account of the testimony he had rendered to the Divine Word. We see in the works of Clement of Alexandria, and of Origen allusions in the same sense. No writer of the first three centuries is known that assigns to the Apocalypse another place or another date" (Revelation in Smith's "Dictionary of the Bible," vol. 3, p. 1036).

www.ingramcontent.com/pod-product-compliance
Lightning Source LLC
Chambersburg PA
CBHW021225300426
44111CB00007B/430